MANUAL FOR TEACHERS

TO ACCOMPANY THE TWELFTH EDITION OF

CASES AND MATERIALS

ON

FUNDAMENTALS
OF
FEDERAL INCOME TAXATION

By

JAMES J. FREELAND
Late Professor of Law
University of Florida

DANIEL J. LATHROPE
Professor of Law
Hastings College of the Law

STEPHEN A. LIND
Albert R. Abramson Distinguished Professor of Law
Hastings College of the Law

RICHARD B. STEPHENS
Late Professor of Law
University of Florida

New York, New York
FOUNDATION PRESS
2002

 *TEXT IS PRINTED ON 10% POST CONSUMER RECYCLED PAPER*

INTRODUCTION

This 2002 edition of the Manual is published to complement the 2002 Twelfth Edition of the FUNDAMENTALS, but we see no reason to change much what we have said in Manuals prepared for use with earlier editions of and supplements to the FUNDAMENTALS. As we have said earlier:

> Of course a book such as this may present a theme or a melody but it leaves for development by the user the matter of rhythm, harmony, and orchestration. The Manual does not purport to supply these elaborations, and it is assumed that rather different courses may be taught from the FUNDAMENTALS on the basis of the rather different interest, experience, and skills of its users. Nevertheless, two things are supplied here. One is a reference to ancillary matters and to recent developments which bear on matters discussed in the FUNDAMENTALS. Another is suggested answers (sometimes only approaches) to the problems and questions raised in the book. The suggestions have two purposes: (1) to enable busy and relatively inexperienced instructors to ascertain that they are not overlooking anything of importance in dealing with a question and (2) to offer a little guidance where the purpose of a question may be obscure. (We have in mind Browning's admission that when written some of his poems were understood only by him and God and later only by God.)

At the same time we think it is important to alert teachers of some of the more significant changes made in this edition of the FUNDAMENTALS which are as follows:

Chapter	*Changes*
Chapter 4	Qualified retirement plan services are added to excludable fringe benefits in Chapter 4 A.
Chapter 5	Chapter 5B is updated for the Section 127 amendment to allow an exclusion for the expense of graduate level courses.

Chapter 6	The year 2010 repeal of Section 1014 and replacement with Section 1022 is briefly considered in Chapter 6 B 4.
Chapter 9	A more detailed discussion of personal injury damage recoveries is included in Chapter 9 C.
Chapter 11	The discussion of tax benefits for costs of higher education expenses is updated in Chapter 11 C.
Chapter 13	The *Morrill* case is resurrected in Chapter 13 B.
Chapter 14	*Exacto Spring Corp. v. Commissioner* is added to Chapter 14C. Chapter 14E2 has been updated to reflect the 2002 changes in depreciation of personal property.
Chapter 16	The Chapter 16 B discussion of the deduction of interest on education loans is updated.
Chapter 18	New Chapter 18 D adds the Section 222 qualified tuition and related expenses deduction and a problem. Old Chapter 18 D and E becomes Chapter 18 E and F. *Sinyard v. Commissioner* is added to Chapter 18 F.
Chapter 20	The Chapter 20 B 3 changes in deferred compensation rules are added.
Chapter 24	Chapter 24 A and B have been updated to reflect that Section 453 is again available to accrual method taxpayers. The Chapter 24 B rules related to election out of Section 453 are updated.
Chapter 27	Chapter 27 A is updated to reflect changes in tax rates, the phase-out of Sections 68 and 151(d), and the marriage penalty. Chapter 27 B is updated to reflect changes in the credit provisions. Chapter 27 C is amended to reflect changes in the AMT exemption amount.

Chapter 28   Chapter 28 B2 updates the innocent spouse rules to reflect minor changes made by the 2000 Legislative.

Some of us, who have used the FUNDAMENTALS for a number of years have experimented with a new way to teach the course using the current Text. We essentially have taught the "fundamental" Fundamentals (gross income, assignment of income, deductions, timing, characterization and some areas related to characterization such as Section 453) over about 2/3 of the time allocated to the course and then assigned a major Overview Problem identical or similar to the Revised Overview Problem at page 4 of the Teachers' Manual (which can be required to be turned in with a written answer or merely discussed in class) at the end of that period. This method of teaching the course has the advantage of presenting the students the big picture of the course about two-thirds of the way through the term. This is followed by coverage of some specific areas (e.g., real estate, family law, deferred compensation) examining the areas with the perspective of all their relevant tax consequences (income or deduction, timing, characterization, etc.). Obviously, the areas that are covered in the specialized areas (e.g., Sections 121, 1031, 71, 215, 83, etc.) should not be covered in the first portion of the course. Below are some suggestions for one-hour assignments of specialized areas. The list is not exhaustive, but is merely illustrative of the areas one might cover.

1.   Taxation of Real Estate
      Hour #1:
            Text pages 891-897.
            Problem 2 on page 911.
      Hour #2:
            Text pages 904-910.
            Problems 3, 5, and 6(a) and (b) on pages 911-913.
      Hour #3:
            Text pages 221-226.
            Problems 1 and 2 on page 226-227.
            Skim Text pages 520-524.
            Text pages 466-469.
            Problem 2 on page 475.
      Hour #4:
            Text pages 496-499.
            Problem 3 on page 505.
            Text pages 608-610.
            Skim Text pages 822 and 827-831.

2.   Taxation of Charitable Giving
      Hour #1:
            Text pages 803-819.
            Problem 1 on pages 819-820.
      Hour #2:
            Problems 2-5 on pages 820-821. Omit Problems 2(g) and 4(c).

3.   Deferred Compensation
      Hour #1:
            Text pages 668-674, 869-875.

4.   Taxation of Education Expenses
      Hour #1:
            Text pages 113-115.
            Problem 1(a), (b) on pages 115-116. Section 152(d).
            Skim top of Text page 180.
            Skim Text pages 385-392, §§ 132(a)(3), (d).
            Text page 500. Section 62(a)(17).
            Problem 4 on page 505-506.
            Text pages 228-231.
            Problem 1(a), (b), (c), (e), (h) on page 235.
            Text pages 566-567.
            Problems 1 & 2 on pages 567-568.
      Hour #2:
            Text pages 231-235.
            Problem 2 on page 235-236.

5.   Tax Consequences of Litigation
      Hour #1:
            Text pages 182-185.
            Problem 1 on pages 185-186.
            Text pages 186-189. Skim Text pages 189-192.
            Problem 1 on pages 193-194.
      Hour #2:
            Text pages 192-193.
            Problem 3 on page 194.

6.   Tax Consequences of Divorce
      Hour #1:

             Text pages 195-200. Section 62(a)(10).
             Problems 1 on pages 203-204.
             Skim Text pages 200-203.
             Text pages 205-207.
             Problem 1 on page 207.
             Text pages 212-214. Section 152(e)(1) and (2).
             Problem 1(a), (b), and (d) on page 214.
      Hour #2:
             Text pages 208-212.
             Problem 1 on page 212.
             Skim Text pages 214-217.
             Text pages 457-465.
             Problem 2 on page 466.

We are grateful to colleagues and others who have raised questions of errors and omissions in prior Manuals. We especially want to thank Bill Baker of De Paul, Bryan Camp of Texas Tech, Susan Kalinka of Louisiana State, Dick Kaplan of Illinois, Charles A. Wry, Jr. of Boston University, and Kevin Yamamoto of South Texas for their valuable input. In preparation of this edition of the Manual, industrious research assistance was provided by Richard Moore and John Schuering. In addition invaluable secretarial assistance was rendered by Cecilia Bruno, Ted Jang and Suzanne Menne.

TABLE OF CONTENTS

Page

PART ONE: INTRODUCTION

Chapter 1   Orientation 1

PART TWO: IDENTIFICATION OF INCOME
SUBJECT TO TAXATION

Chapter 2   Gross Income: The Scope of Section 61 11

Chapter 3   The Exclusion of Gifts and Inheritances 18

Chapter 4   Employee Benefits 25

Chapter 5   Awards 34

Chapter 6   Gains from Dealings in Property 38

Chapter 7   Life Insurance Proceeds and Annuities 53

Chapter 8   Discharge of Indebtedness 59

Chapter 9   Damages and Related Receipts 65

Chapter 10   Separation and Divorce 70

Chapter 11   Other Exclusions from Gross Income 82

PART THREE: IDENTIFICATION OF THE
PROPER TAXPAYER

Chapter 12   Assignment of Income 95

Chapter 13   Income Producing Entities 103

PART FOUR: DEDUCTIONS IN COMPUTING TAXABLE INCOME

Chapter 14 Business Deductions 114

Chapter 15 Deductions for Profit-Making, Nonbusiness Activities . . 162

Chapter 16 Deductions Not Limited to Business or Profit-Seeking Activities 175

Chapter 17 Restrictions on Deductions 187

Chapter 18 Deductions for Individuals Only 201

PART FIVE: THE YEAR OF INCLUSION OR DEDUCTION

Chapter 19 Fundamental Timing Principles 229

Chapter 20 How Inelectable is the Integrity of the Taxable Year? . . 248

PART SIX: THE CHARACTERIZATION OF INCOME AND DEDUCTIONS

Chapter 21 Capital Gains and Losses 257

Chapter 22 Characterization on the Sale of Depreciable Property . . . 276

Chapter 23 Deductions Affected by Characterization Principles 293

PART SEVEN: DEFERRAL AND NONRECOGNITION OF INCOME AND DEDUCTIONS

Chapter 24 The Interrelationship of Timing and Characterization . . . 315

Chapter 25 Disallowance of Losses 331

Chapter 26 Nonrecognition Provisions 337

**PART EIGHT: CONVERTING TAXABLE INCOME
INTO TAX LIABILITY**

Chapter 27   Computations 355

**PART NINE: FEDERAL TAX PROCEDURE AND
PROFESSIONAL RESPONSIBILITY**

Chapter 28   Procedure and Professional Responsibility 367

PART ONE: INTRODUCTION

Chapter 1.   Orientation

Page 1:

If the *Cesarini* case at the beginning of Chapter 2 is assigned along with Chapter 1 for the first class, it can be utilized to develop an appreciation of the comments in the section on "Tools" in Chapter 1. As the course moves along, there will be time enough to make some brief references to constitutional questions and to emphasize the historical development and extraordinary drafting effort that have produced the current Internal Revenue Code, as suggested in "A Glimpse Backward." A word or two on that effort is sometimes needed to persuade students that, however difficult the statutory language may be, the Code is not a sloppy piece of draftsmanship. Frankly, however, as we acknowledged several years ago, the Code becomes less salable as time goes on.

Cesarini, of course, begins the quest for gross income, the subject of Part Two of the book. Beginning students may need to have gross income related to the matter of the ultimate determination of tax liability. This can be accomplished by use of the note on "The Road Ahead" which presents that skeleton of the course as follows:

	Gross Income	(Part Two)
less	Deductions	(Part Four)
equals	Taxable Income	(Part Four)
Rates applied to Taxable Income		
determine	Tax Liability	(Part Eight)
less	Credits	(Part Eight)
equals	Tax Due	

Page 46:

At the end of this Chapter and at the end of the course, one may want to provide students with an overview problem providing a summary of materials to be covered in the course. The problem below and the revision of the problem may be duplicated for class distribution. The answers to the problems follow the problems:

OVERVIEW PROBLEM

Taxpayers, a married couple, have two young children and several potentially taxable events that occur during the current year. Husband is a federal government employee who has a $50,000 per year salary. Wife owns a sole proprietorship catering business that generates $125,000 of gross receipts in the year, although there are various expenses related to the business that are considered below. In doing this problem, assume no post-1986 inflation has occurred, and that taxpayers file a joint return in the year 2002.

A. The first step in determining Tax Liability is a determination of Gross Income. Determine Taxpayers' Gross Income, if, in addition to the amounts above, the following amounts are received during the year:

   (1) Wife receives a $500,000 inheritance from her parents' estate.

   (2) Wife earns $10,000 of interest on the inheritance above which is deposited in CDs.

   (3) Taxpayers receive $10,000 of dividends on investments.

   (4) Taxpayers receive $25,000 of interest on tax-exempt bonds.

   (5) Wife receives a $5,000 award as Successful Businesswoman of the Year.

   (6) Husband recovers $3,000 in settlement of a physical personal injury suit.

B. After computing Gross Income, Taxpayers must determine their Adjusted Gross Income (Section 62) and Taxable Income (Section 63). Determine those amounts based on the following expenses of Taxpayers. Assume the exemption amount is $2,000 per exemption and the standard deduction amount for spouses filing a joint return is $5,000. See Section 67 for computation of Taxpayers' itemized deductions, but disregard Section 68 which is inapplicable here.

   (1) Wife incurs the following expenses in the catering business: (a) $30,000 cost of food; (b) $18,000 of rent; (c) $1,000 of utilities; and (d) $31,000 of salaries.

(2)   Wife purchases new equipment at a cost of $100,000. The equipment has a 5-year recovery period (hint: first-year depreciation under § 168 is 20 percent of cost; ignore § 179).

(3)   Husband incurs $2,000 of expenses to attend a seminar related to his employment.

(4)   Husband spends $200 for books and magazines related to his employment, and Taxpayers spend $100 in other sports and house decorating periodicals.

(5)   Taxpayers pay $10,000 of interest on the mortgage of their residence and $3,000 of property taxes.

(6)   Taxpayers pay $1,000 in sales taxes on nonbusiness items.

(7)   Taxpayers give $3,000 of cash to various charities.

(8)   Taxpayers pay $4,000 of tuition for their children's secondary schools,

(9)   Taxpayers incur $2,000 in medical expenses.

(10)   Taxpayers spend $20,000 to add a garage and guest room to their residence.

C.   Third, determine Taxpayers' Tax Liability for 2002, under Section l(a) which appears at page 935 of the Text and which applies to taxpayers who file a joint return.

D.   Finally, credits are allowed to directly reduce tax liability. See the Section 24 credit which is applicable here. Will Taxpayers actually have to pay any tax if Husband's employer withheld $8,000 in taxes and Wife paid $10,000 in estimated taxes? See Section 31. What result to Taxpayers?

REVISED OVERVIEW PROBLEM

At the end of the course, one may want to add the following additional facts to the problem above to add both characterization and other issues.

(a)   In the gross income portion of the problem add:

(7)   Taxpayers acquired a building in 1987. They took $40,000 of depreciation on the building. The building had a $10,000 adjusted basis and the land beneath it had a $20,000 adjusted basis when Taxpayers sold them for $55,000 and $30,000 respectively, with Taxpayers receiving $50,000 of cash and Buyers assuming Taxpayers' $35,000 nonrecourse liability on the property.

(8)   Taxpayers sold some stock purchased several years ago for $20,000 at a sale price of $15,000.

Recompute Taxpayers' Gross Income, Adjusted Gross Income, Taxable Income, Tax Liability, and the amount of any Tax Due or Refund. Note that Section 68 and Section 1(h) now become applicable.

(b)   What difference in results if the building in item (7), above, had been exchanged for another building and land of equal values also subject to a $35,000 nonrecourse liability?

Answers to the OVERVIEW PROBLEM:

Taxpayers' Gross Income is $200,000, determined as follows:

Both Husband's salary and Wife's business income, $175,000, are included in gross income. In addition,

(1)   Wife's inheritance is excluded from gross income by § 102(a).

(2)   The $10,000 of interest generated by the inherited property is included in gross income under § 61(a)(4). See also § 102(b)(1).

(3)   The $10,000 of dividends are gross income under § 61(a)(7).

(4)   The interest on the tax-exempt bonds is excluded from gross income by § 103(a).

(5)   The $5,000 award to Wife is included in gross income under § 74(a). It does not qualify for the § 74(b) exclusion.

(6)   Husband's physical personal injury settlement of $3,000 is excluded by § 104(a)(2).

Taxpayers must determine whether their expenses are deductible and whether the deductions are above or below the line, and they must compute their itemized deductions. First, deductible amounts:

(1)   Wife's $80,000 of expenses are all deductible as ordinary and necessary business expenses under § 162(a).

(2)   Wife's equipment qualifies for $20,000 of depreciation deductions under § 168 (20% of the cost is depreciable in the year of acquisition).

(3)   Husband's $2,000 of business expenses are ordinary and necessary expenses incurred by an employee deductible under § 162(a).

(4)   Husband's $200 of books and journals related to work are deductible as ordinary and necessary business expenses under § 162(a), but the $100 for other periodicals is a nondeductible personal expense under § 262.

5

(5)   Taxpayers' $10,000 of mortgage interest is deductible under § 163(h) and the $3,000 of property taxes are deductible under § 164(a)(1).

(6)   Sales taxes on goods for personal use are nondeductible. See §§ 164, 262.

(7)   Taxpayers' $3,000 cash gift to charity is deductible under § 170.

(8)   Taxpayers' children's tuition expense is a nondeductible personal expense. § 262.

(9)   Taxpayers' medical expenses are nondeductible because they do not exceed 7.5% of Taxpayers' $100,000 adjusted gross income. § 213(a). (Adjusted gross income is determined below.)

(10)   Taxpayers' addition to their home is a nondeductible capital personal expenditure. § 262.

Having determined the extent to which the above items are deductible, the next step is to determine which items are deductible above-the-line under § 62:

(1)   Wife's $80,000 of business expenses are deductible under § 62(a)(1).

(2)   Wife's $20,000 depreciation expenses are deductible under § 62(a)(1).

(3) and (4)   As Husband is an employee, his business expenses are not allowed under § 62(a)(1) or (2) and they are itemized deductions.

(5) and (7)   These deductible items are not listed under § 62 and they are itemized deductions.

Taxpayers' Adjusted Gross Income is $100,000 equal to $200,000 less the $100,000 of § 62 above-the-line deductions.

The next step is to determine the amount of Taxpayers' itemized deductions. Those deductions include:

(3)	Husband's seminar expenses:	$ 2,000
(4)	Husband's books and journals:	200
(5)	Taxpayers' mortgage interest:	10,000
(6)	Taxpayers' property taxes:	3,000
(7)	Taxpayers' charitable deductions:	3,000
		$18,200

However, § 67 imposes a 2% floor on "miscellaneous" itemized deductions which are itemized deductions other than those listed under § 67(b). Items (5) through (7) are listed under §§ 67(b)(1), 67(b)(2), and 67(b)(4), respectively and may be deducted in their entirety ($16,000). The remaining items ((3) and (4)) total $2,200 and they exceed 2% of adjusted gross income ($2,000) by only $200. Thus, total itemized deductions are $16,200. Since the total itemized deductions exceed the $5,000 standard deduction allowed to married taxpayers filing a joint return, Taxpayers would deduct their $16,200 of itemized deductions. § 63. Section 68 is inapplicable here because Taxpayer's adjusted gross income does not exceed $100,000. See §§ 68(a)(1) and (b)(1).

Taxpayers filing a joint return are allowed 2 personal exemptions (Reg. § 1.151-1(b)) and 2 dependency exemptions for their children, totaling $8,000 in exemptions. As a result Taxpayers have $75,800 of Taxable Income, determined as follows:

Adjusted gross income:	$100,000
Itemized deductions:	[16,200]
Exemptions:	[8,000]
Taxable Income:	$ 75,800

Employing the § 1(a) tax rates applicable to Taxpayers filing a joint return, Taxpayers have $14,262 of Tax Liability computed as follows:

$6,405 plus $7,857, i.e., 27% of $29,100 ($75,800 minus $46,700).

That amount of tax liability is reduced by a $1,200 credit under the § 24 Child Tax Credit ($600 for each child in 2002). No § 24(b) phaseout of the credit would occur. In addition, as a result of the withholding and estimated taxes of $18,000, Taxpayers have a § 31 credit of $18,000 and will receive a $4,938 refund for the year. This part of the problem demonstrates that the order in which credits are taken is important.

Answer to the REVISED OVERVIEW PROBLEM:

Taxpayers' original Gross Income was $200,000. As a result of the revised items ((7) and (8)), it is increased to $250,000 determined as follows:

(7)   Taxpayers have a total amount realized of $85,000, cash of $50,000 plus mortgage relief of $35,000 under *Crane*. The gain on the building is the difference between the amount realized, $55,000, and the adjusted basis of $10,000 or a gain of $45,000. In characterizing the gain, there is $45,000 of § 1231 gain. There is also a $10,000 ($30,000 less $20,000) § 1231 gain on the land. Since the gains are the only main hotchpot § 1231 items, they are characterized as $55,000 of LTCGs in the main hotchpot. Since $40,000 of the building gain relates to depreciation on the building, that $40,000 potentially is § 1(h)(7) "unrecaptured § 1250 gain."

(8)   Taxpayers also have a LTCL of $5,000 (deductible under § 165(c)(2)) on the stock sale.

The above capital gain and loss items are netted upon entering gross income. There is:

LTCG:	$55,000	STCG:	0
LTCL:	[5,000]	STCL:	[$ 0]
NLTCG:	$50,000	NSTCL:	[$ 0]

Thus, there is a § 1222(11) net capital gain of $50,000 which is included in gross income, increasing Gross Income to $250,000.

Taxpayers' Adjusted Gross Income is $150,000 ($250,000 less $100,000). As a result of an increased adjusted gross income, the exemptions remain at $8,000 (see § 151(d)(3)(C)(i)), but the itemized deductions are reduced. First, the miscellaneous itemized deductions of $2,200 do not exceed 2% of the $150,000 of Adjusted Gross Income and the itemized deductions are reduced under § 67 to $16,000. Further, the itemized deductions are reduced under § 68 by $1,500 (3% of the excess of the $150,000 adjusted gross income over $100,000) from $16,000 to $14,500. That results in Taxable Income of $127,500, determined as follows:

Adjusted gross income:	$150,000
Itemized deductions:	[14,500]
Exemptions:	[8,000]
Taxable Income:	$127,500

§ 1(h)(1): Tax Liability on the $127,500 of Taxable Income is determined as follows:

(A) $14,721: A tax determined under § 1(a) on the *greater* of:
  (i) $77,500, taxable income reduced by net capital gain ($127,500 less $50,000)
  (ii) $36,900, the *lesser* of
    (I) $46,700, taxable income taxed below 25% under § 1(a)
    (II) $165,000, $175,000 (taxable income) less $10,000 (adjusted net capital gain = $50,000 of NCG less $40,000 of unrecaptured § 1250 gain)

The § 1(a) liability on $77,500 is $14,721, $6,405 plus $8,316 (27% of $30,800). The tax on the remaining $50,000 of net capital gain is determined as follows. The $5,000 of LTCL from the stock wipes out $5,000 of the $15,000 LTCG that would normally be taxed at 20% leaving $10,000 to be taxed at the 20% rate and the $40,000 unrecaptured § 1250 gain to be taxed at the 25% rate. As a result:

§ 1(h)(1)(C): 20% of $10,000 equals $2,000
§ 1(h)(1)(D): 25% of $40,000 equals $10,000

Total Tax Liability:
    ($14,721 + 2,000 + 10,000) $26,721

Assuming (unlikely) that Taxpayers did not increase their estimated tax payments, they would have a tax liability after their $18,000 of § 31 credit of $8,721. They would not be allowed a § 24 child credit because their modified adjusted gross income is in excess of the phase-out amount. § 24(b).

In the alternative, if the building and land had been exchanged for another building and land of equal value also with a $35,000 nonrecourse mortgage, Taxpayers would have had a § 1031 like kind exchange. Since the liabilities are equal (see Reg. § 1.1031(d)-2 Example (2)), there is no boot and the entire gain is deferred. Taxpayers have a $30,000 adjusted basis (§ 1031(d)) and a tacked holding period (§ 1223(1)) in the building and land received. As a result, Taxpayers have a NLTCL of $5,000. Under § 1211(b) only $3,000 of the total $5,000 net loss is currently deductible and under § 1212(b) Taxpayers will have a $2,000 LTCL carryover. Again, the § 1211(b) $3,000 loss is deducted going into gross income with the result that Taxpayers have a Gross Income of $197,000, an Adjusted Gross Income of $97,000, and Taxable Income of $72,740 ($97,000 less $16,260 and $8,000). Under § 1(a) Taxpayers' Tax Liability is $13,435.80, the sum of $6,405 plus $7,030 (27% of $26,040 ($72,740 less $46,700)). Taxpayers will be allowed a $1,200 § 24 credit reducing tax liability to $12,235.80. As a result of their § 31 credit of $18,000, Taxpayers will receive a $5,764.20 tax refund.

PART TWO: IDENTIFICATION OF INCOME SUBJECT TO TAX

Chapter 2.   Gross Income: The Scope of Section 61

Page 48:

> See Thuronyi, "The Concept of Income," 46 *Tax L. Rev.* 45 (1990); McCombs, "An Historical Review and Analysis of Early United States Tax Policy Scholarship: Definition of Income and Progressive Rates," 64 *St. John's L. Rev.* 471 (1990).

Page 48:

> One question likely to be raised is whether it is constitutional to tax as "income" gain attributable solely to inflation. The Tax Court surprised no one holding expressly that it is. Hellerman v. Comm'r, 77 T.C. 1361 (1982).

Page 60:

> The *Charley* case is discussed in a note by Rosenzweig, "Employee-Owner of Company Taxable on Frequent Flyer Miles 'Sold' Back to Company: *Charley v. Commissioner*," 50 *Tax Law.* 677 (1997).

Page 63:

> See Coven, "Redefining Debt: Of Indianapolis Power and Fictitious Interest," 10 *Virg. Tax Rev.* 587 (1991), and Yin, "Of Indianapolis Power and Light and the Definition of Debt: Another View" 11 *Virg. Tax Rev.* 467 (1991) both critical of the *Indianapolis Power* result, but for different reasons."

PROBLEMS

Page 65:

1.   Yes; the result relates to the nature of the property itself and the concept of realization. The Cesarinis acquired all interests in the piano they purchased and they realize no income on that property until they dispose of it. In the problem, the Cesarinis would have no income as a result of their discovery that they had the original Steinway; the realization of that gain awaits disposition of the piano. On the other hand, the Cesarinis did not

purchase the money or for that matter any property other than the piano. The money or any other property they found *in* the piano was someone else's property which they *found* on their property. They did not acquire it under state law applicable in *Cesarini* until they found it; and they realized income when they were able to assert an interest in it against others by reducing it to "undisputed possession." It then became gross income to them and, not being purchased, was in the nature of a taxable windfall like the treble damages in *Glenshaw Glass*. Reg. § 1.61-14(a).

This would seem an appropriate time to introduce the concepts of realization and recognition. Gain is not taxed until "realized" and, it is then not taxed until "recognized." This presents a kind of tax deferral to compare with immediate recognition of gain and a complete exclusion from gross income (see, for example, §§ 74(b) and 102(a)).

2.   Yes, she must include $200 in gross income. Obviously the answer would now be compelled by § 74. However, as that section has not been covered yet, this question is intended to be considered by the student under the broad doctrine of *Glenshaw Glass*. It is also premature to raise the old gift argument under § 102. Cf. Ray W. Campeau, 24 T.C. 370 (1955), nonacq., 1958-1 C.B. 7. This may be a good point at which to raise the question whether income can be received other than in the form of cash; and, if so, how the amount of such income is measured.

As to the second part of the question, estate tax Reg. § 20.2031-1(b)'s definition of fair market value may be cited. The regulation provides:

> The fair market value is the price at which the property would change hands between a willing buyer and a willing seller, neither being under any compulsion to buy or to sell and both having reasonable knowledge of relevant facts.

3.   The $40,000 salary is compensation includible in Employee's gross income. Both the additional items are means of compensating Employee similar to the indirect compensation in the *Old Colony Trust Co.* case, and both are includible within gross income. The stock represents a bonus which constitutes $20,000 of compensation other than in the form of cash. (This problem does not raise an issue with respect to the more complex stock option arrangements, which are noted at page 674 of the Text, or § 83, which is considered at page 869 of the Text.) In addition the car, even though given to Employee's spouse, is an indirect form of compensation to Employee. While the question of who is taxed on the income may be

ignored here, Employee is taxed and the spouse's gain should be viewed as an indirect gift by Employee, excluded from the spouse's gross income by § 102. See Chapter 12. Again, as in problem 2, above, the amount of income, $15,000, is measured by the fair market value of the property received.

4(a). The kickbacks are compensation for services rendered by Adjuster and are required to be included in Adjuster's gross income. Under *Glenshaw*, it is obviously not even necessary to label the kickback compensation and about the only room for controversy in this area is the factual question whether kickbacks were received. That question arose in the case of William E. Dwyer, 32 T.C.M. 266 (1973).

4(b). Even though the kickbacks violated local law, they are still required to be included within Adjuster's gross income. Income, even though acquired from an illegal source, is taxable under the broad rationale of the *James* case discussed in the Note preceding this set of problems. See U.S. v. Wyss, 329 F.2d 658 (7th Cir. 1957).

5(a). Owner realizes $4,000 of income as rent; income may be received not merely in the form of cash, but in property or improvements as well. Since the improvements are intended to constitute rent, they are included within Owner's income. Reg. § 1.61-8(c). Note that if the improvements were not intended as rent they would be excluded from gross income by § 109 which is considered problem 1(e) at page 121 of the Text.

5(b). Owner would still have realized $4,000 as rental income, if the *value* of the improvements is still $3,000. Gross income is measured by the fair market value of what is received, not the cost of what is given up.

5(c). Tenant's gross income would be $2,500 under these facts. It may be premature to consider the consequences here in detail, but students will later discover that he will be seen as having performed services to satisfy an obligation. He has a basis of $500 for $3,000 of rental value, and would have $2,500 of income from his services.

6(a). Flyer has no gross income. The mileage credits are a part of what Flyer purchases with the regular ticket. In effect, part of Flyer's cost of the ticket is allocated to the ticket and part of the cost of the ticket is allocated to the mileage credits. Cf. Rev. Rul. 76-96, 1976-1 C.B. 23, treating a rebate from a manufacturer as a reduction in purchase price, and Priv. Ltr. Rul. 9920031 (Feb. 22, 1999), allocating the taxpayer's cost of a mutual fund investment which awarded frequent flyer points between the cost of the mutual fund and the points.

6(b).   Under general § 61 / *Glenshaw Glass* principles, Flyer should have gross income to the extent of the fair market value of the credits. The IRS however, has announced that it will not assert that gross income includes the receipt or personal use of frequent flyer miles or other in-kind promotional benefits (e.g., rental cars or hotels) attributable to the taxpayer's business or official travel. Announcement 2002-18, 2002-10 I.R.B. 1. In the announcement, the IRS acknowledges that there are "numerous technical and administrative issues relating to these benefits on which no official guidance has been provided. . . ." These issues include timing of income, valuation of income inclusions, and identifying benefits attributable to business expenditures versus personal expenditures. Because of these issues, the IRS is not pursuing the taxation of these benefits. The announcement also states that any future guidance on the taxability of these benefits will be applied prospectively. Id.

The announcement states that this relief does not apply to travel or other promotional benefits that are converted to cash, to compensation that is paid in the form of travel or other promotional benefits, or "in other circumstances where these benefits are used for tax avoidance purposes." Id. The facts of the problem do not seem to raise any of these exceptions.

6(c).   Under general principles, the fact that the credits are nonassignable would raise valuation issues which might exclude them from gross income. Under Announcement 2002-18 (discussed in problem 6(b), above), the valuation issues are not reached because the IRS's current policy is to simply not tax the credits, except in certain limited abusive circumstances. As noted in problem 6(b), above, the valuation issues are one of the bases for the IRS's current position that the credits will not be taxed.

6(d).   Under general principles, the use of the credits might produce gross income if the fact of nonassignability had allowed Flyer to exclude the credits when they were received. However, Announcement 2002-18 (see problem 6(b), above) applies to use of frequent flyer credits to take a flight, as well as receipt of the credits. Thus, Flyer does not have to include anything in gross income as a result of the trip, unless one of the exceptions in Announcement 2002-18 applies.

Rev. Rul. 80-52, 1980-1 C.B. 100, dealing with a similar barter club situation adds a timing facet in a situation where the club uses credit units in its barter system. It holds that the value of credit units received are included in income in the year the units are credited to a taxpayer's account.

Rev. Rul. 83-163, 1983-2 C.B. 26, requires a member of a barter club to include the fair market value of services that the member receives in gross income in the year the services are received, although the services that the member is to perform may not be rendered until a future date. Both these rulings involve timing aspects of barter clubs and consideration of them might be preferable in conjunction with Chapter 19 of the Text.

For articles on barter clubs, see Keller, "The Taxation of Barter Transactions," 67 *Minn L. Rev.* 441 (1982); Newman, "Determining Value in Barter Transactions: A Response to Robert Keller's The Taxation of Barter Transactions," 68 *Minn. L. Rev.* 711 (1984); and Kaufman, "'Living on the Cheap,' Is Barter Better?: Revenue Rulings and a Selective Analysis of the Effect of TRA 84 on Barter Transactions," 37 *U. Fla. L. Rev.* 641 (1985).

PROBLEMS

1(a).   A respectable argument can be made that a cash method taxpayer realizes income upon harvesting the crop, when the fruit of the taxpayer's labor is severed from the land and reduced to possession as separate property. However, practice supported by a lengthy history is against this view which would present practical difficulties. No gross income at this stage. See Reg. § 1.61-4(a)(1).

1(b).   Vegy has no income when she and her immediate family consume vegetables which she has grown. This is in the nature of imputed income which the government does not attempt to tax. Imputed income has been defined as:

> a flow of satisfactions from durable goods owned and used by the taxpayer, or from goods and services arising out of the personal exertions of the taxpayer on his own behalf. (Marsh, "The Taxation of Imputed Income," 58 *Pol. Sci. Q.*

514 (1943).)

The rule is applied within a family unit. Similarly, in the *Independent Life Insurance Co.* case at page 66 of the Text it was held that the rental value of property used by its owner is not income within the meaning of the Sixteenth Amendment.

1(c).   If Vegy sells the vegetables, she has $100 of gross income as a sale of property generated from her personal efforts, assuming she has no basis for the vegetables.

1(d).   Both Vegy and Charlie have $100 of gross income. They have engaged in an exchange which is essentially a cross sale. Although this may be difficult for a student to see, it is easily recognized if cash is put into each side of the transaction. Thus, it is just as though Vegy sold the vegetables for $100 of cash and used the cash to purchase $100 worth of tuna. Reg. § 1.61-4(a)(1). See also *Rev. Rul. 79-24* at page 66 of the Text. Unreported barter transactions are of concern to the Treasury.

1(e).   In return for rendering her services at the market, Vegy is receiving a rent-free use of the Grocer's space. Vegy is conferring a benefit on Grocer by making his market more desirable for customers because it offers a wider range of goods. Grocer is compensating Vegy for those benefits by providing her with rent-free use of the market. This compensation would be income of $50 under *Rev. Rul. 79-24* at page 66 of the Text and the *Dean* case at page 67 of the Text.

It may be premature to recognize a § 162 business deduction which Vegy could claim in effect offsetting the income which she must report. Nevertheless, in the *J. Simpson Dean* case at page 481 of the Text, Judge Raum asserts the existence of such a potential offsetting deduction as a reason for not finding any income. Students may be left to ponder the question whether the Raum analysis is persuasive.

Grocer has tax consequences similar to those of Vegy.

2(a).   Both Doctor and Lawyer would have $200 of gross income. This is an exchange of services, where each of the parties has rendered services and received services in return. The value of the services received is compensation for the services rendered and it is required to be included in gross income. See *Rev. Rul. 79-24* at page 66 of the Text.

2(b).   Lawyer does not have any income from filing her own return. This is an example of imputed income which the government does not attempt to tax. See the discussion of problem 1(b), above.

Chapter 3.   The Exclusion of Gifts and Inheritances

Page 70:

> The Text raises the question whether Congress constitutionally could
> tax the receipt of gifts and inheritances as income. Especially in view
> of the Supreme Court's more recent broad definition of what constitutes
> income, the general opinion is that such a tax would be valid. See Del
> Cotto, "The Trust Annuity as Income: The Constitutional Problem of
> Taxing Gifts and Bequests as Income," 23 *Tax. L. Rev.* 231 (1968).
>
> Gifts pretty clearly are taxable accessions to wealth; but § 102(a) is a
> long-standing Congressional choice generally to exclude such receipts
> from gross income as they always have been. See § 22(b)(3) (1939).
> In conjunction with this discussion one should at least inform students
> of wealth transfer taxation under Chapters 11-14 of the Internal
> Revenue Code. Some have suggested that the wealth transfer taxation
> provisions should be repealed and to generate the lost revenues, §
> 102(a) should also be repealed. See Dodge "Beyond Estate and Gift
> Tax Reform: Including Gifts and Bequests in Income" 91 *Harv. L.R.*
> 1177 (1978); Hudson, "Tax Policy and the Federal Income Taxation of
> Wealth," 19 *Willamette L.R.* 1 (1983).

PROBLEM

Page 81:

1.   *Duberstein* demonstrates that in tax controversies turning on questions
      of fact appellate courts rarely overturn findings of the trial court. An
      appellate court will reverse the trial court's fundamental findings of
      fact: (1) in a jury trial, only when reasonable persons would reach
      conclusions different from the conclusions of the jury; or (2) in a bench
      trial, only if the findings of the judge are clearly erroneous.

PROBLEMS

Page 82:

1.   The issue in this problem is whether, on the facts presented, § 102(a) or
      § 102(c) applies. The facts and circumstances surrounding the gift are

critical, just as they are critical in general under *Duberstein*. For example, suppose Son receives his television at the workplace, under facts and circumstances identical with those of all the other employees. The broad language of § 102(c) requires employees to include in gross income "any" transfer by or for an employer to or for the benefit of that employee. In these assumed circumstances, § 102(c) applies. Son, as an employee, therefore cannot exclude the value of the television, $500, from gross income. A similar analysis applies to the other employees receiving $100 sets under such circumstances. This result is similar to regulations interpreting the general provisions of the 1954 Code. See Reg. § 1.61-2(a)(1), T.D. 6416, 1959-2 C.B. 126. For example, if the sets are in the nature of Christmas bonuses, then each employee, including Son, must include the fair market value of his set in gross income.

Assume alternatively, that Son receives the set under Employer's Mother's Christmas tree. It is likely that § 102(a), and not § 102(c), applies to exclude the $500 television from Son's gross income. In such circumstances, Prop. Reg § 1.102-1(f)(2) creates an exception from § 102(c) for "extraordinary transfers to the natural objects of an employer's bounty ...if the employee can show that the transfer was not made in recognition of the employee's employment." In such circumstances, the application of § 102(a) over § 102(c) depends on Son's ability to negate the factual existence of a transfer from employer to employee, qua employee, and establish a gift in whole or in part.

Assuming § 102(c) requires inclusion of the fair market value of the set in Son's gross income, Son might argue for partitioning the single transfer. Specifically, Son would argue to bifurcate the transfer of the $500 set into part gift ($400) and part compensation ($100). No cases address such a claimed partition, but the facts in this problem suggest an ideal situation for partitioning although it is also questionable whether the regulations would permit a partitioning.

One further issue for consideration is the potential application of §§ 132(a)(4) and (e). If the sets are "de minimis fringe benefits", the employees may exclude them from gross income, notwithstanding § 102(c). The Conference Report to the 1986 Act gives two examples of de minimus fringe benefits. One example involves new employee achievement awards, and the other traditional retirement gifts. H. Conf.

Rep. No. 841, 99th Cong., 2nd Sess. II-18-19 (1986). Neither example fits the facts of this problem and, although the potential exists for application of § 132(e), the section probably does not govern these facts. See the answer to problem 4, below.

We criticize the apparent lack of legislative contemplation concerning § 102(c), although the Prop. Reg. § 1.102-1(f)(2) exception helps to alleviate the uncertainty of the code section.

2. Tips are gross income, includible under § 61. The maitre d' and the croupier might argue for the § 102(a) exclusion. Lucky Louie may indeed have intended the tip as a gift. However, by overwhelming weight of judicial authority, gratuities paid to barbers, beauticians, casino dealers, taxicab drivers, hotel, railroad, restaurant and ship employees, and the like constitute gross income. See Andrews v. U.S., 295 F.2d 819 (Ct. Cls. 1961), cert. den., 396 U.S. 829 (1962); Olk v. U.S., 536 F.2d 876 (9th Cir. 1976), cert. den., 429 U.S. 920 (1976) (tokes and tips to casino dealers are gross income.) Even in the absence of evidence, the Tax Court holds that waiters receive approximately 10% of their sales as tips. Cesanelli v. Comm'r, 8 T.C. 776 (1947). "Tips" does not appear as an item of gross income in § 61, but is an example of the judicial gloss added to § 61. See also Reg. § 1.61-2(a).

There are tip-reporting requirements for both employees and employers. See § 6053 and Reg. § 31.6053-3. "Tokes" also are gross income includible under § 61. *Olk* involves a craps dealer. As a dealer, the dealer was not permitted to fraternize with patrons and was required to remain separated from them when taking breaks or eating. Dealers were required to treat all patrons equally and could not render any personalized service of any kind to a patron. Only between 5% and 10% of those who gambled gave anything to a dealer. Any monies (tokes) given to the dealer in *Olk* were placed in a common fund and divided equally among all dealers at a table.

The District Court in *Olk*, 388 F.Supp. 1108 (D. Nev. 1975), rejected the government's contention that tokes were merely tips and thus taxable as income. It defined a "tip" as a payment to an individual who has rendered a service either because of the quality of the service or as a result of a social compulsion. Tokes were distinguished from tips on the ground that the dealer does not render a personal service, but merely

20

carries out the duties of employment. The District Court thus found that tokes are not an incident of the services performed by the dealer, and held that they constitute gifts under § 102(a).

The Ninth Circuit properly reversed, holding that "tokes", like tips, are income. The court concluded that they are not acts of "detached generosity", as required by *Duberstein*, but rather are "involved and intensively interested acts." 536 F.2d 876 (9th Cir. 1976), cert. den., 97 S.Ct. 317 (1976). See also Williams v. Comm'r, 41 T.C.M. 312 (1980), reaching the same result as in *Olk*.

3.   Once again, § 102(c) has potential appli-cation to Reverend, as an employee of the congregation. Reverend should invoke a pre-*Duberstein* (and therefore pre-1986 Act) decision, Schall v. Comm'r, 174 F.2d 893 (5th Cir. 1949). Under *Schall*, the $5,000 is not income. Id; see also Rev. Rul. 55-422, 1954 C.B. 14. Under *Schall* and Rev. Rul. 55-422, the Service generally will not assert employer-employee arguments to a clergy's relationship with her congregation. Apparently, the Service considers such a relationship as different in nature and more personal than the normal employer-employee relationship. Extending the rationale of *Schall* forward to the 1986 Code, the Prop. Reg. § 1.102-1(f)(2) exception should apply here and §102(c) should not govern the result in this problem. Reverend may exclude her $5,000 as a gift under § 102(a).

4.   As to the amount, the facts raise a *Kralstein* issue. Max Kralstein v. Comm'r, 38 T.C. 810 (1962). Under *Kralstein*, the motive of each contributor receives an independent examination to determine whether a particular transfer satisfies the "gift" criteria of *Duberstein*. In other words, the *Kralstein* issue concerns a single transfer by multiple transferors. *Kralstein* involved the receipt by the taxpayer of cash and personal property at a testimonial dinner. The funds used were furnished by many persons and entities whose motives and intentions were not uniform. Applying *Kralstein* to this problem, Retiree has gifts from employees, and not transfers from the employer, to the extent that § 102(a), and not § 102(c), applies. Retiree's exclusion amount therefore is dependent upon the motives of each and every fellow employee; but seemingly Retiree may exclude the $3,000.

Traditional retirement gifts (the gold watch, etc.) result in exclusions

21

from gross income as de mimimis fringe benefits. § 132(e); H. Conf. Rep. No. 841, 99th Cong., 2d Sess. II-18 (1986). "The committee expects that the exclusion under section 132(e) for a de minimis fringe benefit will apply, under appropriate circumstances, to traditional retirement gifts presented to an employee in his or her retirement after completing lengthy service, where the section 74(c) exclusion for length of service does not apply because the employee received such an award within the prior four years." S. Rep. No. 313, 99th Cong., 2d Sess. 53-54 (1986). The exclusion under § 74(c), for employee achievement awards, is not available for awards of cash, gift certificates, or equivalent items. Id. at 51. Of significance is that most of the examples in the legislative history to the 1986 Act involve gold watches. Apparently, Congress targets gold watches, and not cash awards, as qualifying under § 132(e). The best view in this circumstance is to consider cash awards as not qualifying for the de minimis exception under § 132(e). Section 102(c) then governs, giving Retiree § 61 gross income of $2,000 from Employer.

PROBLEMS

Page 91:

1(a). In the usual case (but see (e), below), § 102(a) expressly excludes this bequest from gross income.

1(b). Section 102(a) also expressly excludes this inheritance from gross income.

1(c). This settlement would also be excluded from income by § 102(a), if what Daughter received rested on her rights as one of the intestate successors. See Lyeth v. Hoey, 305 U.S. 188 (1938), at page 83 of the Text. The result in *Lyeth* seems almost obvious, but the case is a landmark case on the interpretation of a term in the federal taxing statute, and on the role of state law in federal tax controversies.

1(d). This amount probably is not gross income. The bequest appears to rest on affection and is not in response to an agreement to provide compensation. Cf. Rev. Rul. 57-398, 1957-2 C.B. 93.

1(e). This amount is gross income to Daughter under *Wolder*. See also Rev.

Rul. 67-375, 1967-2 C.B. 60, which properly indicates that there is no § 102 magic in acquiring compensation under a will provision. See problem 3, below, for a discussion of the effects of § 102(c) on *Wolder*.

1(f).   This amount also would be gross income to Daughter. See Cotnam v. Comm'r, 263 F.2d 119 (5th Cir. 1959), cited in *Wolder*.

1(g).   Again, $10,000 is gross income to Daughter. Settlement of Daughter's claim does not alter the nature of the receipt of income. See Cohen v. U.S., 241 F.Supp. 740 (E.D. Mich. 1965); Priscilla Hansen, 33 T.C.M. 43 (1974).

1(h).   This amount is gross income for services. Some students may be interested in the relationship of this problem to the Federal Estate Tax. In general, the relationship is: (1) income to recipient, estate tax deduction under § 2053; (2) excluded bequest to recipient, no estate tax deduction. For the income tax effects of waivers of executor's fees see Rev. Rul. 66-167, 1966-1 C.B. 20, at page 250 of the Text. The Tax Court upheld the validity of a waiver of the right to receive a statutory executor's fee and its exclusion from the gross income of the executor. Breidert v. Comm'r, 50 T.C. 844 (1968). Cf. § 102(c) and problem 2, below.

1(i).   Under United States v. Merriam, 263 U.S. 179 (1923), discussed in *Wolder*, the $20,000 amount would not be included in gross income. *Merriam* did not include a like amount in gross income, because services were not expressly required in order to receive the money. As *Wolder* suggests, the result in *Merriam* is of doubtful validity today. Even if services are not required, sufficient § 102 intent as considered in the *Duberstein* case probably is not present, and under *Glenshaw Glass,* the full amount may be gross income. Cf. § 102(c) and problem 3, below.

2.   No. Taxpayer has gross income not excluded by § 102. The underlying claim for Taxpayer's suit is a quantum meruit claim for past services rendered and, as such, the settlement is included in gross income. Cf. *Wolder*. See Green v. Comm'r, 54 TCM 764, aff'd 846 F.2d 870 (2d Cir. 1988), cert. den. 10/3/88.

3.   Section 102(c) does not necessarily apply in *Wolder*. Section 102(c)

may simply add more fuel to the litigation fire. At issue now are traditional notions of employee-employer relations. Whether the taxpayer in *Wolder* actually is an employee of Boyce depends on the facts of their arrangement. Their relationship may be considered one of an employer and employee, but also may be considered an agency relationship, an independent contractor, or some other type of contractual relationship. In these circumstances if taxpayer is an employee, taxpayer would not qualify for an exclusion under Prop. Reg. § 1.102-1(f)(2) because the payments are in recognition of employee's employment. Again we are critical of inadequacies in the legislative process which might well have provided guidance on the interpretation of § 102(c) in the legislative history. Regardless of the factual outcome, the Service now has another weapon to use against taxpayers in future litigation involving gifts with business or employment overtones.

Page 92:

> See McCoy, "Executive Perks and the Fringe Benefit Rules" 42 *N.Y.U. Inst. on Fed. Tax'n.* Ch. 39 (1984); McKinney, "Certainty Provided as to the Treatment of Most Fringe Benefits by Deficiency Reduction Act," 61 *J. Tax*'n 134 (1984); See also Cairns, Riordan and Riordan, "Maximize Mileage from Transportation Fringe Benefits" 58 *Tax'n for Accts.* 25 (1997).

PROBLEM

Page 101:

1(a).   This qualifies for exclusion under § 132(a)(1). It satisfies the § 132(b) definitional requirements and, assuming it is nondiscriminatory *or* that Employee is not a highly compensated employee (see § 132(j)(1) and (6) and § 414(q)), it is excludable.

1(b).   The value of the room is not excludable from Employee's gross income as a § 132(a)(1) exclusion. The hotel foregoes other revenue (by bouncing the guest) in allowing Employee to use the room thereby indirectly incurring a cost. § 132(b)(2). See Reg. § 1.132-2(a)(5). Nevertheless Employee seemingly may exclude 20% of the hotel room cost under § 132(a)(2). See Reg. § 1.132-2(a)(2), § 132(c), and problem (i), below.

1(c).   The fact that the fringe benefit takes the form of the rebate rather than tax free use is not a substantive difference and there is an exclusion. The legislative history is clear on this, as is Reg. § 1.132-2(a)(3).

1(d).   There is an exclusion here. Under § 132(h)(2)(A), use by an employee's spouse or dependent children of a § 132(a)(1) fringe is treated as use by an employee.

1(e).   This is excluded as a result of the reciprocal written agreement provision of § 132(i).

1(f).   Seemingly, this is a discriminatory fringe for the benefit of highly compensated employees. The rule of § 132(j)(1) denies an exclusion for a § 132(a)(1) or (2) fringe. In addition, there is no apportionment (i.e. 40% exclusion). The entire amount is included in gross income. Reg. § 1.132-8(a)(2).

We say that this is "seemingly" discriminatory because the facts only state that the employee is an officer. To be discriminatory the payment must be made to a "highly compensated employee" (see § 132(j)(1) and (6)), which is defined in § 414(q). See especially § 414(q)(1)(D) and (5). We'll make the assumption that this is a highly compensated employee.

1(g).   The cost of the hotel room is included in Employee's gross income. Since it is not in Employee's line of business it fails to meet the § 132(b)(1) test for exclusion. It also fails to qualify for a § 132(c) "qualified employee discount" because it is not in Employee's line of business. § 132(c)(4).

1(h).   Assuming it is nondiscriminatory (see § 132(j)(1)) and assuming Employee's hotel services are substantial, this is excluded because Employee is deemed to work in both lines of business. See Reg. § 1.132-4(a)(1)(iv).

1(i).   The legislative history of § 132(a)(2) and (c) indicates that insurance policies are treated as services for purposes of qualified employee discounts. As the amount of the discount is only 20%, it fully qualifies for a § 132 exclusion. § 132(c)(1)(B). Pre-§ 132 Comm'r v. Minzer, 279 F.2d 338 (5th Cir. 1960), held an insurance agent had income to the extent that the price of a policy to the agent was reduced by the agent's commission. Query the interrelationship of Minzer and § 132(a)(2) and (c). Seemingly § 132 has nullified Minzer. See also § 132(j)(1).

1(j).   Employee has a $1,000 qualified discount but only $800 may be excluded from gross income under § 132(c)(1)(A). The gross profit percentage defined in § 132(c)(2) is:

$$\frac{\text{aggregate sales price less cost}}{\text{aggregate sales price}}$$

$$\frac{\$1,000,000 - \$600,000}{\$1,000,000} = 40\%$$

and 40% of the $2,000 normal price, which is $800, qualifies for the exclusion. The remaining $200 of discount is included in gross income. Although premature at this point, it should be pointed out that Employee's cost basis for the video cassette recorder should be $2,000. To reduce basis by the amount excluded would change the exclusion to essentially a deferral. See problem 1(g) at page 121 of the Text.

1(k). This is an example of a working condition fringe under § 132(a)(3) and (d). Query whether the amount is gross income in the first place? See *Allen J. McDonell* in the first part of Chapter 5. If it is, it is excluded because had Employee incurred the expenses, Employer would have been able to deduct them under § 162.

1(l). This is a de minimis fringe under § 132(a)(4) and (e).

1(m). Query whether this is a de minimis fringe? Is it a holiday gift with a low fair market value? See Reg. § 1.132-6(e)(1).

1(n). The amount is a qualified transportation fringe under § 132(a)(5) for "qualified parking" (see § 132 (f)(1)(C)) as defined in § 132 (f)(5)(C) to include "parking provided to an employee on or near the business premises of the employer." The exclusion is not subject to the discrimination limitation. The exclusion is limited (subject to an inflation adjustment in § 132 (f)(6)) to $175 per month.

1(o). This amount is excluded in part as a qualified transportation fringe under § 132(a)(5), specifically as a transit pass. See §§ 132(f)(1)(B) and (5)(a). The exclusion is subject to a limit of $100 per month for years after 2001 with inflation adjustments under § 132(f)(6). Assuming the vouchers here cost $110 per month, only $1,200 of the $1,320 is excluded from gross income. § 132(f)(2)(A). The remaining $120 is included in Employee's gross income, and it may not be excluded under any other subpart of § 132. § 132(f)(7).

1(p). This is an excluded on-premises athletic facility under § 132(j)(4).

Page 102:

One may want to point out two aspects of § 119 not otherwise covered in the problems. First, § 119(b)(2) makes immaterial for purposes of the convenience of the employer test the fact that a charge is made for employer-furnished meals or that an employee may accept or decline such meals. This subsection supersedes Reg. § 1.119-1(a)(3)(i), which states that meals an employee can opt to accept and pay for are conclusively deemed not to be for the convenience of the employer. Second, § 119(b)(3) provides that, if an employee is required to pay a fixed charge for meals, whether the employee accepts or declines them, the fixed charge is excluded from the employee's gross income, *as long as* the meals are deemed to be for the convenience of the employer.

Page 105:

In Rowan Companies, Inc. v. U.S., 452 U. S. 247 (1981), the Supreme Court held that if the value of an employee's meals and lodging is excludable under § 119, the employer needn't include the value of the meals and lodging in computing the employee's "wages" for purposes of social security (FICA) and federal unemployment (FUTA) taxes. The Service has issued Rev. Rul. 81-222, 1981-2 C.B. 205, to express a rule in conformance with the *Rowan* case.

Page 105:

In Boyd Gaming v. Comm'r, 177 F.3d 1096 (9th Cir. 1999), the Ninth Circuit held that where a casino operator's employees were required to stay on the premises for meals during work hours, more than one-half of the employees were required to do so for the convenience of the employer for a "substantial non-compensatory business reason." See Reg. § 1.119-1(e)(2). As a result, the now 50% cap on the deductibility of meals under § 274(n) was inapplicable and the meals were totally deductible by the employer. See §§ 274(n)(2)(B), 132(e)(2). The Service has acquiesced in the decision. See Announcement 99-77, 1999-2C.B. 243. The *Boyd Gaming* result was codified in 1998 by § 119(b)(4) which provides that if more than ½ of the meals furnished to employees on an employer's business premise are furnished for the convenience of the employer, then all meals furnished on the business premises are treated as furnished for the convenience of the employer.

PROBLEMS

Page 106:

1(a). Employee would have $3,000 of income. This is in the nature of a bargain rental arrangement under which the net value is income to the employee unless excluded by § 119. A part of the purpose of this problem is to acquaint students with the need to identify and apply all elements of a taxing statute. Simple here, the approach becomes more difficult in more complicated provisions. As it is assumed the § 119 requirement that Employee accept the lodging as a condition of employment is missing, Employee has income. This income would increase Employee's gross income by $3,000, the amount of nonexcludable net value which Employee is receiving from Employer.

1(b). In this situation, it is still possible that the convenience of the employer test is not met. Convenience of the employer connotes a substantial noncompensatory business reason for requiring the employee's presence. Moreover, as regards the required acceptance of the lodging, while it is doubtful that the Commissioner would look behind the terms of most employment contracts (but see § 119(b)(1)), this may be a place to raise the pervasive doctrine of substance versus form. If the specific contractual condition were a mere sham it would not control. The sham issue would most likely be raised in a sole shareholder employee situation or in an intra-family situation.

1(c). This problem raises the issue whether groceries constitute "meals" under § 119. The Tax Court position is that they do not. Michael A. Tougher, Jr., 51 T.C. 737 (1969), aff'd per curiam, 441 F.2d 1148 (9th Cir. 1971), cert. den., 404 U.S. 856 (1971). The Tax Court's conclusion is based on the reasoning that the term "meals" should be given its ordinary meaning of ready-to-eat servings of food. The Third Circuit, however, has rejected this approach and allowed the taxpayer to exclude the value of groceries, as well as non-foodstuffs which are an integral part of either "meals" or "lodging." Jacob v. U.S., 493 F.2d 1294 (3d Cir. 1974). The Third Circuit relied in part on the state troopers cases cited in problem 3, below, which no longer have validity in the aftermath of Commissioner v. Kowalski, 434 U.S. 77 (1977). Although the Supreme Court did not consider this issue in *Kowalski*, nevertheless the tone of its decision gives more weight to the Tax Court

29

position.

Section 119 applies to the lodging. Note as well that § 119(a) specifically makes the exclusion applicable to meals and lodging furnished to the taxpayer and *the taxpayer's spouse and dependents.*

1(d).   If in the year the Employee accepted the position and commenced work Employer transferred the residence outright without any conditions to Employee, then the full value of the value of the residence would be included in Employee's gross income for that year. This is straight compensation unaffected by § 119 which as to lodging contemplates only an employee's use of property in which the employer has some rights. This is a clear inference from the "business premises" requirement. It is premature to consider that it is also possible Employer would have a gain on the transfer of the residence if the residence's value exceeded the Employer's basis in it. See the *International Freighting Corporation* case at page 133 of the Text.

2.   This question raises several issues related to the application of § 119 to this situation. It involves not only the specific requirements listed in Reg. § 1.119-1(a)(1) and (b), but in addition the "employee" requirement. Section 119 as well as other sections to be covered in the course (for example § 79 dealing with group term life insurance and §§ 104-106 dealing with health insurance and benefits) apply only to an "employee." A self-employed person is of course not an employee of himself or herself. (But see § 127(c)(3).) At the same time a person may be an employee of a corporation which is a separate taxable entity (see the *Dean* case at page 67 of the Text), even though he or she is a substantial or sole shareholder or a director of the corporation. If meals and lodging are provided to the individual in his or her capacity as an employee they may be excludable if the other § 119 requirements are met. However, if they are provided to the individual in some other role, such as director or shareholder, they are outside the exclusion. Cf. Maurice A. Enright, 56 T.C. 1261 (1971), where premiums paid on group term life insurance policies on the life of an employee-director were made because of his status as a director, not as an employee, and they were not excludable from his gross income under § 79. Thus by incorporating her business, Planner became an "employee" of the corporation and it is assumed the meals and lodging are provided to her in that role. Note that if she had not incorporated her business, § 119

would not apply to her. This is discussed in the concluding paragraph of this answer. Incidentally it has been held that § 119 may apply to a partner in a partnership business entity where a partner is both an owner partner and an employee of the partnership and where meals and lodging are provided to the partner in his or her role as an employee of the partnership. Armstrong v. Phinney, 394 F.2d 661 (5th Cir. 1968). Cf. § 707(a); contra, Wilson v. U.S. 376 F.2d 280 (Ct. Cls. 1967).

Jack B. Lindeman, 60 T.C. 609 (1973), acq. 1973-2 C.B. 2, held that a residence adjacent to the motel and used by the taxpayer for business purposes is "on the business premises" of the corporate employer as required by § 119. It is within the perimeter of the property on which both the corporation and employee conduct a significant portion of their business. The fact that the residence was acquired after the motel and principally to house the employee should not preclude it from being part of the business premises.

Since the corporation is owned solely by the taxpayer, she is both a corporate owner and corporate employee. Both the condition of her employment test for lodging and the convenience of the employer test for meals and lodging are difficult to apply when one person assumes both roles. The Commissioner can be expected to look closely at whether these requirements are met when the same person plays a dual role and the situation may lack arms' length bargaining. However, whether the requirements are met here can be partially answered by examining other similar businesses. As this is a common requirement in the motel business, it would seem that taxpayer's assertion that the requirements are met is legitimate. Incidentally, the regulations provide that if the requirements for exclusion of lodging are met the exclusion will automatically apply to any meals furnished without charge to the employee on the premises. Reg. § 1.119-1(a)(2)(i), last sentence. It is assumed that the food provided here is meals. See problem 1(c), above.

This problem may cause some concern to students. The effect of what Planner has done as a result of incorporating her business is to allow the corporation as an entity to write off her personal meals and lodging expenses. This is because the corporation may deduct the costs as a § 162 deduction reducing the business income and yet Planner has no income. Although the result is sound under the statute one may question whether a mere change in form of a business entity should cause such a difference in result in a taxpayer's overall tax consequences. One may also question whether incorporation is warranted given the current corporate rates in comparison to the individual rates (compare the § 1 rates to the § 11 rates) and may want to discuss general choice of entity considerations.

3.   The cases listed in the problem involve two issues: (1) whether meals and lodging must be furnished "in kind" and (2) whether privately-owned restaurants adjacent to state highways are "on the business premises of the employer." The Third Circuit had aligned itself with the Fifth, Eighth, and Tenth Circuits and against the First Circuit and the Tax Court in holding that § 119 was applicable. Kowalski v. Comm'r, 544 F.2d 686 (3rd Cir. 1976). But a year later the Supreme Court reversed the Third Circuit and agreed with the Tax Court that the reimbursements were required to be included in gross income. In its syllabus of the case the Supreme Court stated at 434 U.S. 77:

1.   In the absence of a specific exemption, the cash meal allowance payments are included in gross income under § 61(a), since they are "undeniabl[y] accessions to wealth, clearly realized, and over which the trooper has complete dominion." *Commissioner v. Glenshaw Glass Co.*, 348 U.S. 426, 431.

2.   The payments are not subject to exclusion from gross income under § 119, since § 119, by its terms, covers meals furnished by the employer and not cash reimbursements for meals.

3.   No specific exemption for the payments can be claimed on the basis of the once-recognized doctrine that benefits conferred by an employer on an employee "for the convenience of the employer" are not income within the meaning of the Internal Revenue Code, since it appears from the legislative history of § 119 that it was intended comprehensively to modify the prior law, both expanding and contracting the exclusion for meals previously provided, and therefore it must be construed as a replacement for the prior law, designed to end the confusion that had developed respecting the convenience-of-the-employer doctrine as a determinant of the tax status of meals.

Due to the nature of its holding, the Supreme Court did not need to address the issues whether restaurants along the state highway are on the business premises and whether the cash meal allowances were for the convenience of employer, but the Court did say that for the latter test of § 119, meal allowances would have to be demonstrated to be necessary to allow a taxpayer to "properly perform his duties." The Ninth Circuit distinguished *Kowalski* on its facts and excluded mandatory payments into a firehouse mess fund from employee's gross income citing Reg. § 1.119-1(a)(3). Sibla v. Comm'r, 611 F.2d 1260 (9th Cir. 1980).

As to the "business premises" issue, the First Circuit in Wilson v. U.S., 412 F.2d 694 (1969), strictly defined business premises as not encompassing restaurants adjacent to state highways. Other circuits have disagreed. See U.S. v. Barrett, 321 F.2d 911 (5th Cir. 1963); U.S. v. Morelan, 356 F.2d 199 (8th Cir. 1966); U.S. v. Keeton, 383 F.2d 429 (10th Cir. 1967). The Sixth Circuit in the *Anderson* case, cited in the Note at page 105 of the Text, would appear to agree with the Fifth, Eighth, and Tenth Circuits by defining business premises to include places where the employee performs some significant portion of his duties, but the First Circuit disagrees in *Wilson* stating that restaurants along the state highway are not on the business premises because, even under the *Anderson* definition of business premises, "The restaurant was not a `place where the employee performs a significant portion of his duties.' Rather, taxpayer was there because he was off duty." (412 F.2d 694 at 696). The Tax Court, incidently, found it unnecessary to rule on the issue in Ghastin v. Comm'r, 60 T.C. 264 (1973).

Chapter 5.   Awards

PROBLEMS

Page 112:

1.   The first issue is whether Picabo's award is for a type of achievement
within § 74(b). Wills v. Comm'r, 411 F.2d 537 (9th Cir. 1969), and
Hornung v. Comm'r, 47 T.C. 428 (1967), both held that an award
received by a professional athlete for athletic achievement is not within
a § 74(b) classification, - neither a "civic" nor an "artistic" achievement.
Both cases involve awards to professional athletes. It may be argued
that an award to an amateur athlete qualifies as a "civic" achievement,
defined as an achievement that is a positive action which is exemplary,
unselfish, and broadly advantageous to the community. See Simmons
v. United States, 308 F.2d 160 (4th Cir. 1962). We think that the
chances of success for classification as a civic achievement are slim.

A second issue is whether Picabo's 15 minute acceptance speech
constitutes "substantial future services" by Picabo. It is unlikely that an
acceptance speech constitutes *substantial* future services. Rev. Rul. 58-
59, 1958-1 C.B. 40, states, in effect, that the appearance by a recipient
of an award or the recipient's representative to receive and accept the
award does not constitute the rendering of substantial future services.
While making a brief acceptance speech is more than accepting the
award, it is probably within the scope of the Ruling.

If Picabo met the requirements of § 74(b), then the $5,000 would be
excluded from her gross income by § 74(b). She would not be allowed
a § 170 charitable deduction. If, the award is included in gross income
under § 74(a), then Picabo will be allowed a charitable deduction under
§ 170. However the deduction is subject to the § 170(b) limitations (see
Chapter 23B), and it will result in a reduction of her taxable income
only if she "itemizes" her deductions. (See Chapter 18F). If Picabo
itemizes her deductions and can fully deduct the amount of the award,
then the inclusion-deduction consequences create a "wash" having the
same consequences as exclusion under § 74(b) with no § 170 deduction.

2(a).   The $300 gift certificate is likely gross income to Cliff under § 74(a).
It is not excluded by the § 74(c) exception. In order to qualify under §

34

74(c), Cliff's award must be of tangible personal property; a gift certificate is representative and not tangible, and it does not qualify. See Prop. Reg. §1.274-8(c)(2). However, it is arguable that the $300 is excludible from gross income as a de minimis fringe benefit under § 132(e).

2(b).   The gold watch (which is incidentally within the dollar limitations of § 274(j)(2)(A)) qualifies for a § 74(c) exclusion as an employee length-of-service award. It is tangible personal property, awarded at a meaningful presentation and seemingly not disguised compensation. It is both excludable by Cliff and deductible by Gusher.

2(c).   The § 74(c) exclusion is inapplicable because an employee length of service award qualifies for an exclusion only if the employee has been in the employer's service for five years and has not received a similar award in the current and prior four years. § 274(j)(4)(B). Here Cliff fails the five year test.

Page 113:

In Knapp v. Comm'r, 89-1 U.S.T.C. ¶ 9169 (2nd Cir. 1989), aff'g. 90 T.C. 430 (1988), Associate Dean and Professor Knapp had to include in gross income payments made by N.Y.U. Law School, his employer, to other educational institutions attended by his children in the year 1979. Such assistance payments did not fall within the exclusion for scholarships provided in § 117 for that year. See Reg. § 1.117-3(a). Subsequent to the issue year in *Knapp*, § 117 was amended by the addition of subsection (d). See § 117(d)(1), (2). Section 117(d)(1), had it been in effect for the issue year of *Knapp*, seemingly could have changed the result or outcome of the case. However, § 117(d)(1) would not have been applied to *Knapp* because the N.Y.U. plan applied only to high level administrators and to professors. This in turn made the plan discriminatory in favor of highly compensated employees. The plan would flunk § 117(d)(3) with the result that § 117(d)(1) would not apply.

PROBLEMS

Page 115:

1(a).   Momentarily, disregarding the research work that Student is required to do, $3,000 of the scholarship earmarked for tuition and books would be excluded from gross income. § 117(b)(2)(A) and (B). However, Student must include the $3,000 earmarked for room and board. Since Student is required to do $3,000 worth of research work the issue is whether: (1) it is done to receive the tuition and books, which would result in its inclusion in gross income, (2) it is done to receive the room and board (included in income in any event), or (3) it is prorated between the two receipts one-half to each. Student's total gross income under (1), above, would be $6,000; under (2), above, $3,000; and (3), above, $4,500. Seemingly, if for the receipt of the $6,000 the research were required to be done *specifically* for the room and board, Student would be required to include only $3,000 in gross income. Perhaps the institution awarding the scholarship should plan accordingly. Furthermore, the regulations imply that if Student can show that $3,000 was not for services and that Student incurred $3,000 for tuition and books, then that $3,000 can be excluded. Prop. Reg. § 1.117-6(d)(5) Example (5)

1(b).   This makes no difference after 1986. The result is the same as in problem 1(a), above. Prior to the 1986 Act an exception was allowed in such circumstances where the work was required of all students.

1(c).   The issue is whether an athletic scholarship is compensation for services. In Rev. Rul. 77-263, 1977-2 C.B. 47, an athletic scholarship was said to be excludable under pre-1986 Act § 117 where the university expects but does not require the student to participate in a particular sport, requires no particular activity in place of participation, and does not cancel the scholarship if the student does not participate. The facts are inadequate to indicate whether these requirements are met. If they are met then $3,000 is excluded as in problem 1(a), above, and the $3,000 for room and board is included. If they are not met, the football scholarship constitutes gross income for services or gross income under the *Glenshaw Glass* definition.

1(d).   Although this amount is indirect reciprocal compensation, § 117(d)

36

nevertheless excludes the $2,500 tuition reduction from Student's gross income. The plan is nondiscriminatory, § 117(d)(3); Student is an employee under § 132(h)(2)(A) as incorporated by § 117(d) (2)(B); and the amount is awarded by an educational institution as defined in § 170(b)(1)(A)(ii). Furthermore, Student is not required to perform any services and thus § 117(c) is inapplicable to this § 117(d) situation. Although Prop. Reg. § 1.117-6(d)(2) lst sentence interprets services broadly under § 117(c), seemingly Student's spouse has been reasonably compensated and the tuition scholarship is excluded. See Prop. Reg. § 1.117-6(d) Example (6).

2(a).   This is compensation for future services and thus would not fit the § 117 exclusion because of § 117(c). Prop. Reg. § 1.117-6(d)(2) and -6(d)(5) Example (2). However, Lawyer could argue that her stipend would qualify under § 127 as part of an educational assistance program. If the requirements under § 127(b)(2)-(6) are met and, if the amount is used for tuition, fees, books, supplies, equipment, and similar expenses (§ 127(c)(1)(A)), Lawyer could exclude $5,250 (the § 127(a)(2) maximum) of the $10,000 from gross income. The remaining $4,750 would be included in gross income. Prop. Reg. §1.117-6(d)(5) Example (2).

2(b).   The test for this stipend to qualify for an exclusion is whether it represents compensation for past, present, or future services. Prop. Reg. § 1.117-6(d)(2). Although this would not be considered as compensation for future services, a court could consider this compensation for past or present services. You must ask: Is there a gratuitous flavor? Is the stipend primarily for the benefit of the grantor? Even if a court were to label the stipend compensation under § 117, Lawyer could still argue that § 127 would apply in order to exclude $5,250 of the stipend from gross income as in problem 2(a), above.

2(c).   The stipend here is clearly not compensation, and thus there is no § 117 exclusion problem. The amount is still potentially income as a prize except to the extent that § 117 applies. Note the introductory clause of § 74(a). The amount of the § 117(a) exclusion depends on the extent to which the stipend is a "qualified scholarship." If the stipend does not preclude use of the proceeds for tuition, books, etc. (one cannot imagine that it would!) then to the extent it is so used the amount is excluded from gross income.

PROBLEMS

Page 121:

1(a). Owner's § 1001(a) gain is $6,000, the difference between the § 1001(b) $16,000 amount realized (the money received) and the § 1011(a) $10,000 adjusted basis. Owner's adjusted basis was determined by the § 1012 cost of property, no adjustments being required. In a cash purchase situation one is not concerned with a *Philadelphia Park* "exchange" cost basis problem because the amount of cash establishes the cost basis. It is premature to consider the character of the gain at this point. See Chapter 21. Brokerage or attorney fees in purchasing or retaining property are a part of its cost and are taken into account in the determination of basis under § 1012.

1(b). Owner would again have a $6,000 gain. Owner's total cost basis for the land is $10,000. The cost of the option is simply a part of the cost of the land and, as such, is included as a part of the cost basis. Mead Coal Co. v. Comm'r, 72 F.2d 22 (4th Cir. 1934). Owner's gain is the difference between the $16,000 amount realized and the $10,000 adjusted basis.

1(c). The option itself is property. If Owner sells the option for $1,500 Owner has a $500 gain on its sale, which is the difference between the amount realized of $1,500 under § 1001(b) and the adjusted basis of $1000 under § 1011(a). Characterization and timing problems in option transactions arise in problem 2 at page 756 of the Text.

1(d). Owner's § 1001(a) gain would be $6,000. Owner's § 1012 cost basis of $10,000 is increased by the $2,000 capital expenditure under § 1016(a)(1) to give Owner a § 1011(a) adjusted basis of $12,000. The difference between the $18,000 amount realized and $12,000 adjusted basis is a $6,000 gain.

1(e). Owner would have an $8,000 gain on the sale of the land.

Owner would have an $8,000 gain on the sale of the land.

The annual cash rental payments were included in income but have no effect on Owner's basis for the property. Cf. § 1016.

Since the clearing expenses were excluded from income by § 109, § 1019 properly provides that the basis of the property is not to be increased. Thus, Owner's basis for the property remains $10,000 and, as the amount realized is $18,000, Owner has an $8,000 gain. The effect of this is that Owner postpones recognition of the $2,000 improvement gain until Owner's disposition of the property. Compare the exclusion in problem 1(g), below.

Under the broad definition of income reflected in the *Glenshaw Glass* case, improvements made by a lessee on a lessor's land, even if not made as rental payments, constitute income to the lessor when the lessor reacquires the property upon termination of the lease. Helvering v. Bruun, 309 U.S. 461 (1940), so held. See Schlesinger, "Consequences to Lessor of Lessee Construction" 17 *N.Y.U. Inst. on Fed. Tax.* 697 (1959). The *Bruun* result may create some difficult problems for a lessor, such as determining the value of the improvements, bunching of income into a single taxable year, and tax liability without the receipt of cash or readily convertible property. Recognizing these difficulties, Congress in 1942 enacted § 109 which provides that improvements, other than those intended as rent, made by a lessee on a lessor's real property are to be excluded from the lessor's gross income. A companion provision, § 1019, specifies that, if § 109 applies, the lessor receives no increase in the basis of the property as a result of the improvements. The overall effect of § 109 and § 1019 is that nonrental improvements are not required to be included in income at the time they are received but, when the lessor subsequently disposes of the property, they will generate income (or reduce loss) to the extent that they have increased the value of the property, unless another exclusionary rule such as § 102 applies. The above problem illustrates how that occurs.

If § 109 had been inapplicable and the $2,000 included in Owner's income, Owner would have had a $12,000 cost basis in the property, see Reg. § 1.61-2(d)(2)(i), and a $6,000 gain upon its subsequent sale. Thus under either result the total income is the same, but there are timing and (although premature) characterization differences.

1(f).   Owner has a $6,000 gain on the sale of the land. The amount realized under § 1001(b) is the money Owner received ($16,000), and the adjusted basis under § 1011(a) is Owner's "cost" ($10,000) which is what in substance Owner paid for it (§ 1012). It is difficult for students to grasp that when one is compensated for services with property and is required to include the fair market value of the property in income under § 61, one has a cost basis for the property equal to the amount included in income. For example, Mr. Duberstein would have had a cost basis in his Cadillac equal to its fair market value on its receipt. This concept is more easily understood if it is realigned as a situation in which the taxpayer receives cash for services (equal to the fair market value of the property) and then purchases the property with the cash with which the taxpayer was originally compensated. Thus, in basis matters, "cost" has a special *tax* meaning, and here a return of capital tax free is permitted to the extent of the taxpayer's taxed cost for property. See Reg. § 1.61-2(d)(2)(i).

An additional issue is whether the income tax paid upon receipt of the land as compensation is added to the basis of the land under § 1016(a)(1). It is not. Again, comparison can be made to a case in which a person receives cash as compensation and then uses the cash to buy a car. The tax paid on the cash would not be a part of the car's cost basis. (It is of course possible for Congress to let tax paid affect tax basis. A portion of the federal gift tax paid is allowed as an increase to a donee's basis under the express provisions of § 1015(d)(6) but, as basis is a cost of acquisition notion, even § 1015(d) limits the permitted increase so that basis cannot exceed the fair market value of the property. See § 1015(d)(6)(B). Cf. § 1015(d)(1)(A) parenthetical. These parenthetical remarks are relevant to the next set of problems.)

1(g). Owner would be taxed on a $6,000 gain on the sale of the property. The $1,000 employee discount is added to the basis which is $10,000. Failure to add the $1,000 to basis would convert the exclusion to a mere postponement or deferral of gain. See §§ 109 and 1019 in problem 1(e), above, where Congress intends a mere deferral. Here an exclusion is intended and Owner has a $10,000 basis and a $6,000 gain.

Page 122:

Note that § 1015(d)(6) added by T.R.A. 1976 reduced the amount of the § 1015(d) federal gift tax increase to the carryover basis. Under § 1015(d)(6) only the portion of the gift tax attributable to the net appreciation on the gift property generates an increase in basis. Thus, if property with a $40,000 adjusted basis, worth $100,000 is given to a donee and $10,000 of federal gift tax is paid on the transfer only the portion of the net appreciation in value of the gift ($60,000) over the amount of the gift ($100,000) times the tax ($10,000) results in a basis adjustment. Under prior law which applied to transfers through 1976, Donee's basis would have been $50,000; however, for post-1976 transfers § 1015(d)(6) limits donee's basis to $46,000. The House Committee Report states, questionably, that the adjustment was allowed initially so that the same property was not subject to both gift and income tax (i.e., to prevent imposition of a tax on a tax) but that prior law was too generous in the adjustment since only the appreciation was subject to the income tax. Actually, the full amount of gift tax paid seems to increase the "cost" of the gift property. Cf. Duke v. Comm'r, 200 F.2d 82 (2d Cir. 1952), cert. den., 345 U.S. 906 (1953). For an article taking an opposite approach and concluding that Congress was, if anything, too generous under § 1015(d)(6), see Collings, "Basis of Property Transferred at Death Under the Tax Reform Act of 1976", 28 *Mercer L.R.* 917 at 947 (1977). Section 1015(d)(6) is explored in problem 3 at page 153 of the Text.

PROBLEMS

Page 128:

1(a)   (1).   Donee's § 1001(a) gain is $15,000, the difference between the $35,000 amount realized and the $20,000 transferred adjusted basis determined under § 1015(a).

(2).   Donee's § 1001(a) loss is $5,000, the difference between the $20,000 adjusted basis determined under § 1015(a) and the $15,000 amount realized.

(3).   Donee's § 1001(a) gain is $5,000, the difference between the $25,000 amount realized and the $20,000 transferred adjusted basis determined under § 1015(a).

1(b)   (1).   Donee's § 1001(a) gain is $5,000, the difference between the $35,000 amount realized and the $30,000 adjusted basis determined by applying the general rule of § 1015(a). The exception to the general rule of § 1015(a) is inapplicable because the donor's basis is always used for purposes of determining gain.

(2). Donee's § 1001(a) loss is $5,000. The adjusted basis is $20,000 the fair market value of the property at the time of the gift, determined by applying the exception to the general rule of § 1015(a). The difference between Donee's adjusted basis of $20,000 and the amount realized of $15,000 is a $5,000 loss. An effect and probably an objective of this exception is to foreclose the convenient shifting around of losses among family members. On the other hand, on these facts Donee can hardly be seen to have suffered an economic loss greater than the decline in value while holding the property. Compare the treatment of gain in both respects. (Consider also whether Donor might better have sold the property and made a cash gift to Donee.)

(3). Donee has neither gain nor loss. There is a natural student inclination here to take short cuts rather than carefully to apply the statutory basis rules. All will determine there is no gain under the general rule of § 1015(a), as the Donor's basis exceeds the amount realized by Donee. Turning to the exception, some think they find a $4,000 gain on the ground that under the exception the Donee's basis of $20,000 is $4,000 less than the amount realized. The error, obviously, is in failure to give effect to the phrase "for the purpose of determining loss," and the answer is "no loss either," not that there is a gain of $4,000 under the exception. This seeming anomaly affords a good chance to require students to deal more precisely with the statutory language and better to articulate their conclusion. Reg. § 1.1015-1(a)(2) Ex. is explicit of course, but students should not be permitted to use it as a "reason" for their correct answers. A sale at any price between $20,000 and $30,000 will result in neither gain nor loss.

2(a). Father's gain would be zero and Daughter would have a $120,000 basis in the property. Reg. § 1.1001-1(e) indicates that Father has a gain only to the extent that his amount realized ($120,000) exceeds his adjusted basis ($120,000) for the property. Thus no gain is realized. Under Reg. § 1.1015-4 Daughter has a $120,000 basis in the property, the greater of the amount Daughter paid for the property ($120,000) or the Father's adjusted basis for the property at the time of the transfer ($120,000).

2(b).   In substance the above transaction may be viewed as a sale of two-thirds of the property and a gift of the other one-third of the property by Father. This is not the law, but how would it work out? So viewed, Father would have a $40,000 gain on the sale, i.e., a $120,000 amount realized less the $80,000 adjusted basis allocated to two-thirds the property; and Daughter would have a $160,000 total basis in the property acquired, i.e., a $120,000 § 1012 cost basis in two-thirds and a $40,000 § 1015(a) gift basis in the other one-third. Assuming equal basis and value of all parts of the tract of land these are exactly the consequences that would follow a physical division of the land and a gift of one-third and a sale of the other two-thirds. This analysis of the transaction is more realistic and has been accepted by Congress, but only in the case of a transfer that is in part a gift and in part a sale to a charity. See § 170(e)(2) and § 1011(b). The result in the regulations favors the donor at the expense of the donee (but of course it is probably all in the family).

Page 130:

Recall that Farid relinquished her marital rights and promised to marry Kresge in consideration for the stock she received from him in a premarital transfer. The court found, for income tax purposes, that Farid held the shares not as a donee but as a purchaser. She had given fair consideration for the stock and therefore had a § 1012 cost basis rather than a § 1015 transferred basis in the stock.

The legislative history indicates that a transfer of property for the relinquishment of marital rights during marriage or incident to divorce is a transfer qualifying for § 1041 treatment. H. Rep. No. 98-432, Part 2, 98th Cong., 2d Sess 1491-1492 (1984).

Under a literal reading of the statute, transfers of property incident to an antenuptial agreement would not be subject to the provisions of § 1041 if they occur, as in *Farid-Es-Sultaneh*, prior to marriage. If they occur subsequent to the marriage of the parties, § 1041 applies to a transfer of property from an individual to a *spouse* or a *former spouse* (when incident to a divorce). As to post-marriage transfer, should it make any difference that marital rights are given up in an antenuptial versus a postnuptial agreement? Seemingly not.

Section 1041 treats a transfer of property between spouses as a gift. Maybe antenuptial agreement transfers should be within the coverage of the provision, but then only if the parties do subsequently marry. Clearly, the statute does not currently so provide. And it is a congressional decision whether to amend it to do so.

PROBLEM

Page 130:

(a).   Andre realizes a gain of $3,000 ($7,000-$4,000). However he recognizes no gain due to § 1041(a)(1).

(b).   Steffi takes a transferred basis of $4,000 from Andre under § 1041(b)(2).

(c).   Steffi will have a $3,000 gain if she immediately resells the property. § 1001(a),(c). Thus the gain which Andre did not recognize because of § 1041(a) is recognized when Steffi disposes of the property. It is premature here to point out that Steffi also tacks Andre's holding period. § 1223(2).

(d).   Andre realizes a loss of $1,000, but the loss is not recognized because § 1041(a) applies to losses as well as gains. Note that § 267 would also disallow the loss; however, it is not needed to do the job. See § 267(a)(1), (b)(1) and (c)(4). Steffi will take a transferred basis of $4,000 from Andre. § 1041(b)(2). She will recognize a $1,000 loss if she immediately resells the property. As in a gain situation, § 1041 provides for a transferred basis and defers recognition of a loss until the property is disposed of. Cf. §§ 165(c), 1223(2). Compare the result here with one reached under the § 1015 basis rules.

(e).   Section 1041(a) provides a straight forward rule that no gain or loss is recognized on transfers between spouses. This applies despite what consideration is furnished. So on Andre's transfer of property to Steffi the same result occurs as in problem 1(a) and (b), above. There is no gain to Andre, § 1041(a), and a transferred basis of $4,000 to Steffi.

§ 1041(b)(2). On Steffi's transfer to Andre, the realized gain of $2,000 ($7,000-5,000) is not recognized, § 1041(a), and Andre will take a transferred basis of $5,000 in the property. § 1041(b)(2).

Page 133:

In Cottage Savings Ass'n v. Comm'r, 499 U.S. 554, 111 S. Ct. 1503 (1991), the Supreme Court held that an exchange of one pool of mortgages for another such pool where there were different mortgagors and different properties securing the obligations was a taxable event because the properties were materially different. See Prescott, "Cottage Savings Association v. Commissioner: Refining the Concept of Realization," 60 *Fordham L. Rev.* 437 (1991). Subsequent to the case the Treasury has finalized regulations under § 1.1001-3 providing rules with respect to modifications of debt instruments and whether such modifications are significant enough to constitute favorable exchanges. See Lipton, "The Section 1001 Debt Modification Regulations: Problems and Opportunities," 85 *J. Tax'n* 216 (1996) and Swartz and Thomas, "Determining a 'Significant Modification' Under the Final Cottage Savings Regulations" 14 *J. P'ship Tax'n* 3 (1997).

Page 136:

For beginning students the *Crane* case is most difficult. It is a merry-go-round. The ultimate conclusion that the amount realized includes the amount of the mortgage seems at first absurd. However, it is inescapable if the other facets of the opinion are first presented. The Court deals first with the unadjusted gross basis and the determining question of what is the "property" acquired from the decedent. Next, the opinion moves to adjusted basis, taking account of depreciation deductions computed with respect to the gross basis initially determined. Beginning students need some help to see that these deductions were a tax benefit to the taxpayer effecting a kind of tax recovery of capital. Finally, inclusion of the amount of the mortgage in the amount realized is seen to be only the counterpart of including the mortgage in the initial basis of the property, and the gain identified essentially matches the depreciation advantages previously secured. Two items in *Crane* not to discuss at this point are (1) characterization, especially since those particular comments in *Crane* are partially obsolete; and (2) a sale of property subject to a mortgage in excess of

45

fair market value on which the Court "punted." Postponement of consideration of this issue is brief, however, since it is at issue in the *Tufts* case which follows *Crane* in the Text. *Crane*-type problems are very pervasive in the tax law and students should be assured that their struggle with the case is of more than momentary importance.

Page 145:

Numerous issues arise with respect to a situation where a taxpayer acquires property subject to a nonrecourse liability greatly in excess of the fair market value of the property. Some cases have disregarded the entire liability in determining the taxpayer's basis for the property (Estate of Franklin v. Comm'r, 544 F.2d 1045 (9th Cir. 1975)), while others have allowed taxpayers a basis up to the fair market value of the property (Pleasant Summit Land Corporation v. Comm'r, 863 F.2d 263 (3rd Cir. 1989), cert. den. 493 U.S. 901, 110 S. Ct. 260 (1989); Regents Park Partners v. Comm'r, 63 T.C.M. 3131 (1992)). Other cases in the area are discussed in Cowan," Is Any Part of a Nonrecourse Mortgage Greatly Exceeding FMV Includable in Basis," 77 *J. Tax'n* 260 (1992).

Page 152:

A prior edition of the Text included the *Malone* case where in a gift situation taxpayer transferred property subject to personal liability in excess of the property's basis, which the donee assumed. The excess was held to constitute income to the donor. Malone v. United States, 326 F. Supp. 106 (N.D. Miss. 1971), aff'd per curiam, 455 F.2d 502 (5th Cir. 1972).

Page 152:

See Duhl and Kevall, "Supreme Court Holds That Net Gift Triggers Income to Donor: An Analysis of Diedrich" 57 *J. Tax'n* 130 (1982); Hendrick "Effect of Diedrich's Part Sale/Part Gift Rationale on the Transferee's Basis Computation," 11 *Ohio Northern Univ. L. Rev.* 89 (1984); Carpenter, "Net Gift Gives Rise to Taxable Income to Donor: Diedrich v. CIR" 24 *Boston College L. Rev.* 1429 (1983). Developments in this area prior to Diedrich are discussed in an excellent article by Ward, "Taxation of Gratuitous Transfers of Encumbered Property: Partial Sales and Section 677(a)," 63 *Univ. of Iowa L.*

Rev. 823 (1978); see also Lies, "A Uniform Theory for Determining Whether a Donor Has Taxable Income on a Net Gift," 16 *U.S.F.L. Rev.* 95 (1981).

PROBLEMS

Page 153:

1(a).   Mortgagor's cost basis in the land is $100,000, the $20,000 amount of out of pocket cash paid and the $80,000 amount of nonrecourse liability incurred. Cf. *Crane* where the amount of the nonrecourse liability was a part of the taxpayer's § 1014 basis. The result would be the same here regardless of whether the liability was personal (recourse) liability or whether the liability was incurred directly from the Seller rather than from the Bank.

It should be pointed out that since the liability is already a part of the cost basis of the land, no adjustment to the basis of the land is made when interest or principal payments are made on the mortgage. Deductibility of interest payments is considered in Chapter 16B.

1(b).   The encumbrance of property after its acquisition, even though Mortgagor is free from any personal obligation to repay and even though the mortgage proceeds exceed Mortgagor's basis in the property, does not constitute a disposition of the property and is not a taxable event. The contemporaneous recognition of an obligation to repay the loan (even though not personally liable to do so) precludes a gain at this point. Woodsman Associates, Inc. v. Comm'r, 198 F.2d 357 (2d Cir. 1952). The mortgage also has no immediate effect on the property's $100,000 adjusted basis.

1(c).   If the mortgage proceeds are used to improve the land, they constitute a capital expenditure incurred on the land and the $100,000 adjusted basis of the land is increased by the $100,000 improvement to an adjusted basis of $200,000. § 1016(a)(1).

1(d).   If the mortgage proceeds are used to purchase $100,000 of stocks and bonds, there is no increase in the adjusted basis of the land. It remains $100,000. Of course, the stocks and bonds have a $100,000 cost basis.

1(e).   Mortgagor has a $200,000 gain on the sale of the land. Mortgagor's amount realized on the sale is $300,000, the total of the $120,000 of cash received as well as the amount of the $180,000 of liability relief. *Crane*. The difference between Seller's $300,000 amount realized and the $100,000 adjusted basis of the land is a $200,000 gain to Seller. If Mortgagor were personally liable on the mortgages and Purchaser assumed the liabilities, *Crane* would not be needed here. Mortgagor's liabilities would be discharged in connection with Purchaser's assumption of the mortgages, and the *Old Colony Trust Co.* principle would include the $180,000 within the amount realized.

Purchaser's cost basis in the land regardless of the type of liability would be $300,000, the total of the $120,000 of cash plus the $180,000 of liabilities.

1(f).   Mortgagor most likely has an $80,000 gain on the donative transfer. Several cases have concluded there was such a gain result where the liability was a personal liability, Evangelista v. Comm'r, 629 F.2d 1218 (7th Cir. 1980); Malone v. U.S., 326 F.Supp. 106 (N.D. Miss. 1971), aff'd per curiam, 455 F.2d 502 (5th Cir. 1972), or a combination of personal and nonrecourse liability, Estate of Levine v. Comm'r, 72 T.C. 780 (1979), aff'd, 634 F.2d 12 (2d Cir. 1980). And in Johnson v. Comm'r 495 F.2d 1079 (6th Cir. 1974), the same result was reached in a nonrecourse situation. The implication of *Crane* is that, except where a statute alters the result, e.g. § 465 and see Problem 2(a) on page 180 of the Text, recourse and nonrecourse liabilities should be treated in the same manner. Cf. *Kirby Lumber* at page 165 of the Text. In effect, Mortgagor has realized $180,000 under *Crane* even though Mortgagor was not personally liable on the loans. This results in a part gift, part sale and pursuant to Reg. § 1.1001-1(e) Mortgagor has an $80,000 gain, the difference between the $180,000 amount realized and the land's $100,000 adjusted basis. The result is proper. The $180,000 encumbrances are ones Mortgagor is not obligated to repay and ones in which Mortgagor is no longer concerned; Mortgagor has an amount realized to that extent.

Son's basis in the property is determined under the part gift, part sale Reg. § 1.1015-4. His basis is $180,000, the greater of:

(i)   the amount paid by the transferee for the property: Under

48

Crane Son has incurred a cost of $180,000 (or)

(ii)   the transferor's adjusted basis for the property at the time of the transfer: $100,000 plus the $80,000 gain recognized by the Mortgagor on the transfer equals $180,000. (It is assumed no gift tax is paid).

With respect to this transaction, it can be argued (see problem 2(b) at page 179 of the Text) that it should be treated as two transactions, a $180,000 sale and a $120,000 gift resulting in a $120,000 gain to Mortgagor (amount realized   of $180,000 less $60,000, $180,000/$300,000 of the $100,000 adjusted basis) and a $220,000 adjusted basis to Son ($180,000 of cost basis and a $40,000§ 1015(a) basis, $120,000/$300,000 times $100,000). Similar transfers to charity are now so treated by express statutory provision. See §§ 170(e)(2) and 1011(b).

1(g).   As in problem 1(f), above, Mortgagor has realized $180,000 under *Crane* even though she is not personally liable on the loan. Her gain realized is $80,000 ($180,000 - $100,000), but this gain is not recognized on the transfer of the property to her Spouse. § 1041(a). Spouse takes a $100,000 transferred basis in the land from Mortgagor. § 1041(b)(2).

The effect of Spouse's extinguishing the liabilities is nil. When the property is mortgaged, the amount of the loan proceeds is not included in the income of Mortgagor because Mortgagor has an obligation to repay the loan. Therefore, when the obligation is satisfied there can be no tax effect. See a comment to this effect in *Tufts* at page 145 of the Text. Again, the spouses are a single economic unit and any gain or loss will be recognized when Spouse sells the property.

1(h).   Again using the *Crane* principle, Mortgagor has an amount realized equal to the amount of the liabilities on the property or $180,000. Thus Mortgagor has an $80,000 gain on the transfer. Parker v. Delaney so held.

1(i).   Until the *Tufts* decision, the answer was somewhat in doubt. However, the Supreme Court in *Tufts* provides us with the final answer of $80,000. When a taxpayer sells or disposes of property encumbered by a nonrecourse obligation, the outstanding amount of the obligation is included in the amount realized. The fair market value of the property is irrelevant to this calculation. *Tufts* at page 145 of the Text. But see problem 2 at page 180 of the Text.

2. Yes, Investor has a gain on the sales, because basis must be allocated to the separate parcels to determine gain or loss as each sale takes place. There is no question as to the amount of property disposed of in each parcel and consequently one-third of the total basis or $10,000 must be allocated to each parcel. Reg. § 1.61-6(a). Investor would have a $4,000 gain in year one, a $6,000 gain in year two and a $10,000 basis in the remaining parcel. If at the time of acquisition each of the three acres acquired had different values, the taxpayer's total cost basis would have been allocated to the several acres in proportion to their relative fair market values *as of that time*. Perhaps the need to ascribe a cost basis to separate portions of property all acquired at the same time can be seen better by way of a hypothetical assuming a purchase of several hundred shares of stock which are then sold off piece-meal at a later time.

3(a). Gainer would have a $10,000 gain on his transfer, the difference between his $32,000 amount realized and $22,000 adjusted basis. Gainer's basis is computed under § 1015 by carrying over donor's basis of $20,000 (§ 1015(a)) and increasing it by $2,000 under § 1015(d)(6). The § 1015(d)(6) computation applies the ratio of the net appreciation in the property over the value of the property, $10,000/$30,000, to the gift tax, $6,000, to yield $2,000.

3(b). Shelterer's basis is Shelterer's cost of $32,000.

3(c). The key to this question is the dubious objective expressed in the committee reports that a tax addition to basis should apply only to that part of the gift tax attributable to the value of the gift that will be subject both to gift tax and later income tax. This objective is criticized above at the comment for page 122 of the Text. Section 1015(d)(6) reflects this philosophy, as applied to this problem:

$$\frac{\text{Net appreciation}}{\text{Amount of gift}} \quad x \quad \text{tax paid} \quad = \quad \text{increase in basis}$$

Net appreciation under § 1015(d)(6)(B) is the excess of fair market value of the gift less the donor's adjusted basis immediately before the gift. This raises the issue whether "the fair market value of the gift" means the net value which is used for gift tax purposes (here, $30,000 - $12,000 mortgage) or the gross fair market value of the property involved ($30,000).

A similar issue arises with respect to the meaning of "the amount of the gift" under § 1015(d)(6)(A)(ii).

Is it gross gift ($30,000) or net gift ($18,000)?

If one uses the gross gift approach then the net appreciation under (6)(B) is $30,000 less $20,000 or $10,000. Plugging the $10,000 amount into the (6)(a) formula, there is a $1,000 adjustment:

$$\frac{\$10,000}{\$30,000} \times \$3,000 = \$1,000$$

Under this approach Gainer would have an $11,000 gain on his sale, i.e., $32,000 less $21,000 (his $20,000 basis plus the $1,000 adjustment).

The result is philosophically sound. The equity approach should be used in determining the gift tax liability but there is appreciation on the property itself which is potentially subjected to both taxes and which should get the benefit of an adjustment.

If one uses a net gift approach, then "the amount of the gift" is the net gift or $18,000. Cf. § 2503(a) using the term "amount of gifts" which uses a net amount concept. Using that interpretation, the adjustment is still uncertain. If the donor's basis in the property is allocated pro rata between the $18,000 net gift and the $12,000 sale then the adjusted basis in the gift is $12,000 ($18,000/$30,000 x $20,000), the net appreciation in the gift is $6,000 and the adjustment is $6,000/$18,000 x $3,000 or again = $1,000 (as above) and the Gainer would again have an $11,000 gain on the sale.

However, it is also arguable that in a non charitable part-gift, part-sale the regulations first allocate the donor's basis in the property to the sale portion of the property. See Reg. § 1.1001-1(c). Thus, donor's basis in the sale property would be $12,000 with only the remaining $8,000 of the donor's adjusted basis allocated to the net gift. Using that interpretation, the appreciation in the gift is $10,000 and the adjustment is as follows:

$$\frac{\$10,000}{\$18,000} \text{ x } \$3,000 \text{ or a } \$1,667 \text{ adjustment}$$

Under this approach Gainer would have a $10,333 gain on his sale - $32,000 less $21,667 (his $20,000 basis plus the adjustment.) This result appears to be a better statutory interpretation, although from a policy approach the prior result may be more appropriate.

Shelterer's cost basis is $32,000, i.e., the sum of the cash and the liability on the property.

Page 155:

An article summarizing the income tax consequences of life insurance is Gallagher, "A Primer on Section 101-Federal Income Taxation of Life Insurance Proceeds," 49 *Temple L. Q.* 831 (1976). A more recent article discusses the § 101(g) accelerated death benefits. See Brazelton and Kaenzing, "Accelerated Death Benefits Finally Afforded Exclusion" 75 *Taxes* 57 (1997). See also Gazur, "Death and Taxes: The Taxation of Accelerated Death Benefits for the Terminaly Ill" 11 *Va. Tax Rev.* 263 (1991) (written prior to the enactment of § 101(g)).

Page 155:

It is possible that the "suffered enough" notion underlies the § 101(a) life insurance exclusion. But, and perhaps more importantly, the proceeds are similar to other inherited property that is excluded from gross income by § 102(a) and receives a stepped-up basis under § 1014, although note that this comparison breaks down if there was an inter vivos gift of a life insurance policy because there is still a § 101(a) exclusion with no § 1015 basis because the proceeds are in cash.

Page 157:

The result under § 101(d) is logical and the exclusion, if she lives beyond her life expectancy, is supported by the doctrine of the dirty trick; it would seem unfair to hit Mrs. Married with tax on her full payments at a time in her life when she is elderly, likely least able to pay the tax, and accustomed to the exclusion. The result is justified from a revenue standpoint by the fact that neither she nor her estate is allowed any loss deduction if she dies prior to her life expectancy. Nevertheless compare the result in an annuity situation under § 72(b)(2) and (3) and compare problem 1(d) under the life insurance problems with and problems 1(b) and (c) at the end of the Chapter.

Page 158:

The "Victims of Terrorism Tax Relief Act of 2001" added § 101(i) to the Code. Under that provision gross income does not include amounts paid by an employer by reason of the death of an employee who is a "specified terrorist victim" as defined in § 692(d)(4). § 101(i)(1). The payments may be a lump sum or payments made over time. Id. Section 692(d)(4) defines a specific terrorist victim as one who dies as a result of wounds or injury incurred as a result of the terrorist attack in Oklahoma City on April 19, 1995, the terrorist attacks on September 11, 2001, or as a result of illness incurred due to an anthrax attack occurring after September 10, 2001 and before January 1, 2002. The term does not include any individual indentified by the Attorney General to have been a participant or conspirator in any such terrorist attack or a representation of such individual. § 692(d)(4). In general, the exclusion does not apply to amounts that would have been payable if the individual had died for a reason other than the attack. § 101(i)(2)(A). A special rule opens the limitations period for the Oklahoma City victims for a one-year period after enactment of the provision.

PROBLEMS

Page 158:

1(a). The $100,000 of proceeds are excluded from gross income by § 101(a)(1), as such amounts are paid by reason of Insured's death.

1(b). Under § 101(c) the $10,000 of interest is not subject to the § 101(a) exclusion, and the interest would be required to be included in Beneficiary's gross income in the current year. Like payments of interest in each succeeding year would be treated the same.

1(c). Beneficiary (daughter) would have $8,000 of income in the current year. The § 101(d) exception applies when the life insurance proceeds are paid in an annuity form over a period of years. Under § 101(d) the amount of proceeds ($100,000) is sought to be excluded from gross income, but the actual exclusion is prorated among the total payments expected to be received. Since the daughter's life expectancy is 25 years, $100,000 is divided by 25 to prorate $4,000 to each year as the amount to be excluded in each year. The remaining $8,000 of the $12,000 is included in income.

Both subsections (c) and (d) of § 101 contemplate amounts of the proceeds being held by Insurer. In such circumstances the question may be asked which subsection applies. Reg. § 1.101-3(a) answers that § 101(c) applies only when the insurer holds amounts "without substantial diminution of the principal amount" over the period when interest is being paid. The two provisions are made mutually exclusive by § 101(d)(3).

1(d).   Beneficiary (daughter) would have $8,000 of gross income in the twenty-sixth year. The prorated amount is excluded from gross income without regard to whether the beneficiary lives beyond the life expectancy used in making the calculation. Reg. § 1.101-4(c).

This conclusion in the regulations is difficult to discern in the statute but, at least, it does find support in S.Rep. No. 1622, 83rd Cong., 2d Sess. (1954), p. 181. Note that if she died prior to the 25 year period and did not recover the full $100,000 of proceeds, neither she nor her estate would be allowed any deduction. Cf. Rev. Rul. 72-193, 1972-1 C.B. 58. Compare the current annuity rules under § 72(b)(2) and (3) and see problem 1(b) and (c), on page 163 of the Text.

2(a).   If Pro takes out a policy on Jock's life, any amounts received by Pro would be excluded from gross income. § 101(a)(1). Note that generally Pro must have an insurable interest in Jock to purchase a policy on his life.

2(b).   If, however, Pro purchases an existing, paid-up policy from Jock then $980,000, or the excess of the proceeds received over the consideration paid, is income to Pro under § 101(a)(2), as neither of the § 101(a)(2)(A) or (B) exceptions is applicable. Supporting reasons are elusive; it may be an incidental effect of an effort to discourage trafficking in insurance policies for artificial reasons. Of course, the tax planning answer is obvious: a new policy, not a purchase of the old policy.

2(c).   If Jock is a shareholder in Pro Corporation, the § 101(a)(2)(B) exception to the § 101(a) (2) income recognition rule applies and the proceeds are excluded from Pro's gross income. Suppose Jock owns less than 1% of the stock. Is the exception too liberally expressed?

3(a).   On Insured's sale of the policy to Child, Insured would recognize a gain of $20,000, $60,000 less $40,000. There is no § 101(a)(1) protection on this sale, because the amount is not paid by reason of Insured's death.

At Insured's death when Child receives the $100,000 of insurance proceeds, Child has $40,000 of income under § 101(a)(2) because there has been a transfer for valuable consideration and child's basis is a § 1012 cost basis. Note that if this had been either a gift to Child or a part gift, part sale to Child the proceeds would be excluded by § 101(a)(2)(A).

3(b).   When Insured sells the policy to Spouse for $60,000, § 1041 comes into play. Insured has no income and Spouse takes the policy with Insured's $40,000 basis. See § 1041(a) and (b)(2), respectively. When Insured dies and Spouse collects $100,000, Spouse has no income. Although § 101(a)(2) would seem to require Spouse to include $60,000 ($100,000 less $40,000) in gross income, the § 101(a)(2)(A) exception applies sending Spouse back into § 101(a)(1) and allowing Spouse to exclude the proceeds from gross income.

3(c).   Insured's sale is treated under § 101(g)(1)(A) and (2)(A) as paid by reason of Insured's death and the $40,000 "gain" is excluded under § 101(a)(1). See § 101(g)(2)(B)(i), (ii) and (4)(A). When Viatrical Settlement Provider collects the $100,000 of proceeds at Insured's death, it will have $20,000 of gross income ($100,000 less $80,000) included under § 101(a)(2).

Page 161:

The current plan for taxing annuities seems clearly to be an improvement over the prior "recovery of capital" and "3% of cost" techniques.

PROBLEM

Page 163:

1(a).   T will be taxed on $1,000. Since T has a 24 year life expectancy, T can expect to receive $72,000 in total annuities. The § 72(b) "exclusion

56

ratio" is 2/3, determined by the ratio of the "investment in the contract" ($48,000) to the "expected return" under the contract ($72,000). Thus § 72(b) will exclude $2,000 of the payment (2/3 of $3000) leaving only $1,000 includable in T's gross income under § 72(a).

In explaining the above result the following techniques may be helpful:

(1)   To decipher the statute, reduce the narrative to a formula:

$$\frac{\text{Excluded Amount}}{} = \text{Amount received} \quad \text{X} \quad \frac{\text{Investment in Contract}}{\text{Expected Return}}$$

Section 72 provides definitions for terms used in the equation. Many Code provisions require similar analysis.

(2)   To understand what is happening, check the conclusions: The general objective is tax-free return of capital. A $2,000 exclusion each year for 24 years equals $48,000, the total amount to be excluded. The general aim is to exclude cost as a return of capital and to tax the balance as gain.

1(b).   If T outlives T's life expectancy, T will be taxed on the full $3,000 amount of annuity received in the thirtieth year of annuity payments. § 72(b)(2). Prior law would have continued the exclusion in a manner similar to continuation of the life insurance exclusion. See problem 1(d) for page 158, above. The action of Congress under § 72(b)(2) (even though it was mixed with some § 72(b)(3) equity) seems inappropriate. See the comments at page 162 of the Text.

1(c).   Yes, the estate will get a deduction. § 72(b)(3). If the death occurred after 9 years the estate would be allowed a $30,000 deduction ($48,000 of cost less $18,000 of previously recovered cost) under § 72(b)(4). The deduction qualifies as a net operating loss. § 72(b)(3)(C). We again question the policy of the statutory change. See problem 1(b), above, and page 162 of the Text.

1(d).   If there is a 34 year expectancy, the "expected return" under the contract would be $102,000. The § 72(b) exclusion ratio is 3/4 determined by the ratio of the "investment in the contract" ($76,500) to the "expected return" under the contract ($102,000). Thus the § 72(b) exclusion is 3/4 of each payment or $2,250; and $750 of each $3,000 payment will be included in income under § 72(a), whether the payments are being received by T *and* T's spouse jointly or by T *or* T's spouse as the survivor.

Chapter 8.   Discharge of Indebtness

Page 166:

> For a discussion of the *Zarin* case, see Giangiordano, "Taxation - Discharge of Indebtedness Income," 64 *Temple L. Rev.* 1189 (1991); Kulper, "Taxpayer Rolls the Dice and the IRS Craps Out: Forgiveness of Gambling Debts is Not Income in Zarin v. Commissioner," 1991 *Utah L.R.* 617 (1991); Johnson, "*Zarin* and the Tax Benefit Rule: Tax Models for Gambling Losses and the Forgiveness of Gambling Debts," 45 *Tax L. Rev.* 697 (1990); Barton, "Legal and Tax Incidents of Compulsive Behavior: Lessons from *Zarin*" 45 *Tax Law.* 749 (1992); and Katz, "Did *Zarin* have a *Tufts* Day at a Casino Made Out of *Kirby Lumber?*" 26 *U.C. Davis L.R.* 261 (1993).

Page 179:

> The House Committee Report to the 1993 legislation contains the following numerical example of the qualified real property business indebtedness exclusion under § 108(a)(1)(D) (H.R. 2141, 103 Cong., 1st Sess, 185-186 (1993)):

> > . . . Assume that on July 1, 1993, Individual J owns a building worth $150,000, used in his trade or business, that is subject to a first mortgage securing a debt of J's of $110,000 and second mortgage securing a second debt of J's of $90,000. J is neither a bankrupt nor insolvent and neither debt is qualified farm indebtedness. J agrees with his second mortgagee to reduce the second mortgage debt to $30,000, resulting in discharge of indebtedness income in the amount of $60,000. Under the provision, assuming that J has sufficient basis in business real property to absorb the reduction . . ., J can elect to exclude $50,000 of that discharge from gross income. This is because the principal amount of the discharged debt immediately before the discharge (i.e., $90,000) exceeds the fair market value of the property securing it (i.e., $150,000 of free and clear value less $110,000 of other qualified business real pro-perty debt or $40,000) by $50,000. The remaining $10,000 of discharge is included in gross income.

A provision of the "Victims of Terrorism Tax Relief Act of 2001" allows an exclusion (not found in the Code) for discharge of indebtedness (in whole or in part) of indebtedness if the indebtedness is discharged by reason of the death of an individual as a result of the September 11, 2001 attacks or as a result of anthrax attacks occurring after September 10, 2001 and before January 1, 2002, but only if the discharge is because the individual died as a result of one of the attacks.

PROBLEMS

Page 180:

1(a).   Assuming in each part of this problem that no exception to the *Kirby Lumber* doctrine applies, Poor has $3,000 of gross income under *Kirby Lumber*. If there is an expression of student interest in the creditor's side of a *Kirby Lumber* transaction a brief comment on § 166 may be in order. See Chapter 23A.

1(b).   Poor has $2,000 of gross income under *Kirby Lumber*.

1(c).   Poor has $5,000 of gross income; $2000 under *Kirby Lumber* and $3,000 by the satisfaction of a legal obligation with appreciated property under the *International Freighting Corp.* case at page 133 of the Text. Cf. U.S. v. Davis, 370 U.S. 65 (1962).

1(d).   Poor has $10,000 of income because the $10,000 obligation is discharged as compensation for Poor's services. In effect the compensation was merely prepaid.

1(e).   Poor has $10,000 of income: $8,000 realized by rendering of services as in problem 1(d), above, and $2,000 under the *Kirby Lumber* doctrine.

1(f).   Poor has $3,000 of income under the *Kirby Lumber* doctrine. Poor also has $7,000 of indirect compensation from Employer under *Old Colony Trust Co.* and § 102(c).

2(a).   Owner's amount realized from the disposition of the land includes the amount of liabilities from which Owner is discharged as a result of the disposition. Reg. § 1.1001-2(a)(1). If the property secures recourse liability, then the amount realized does not include the amount that is discharge of indebtedness. Reg. § 1.1001-2(a)(2). In this case, the liability is recourse. Creditor has the right to collect the unpaid debt from Owner personally, the forfeiture of the security does not necessarily extinguish the debt. Therefore, the disposition of the property results in a discharge of liability to the extent of the fair market value of the property, $170,000. Thus the amount realized is $170,000 and Owner realizes gain of $70,000 ($170,000 - $100,000) on the land. The remaining amount discharged, $10,000, is discharge of indebtedness income, and Owner has $10,000 of discharge of indebtedness income. See Reg. § 1.1001-2(c) Ex. (8) and Rev. Rul. 90-16, 1990-1 C.B. 12. Since the land is held for investment purposes, the §108(a)(1)(D) qualified real property business indebtedness exception to the *Kirby Lumber* doctrine would not apply.

The relevance of bifurcating the gain into two segments will be more appreciated once characterization is explored in Chapter 21, infra. Cf. Gehl v. Comm'r, 95-1 USTC ¶ 50,191 (8th Cir. 1995) a Not for Publication decision affirming 102 T.C. 784 (1994), holding that where property was transferred by an insolvent debtor to a creditor with a fair market value in excess of basis but less than the amount of debtor's recourse debt, the debtor had a § 61(a)(5) gain on the property equal to its fair market value less its adjusted basis and only the excess of the debt over the fair market value of the property was *Kirby Lumber* § 61(a)(12) income qualifying for the insolvency exception. The decisions relied in part upon Reg. §§ 1.1001-2(a)(2) and -2(c) Example 8. Also cf. Aizawa v. Comm'r, 99 T.C. 197 (1992), involving a foreclosure on a recourse liability in which the taxpayer was not relieved of the remaining recourse liability and the court concluded that the proceeds of the foreclosure sale constituted the amount realized on the property.

2(b).   Since the liability is a nonrecourse liability, the entire liability is discharged by the transfer of the property to Creditor. The amount realized is therefore the entire amount of the debt, $180,000, and Owner realizes gain of $80,000 ($180,000 less $100,000) on the property. *Tufts*; Reg. §§ 1.1001-2(a)(1), -2 (a)(4)(i) and -2(b); Ltr. Rul 9302001. Cf. Rev. Rul. 91-31, 1991-1 C.B. 19 (involving discharge of

61

nonrecourse indebtedness which did not involve the disposition of the property). Owner has no discharge of indebtedness income. Justice O'Connor's concurring opinion is *Tufts* at page 145 of the Text suggests that the bifurcation approach that applies to a recourse liability should also apply to a nonrecourse liability. An article is also critical of the difference in treatment between recourse and nonrecourse liabilities. See Geier, "Tufts and the Evolution of Debt - Discharge Theory," 1 *Fla. Tax Rev.* 115 (1992). The article traces the evolution of the difference in treatment and concludes that it does not make sense. It concludes that the bifurcated approach currently applied to discharge of recourse debt (part (a) of problem) is better than the collapsed or unbifurcated approach of *Tufts* currently applied to discharge of nonrecourse debt (part (b) of problem).

3(a).   Businessman has $40,000 of *Kirby Lumber* income. He is solvent and there is no applicable exception under § 108. The gift exception seems inapplicable.

Prior to the 1986 legislation this would have been a "qualified business indebtedness" falling within the elective exception which if elected would have resulted in exclusion of the $40,000 of *Kirby Lumber* income and a basis reduction in the ambulances to $60,000. See I.R.C. (1954) § 108(a)(1)(C), now repealed.

3(b).   Here, the § 108(e)(5) purchase price exception is applicable. It applies in a situation which does not involve bankruptcy or insolvency. § 108(e)(5)(B). When Businessman has a $40,000 purchase price adjustment and the adjusted basis of the property is less than the adjustment amount, Businessman has $5,000 of income and a zero adjusted basis in the ambulances. As there is no statutory directive in such circumstances, it is unclear whether the income is *Kirby Lumber* income or income under the tax benefit doctrine, but in either event there is $5,000 of ordinary income.

3(c).   The § 108(d)(3) definition of insolvency is met; therefore § 108(a)(1)(B) applies to exclude the $40,000 discharged amount from gross income. Section 108(b) requires a reduction in tax attributes. Since there are no tax attributes under § 108(b)(2)(A)-(D) then seemingly a basis reduction is required under § 108(b)(2)(E). However, in a Title II case or an insolvency case (in which no § 108(b)(E) election is made), § 1017(b)(2) limits the mandatory basis reduction, and the basis of the assets is not to be reduced below the amount of the liabilities. Thus here, assuming the ambulances are worth $100,000 and the liabilities after the discharge are $185,000 ($225,000 - 40,000), the $100,000 basis of the ambulances is not reduced. Since there is no passive activity loss or credit carryover and no foreign tax credit carry-over, there is no § 108(b)(2)(E) or (F) reduction and there are no income tax consequences to Businessman other than the § 108 exclusion of $40,000.

3(d).   In this situation, the $40,000 of *Kirby Lumber* exception first wipes out the net operating loss of $30,000. See § 108(b)(2)(A). However, there would be no $10,000 basis adjustment to the ambulances because of § 1017(b)(2) which is discussed in problem 3(c), above.

In the alternative, Businessman could elect under § 108(b)(5) to reduce his basis in the depreciable ambulances to $60,000, rather than eliminating his net operating loss. If he so elected, the § 1017(b)(2) limitations would not apply (see the last sentence of § 1017(b)(2)) and the adjusted basis of the ambulances would be reduced to $60,000. Clearly the first solution is the preferable alternative.

3(e).   Under § 108(a)(1)(B) as limited by § 108(a)(3) there is an exclusion of $25,000 for an insolvency situation. There is no exclusion of the additional $15,000 which must be included in gross income under *Kirby Lumber*.

As to the insolvency exception, § 1017(b)(2) again limits the basis reduction as in problems 2(c) and (d), above. The issue is to what extent § 1017(b)(2) requires a basis reduction. The aggregate basis of the property after the discharge to which § 108(a)(1)(B) applies is $100,000 and the liabilities *after* the § 108(a)(1)(B) discharge are also $100,000. Thus there is no basis reduction under § 1017(b)(2).

In the alternative, it is arguable that the assets basis must be reduced to $85,000 (rather than $100,000) to reflect the full $40,000 of debt discharge, not merely the § 108(a)(1)(B) discharge. The issue is whether "the discharge" in § 1017(b)(2)(B) refers to the § 108(a)(1)(B) discharge in the introductory clause of § 1017(b)(2) or to the entire debt discharge by the creditor. Although we can find no direct authority on point, we feel that the latter is the better alternative.

4(a).   If Friend's power to enforce Decedent's $5,000 debt expires due to the running of a statute of limitations, Decedent's estate has gross income of $5,000. As expressed in Estate of Emelil Bankhead, 60 T.C. 535 (1973), the estate is economically enriched by the extinction of the indebtedness and the beneficiaries stand to take more money than they would otherwise have received if the debt had been paid. See also Carl T. Miller Trust v. Comm'r, 76 T.C. 191 (1981). Apparently, it is immaterial whether the statute extinguishes the debt or merely bars an action on it. See Securities Co. v. U.S., 85 F. Supp. 532 (S.D.N.Y. 1948).

4(b).   Although Decedent's estate would again be relieved of a $5,000 obligation and would seemingly have $5,000 of *Kirby Lumber* income, nevertheless Friend's action is probably indicative of sufficient donative intent a la *Duberstein* to fall within the gift exception to *Kirby Lumber* with the result that the estate has no income. See § 102, Reg. § 1.61-12(a).

4(c).   Nephew need report no gross income. This is simply an extension of the gift exception to the *Kirby Lumber* doctrine to include bequests, again under § 102.

This may be some students' first intimation that an estate is an entity subject to income tax. It should be pointed out that generally its overall computation of tax liability is similar to that of an individual. See Chapter 13, infra.

PROBLEM

Page 185:

1(a).   This problem is primarily intended to demonstrate that the inclusion in gross income of a recovery of a judgment or settlement depends upon the nature of the recovery.

The $8,000 recovery of the loan is a mere return of capital and not included in gross income; but the $500 of interest is included in gross income.

1(b).   Debtor has a $6,500 gain on the land which is transferred in satisfaction of the obligation. This is the holding of *International Freighting Corporation* previously encountered in Chapter 6, of the soon-to-be-discussed *Davis* case in Chapter 10 and the *Kenan* case in Chapter 21. It is premature to concern students with the characterization of Debtor's gain and is probably premature to point out that Debtor will possibly have a $500 interest deduction under § 163. Cf. § 163(d) and (h). Plaintiff's basis in the land will be $8,500.

1(c).   Plaintiff's recovery is based on a breach of contract claim and the $8,000 of lost profits is included in gross income.

Punitive damages of $16,000 received on account of a business claim are included in gross income under the Supreme Court's holding in *Glenshaw Glass*, found in Chapter 2 of the Text.

1(d)(1). The damages received in the settlement flow from a breach of a business contract and the $6,000 gain on goodwill is included in Plaintiff's gross income. It is as though Plaintiff had sold the goodwill in which she has a $4,000 basis for $10,000. The first $4,000 of the recovery is a return of capital; the remaining $6,000 is a gain from the goodwill. At this point we continue to ignore characterization of includable recoveries. It should also be pointed out that Plaintiff's basis for any remaining goodwill in the business is zero since she has fully recovered her $4,000 basis.

1(d)(2). If Plaintiff recovers only $4,000, the recovery is merely a recovery of capital, she has no gross income, and her basis in the remaining goodwill (a nondivisible asset) is zero.

1(d)(3). In this situation Plaintiff has a $3,000 recovery of capital, no gross income, and a $1,000 basis in her remaining goodwill.

Page 189:

> In a case of first impression, the Ninth Circuit addressed a different allocation issue. In Niles v. U.S., 710 F.2d 1391 (9th Cir. 1983), the court affirmed a District Court holding that the Service may not allocate a portion of a lump sum jury award to future medical expenses. The taxpayer received a $4 million unallocated jury award in a personal injury suit. The Service contended that a portion of the award should be allocated to future medical expenses to prevent the taxpayer from later deducting that amount of expenses under §213(a). The Service had taken this position in Rev. Rul. 79-427, 1979-2 C.B. 120. However, the Court held that the Service had no authority to allocate any portion of the lump sum award to future medical expenses because allocation was solely a jury function. It allowed deduction of medical expenses in future years denying the Service's claim that the expenses were "compensated for" within § 213(a) by the prior lump sum personal injury award.

PROBLEMS

Page 193:

1(a). The full $100,000 recovery of a physical personal injury is excluded under § 104(a)(2).

1(b). Even though $50,000 of the recovery is related to loss of compensation as a result of a physical personal injury, the full recovery is excluded from gross income under § 104(a)(2).

1(c). The $200,000 of punitive damages from a physical personal injury are specifically included in gross income. § 104(a)(2) (first parenthetical).

1(d).   This recovery is based on emotional distress arising out of a physical personal injury, and it is excluded from gross income as a recovery of *any* damages on account of physical personal injury under § 104(a)(2).

1(e).   The $100,000 recovery for emotional distress is not based on a physical personal injury and, except to the extent it is for amounts actually paid for medical care, it is included in gross income. § 104(a) flush language.

1(f).   This recovery for a non-physical personal injury is included in gross income. The § 104(a)(2) exclusion is inapplicable.

           If, however, Plaintiff alleged a personal physical injury (e.g., an assault from a harmful or offensive touching by the coach), the recovery for the assault would be excluded from gross income by § 104(a)(2).

1(g).   This $1,000,000 recovery is excluded by § 104(c) as it is essentially a physical personal injury recovery, even though it is labeled as punitive damages.

2(a).   They have $1,500 of gross income. This problem illustrates the application of the introductory clause of § 104(a) (and § 105(b)) which reduces the § 104 exclusion by the amount of the previously allowed deduction. Thus, only $1,000 of their recovery is excluded by § 104(a)(2). As the Note in the Text points out, to allow both a deduction and an exclusion of the $1,500 amount would create an unwarranted tax benefit; note that the overall treatment of the $1,500 is a wash both in terms of cash flow and inclusion in and deduction from gross income.

2(b).   They have $400 of gross income that is not excluded under the protective umbrella of § 105(b). Spouse's illness was compensated by both their personal policy and a policy provided by Spouse's Employer. Section 104(a)(3) excluded the full $3,000 received under their personal policy without regard to its disposition or use. Section 105(b) excludes amounts received by Spouse under Employer's policy which reimburses Spouse for medical care, but only to the extent of the cost of such care. To determine which policy's proceeds are used to pay for Spouse's medical care, *Rev. Rul. 69-154*, discussed at footnote 29 on page 191 in the Text, says that the amount of medical expense to be considered paid by the proceeds of each policy is proportionate to the amount of benefits received from each policy. Thus 40 percent (2000/5000) of Spouse's $4,000 expense is deemed paid out of the proceeds of Employer's policy. Section 105(b) excludes $1,600 of the proceeds from Employer's policy and the remaining $400 is included in Spouse's gross income. This allocation affects only the § 105(b) exclusion of amounts received under the Employer's policy. As stated above, the amount received under their personal policy remains fully excluded. The answer of course assumes that § 105(h) restrictions are not encountered.

2(c).   No; when the expenses and recovery occur in the same year § 104 and § 105 allow exclusions but § 213(a) allows a deduction only to the extent that expenses for medical care are "not compensated for by insurance or otherwise." Again, this precludes any double tax benefit.

3(a).   The $1 million recovery would be excluded from Injured's gross income under § 104(a)(2). However, the 5% interest earned each year from the money market account would be interest income included in Injured's gross income. See Rev. Rul. 65-29, 1965-1 C.B. 59. Cf. Rev. Rul. 76-133, 1976-1 C.B. 34.

3(b).   Again, the $1 million recovery would be excluded from Injured's gross income under § 104(a)(2). However, since Injured purchased the annuity, § 72 would apply and the interest element on the annuity in excess of the exclusion ratio would be included in Injured's gross income. Cf. § 72 (b)(2), (b)(3), Rev. Rul. 65-29, 1965-1 C.B. 59.

3(c).   If the case is settled and Injured receives $100,000 a year for life from Defendant the full $100,000 per year is excluded from Injured's gross income. *Rev. Rul. 79-313*. See also the second parenthetical in § 104(a)(2) allowing the § 104(a)(2) amount to be received in "periodic payments." One should take this hypothetical a step further. If Defendant purchased an annuity payable to Defendant for $100,000 a year for Injured's life, and then made payments to Injured, Defendant would have § 72(a) income and Injured would have § 104(a)(2) exclusions. See problem 3(b), above. If the payment were made directly to Injured by the annuity company, the amount would be totally excludable by Injured so long as Injured had a right only to the annuities as paid and no right to the sum producing the periodic payments. Rev. Rul. 76-133, 1976-1 C.B. 34.

See Lichtenstein and Winquist, "Deferred Payment for Damage Suit Offers Significant Advantages for Both Parties" 12 *Tax'n for Law.* 68 (1983); Cane, "How to Use and Benefit from Structured Settlements in Personal Injury Suits" 59 *J. Tax'n* 330 (1983).

Page 196:

> The Third and Sixth Circuits have held that a collateral attack on the language of a divorce settlement agreement involving tax consequences is not permitted unless the agreement is voidable because of mistake, undue influence, fraud, or duress. Comm'r v. Danielson, 378 F.2d 771 (3rd Cir. 1967) and Schatten v. U.S., 746 F.2d 319 (6th Cir. 1984). But see Green v. Comm'r, 855 F.2d 289 (6th Cir. 1988), not applying the *Schatten* rule to a divorce decree merely labellig a payment as a property settlement. These decisions have continued viability with respect to divorce instruments executed after 1984.

PROBLEMS

Page 203:

1(a).   If Andy and Fergie are not living in the same household, and there is no liability to make post-death payments, this qualifies as an "alimony or separate maintenance payment" as it meets all the requirements set forth in § 71(b). It is a cash payment, made pursuant to a "divorce or separation instrument" as defined in § 71(b)(2) which does not designate the payment as "non-alimony".

1(b).   This does not qualify as an "alimony or separate maintenance payment" because § 71(b) expressly provides that only cash payments qualify as alimony. Temp. Reg. § 1.71-1T(b), Q & A-5 states that transfers of a debt instrument of a third party *or* execution of a debt instrument by the payor do not qualify as alimony or separate maintenance payments. As cash payments of principal are made with respect to the note, § 71 and 215 come into play.

1(c).   Again, the payments do not qualify as alimony because they were not made in cash. Temp. Reg. § 1.71-1T(b), Q & A-5 also states that transfers of property do not qualify as alimony or separate maintenance payments.

1(d).   Section 71(b)(1)(B) provides that the parties may designate the payments as not includable in the recipient spouse's gross income under

§ 71(a) and not deductible under § 215(a) by the payor spouse. Such payments do not constitute alimony or separate maintenance payments.

1(e).   The payments would still be characterized as "non-alimony" even though the purpose of the non-deductibility provision is to avoid the imposition of federal income taxes on the payments. The very purpose of § 71(b)(1)(B) is to give the husband and wife an easy election of consequences, i.e., deductible and includable or nondeductible and not includable.

1(f).   The payments originally do not qualify as alimony or separate maintenance payments. Section 71(b)(1)(D) provides there must be no liability to make payments after the death of the payee spouse if the payments under the instrument are to receive alimony status. Since the decree contains no such provision and assumedly it is not supplied by local law, the payments here do not achieve alimony status.

1(g).   Here the payments qualify as alimony payments. The 1986 Act deleted a 1984 requirement that such terminations must be expressly provided in the divorce or separation instrument. Termination by operation of local law satisfies the § 71(b)(1)(D) requirement.

1(h).   The $25,000 cash payment would partially qualify as an "alimony or separate maintenance payment." A $10,000 portion receives alimony treatment because the divorce decree expressly states that these payments are to terminate upon Fergie's death should she die prior to the expiration of the 10-year period. However, as to the remaining $15,000, it is not a payment that will terminate upon Fergie's death, and it is not accorded alimony status. § 71(b)(1)(D).

1(i).   The payments do not qualify as alimony or separate maintenance payments.   Section 71(b)(1)(C) precludes otherwise qualifying payments from receiving alimony treatment for spouses legally separated under a divorce or separate maintenance decree, if they are living in the same household. Nor would it make a difference if Andy and Fergie are living on different floors in the same house. Temp. Reg. § 1.71-1T(b), Q and A-9 indicates that a dwelling unit formerly shared by both spouses will not be considered two separate households even if the spouses are physically separated from each other within the dwelling unit.

1(j). The payments probably (see the next paragraph) qualify as alimony or separate maintenance payments, as the § 71(b)(1)(C) prohibition applies only to those who are legally separated or divorced. Those who are living under a mere written separation agreement or a decree for support under § 71(b)(2)(B) and § 71(b)(2)(C), respectively, may continue to live in the same household without jeopardizing the alimony status of otherwise qualifying payments.

Note, however, that alimony status is achieved only if the spouses do not file a joint return. § 71(e). This rule is sensible because if a joint return were filed, there would be an inclusion/deduction "wash" on the joint return.

2(a). The payments are deductible by Tina under § 215 and included in Ike's gross income under § 71(a) in each of the three years. However § 71(f) recapture also comes into play in year three when Tina must take an amount into income and Ike receives a deduction. The amount involved is $62,500, computed as follows:

Recapture from year two, § 71(f)(4):

§ 71(f)(4)(A):	$40,000
Less § 71(f)(4)(B): 10,000 + 15,000 =	25,000
Equals § 71(f)(2)(B):	$15,000

We begin with the recapture from year two because it is impossible to compute the year one recapture without knowing the amount, if any, of year two recapture. See § 71(f)(3) (B)(i)(I).

Recapture from year one, § 71(f)(3):

§ 71(f)(3)(A): (first year)	$80,000
Less: § 71(f)(3)(B):	

The sum of:

(i) $17,500, the average (1/2) of: (I) the 2nd year $40,000 less the 1st year $15,000 plus (II) the 3rd year $10,000 (i.e. 1/2 of $35,000)

Plus

72

| (ii) | $15,000 | $32,500 |

| Equals § 71(f)(2)(A): | | $47,500 |

Under § 71(f)(2) the total excess alimony payments which must be recaptured in year three are $15,000 from year two plus $47,500 from year one or a total of $62,500. As a practical matter, note that if the $10,000 in year three is Ike's only income and if Ike has a § 71(f) deduction of $62,500, the deduction may be almost entirely wasted because it does not qualify for a § 172 carryover.

2(b). This problem illustrates that minor reductions in alimony will not trigger the recapture rule. The payments are deductible by Tina under § 215 and included in Ike's gross income under § 71(a) in each of the three years. Here, the § 71(f) recapture rule is inapplicable and there is no recapture in year three. By the numbers:

Recapture from year two, § 71(f)(4):
        § 71(f)(4)(A): $70,000
        Less § 71(f)(4)(B): $60,000 plus $15,000   75,000
        Equals § 71(f)(2)(B)   zero

Recapture from year one, §71(f)(3):
        § 71(f)(3)(A): $80,000
        Less § 71(f)(3)(B):
        § 71(f)(3)(B)(i):
                ½ of $70,000 and $60,000, i.e.
                ½ of $130,000 is $65,000

Plus

        § 71(f)(3)(B)(ii): $15,000   80,000
        Equals § 71(f)(2)(A)   zero

Under § 71(f)(2) there are no excess alimony payments which must be recaptured.

2(c). This problem illustrates that rear loading will not trigger the § 71(f) recapture rules. Again Tina may deduct and Ike has gross income on the payments in the three years. There are no excesses from year two

73

to year three and none from years one and two to year three and thus no recapture.

2(d). This problem illustrates that even though there is front loading from year one to year two, if there is sufficient rear loading in year three, recapture does not occur. Again Tina has § 215 deductions and Ike § 71(a) gross income in each of the years. There is no recapture in year three:

Recapture from year two, § 71(f)(4):   none
There is no excess of year two over year three.

Recapture from year one, § 71(f)(3):   none
    § 71(f)(3)(A): $80,000
    Less
    § 71(f)(3)(B)(i):
        ½ of $50,000 and $80,000
        i.e. ½ of $130,000 or $65,000
    Plus

    § 71(f)(3)(B)(ii): $15,000 $80,000
    Equals § 71(f)(2)(A):   zero

2(e). These payments are still gross income to Ike and deductible by Tina. However, they are *not* subject to the alimony recapture rules of § 71(f)(2). Section 71(f)(5)(C) excepts from the application of the alimony recapture rules payments that are fixed as a set percentage of income from a business owned by the payor spouse as long as the payments are required to be made for a period of not less than three years.

2(f). The entire amount of each payment ($80,000) qualifies for alimony treatment. The alimony recapture rules are not invoked where payments terminate within the three post-separation year period due to the death of either spouse. § 71(f)(5)(A).

2(g). All the payments qualify in full as alimony or separate maintenance payments and are subject to § 215(a) and § 71(a). The alimony recapture rules do not apply to payments under § 71(b)(2)(C). See §

71(f)(5)(B).

2(h). None of the year one payment will be accorded alimony status. The $120,000 payment in year one fails to pass the § 71(b)(1)(C) hurdle (see problem 1(i), above) and thus fails to qualify as an alimony or separate maintenance payment. Those in years 2 through 4 do qualify as alimony and are gross income to Ike and deductible by Tina. There is no recapture because the recapture rules apply only to "post-separation years" as defined in § 71(f)(6), are the first three years to which § 71(a) and § 215 apply. Thus the three years to be tested under § 71(f) are years two through four. Since there is only a $10,000 reduction in each of those years there is no recapture. See problem 2(b), above. Although front-loading is naughty, a little bit of front-loading is A-o.k.

PROBLEMS

Page 207:

1(a). The rental payments paid by Tom qualify as alimony or separate maintenance payments with the result that they are deductible by Tom under § 215(a) and includable in Nicole's gross income under § 71(a). Temp. Reg. § 1.71-1T(b), Q & A-6 specifically indicates that cash payment made by the payor spouse to a third party such as a lessor, under the terms of the divorce or separation instrument may qualify as a payment of cash received "on behalf of a spouse." § 71(b)(1)(A). This is an example of indirect alimony and, unless Tom is Nicole's landlord, this is alimony. Other examples include payment of medical expenses, insurance premiums and other obligations.

1(b). The $1,000 mortgage payments would also receive alimony treatment for the reasons stated in problem 1(a), above. Temp. Reg. § 1.71-1T(b), Q & A-6 gives as an example of payments to third parties which qualify for alimony status, the payment of the payee spouse's mortgage liabilities by the payor spouse. Since Nicole owns the house, the benefits are received by her indirectly and do not flow to Tom. Compare the result in problem 1(c), below.

1(c). These payments do *not* qualify as alimony or separate maintenance payments and thus do not come within the coverage of § 215(a) and § 71(a). Temp. Reg. § 1.71-1T(b), Q & A-6 indicates that any payments to maintain property owned by the payor spouse but used by the other spouse do not constitute payments on behalf of the other spouse. See the cases cited at footnote 4 at page 207 of the Text.

2(a).   The issue here is whether the $60,000 Roseanne expended for the insurance policy constitutes "alimony." It clearly does not. Section 71(b)(1) allows only payments made in *cash* to qualify as alimony. The transfer of the insurance policy is more in the nature of a property settlement. See § 1041. Thus, the $60,000 expended by Roseanne will not be deductible by her nor will it be includable in Tom's gross income.

2(b).   In this case, the entire $70,000 (the $10,000 annual payment plus the $60,000 transferred to Tom to purchase the insurance policy) will likely be accorded alimony status and thus be deductible by Roseanne under § 215(a) and includable in Tom's gross income under § 71(a). By making a simple alteration of the form of the transaction (from a transfer of the policy to a transfer of cash to purchase the policy) the parties have affected the tax treatment of the payment.

Or have they? If there is a prearranged binding agreement or understanding that Tom will purchase life insurance then in substance the situation is identical to problem 2(a), above, and the results should be the same.

The question of substance over form is never far below the surface and, even if the Commissioner has never heard of Longfellow, the Commissioner has been known to suggest that "things are not what they seem."

Note, however, that if the $60,000 cash payment is alimony and if it had occurred in year one or year two, it would have triggered the recapture rule of § 71(f) in year three. See problem 2 at page 204 of the Text.

2(c).   Again, the $5,000 initially expended on the policy will not be accorded alimony treatment for the reasons stated in problem 2(a), above. However, the $5,000 of cash that Roseanne transfers to Tom each year to enable him to pay the premiums on the policy will be accorded alimony status as these transfers meet all the requirements set forth in

§ 71(b) and he is the owner of the policy.

2(d).   The $5,000 premiums paid directly to the insurance company will qualify as alimony or separate maintenance payments and therefore be governed by § 71(a) and § 215(a). Temp. Reg. § 1.71-1T(b), Q & A-6 indicates that premiums paid by the payor spouse for life insurance on the payor's life made under the terms of a divorce decree qualify as payments made "on behalf of" the payee spouse to the extent the payee spouse is the owner of the policy. See I.T. 4001 in the Text.

2(e).   The premiums paid do not receive alimony or separate maintenance treatment because they are not deemed to be made to or on behalf of the payee spouse. The premiums would receive alimony status only if Tom is the beneficiary and is also the owner of the policy holding all the incidents of ownership. Temp. Reg. § 1.71-1T(b), Q & A-6.

PROBLEM

Page 212:

1(a).   Michael will recognize no gain on the transfer of the land. § 1041(a)(2). This section provides for nonrecognition treatment on the transfer of property from an individual to a former spouse, if the transfer is "incident to divorce." Section 1041(c)(1) specifically provides that a transfer of property is incident to divorce if it occurs within one year of the date on which the marriage ceases, which is the case here. Lisa Marie will recognize no income on the transfer, § 1041(b)(1), and will take a transferred basis of $100,000 for the land under § 1041(b)(2).

Lisa Marie will recognize a gain of $500,000 on her sale of the property. Although premature (see Chapter 21), it will be a capital gain if the land is a capital asset in the hands of Lisa Marie. If it is a capital gain, it will be long-term capital gain as, under § 1223(2), Lisa Marie will be permitted to "tack" Michael's holding period for the land.

1(b).   Michael will not have a recognized loss on the transfer of the property to Lisa Marie. It is foreclosed by § 1041(a)(2) and § 1041(c)(1). Lisa Marie will have no gross income as, for income tax purposes, § 1041(b)(1) treats the transfer as a gift; and Lisa Marie's basis in the land will be $500,000. Lisa Marie will recognize a loss (probably long-term capital loss, see problem 1(a), above) of $150,000 on the sale of the property. The fact that the transfer is made to satisfy a debt obligation of Michael is of no consequence since all transfers made within one year of the cessation of the marriage are conclusively presumed to be incident to the divorce. § 1041(c)(1). See Temp. Reg. § 1.1041-1T(b) Q & A-6.

Contrast the basis consequences under § 1041 with the consequences that follow a gift between unrelated parties. Under § 1015(a), the loss on the sale of the property would be only $50,000, if Lisa Marie were not an ex-spouse.

1(c). The issue here is whether the transfer is "incident to the divorce." If, as here, the transfer does not fall within the 1-year rule of § 1041(c)(1), the question becomes whether the transfer is "related to the cessation of the marriage" under § 1041(c)(2). Temp. Reg. § 1.1041-1T(b), Q & A-7, indicates that a transfer is related to the cessation of the marriage if it is pursuant to a divorce or separation instrument and occurs not more than six years after the date on which the marriage ceases. Since the transfer here was pursuant to the divorce decree and occurred within the six year period, the Treasury's present view is that § 1041 will apply. Michael will recognize no gain on the transfer of the property to Lisa Marie, and Lisa Marie will receive the land as a gift with a basis in the stock of $100,000 pursuant to § 1041(a) and (b)(1) and (2).

1(d). The results are the same as in problem 1(c), above. The requirements of Temp. Reg. § 1.1041-1T(b), Q & A-7, are again met. The written instrument incident to the divorce decree is a "divorce or separation instrument." § 71(b)(2)(A). Thus the transfer is pursuant to such an instrument and occurs within six years after the date the marriage ceases. See Young v. Comm'r, 113 T.C. 152 (1999).

1(e). This would also probably result in a nontaxable transaction. Temp. Reg. § 1.1041-1T(b), Q & A-7 also indicates that a transfer occurring more than six years after the cessation of the marriage is presumed to be unrelated to the cessation of the marriage. Since the transfer here occurred outside the six year period, the presumption applies. However, since the transfer is pursuant to the divorce decree, seemingly § 1041 would still apply. Temp. Reg. § 1.1041-1T(b), Q & A-7 goes on to provide that the presumption "may be rebutted only by showing that the transfer was made to effect the division of property owned by the former spouses at the time of the cessation of the marriage." The problem facts are within this requirement. See Ltr. Rul. 9306015 for a situation where a transfer was outside the six year period and § 1041 was inapplicable.

PROBLEM

Page 214:

1(a). Assuming all other requirements under § 71(b) are met, $6,000 of each $10,000 payment qualifies as an alimony or separate maintenance payment and thus will be deductible from Sean's gross income under § 215(a) and includable in Madonna's gross income under § 71(a). The other $4,000 is not income to Madonna or deductible by Sean as § 71(c)(1) provides, in effect, that amounts fixed for the support of payor spouse's children are *not* alimony.

1(b). Only $6,000 of the $10,000 payment will be treated as alimony under § 71 and § 215. Although the $4,000 is not fixed in the agreement as payable for the child, § 71(c)(2)(A) provides that if an amount specified in an instrument will be reduced upon the child reaching a certain age, marrying or dying, then an amount equal to the amount of such reduction, the $4,000, will be *deemed* to have been fixed in the instrument as payable for child support.

1(c). Again, only $6,000 of the $10,000 payment will be treated as alimony under § 71(a) and § 215(a). Section 71(c)(2)(B) provides that if payments specified in the instrument are reduced at a time that can be clearly associated with the happening of a contingency relating to a child of the payor, an amount equal to such reduction (or reductions) will be *deemed* to have been fixed in the instrument as payable for child support. Temp. Reg. § 1.71-1T(c), Q & A-18 provides that a payment will be treated as reduced at a time that can clearly be associated with the happening of a contingency relating to a child of the payor in only two situations. The first situation is where payments are to be reduced not more than six months before or after the child is to attain the age of 18, 21 or the local age of majority. The second situation, involved here, is where the payments are to be reduced on two or more occasions occuring not more than one year before or after a different child of the

79

payor spouse attains a certain age (the same age for each child) between the ages of 18 and 24, inclusive. In the problem, we find that Daughter will attain the age of 18 on June 17, 2008. This is less than one year after January 1, 2008, the date on which the payments will be reduced to $8,000 per year. Son will attain the age of 18 on March 5, 2011. This is less than one year prior to January 1, 2012, the date on which the payments will be presumed to be reduced; it is a time clearly associated with the happening of a contingency relating to a child of the payor. See Temp. Reg. § 1.71-1T(c) Q & A-18 Example. The temporary regulations also state that this presumption may be rebutted by showing that the dates on which the payments are to be reduced were determined independently of any contingencies relating to the payor spouse's children. Temp. Reg. § 1.71-1T(c), Q & A-18.

1(d). Only $1,000 of the $5,000 paid by Sean will be treated as an alimony or separate maintenance payment. This is due to the special allocation rule found in § 71(c)(3). The rule provides that where payments are less than the amount specified in the instrument, the payments are first allocated to the amount fixed as payable for child support and then, if there is any excess, it is allocated to the amount payable as alimony. In this problem, the $5,000 is first allocated to the $4,000 fixed as support for the child, and then the excess payment of $1,000 is allocated to the alimony component.

Page 217:

In another context (income tax rates payable by unmarried individuals as opposed to those payable by married individuals either filing jointly or separately), the Tax Court held that parties who had twice obtained foreign divorces prior to the end of a tax year and remarried in the beginning of the next tax year did not have valid divorces for federal tax purposes. In so holding, the court sidestepped the sham transaction doctrine and based its decision on a finding that the state of domicile (Maryland) would not have recognized the validity of the foreign divorces. Boyter v. Comm'r, 74 T.C. 989 (1980). However on appeal, the Fourth Circuit Court of Appeals remanded for consideration of the question whether the divorces and subsequent remarriages fell under the sham transaction doctrine. Boyter v. Comm'r, 668 F.2d 1382 (4th Cir. 1982); See page 934 of the Text. While the *Boyter* case is not a § 71 case, it may stand for the proposition that Federal courts, for Federal tax purposes, may disregard a divorce found effective for state law purposes.

Page 221:

The "Victims of Terrorism Tax Relief Act of 2001" has added § 139, the most recent exclusion provision to the Code. Section 139(a) provides an exclusion for a "qualified disaster relief payment" received by an individual. The Technical Explanation of the Act prepared by the Joint Committee on Taxation (page 15) provides:

> Qualified disaster relief payments include payments, from any source, to, or for the benefit of, an individual to reimburse or pay reasonable and necessary personal, family, living, or funeral expenses incurred as a result of a qualified disaster. Personal, family, and living expenses are intended to have the same meaning as when used in section 262. Personal expenses include personal property expenses.

> Qualified disaster relief payments also include payments, from any source, to reimburse or pay reasonable and necessary expenses incurred for the repair or rehabilitation of a personal residence, or for the repair or replacement of its contents, to the extent that the need for the repair, rehabilitation, or replacement is attributable to a qualified disaster. For purposes of determining the tax basis of a rehabilitated residence, it is intended that qualified disaster relief payments be treated in the same manner as amounts received on an involuntary conversion of a principal residence under section 121(d)(5) and sections 1033(b) and (h). A residence is not precluded from being a personal residence solely because the taxpayer does not own the residence; a rented residence can qualify as a personal residence.

> Qualified disaster relief payments also include payments by a person engaged in the furnishing or sale of transportation as a common carrier on account of death or personal physical injuries incurred as a result of a qualified disaster. Thus, for example, payments made by commercial airlines to families of passengers killed as a result of a qualified disaster would be excluded from gross income.

Qualified disaster relief payments also include amounts paid by a Federal, State or local government in connection with a qualified disaster in order to promote the general welfare. As under the present law general welfare exception, the exclusion does not apply to payments in the nature of income replacement, such as payments to individuals of lost wages, unemployment compensation, or payments in the nature of business income replacement.

Qualified disaster relief payments do not include payments for any expenses compensated for by insurance or otherwise. No change from present law is intended as to the deductibility of qualified disaster relief payments, made by an employer or otherwise, merely because the payments are excludable by the recipients. Thus, it is intended that payments excludable from income under the provision are deductible to the same extent they would be if they were includable in income. In addition, in light of the extraordinary circumstances surrounding a qualified disaster, it is anticipated that individuals will not be required to account for actual expenses in order to qualify for the exclusion, provided that the amount of the payments can be reasonably expected to be commensurate with the expenses incurred.

Particular payments may come within more than one category of qualified disaster relief payments: the categories are not intended to be mutually exclusive. Qualified disaster relief payments also are excludable for purposes of self-employment taxes and employment taxes. Thus, no withholding applies to qualified disaster relief payments.

Under the bill, a qualified disaster includes a disaster which results from a terroristic or military action (as defined in section 692(c)(2), as amended by the bill), a Presidentially declared disaster, a disaster which results from an accident involving a common carrier or from any other event which would be determined by the Secretary to be of a catastrophic nature, or, for purposes of payments made by a Federal, State or local government, a disaster designated by Federal, State or local authorities to warrant assistance.

The exclusion from income under section 139 does not apply to any individual identified by the Attorney General to have been a participant or conspirator in the terrorist-related aircraft crashes of September 11, 2001, or any other terrorist attack, or to a representative of such individual.

Page 221:

It has been held that the predecessor of § 121 (§ 1034) does not apply to a transaction in which taxpayer sells the land underlying the taxpayer's house at a gain and moves the house to a newly purchased piece of land. The court concluded that the sale of only the land was not a sale of "property used by the taxpayers as a principal residence." Stuart M. Hughes, 54 T.C. 1049 (1970), aff'd per curiam, 450 F.2d 980 (4th Cir. 1971). This holding would apply to deny the use of § 121 as well.

In 1984, former President Bush, then Vice President, was involved in a § 121 (then § 1034) "principal residence" dispute with the Service. The Service disallowed deferral of a $596,101 capital gain from the sale of President Bush's Houston home. The President claimed that the proceeds were used to buy a replacement house in Maine, but the Service ruled the Maine home was not a new principal residence. The Service's position was that the vice presidential residence in Washington, DC was the President's principal residence. The Washington Post, Oct. 4, 1984, at A 1.

PROBLEMS

Page 226:

1(a). Taxpayers have a realized gain of $400,000. Taxpayers may exclude all of their gain under § 121(a) because they meet the joint return, ownership, and use requirements of § 121(b)(2), they do not otherwise violate § 121(b)(3), and their gain is within the $500,000 exclusion.

1(b). The entire $400,000 of realized gain may be excluded under § 121(a) because the § 121(b)(2) requirements are again met. The point here is that § 121 can be used on multiple occasions if its requirements are met.

1(c). Taxpayers would have to include their $400,000 gain in gross income because the two-year ownership and use requirements are not met. § 121(a). This assumes there are no exigent circumstances under § 121(c)(2)(B). See Problem 2, below.

1(d). The gain would be $800,000 of which $500,000 would qualify for the § 121(b)(2)(A) exclusion and $300,000 would be included in gross income. This illustrates the problem for people who have consistently traded up using old § 1034. Note § 121(g) allowing tacking of ownership and use from rollover residences. Under § 121(g), if Taxpayers' second residence had been owned and used for less than 2 years, they could tack ownership and use from the prior residences which had qualified for nonrecognition under § 1034.

1(e). $400,000 would be included in Taxpayer's gross income. This is not a principal residence and it does not qualify for an exclusion under § 121(a). See Prop. Reg. § 1.121-1(b). If Taxpayers moved to their summer home making it their permanent residence and subsequently met the two-year use and ownership requirements, § 121 would apply to a subsequent sale of that residence.

1(f). The depreciation is subject to the recapture provision of § 121(d)(6). Taxpayer has a $210,000 realized gain and meets the § 121 requirements, but the amount of depreciation of $10,000 does not qualify for the exclusion and it must be included in gross income. Thus Taxpayer has $200,000 of exclusion and $10,000 of gross income.

2(a). This problem is intended to familiarize students with the exclusion rules contained in § 121(c). Single's move was related to a change in the place of employment (§ 121(c)(2)(B)) and even though Single failed to satisfy the two-year ownership and use requirements, § 121(c)(1) allows Single to exclude 1 year/2 years times the exclusion amount of $250,000 or $125,000. See Prop. Reg. § 1.121-3(a) and (b) Ex.1. Since all of Single's $100,000 gain is below the allowable exclusion, none of the gain is recognized.

2(b). Under the rationale of problem 2(a), above, Single may exclude only $125,000 of the $200,000 gain on the sale, and Single must include $75,000 in gross income.

3(a). Here Taxpayer would satisfy the use and ownership requirements. However, Spouse does not satisfy the use requirement. § 121(b)(2)(A)(ii) requires both spouses to satisfy the use requirement in order to qualify for the $500,000 exclusion. As a result, § 121(a) and (b)(1) are met, but § 121(b)(2) is not met and only $250,000 of the $400,000 gain is excluded from gross income. Thus, $150,000 would be included in gross income. § 121(b)(2)(B).

It might appear that § 121(d)(1) would assist the taxpayers. However, the more specific language of § 121(b)(2) would apply here and § 121(b)(2)(A)(ii) is not met. Seemingly such language assists taxpayers where each satisfies the § 121(a) requirements and they both sell their principal residences and file a joint return. In such circumstances each taxpayer would be allowed a $250,000 exclusion. See § 121(b)(2)(B), the Conf. Report in the legislative history, and Prop. Reg. § 1.121-2(b)(2) and (3).

3(b). Since both spouses now meet the use requirements of § 121(b)(2)(A)(ii), and Taxpayer meets the ownership requirement of § 121(b)(2)(A)(i), their full $400,000 gain is excluded as it is within the $500,000 exclusion. § 121(b)(2) does not require the spouses to be married while satisfying the § 121 use requirement. See Prop. Reg. § 1.121-2(b)(3) Ex. 2. Since Taxpayer owned the property (it was not owned ½ by each), they must be married and file a joint return in the year of the sale to qualify for the $500,000 exclusion. If they each owned ½ of the residence and they never married, they could each exclude up to $250,000 under § 121(a) and (b)(1) on their separate returns.

3(c). Spouses could each exclude $200,000 of gain as each meets the ownership and use requirements. Spouse may tack Taxpayer's *ownership* period for purposes of the two-year ownership test where there is a § 1041(a) transfer. § 121(d)(3)(A), Prop. Reg. § 1.121-4(b)(1). Thus, Spouse meets both the ownership and use tests of § 121(a). Taxpayer meets both the ownership and the use tests as well and Taxpayer may also exclude Taxpayer's $200,000 gain. Note that if Taxpayer had failed to meet the use test, under § 121(d)(3)(B) Taxpayer could tack Spouse's use of the property on to Taxpayer's use.

3(d). Both spouses realize a $200,000 gain on the sale. Taxpayer can exclude the $200,000 gain because the use and ownership requirements are met. Spouse would also meet the ownership requirement (see § 121(d)(3)(A)) and would meet the use requirement (see § 121(d)(3)(B)). Thus Spouse could also exclude Spouse's $200,000 gain.

4.   A § 121 exclusion is unavailable here. Although § 121(d)(8)(A) generally allows an exclusion on the sale of a remainder interest in a principal residence, § 121(d)(8)(A) is inapplicable if the sale is between related parties. § 121(d)(8)(B). Since Estate Planner and Son are related individuals under § 267(b) (see § 267(b)(1) and (c)(4)), the transfer between them is ineligible for a § 121 exclusion.

PROBLEMS

Page 235:

1(a).   Since Student is in law school and the year is not one of Student's first two years of higher education, no Hope Scholarship credit is allowed. § 25A(b)(2)(C). However, if the current year is 2002, a nonrefundable Lifetime Learning credit of $1,000 would be allowed (20% of expenses up to $5,000). § 25A(c)(1). If the current year is after 2002, the credit would be $2,000 (20% of expenses up to $10,000). Id. There would be no phase-out of the credit. See § 25A(d).

Taking the problem a step further, if in 2002 Spouses had $3,000 of § 31 withholding on wages and a $2,500 tax liability, their income tax refund would be increased from $500 to $1,500 as a result of the credit. If the current year is after 2002, the income tax refund would be increased to $2,500 as a result of the credit.

1(b).   The fact that the tuition is paid from a student loan does not disallow the $1,000 credit. Cf. § 25A(g)(2). One also might want to mention the § 221 interest deduction considered in Chapter 16B.

1(c).   The qualifying expenses are reduced by any § 117 scholarship. § 25A(g)(2)(A). Thus, only $3,000 of expenses qualify and a $600 credit would be allowed (20% of $3,000) regardless of the year involved.

1(d).   Parents' payment is a § 102 gift and it does not reduce the amount of Student's qualifying expenses. § 25A(g)(2)(C) parenthetical. Thus, a

$1,000 credit is still allowed in 2002 or a $2,000 credit in years after 2002.

1(e).   If Spouses have a modified adjusted gross income of $100,000, the credit is fully phased out. § 25A(d)(1) and (2). If the modified adjusted gross income had been $92,000, the $1,000 potential credit in the year 2002 would be reduced to $400 (and the $2,000 potential credit after the year 2002 would be reduced to $800), because $12,000/$20,000 or 60% of the credit would be disallowed under § 25A(d)(1) and (2).

1(f).   The Lifetime Learning credit is a per taxpayer (not a per student) credit. § 25A(c)(1). Since both spouses are "the taxpayer" on a joint return, the results should be the same as in (a), above, a $1,000 credit or a $2,000 credit, depending upon the year involved. Cf. § 25A(d)(3) where "the taxpayer" would be the two spouses filing a joint return; however, compare Reg. § 1.151-1(b) where two personal exemptions are allowed for the spouses filing a joint return.

1(g).   Spouse's tuition would qualify for a Hope credit since the costs are incurred within the first two years of Spouse's education. § 25A(b)(2)(C). $1,500 of Spouse's first $2,000 will qualify for a Hope credit. § 25A(b)(1). A question might be raised whether if the current year is 2002, Spouses may also claim a Lifetime Learning credit for 20% of the remaining $8,000 of expenses up to the $5,000 limit allowing them a Lifetime Learning credit of $1,000 and total credits of $2,500? No. § 25A(c)(2)(A) disallows the Lifetime Learning credit when a Hope credit is allowed for a student's qualified tuition and related expenses. The legislative history confirms this conclusion. Conf.Comm.Rept. 105-220 at 346. Note that a Hope credit could be claimed for one student's expenses and a Lifetime Learning credit for another student's expenses. However, if the year involved was after 2002, the Spouses would elect to use the Lifetime Learning credit of $2,000 rather than the $1,500 Hope credit. See problem 1(a), above.

1(h).   As in problem 1(a), above, Spouses would qualify for a $1,000 or $2,000 § 25A credit depending on the year involved. If the current year is 2002, the credit would reduce tax liability to $2,000 and result in a $1,000 refund under refundable § 31. If the current year is after 2002, the credit would reduce tax liability to $1,000 and result in a $2,000 refund under refundable § 31. See footnote 10 on page 229 of

88

the Text.

2.   This is something of an open-ended problem with no definitive answer, just a variety of thoughts. One's Clients will need to consider several factors. First, note that none of the alternatives offer any current year tax benefit to Clients. The tax benefits occur in the year that educational expenses are incurred.

In determining whether to purchase a § 135 bond, to contribute to a § 529 Qualified Tuition Plan, or to invest in a § 530 Education Savings Account, Clients should consider a variety of factors:

(a)   The type of the higher education costs that qualify for an exclusion;

(b)   The potential amount of the exclusion;

(c)   The phase-out of the exclusion for contributions and distributions;

(d)   The interrelationship with other benefits such as the Section 25A tuition credits;

(e)   The possibility of rolling over excess amounts into a program benefiting another member of the beneficiary's family.

(1).   Interest income from a § 135 bond is excluded only to the extent that the bond proceeds are used to pay for tuition and fees. § 135(c)(2)(A). Whereas an exclusion is allowed under both §§ 529 and 530 not only for tuition and fees, but also for books, supplies, equipment, special education needs and, generally, room and board. §§ 529(e)(3), 530(b)(2)(A), (4). With respect to all 3 types of benefits, such amounts are first reduced by any amounts excluded by §§ 117, 127, etc., but not § 102. See §§ 135(d)(1), 529(c)(3)(B)(v)(I), 530(d)(2)(C)(i), 25A(g)(2). In the case of an Education Savings Account, such amounts also include expenses for elementary and secondary education expenses. § 530(b)(2)(A), (4).

(2).   Under § 135, the full amount of the interest on the bond is potentially excludable. § 135(a). To the extent taxable, the interest is taxed to the bondholder who is receiving the payments. Under §§ 529 and 530, contributions to a Qualified Tuition Plan or an Education Savings Account are gifts to the beneficiary of the Plan or Account. Earnings are excluded when earned and when disctributed are excluded to the extent that they are used to pay qualified higher education expenses. Any excess distributions are taxed using § 72 principles. §§ 529(c)(3), 530(d). The excess is taxed to the beneficiary of the proceeds. Id. Any income which is taxed is subject to a 10% penalty. §§ 529(c)(6)(only after the year 2003), 530(d)(4).

(3).   With respect to both § 135 bonds and § 530 Education Savings Accounts, there are phase-outs. The interest exclusion on bonds is phased out in *the year of distribution* if the bondholder's modified adjusted gross income is between $40,000 and $55,000 ($60,000 and $90,000 if a joint return). § 135(b)(2)(A). The amounts are adjusted for inflation after 1990. § 135(b)(2)(B). The *contribution* that may be made to an Education Savings Account is $2,000 per year, but it is phased out when the contributor's modified adjusted gross income is between $95,000 and $110,000 ($190,000 and $220,000 if a joint return). § 530(c). A major advantage to the alternative of using Qualified Tuition Plans is that there are no phase-outs with respect to either contributions or distributions related to § 529 Qualified Tuition Plans.

(4).   If the proceeds are from a Qualified Tuition Plan or an Education Savings Account, a § 25A credit may be fully allowed. However, to the extent that a § 25A credit is taken with respect to qualified education expenses, no § 135 exclusion or § 529 or § 530 exclusion is allowed with respect to such expenses. §§ 135(d)(2), 529(c)(3)(B)(v)(II), 530(d)(2)(C)(i)(II). Alternatively, a taxpayer could elect to forgo a Section 25A credit and opt for the benefits of Section 135, Section 529, or Section 530. See § 25A(e). In addition, no contribution may be made to a § 530 Education Savings Account for a beneficiary if a contribution is made in a year by anyone to a § 529 Qualified Tuition Plan for the beneficiary. See note 74 at page 234 of the Text.

(5).   Although not covered in detail in the Text, there is a possibility of rolling over both a Qualified Tuition Plan and an Education Savings Account to other members of a beneficiary's family. See §§ 529(c)(3)(C), 530(d)(5). Essentially § 135 bonds have this same feature because the bond interest is not restricted to a particular beneficiary when the bond is purchased. It is only restricted when used for the taxpayer and the taxpayer's spouse and dependents. § 135(c)(2). Thus, in effect, the bonds may be rolled over between members of the family, although family is not defined as broadly under § 135(c)(2) as under § 529(e)(2) and § 530(d)(4).

Page 238:

The general exclusion of § 103 has withstood attack. Indeed, it does allow high tax bracket taxpayers entirely to avoid tax, and certainly can be challenged on that basis. However, it also allows state and local governments to borrow at lower than the going interest rates and thereby constitutes an indirect federal subsidy to state and local governments. This subsidy effect of § 103 has, to date, been a strong enough policy justification to assure § 103's continued life. But see § 57(a)(5) potentially subjecting interest on some normally tax exempt bonds to the Alternative Minimum Tax which is considered in Chapter 27C of the Text.

Page 238:

Interest received from a state as a part of a condemnation award is not exempt as interest on an "obligation" of a state under § 103, says the Treasury, because § 103 encompasses only obligations arising out of an exercise of a state's borrowing power. Rev. Rul. 72-77, 1972-1 C.B. 28.

Page 240:

One may want to reproduce and distribute to students the following excerpt deleted from this edition of the Text:

EXCERPT

The foregoing comments all concern circumstances in which

Federal income taxes may impinge on the states only indirectly, by way of imposing a tax on an individual or other recipient on amounts *paid* by a state, such as salary or bond interest. What about taxing the *state's* income? From a legislative viewpoint, statutes handle this matter loosely.

A great many organizations enjoy express statutory exemption from Federal income tax.[1] These provisions may encompass some state-owned instrumentalities, but they do not embrace the states as such.[2] This does not mean, however, that the states are subject to tax on their net receipts. Instead, it reflects a state exemption, generally assumed. At one time, even the Treasury Department considered this exemption to rest on the constitutional doctrine of intergovernmental immunity.[3] Treasury changed its position and later considered the state's exemption to rest on an interpretation of the Code, which failed to make the state a taxpayer.[4]

As to some types of income, Section 115(1) supports the state's exempt status. Section 115(1) excludes from gross income a state's receipts from any public utility and from the exercise of any "essential governmental function."[5] At present, there is only one instance in which amounts received by states or state agencies are in fact subjected to Federal income tax.[6] Obviously, as long as Congress and the

---

[1] See I.R.C. § 501(c) and (d).

[2] See Rev. Rul. 60-351, 1960-2 C.B. 169, 173; but cf. Estate of Leslie E. Johnson, 56 T.C. 944 (1971).

[3] G.C.M. 13745, XIII-2 C.B. 76 (1934).

[4] G.C.M. 14407, XIV-1 C.B. 103 (1935): and see Rev. Rul. 71-132, 1971-1 C.B. 29, superseding G.C.M. 13745, supra note 3, reaching the same result as the earlier G.C.M. but without reference to the immunity doctrine.

[5] I.R.C. § 115(1).

[6] See I.R.C. § 511(a)(2)(B) which taxes the "unrelated business income" of state colleges and universities.

Treasury do not attempt to subject a state's receipts to the Federal income tax, actual questions regarding the scope of the federal power to do so cannot arise. Should such questions arise, they probably will not be answered strictly on a state immunity basis.

Several decisions suggest that some state income may be vulnerable to the Federal income tax. One such decision is New York v. United States.[7] In that decision, the Court held that the State of New York, in its sale of mineral waters from Saratoga Springs, was not immune from a Federal excise tax on the sale of soft drinks. In the employee salary cases, the Court finally rejected as a criterion of taxability the question whether the activity in which the employee was engaged constituted an essential governmental function, but the question of essentiality may still have some relevance. Sustaining the excise tax in *New York*,[8] the court stated:

> There are, of course, state activities and state-owned property that partake of uniqueness from the point of view of inter-governmental relations. These inherently constitute a class by themselves. Only a state can own a statehouse; only a state can get income by taxing. These could not be included for purposes of federal taxation in any abstract category of taxpayers without taxing the state as a state. But so long as Congress generally taps a source of revenue by whomsoever earned and not uniquely capable of being earned only by a state, the Constitution of the United States does not forbid it merely because its incidence falls also on a state.

Consider the retail liquor business against this background. In State A liquor stores are state-owned and operated. In State B they are publicly licensed but privately owned and operated. Under present circumstances does this appear to give rise to an inequitable application

---

[7] 326 U.S. 572, 66 S.Ct. 310 (1946).

[8] Id. at 582 and 66 S.Ct. at 314.

of the Federal income tax laws?[9] If you think so, what do you think should be done about it?

These are at best fragmentary comments on a tax area that produces very great amounts of administrative, judicial and academic literature.[10]

---

[9] See Rev. Rul. 71-132, supra note 4. This is inequitable in the sense that consumers in some states may be indirectly paying a Federal income tax on their booze, while consumers in states with state stores may not be. However, it is possible that the state stores may charge the same prices as private stores (thereby directing the amount that would otherwise be paid as Federal taxes to the states) and, anyway, the federal income tax on the retailer has such a minimal effect on the consumer that the situation hardly seems inequitable. In addition if it were highly inequitable most states would likely convert to state owned liquor stores, an option open to them.

[10] Some important articles that examine the cases and competing philosophies in depth include: (1) The classic analysis of the intergovernmental immunities doctrine up to 1946, in Powell, "The Waning of Intergovernmental Tax Immunities," 58 Harv. L. Rev. 633 (1945), and Powell, "The Remnant of Intergovernmental Tax Immunities," 58 Harv. L. Rev. 757 (1945); (2) Frank, "Reciprocal Taxation of Governments," 40 Taxes 468 (1962); (3) Ratchford, "Intergovernmental Tax Immunities in the United States," 6 Nat.Tax.J. 305 (1953); (4) Surrey, "Federal Income Taxation of State and Local Government Obligations," 36 Tax Policy 3 (May-June 1969).

PART THREE: IDENTIFICATION OF THE PROPER TAXPAYER

Chapter 12.   Assignment of Income

Page 242:

Policy reasons supporting progressive rates are explored in the Blum and Kalven article (see Fn. 2) under such headings as the benefit theory, the sacrifice theory, the ability to pay theory, and the economic stability and equality theory. The authors recognize that the theories fall somewhat short of furnishing a full policy reason supporting progressive rates. The constitutional case for progressive taxation is discussed in Martinez, " 'To Lay and Collect Taxes': The Constitutional Case for Progressive Taxation," 18 *Yale Law & Pol. Rev.* 111 (1999).

Page 244:

The principle expressed in *Lucas v. Earl* no longer has much importance in the husband-wife circumstances of that case, because (1) under present California community property law husband-wife income *is* divided in the manner attempted by the taxpayers' in *Earl* (see Poe v. Seaborn, 282 U.S. 101 (1930)) and (2) in any event, since 1948 optional husband-wife income splitting has been possible by way of the joint return. Nevertheless, the rule of the case, disallowing for tax purposes the assignment of income from services, prevails in other intrafamily and similar circumstances, such as attempted assignment by father to son.

Since the contract in *Earl* was entered into in 1901 prior to the 1913 enactment of the Income Tax, the contract was not effected for tax purposes, unless the Earls had fantastic foresight.

Page 250:

Contrast the result reached in the revenue ruling set out on this page with Reverend Gerald P. Fogarty's situation in Fogarty v. U.S., 780 F.2d 1005 (D.C. Cir. 1986). The Reverend accepted a teaching position with the University of Virginia Department of Religious Studies. He was paid a salary by the University but, as a Roman Catholic Priest, he was bound by a vow of poverty. Thus, his entire salary was actually remitted to his tax exempt religious Order. The Court addressed the issue whether the priest contracted with the University as an individual or as an agent of his Order. Finding that the University contracted with Reverend Fogarty as an individual, the Court held that his teaching salary was taxable to him individually. In a case following *Fogarty*, a Roman Catholic nun was taxed on compensation as a nurse-midwife even though under a vow of poverty she transferred the funds to her order. Schuster v. Comm'r, 800 F.2d 672 (7th Cir. 1986).

PROBLEM

Page 254:

1(a). If Executive prior to earning her salary directs that $20,000 of it be paid to her aged parents she will be taxed on the $20,000 under the principle of *Lucas v. Earl* even though the salary is paid to her parents. Since Executive is taxed, her parents are not taxed but merely receive a gift.

In a similar situation in Rev. Rul. 73-174, 1973-1 C.B. 43, an employer purchased a group term life insurance policy for an employee beyond the $50,000 § 79 limitation. When the employee assigned all the employee's rights under the policy it was properly held that the portion of the cost of the insurance in excess of the § 79 limitation was nevertheless income to the employee under § 79(a).

1(b). The result here is unclear. If *Giannini* is perceived as a mere disclaimer case, then these facts may not be within *Giannini* because there is some degree of direction on Executive's part in requiring that the property must go to a charity. The Service would take this position.

The Service appears to be narrowly limiting any *Giannini* exception to the *Lucas* rule. In Rev. Rul. 79-121, 1979-1 C.B. 61, a taxpayer was entitled to an honorarium for speaking to a professional society, which the taxpayer requested the society donate to one of five charities he listed. Although the Ruling is not clear whether the charitable assignment occurred before or after the speech, nevertheless the taxpayer was held taxable on the honorarium and was then allowed a § 170 deduction. As discovered in Chapter 23B, this is not invariably a wash.

In the alternative, this problem may fit within the *Giannini* facts and, if so, the income from the future services is successfully assigned, perhaps more accurately, timely "rejected." The *Giannini* exception requires a taxpayer to disclaim the income both prior to earning it and without naming any recipient. Arguably directing payment to "any charity the Board of Directors... selects" is the same as suggesting "that the corporation do something worthwhile with the money."

If Executive were a member of the Board it is arguable that she could indirectly determine the recipient of the income thereby in effect assigning it, requiring taxation to Executive. There are some reasons to wonder about the result in *Giannini* itself; note for example that Giannini was a director of Banitaly Corporation at the time of his successful assignment of income.

1(c).   This problem involves the issue whether Executive's actions fall within the *Giannini* case excluding the bonus from her income. Normally, for *Giannini* to apply the disclaimer must occur prior to rendering the services (see problem 1(b), above). However, even though the payment is a bonus for services previously rendered by Executive, it was not contracted for by her. Assuming *Giannini* applies in (b), above, Executive should be able to disclaim the bonus when she is first aware of her right to it (compare other windfalls); the fact that she has rendered services that generated the right to it should not alter that result. However, if Executive customarily received a bonus and therefore it was anticipated, even though the exact amount was unknown, it probably would have to be disclaimed prior to rendering the services to qualify for the *Giannini* exception.

1(d).   Corporation is taxed on the $1000 honorarium. This is easily within the scope of *Rev. Rul. 74-581* at page 252 of the Text. Even though Executive receives the funds she does so as an agent of Corporation because she is required by contract to turn the money over to Corporation. If she were not bound by contract or an understanding to turn the money over to Corporation, we would reach the opposite result and Executive would be taxed on the honorarium.

Page 264:

A way to look at *Susie Salvatore*, is to recognize that, when the question is who is taxed on the gain on a sale, there is a kind of who-*sold*-it? doctrine, which is similar to the who-*owned*-it? doctrine that applies to determine who is taxed on income *from* property, such as rent or interest. Realistically, a la *Court Holding*, Susie was seen to have made the sale, though she sought in part to carry it out through others. In another view, the gain bargained for was fully mature and ripened fruit, not transferable for tax purposes under the assignment-of-income doctrine.

Page 272:

See Ferguson v. Comm'r, 174 F 3d 997 (9th Cir. 1999), where taxpayers transferred appreciated stock to a charity at a time when a tender offer was outstanding and over 50 percent of the corporate stock had been tendered. The charity received and sold the stock, but the court held that under assignment of income principles, the shares were sold by the taxpayers and the gain was taxed to them as well.

Page 274:

See the Text at page 868. It discusses § 1286 which provides a set of rules applicable to sales of bond interest coupons or of bonds where the coupons are stripped from the bonds.

PROBLEMS

Page 274:

1(a).   As Father did not transfer the bond which is the income producing property, he will be taxed on the interest. Since none of the coupons is due at the time of the gift (we assume Father cashed the April 1 coupon), there is no income to Father until Daughter receives the interest income. The *Horst* opinion implies this result and Annie A. Colby, 45 B.T.A. 536 (1941), holds that there is no income to Father at the time of the gift. See also Rev. Rul. 58-275, 1958-1 C.B. 22. Although premature here, an issue can be raised whether Father's or Daughter's accounting method determines the time of taxation of the income. There is no authority on point but since Father is treated as owning the income, his accounting method should determine the timing issue.

Loose language in the *Horst* opinion has at times generated the thought that a gift without more might effect a realization of gain. That is not the message of *Horst*. Its real teaching is in a sentence near the end of the opinion, if that sentence is read with proper (added) emphasis:

> When by the gift of the coupons, [Donor] has separated his right to interest payments from his investment *and procured the payment of the interest to his donee*, he has enjoyed the economic benefits of the income...

See also the second to the last paragraph of *Rev. Rul. 69-102* at page 268 of the Text.

1(b).   Since Father has made a gift of the bond along with the interest he would not be taxed on the income as he has transferred the underlying property, the "tree," with which goes the "fruit." Compare *Blair* with *Horst*. Assuming Daughter is a cash method taxpayer, the interest will be taxed to Daughter on her actual or constructive receipt of it.

1(c).   Since Father transferred ½ of the bond, he has effectively assigned ½ of the interest income to Daughter. See the *Blair* case involving an assignment of a portion of the underlying property. Under the *Horst* rationale, the other ½ of the interest would be taxed to Father when it becomes payable to Daughter. See problem 1(a), above.

1(d).   Father would have $600 of income in the current year under the *Stranahan* case. This situation is distinguishable from the other situations above because the Father has received adequate and full consideration for his transfer. Even if the sale of the interest coupons had occurred after they were ripe, the result should be the same, because adequate consideration was received for them. Even though the transaction allows Father to telescope his prospective income, nevertheless the *Stranahan* case holds that, if the transaction is not a sham, it will be recognized for federal tax purposes. On receipt of the interest, Daughter would be able to subtract her cost basis, ($300 per coupon) leaving *her* with income of $200 from the two coupons ($800 - $600).

A student note critical of the *Stranahan* result is Hemmings, "Sale Assignment of Future Income: Aberation or Sound Tax Avoidance

Device," 35 *Pitt. L. R.* 220 (1973). The case receives a more favorable evaluation in Kayle, "The Taxpayer's Intentional Attempt to Accelerate Taxable Income" 46 *Tax Law.* 89 (1992).

1(e). In general, if Father had made a gift of the bonds with the interest he would not be taxed on the income as he has transferred the underlying property, the "tree," with which goes the "fruit". Compare *Blair* with *Horst*. However, with respect to the current six month's interest coupon, payable on April 1, ½ of it or $200 represents "ripe" fruit, interest that has accrued at the date of the December 31 gift, even though there is no right to receive the interest until three months later. See *Rev. Rul. 69-102*. When that interest coupon is paid, ½ of it will be taxed to Father and the other ½ to Daughter. All subsequent interest coupons will, of course, be taxed to Daughter.

1(f). Father's $1000 gain is taxed to him even though the sale proceeds are paid to Daughter. He completed the sale. The appreciation in the value of the property was realized prior to the gift and was "ripe" and therefore unassignable. As *Susie Salvatore* illustrates, if Father owned the bond at the time the sale was completed, the gain on the sale would be taxed to him no matter to whom he directed the proceeds be paid.

1(g). It is possible that the negotiations for a sale may have proceeded to a point that, although the sale is not complete, nevertheless the agreement is so firmed up that it will be treated as complete for tax purposes. Consequently, Father's entering into substantial negotiations with Buyer may generate income to Father even though no binding contract is signed and the property is transferred to Daughter who carries out the sale. Compare Comm'r v. Court Holding Co., 324 U.S. 331 (1945), with U.S. v. Cumberland Public Service Co., 338 U.S. 451 (1950). Cf. Horace E. Allen, 66 T.C. 340 (1976).

2. This problem involves the question when a dividend becomes nonassignable for income tax purposes. There are several possibilities: the declaration date, the record date, the payment date, and the date of actual receipt. The general rule is that right to receive the dividend is determined as of the record date and the tax law follows that principle. Bishop v. Shaughnessy, 195 F.2d 683 (2d Cir. 1962). However, in the case of a closely held corporation, the declaration date rather than the record date may be the significant ownership date if any other view

would simply authenticate a ruse. Estate of Smith v. Comm'r, 292 F.2d 478 (3rd Cir. 1961). See Lyon and Eustice, "Assignment of Income: Fruit and Tree as Irrigated by the P.G. Lake Case," 17 *Tax L. Rev.* 293 at 362-366 (1962).

Since the corporation is substantially owned by the majority shareholder, the problem is similar to *Estate of Smith* and the declaration date probably should determine taxability, even though there may be subsequent record and payment dates. This is especially true in view of the spokesman's language that the dividend will "*go back*" to the company. Of course, such a return then represents a contribution to capital increasing Mr. Hefner's basis in his corporate interest.

If the record date is subsequent to the declaration date and if the general rule of *Bishop v. Shaughnessy* is applied because the corporation is not sufficiently closely held, then rejection of the dividend prior to the income being ripe would avoid an assignment of income. It might be argued that a disclaimer of income (as here) is to be distinguished from an assignment of income and that, even though the income is "ripe", its mere disclaimer as opposed to assignment should not result in taxation to Mr. Hefner. Cf. *Giannini*. However, this disclaimer is in the nature of a gift to the other share-holders of the corporation. Cf. Reg. § 25.2511-1(h)(1); but cf. § 2518.

3(a).   A transfer of a patent is treated as a transfer of property despite the fact that there is a strong element of personal services in developing patents. Carl G. Dreymann, 11 T.C. 153 (1948); cf. Rev. Rul. 54-599, 1954-2 C.B. 52, similarly treated an assignment of an interest in a copyright. Thus the transfer to Son is effective in assigning to Son the income from the sale. (Although § 1235 has some relevance here, it seems premature to inject it into the discussion.)

3(b).   Somewhat surprisingly, the courts have held that the assignment of such a royalty contract is an assignment of property with the result that Son would be taxed on the income. Heim v. Fitzpatrick, 262 F.2d 887 (2d Cir. 1959); cf. Comm'r v. Reece, 233 F.2d 30 (1st Cir. 1956). An argument can be made that the income is ripe under *Susie Salvatore*, although the courts with apparent reluctance equate the transfer of the royalty contract to a transfer of income-producing property, the patent itself. See Lyon and Eustice, "Assignment of Income: Fruit and Tree as Irrigated by the P.G. Lake Case," 17 *Tax. L. Rev.* 295 at 374.

Chapter 13.   Income Producing Entities

Page 276:

> At first blush, use of the partnership receptacle as an assignment of income device would appear to be highly effective. Why not just agree to a convenient income allocation with an eye to exemptions, standard deductions, and applicable rate brackets? However, as the problems at page 302 of the Text illustrate, § 704(e) puts restrictions upon assignment of income through the partnership entity, which largely echo "common law" assignment of income principles illustrated in Chapter 12.

Page 277:

> Some recent articles on limited liability companies are: Brenman, "Limited Liability Companies Offer New Opportunities to Business Owners." 10 *J. P'ship Tax'n* 301 (1994); Kurtz, "The Limited Liability Company and the Future of Business Taxation: A Comment on Professor Berger's Plan." 47 *Tax L. Rev.* 815 (1992); Klein and Zolt, "Business Forms, Limited Liability, and Tax Regimes: Lurching Toward a Coherent Outcome?" 66 *U. Colo. L. Rev.* 1001 (1995).

Page 278:

> There are many restrictions on assigning income to corporate entities (e.g. §§ 531, 541, 1551). Nevertheless, corporations are taxpaying entities creating additional units to which income may be assigned and through which income may be divided among the beneficial owners, the shareholders.

Page 291:

> The last sentence of § 671 provides that §§ 673-679 are the exclusive sections for taxing the income of a trust to the grantor or a third party on the basis of dominion and control over the trust. Thus, the common law doctrine of the *Clifford* case was completely preempted by the statute. But see Reg. § 1.671-1(c). After the 1986 Act, an assignment of an income interest with the retention of a reversionary interest in the grantor is virtually a dead letter. See the current § 673 5% test as

compared to the prior 10-year rule.

Section 671(a), last sentence, does not make § 61 wholly inapplicable to the taxation of trust income. If A sets up a trust to discharge the obligation of B to support child C, B may be taxed on the trust income under § 61, not because B has "dominion and control," but under the *Old Colony Trust Co.* doctrine. *Old Colony* treats a taxpayer as in receipt of amounts paid by another to discharge the taxpayer's obligation. See Rev. Rul. 56-484, 1956-2 C.B. 23.

PROBLEMS

Page 294:

1(a). Grantor would be taxed on the income when the clients pay the fees in the succeeding year. The transfer to the trust constitutes a mere assignment of income from services which continues to be taxable to the transferor-grantor. Helvering v. Eubank, 311 U.S. 122 (1940). This problem shows that to tax Grantor the Commissioner need not reach for the grantor trust provisions unless honest-to-god property has been transferred to the trust. Reg. § 1.671-1(c). The receivables are property, but are "income property" rather than "property property". The income is taxed to Grantor, not to Son. Son receives instead an excluded gift under § 102(a).

1(b). As in problem 1(a), above, only a right to "income", not "property", has been transferred to the trust. Under the rationale of *Horst* the transfer of the right to the rental income without a transfer of the building is a transfer only of a naked right to income. Grantor will continue taxable on the income. Reg. § 1.671-1(c).

1(c). The underlying property is transferred to the trust along with the right to the income from it. None of the grantor trust provisions come into play. Son will be taxed on the rental income distributed to him by the trust.

1(d). Here, although property is transferred to the trust, it carries with it income already earned. It is property dripping with income. The income earned at the date of the transfer (the accrued rent) is taxed to Grantor on its receipt by the trust. It is fruit too ripe to ship. Cf.

Watson v. Comm'r, 345 U.S. 544 (1953), which preceded § 1231(b)(4).

1(e).   Grantor's right to revoke the trust makes § 676(a) of the grantor trust provisions applicable. Grantor will be taxed on the trust's income under § 671 whether or not common law tax principles would have treated Grantor's transfer as fully effective.

1(f).   The ability of Grantor to control the beneficial enjoyment of the trust property, unchecked by any adverse party (see § 672(a)), makes § 674(a) of the grantor trust provisions applicable. Section 671 taxes Grantor on the income from the trust.

1(g).   Grantor is taxed on the income from the trust. Grantor is treated as the owner of the trust under § 673(a). She has a reversionary interest in the trust property the value of which exceeds 5 percent of the trust property at the inception of the trust. § 673(a). Thus, Grantor is taxed on the income from trust. § 671.

1(h).   Since the value of the reversion is greater than 5% of the value of the trust property at the inception of the trust, § 673(a) applies and Grantor is again taxed on the trust income under § 671. The § 673(b) exception is inapplicable because the reversion is not one which can take effect only upon the death of a lineal descendant of the Grantor before the descendant reaches age 21. See problem 1(i), below.

1(i).   Section 673(b) contains an exception to the general rule of § 673(a) which is applicable here. The exception concerns reversionary interests taking effect upon the death of a minor lineal descendant beneficiary who holds all present interests in the trust, but only if the death of such beneficiary occurs before the beneficiary reaches age 21. Consequently, Grantor is not treated as the owner of the trust by reason of the reversionary interest and Son will be taxed on the income. § 673(b). Query, as a practical matter, whether the value of Grantor's reversionary interest exceeds 5% triggering § 673(a) in the first place?

1(j).   Grantor is taxed. This is an illustration of a broad administrative power which § 675 brings within the scope of the grantor trust provisions. See § 675(1).

1(k). The answer is uncertain in this problem. Section 677(a) generally treats the grantor as the owner of any portion of a trust whose income is *or may be* distributed to, or held, or accumulated for, the grantor or grantor's spouse. Section 677(b), on the other hand, deals with discretionary trust amounts expended for the support or maintenance of one, other than grantor's spouse, whom grantor is legally obligated to support. However, § 677(b), unlike § 677(a), taxes Grantor only on income actually applied or distributed.

The issues in this problem are:

(1)   When income is used to pay minor Son's tuition at a private high school, whether the payment constitutes the satisfaction of a legal duty of Grantor to support Son? Reference to local law is necessary.

(2)   Whether Grantor is under a contractual obligation, express or implied, to pay for Son's tuition? Section 677(a) applies when income of a trust may be expended to discharge obligations of the grantor other than those falling within § 677(b). Reg. § 1.677(b)-1(d).

In Morrill v. U.S., 228 F. Supp. 734 (D.C. Me. 1964) at page 283 of the Text, grantor was taxed under § 677(a) because trust income was used to discharge his *contractual* obligation to pay tuition for his children at private colleges and schools. The Court did not decide the issue whether grantor was obligated under state law, as a matter of support, to pay his children's college and school tuition. However, Wyche v. U.S., 1974 CCH Vol. 9 at para. 7911 (Ct. Cl. Comm'r Rep. 1974), held grantor not taxable on income used to pay for private school tuition or for music and dancing lessons for his children. In *Wyche*, South Carolina law did not require grantor to send his children to private school or to provide music and dancing lessons. Furthermore, the court found that the grantor was not contractually obligated to pay such fees. This area is tricky. Particular attention is called to Reg. §§ 1.677(b)-(1)(d) through (f).

Finally, note that the "kiddie tax" may have application, depending upon the beneficiary's age. See § 1(g)(2)(A).

1(ℓ).   Grantor is taxed on the income. This is the message of § 677(a)(1), as indicated above, because the income may be distributed to Grantor's spouse. A question might be raised whether § 678 taxes Husband on the income, as he has untrammelled power to vest the income in himself. Support for this approach appears in legislative history, which indicates that § 677(a) is inapplicable to tax Grantor if another Code provision requires the Grantor's husband to report the income. H. Rep. No. 91-413, 91st Cong., 1st Sess., 1969-3 C.B.200, 261. However, § 678(b) expressly takes Husband off the hook and leaves Grantor taxable here when the Grantor trust provisions, including § 677, apply.

Moreover, note that § 672(e) specifies treatment of the Grantor as holding the power of her spouse, which in this problem is to direct the trustee to pay the income to Grantor which also triggers §§ 673, 674, and 676.

2.   As this problem suggests, an application of the principles of *Earl*, *Horst*, and other cases in Chapter 12 might still leave room for inappropriate income fragmentization through use of the trust entity. The grantor trust provisions additionally require that, in order effectively to assign income from a trust, the grantor must do something more than formally relinquish legal title to the property; the grantor must substantially relinquish benefits and interests in and controls over the property that the grantor transfers to the trust. This is especially so after the 1986 amendment to § 673. These problems are, of course, not in depth studies of the grantor trust provisions, but appear here to caution the student that, when thinking up a great tax saving device, Congress has probably already been there. A New England conscience is a great help in anticipating Congressional answers to devices that look a bit too good to be true; that's what feels so bad when everything else feels so good.

PROBLEMS

Page 302:

1(a).   Reg. § 1.704-1(e)(1)(iv) properly provides that capital is not a material income-producing factor in a partnership in which the income of the partnership is derived principally from compensation for the services of partners. Section 704(e)(1) would not require recognition of the Father-Son partnership. However, § 704(e) is an affirmative provision, and it does not necessarily prevent recognition of a family partnership engaged only in services. All that can be said here is that § 704(e) is of no help in asserting tax recognition of the partnership. That leaves us with the *Culbertson* test. Here, as Son is a nonparticipant, the parties have not in good faith joined together to carry on a business as partners, and their status as partners would not be accorded income tax recognition.

1(b). If Father and Daughter are active practitioners they can be partners within the *Culbertson* test; § 704(e) simply does not affect their tax status. See the discussion at problem 1(a), above.

1(c). Father's mere assignment of a lease to a partnership in a situation where Father retains the underlying property does not create a valid family partnership under §704(e), because only a raw right to income and no capital or income-producing property is transferred to the partnership. It is not a partnership in which "capital is a material income-producing factor". This probably should be viewed as a transfer of a mere right to income, i.e., "income property", an ineffective income assignment under common law tax principles, unless there are management and other activities in which all participate. That might make them common law tax partners in a service business.

1(d). The § 704(e)(1) requirement is met. A partnership in which capital is a material income-producing factor is described in the regulations at Reg. § 1.704-1(e)(1)(iv). In essence, decision rests upon the question whether the use of income-producing property contributes substantially to the partnership's earnings. Here, that requirement is met.

1(e). If Father retains the right to make all business decisions, including the right to use income to expand the center, neither donee partner "*owns a capital interest*" in the partnership within § 704(e)(1). See Reg. § 1.704-1(e)(2).

1(f). As parts (a), (d), and (e) of this problem suggest, § 704(e) incorporates the *Earl*, *Horst*, and *Clifford* principles. A partnership will not be

108

recognized under § 704(e) if there simply is an assignment of income from services (*Earl*), if there is a mere raw assignment of income from property without the underlying income-producing property (*Horst*), or if the donor partner retains *Clifford*-type controls.

2(a).　Section 704(e)(2), by analogy to *Earl*, requires a reasonable allocation ($20,000) to Mother for her services prior to the tax division of the partnership's profits. This would leave the balance ($80,000) to be allocated in one-fourth interests among the partners. Thus, for tax purposes and at variance with their economic rights, Mother would report $40,000 of gross income. This is so regardless of how the $100,000 of income is actually distributed. To the extent that Son and Daughters receive in excess of $20,000, the excess is a gift from Mother, excluded from their incomes by § 102(a).

2(b).　The second exception of § 704(e)(2) requires that, whatever her rights under the agreement, Mother report as gross income an amount not less than that commensurate with her capital interest. Cf. *Horst*. As her capital interest is 1/4, $25,000 must be allocated to her. This is so regardless of how the agreement requires the income to be distributed. As a result of the required adjustment, each of the four partners would be taxed on $25,000. The excess amounts actually received by Son and Daughters are gifts from Mother under § 102(a) and not taxed to them.

2(c).　Section 704(e)(2) does not deal with the question of the services rendered by the donee. Son, under *Earl* and Reg. § 1.704-1(e)(3)(i)(b) and (c), should be taxed on amounts that may reasonably be viewed as compensation for his services, just as the statute expressly provides with respect to the donor-partner. The regulation cited adopts that concept and is supported by Woodbury v. Comm'r, 49 T.C. 180 (1967), acq., 1969-2 C.B. XXV.

Under the facts of this problem the income allocation for tax purposes may be shown graphically as follows:

| | Exception 1: | Exception 2: | |
Partner	Services	Capital	Total
Mother	$20,000	$15,000	$ 35,000
Son	20,000	15,000	35,000
Daughter	0	15,000	15,000
Daughter	0	15,000	15,000
			$100,000

Page 303:

In Steinmetz v. Comm'r, 32 T.C.M. 969 (1973), income from the condemnation of property was taxed to the individual shareholders of a corporation rather than the corporation that held the property. The court concluded that the corporation was created merely to hold title to the property, that it engaged in no business activities, and that it should be disregarded for federal tax purposes. See Krovonet, "Straw Corporations: When Will They be Recognized; What Can and Should be Done?" 39 *J. Tax'n* 54 (1973).

Page 304:

Congress enacted § 269A in response to the case of Keller v. Comm'r, 77 T.C. 1014 (1981). In *Keller*, a doctor incorporated as a professional corporation. The corporation was a partner in a medical partnership. The Commissioner attempted to use § 482 to increase the salary allocated to the doctor from his professional corporation. The Tax Court held that § 482, although generally applicable, could not be applied under the facts of the case. There was an arm's length transaction in which the total compensation received was equivalent to what the taxpayer would have received absent incorporation. In *Keller*, the Commissioner was, in effect, attempting to deprive the taxpayer of additional deferred compensation benefits he sought through the corporation. In response to *Keller*, Congress enacted § 269A, allowing the Commissioner to allocate income, deductions, credits, exclusions and other allowances between an employee and a personal service corporation in which the employee owns directly or by attribution 10% of the stock, if the following requirements are met:

110

(1)   Substantially all the services of the personal services corporation are performed for one other corporation, partnership or entity;

(2)   The principal purpose for forming or utilizing the personal service corporation is the avoidance or evasion of federal income tax by reducing income or securing some other tax benefit; and

(3)   The allocation is necessary to prevent avoidance or evasion of federal income tax or clearly to reflect the income of the personal service corporation or any of its employee-owners.

Although § 269A is no longer significant for deferred compensation purposes because the deferred compensation rules for incorporated and unincorporated persons are essentially the same (see page 649 of the Text), nevertheless § 269A still will be effective in making allocations in other situations where personal service corpora-tions are used to postpone or exempt income. There will likely be a further substantial decline in the use of personal service corporations after 1986. See the problems below.

See Ingram, "Preserving the Benefits of Personal Service Corporations After TEFRA," 61 *Taxes* 28 (1983).

Page 308:

The Tax Court has abandoned its prior position and now agrees with several courts of appeal that § 482 may be used to impute interest on tax-free or low-interest loans, even though use of the loan proceeds did not result in the production of income to the debtor. Latham Park Manor, Inc. v. Comm'r, 69 T.C. 199 (1977), aff'd without opinion, Jan. 28, 1980. The case is discussed in King & Dinur, "Tax Court Gives in on Creation-of-Income Issue Under 482; What Decision Means," 48 *J. Tax'n* 66 (1978). Several subsequent Tax Court and Circuit Court cases have reached the same conclusion. Cf. § 7872 and Prop. Reg. § 1.7872-2(a)(2)(iii) providing that both § 7872 and § 482 may apply to the same transaction.

PROBLEM

Page 311:

1. Father plans to incorporate the business, make an election of S corporation status (see § 1362(a) and (b)) and scatter a part of the income. He should be successful. Father can control the business decisions, yet he has transferred income to Son and Daughter. However, if Father does not receive reasonable compensation for the share of capital or services he renders to the corporation, there will be a reallocation of income to property reflect the value of such capital or services. See § 1366 (e).

   By electing S Corporation status, the income will be passed through to Father, Son and Daughter in proportion to their interests in the corporation and taxed at their individual rates. The income is not taxed at the corporate level under the generally higher corporate rates (Cf. § 1374). Absent the S Corporation election, the income would be taxed at the corporate level at the applicable § 11 corporate tax rate. Under C status, the income would also be taxed to the shareholders at their individual rates, upon distribution. One should discuss choice of entity questions in conjunction with this problem and compare the relative corporate and noncorporate rates.

   Another alternative would be for Father to transfer the business to a trust for the benefit of Son and Daughter. Father could conceivably make himself trustee, thus preserving his ability to oversee the video business operation. He would not run afoul of § 675, dealing with administrative powers, if his powers as a trustee are merely fiduciary. Assuming Father is compensated for any services rendered, he would be able to transfer all remaining business income to the children. Cf. § 704(e), § 1366(e).

   An additional alternative would be for Father to create a partnership with Son and Daughter. See the prior subpart of this Chapter for assignment of income problems which might arise on use of the partnership assignment vehicle. A partnership would permit the parties to make special allocations rather than be taxed in accordance with each members proportionate interest. A similar further alternative would be the creation of a limited liability company (LLC). Under Reg. §

301.7701-3(b)(1)(A)(i), an LLC generally would be classified as a partnership offering the advantages of a pass-through entity as well as limited liability.

PART FOUR: DEDUCTIONS IN COMPUTING TAXABLE INCOME

Chapter 14. Business Deductions

Page 319:

> In Jenkins v. Comm'r, 47 TCM 238 (1984), country music star Conway Twitty (a.k.a. Jenkins) was allowed to deduct payments made from his personal funds to reimburse investors in his failed Twitty Burger Restaurant chain. The court allowed the deductions because they were made to protect the star's reputation and success in the country music industry.

PROBLEMS

Page 319:

1. Although arguably the amount was an indirect contribution to capital of the savings and loan, nevertheless in *Conti* the deduction was allowed as an ordinary and necessary business expense to protect and preserve both the taxpayer's existing business activities and his earning capacity. The Court saw the issue as a balancing process in drawing "a line between expenditures to preserve and protect his business reputation [deductible as ordinary and necessary under § 162] and those which will improve and develop goodwill [non-deductible personal expenditures under § 262]." Certainly the immediate need for such a payment and directness to taxpayer's trade or business are also relevant factors. The liberal position of the *Conti* case is discussed in an article by Tucker, "When Can a Taxpayer Deduct Expenses Made to Protect his Personal Business Reputation?" 39 *J. Tax'n* 36 (1973). See also the *Jenkins* (Conway Twitty) case cited above.

    Some other somewhat similar cases and rulings allowing § 162 deductions include: James O. Gould, 64 T.C. 132 (1975), employee of creditor corporation who was also sole shareholder of debtor corporation allowed a § 162 deduction on payment of debtor's debt to creditor because he made the payment to preserve his status as an employee of creditor; Lutz v. Comm'r, 282 F.2d 614 (5th Cir. 1960), dealer in agricultural produce made deductible pay-off of debts of his retain his license to deal in agricultural commodities which he might have lost without the action taken; Rev. Rul. 76-203, 1976-1 C.B. 45, a moving and storage company's partial restitution to uninsured customers for losses when fire destroyed the company warehouses was made to preserve the company's goodwill and protect its business reputation deductible under § 162. But see Orval C. Walker, 32 T.C.M. 690 (1973), in which payments by a bank employee to a bankruptcy trustee were held nondeductible even though he claimed the expenses were incurred to maintain present employment.

In other "ordinary and necessary" cases the I.R.S. has ruled that a corporate executive could deduct the cost of liability insurance to protect against liability arising from wrongful acts committed within the scope of employment. Rev. Rul. 76-277, 1976-2 C.B. 41. But a wood products broker was denied a § 162 deduction for payments to an ordained minister who was hired to raise the employees' spiritual awareness level. A deduction was allowed for the portion of his salary related to other miscellaneous business tasks. Lionel Trebilcock, 64 T.C. 852 (1975), acq. 1976-2 C.B. 3.

2. The Court in *Heidt* stated that since Employee was entitled to reimbursement for use of a personal car which she voluntarily relinquished under a self-imposed rule adopted to avoid criticism from subordinates, her failure to receive the reimbursement "was based primarily on considerations of personal choice and convenience and certainly not out of any necessity of office." (274 F.2d at 28). Employee got no deduction under § 162.

See Harry M. Flower, 61 T.C. 140 (1973), where taxpayer, an independent contractor, was to be reimbursed for legitimate business expenses but only at his retirement, death, etc. Expenses which he incurred were non-deductible in the year incurred because they were in the nature of loans or advances which would subsequently be reimbursed under the agreement.

Page 319:

The *INDOPCO* case is discussed in Manca, "Deductibility of Takeover and Non-Takeover Expenses in the Wake of Indopco, Inc. v. Commissioner, 45 *Tax Law.* 815 (1992); Lipton, et. al., "Supreme Court

Approves Focus in Long-Term Benefit in Takeover Expense Controversy," 76 *J. Tax'n* 324 (1992). Several court decisions have interpreted *INDOPCO*. Recent discussions include:

1. United Dairy Farmers, Inc. v. Comm'r, 267 F.3d 510 (6th Cir. 2001) (taxpayer could not currently deduct (1) soil remediation expenses related to purchased properties; (2) accounting fees related to corporate reorganization, and (3) engineering studies);

2. Wells Fargo & Company v. Comm'r, 224 F.3d 874 (8th Cir. 2000) (salaries paid to corporate officers related to corporate acquisition could be currently deducted; legal fees related to the investigatory stage of the transaction could be currently deducted; expenses after "final decision" was made had to be capitalized);

3. PNC Bancorp, Inc. v. Comm'r, 212 F.3d 822 (3rd Cir. 2000) (bank could deduct as ordinary and necessary expenses its costs for marketing, researching, and originating loans);

4. A.E. Staley Manufacturing Co. v. Comm'r, 119 F.3d 482 (7th Cir. 1997) (target corporation could deduct expenses on resisting hostile takeover; expenses to defend a business preserve the status quo and do not produce future benefits);

5. Ingram Industries v. Comm'r, 80 T.C.M. 532 (2000) (taxpayer allowed to currently deduct extensive maintenance on towboats as "repairs," court stated that *INDOPCO* did not change long-established standards dealing with repairs and maintenance expenses).

Page 319:

Capitalization issues remain high on the Treasury's agenda. Rev. Rul. 2001-4, 2001-3 I.R.B. 295, deals with costs incurred in conjunction with a heavy maintenance visit on an aircraft airframe by a commercial airline. The ruling holds that such costs generally are deductible as ordinary and necessary expenses. However, such costs must be capitalized to the extent they materially add to the value of, substantially prolong the useful life of, or adapt the airframe to a new or different use. Also, costs incurred as part of a plan of rehabilitation, modernization, or improvement must be capitalized.

In Rev. Rul. 2002-9, 2002-10 IRB. 614, the IRS holds that "impact fees" incurred by a taxpayer in connection with the construction of a new residential building are capitalized costs allocable to the building under §§ 263(a) and 263A.

In another important development, in February, 2002, the IRS issued an advance notice of proposed rulemaking in which it announced that in 2002 it expects to propose a notice of proposed rulemaking that will clarify the application of § 263(a) to expenditures incurred in acquiring, creating, or enhancing certain intangible assets or benefits. Announcement 2002-9, 2002-7 I.R.B.536.   The advance notice describes and explains the rules and standards that the IRS and Treasury expect to include in the proposed regulations.   Because of its importance, substantial portions of the advance notice are reproduced below.   One may want to reproduce and distribute the following Excerpt from Announcement 2002-9:

EXCERPT
Announcement 2002-9
2002-7 I.R.B. 536

The IRS and Treasury Department are reviewing the application of section 263(a) of the Internal Revenue Code to expenditures that result in taxpayers acquiring, creating, or enhancing intangible assets or benefits. This document describes and explains rules and standards that the IRS and Treasury Department expect to propose in 2002 in a notice of proposed rulemaking.

A fundamental purpose of section 263(a) is to prevent the distortion of taxable income through current deduction of expenditures relating to the production of income in future taxable years. See Commissioner v. Idaho Power Co., 418 U.S. 1, 16 (1974). Thus, the Supreme Court has held that expenditures that create or enhance separate and distinct assets or produce certain other future benefits of a significant nature must be capitalized under section 263(a). See INDOPCO, Inc. v. Commissioner, 503 U.S. 79 (1992); Commissioner v. Lincoln Savings & Loan Ass'n, 403 U.S. 345 (1971).

The difficulty of translating general capitalization principles into clear, consistent, and administrable standards has been recognized for decades. See Welch v. Helvering, 290 U.S. 111, 114-15 (1933). Because courts focus on particular facts before them, the results reached by the courts are often difficult to reconcile and, particularly in recent years, have contributed to substantial uncertainty and controversy. The IRS and Treasury Department are concerned that the current level of uncertainty and controversy is neither fair to taxpayers nor consistent with sound and efficient tax administration.

Recently, much of the uncertainty and controversy in the capitalization area has related to expenditures that create or enhance intangible assets or benefits. To clarify the application of section 263(a), the forthcoming notice of proposed rulemaking will describe the specific categories of expenditures incurred in acquiring, creating, or enhancing intangible assets or benefits that taxpayers are required to capitalize. In addition, the forthcoming notice of proposed rulemaking will recognize that many expenditures that create or enhance intangible assets or benefits do not create the type of future benefits for which capitalization under section 263(a) is appropriate, particularly when the administrative and recordkeeping costs associated with capitalization are weighed against the potential distortion of income.

To reduce the administrative and compliance costs associated with section 263(a), the forthcoming notice of proposed rulemaking is expected to provide safe harbors and simplifying assumptions including a "one-year rule," under which expenditures relating to intangible assets or benefits whose lives are of a relatively short duration are not required to be capitalized, and "de minimis rules," under which certain types of expenditures less than a specified dollar amount are not required to be capitalized. The IRS and Treasury Department are also considering additional administrative relief, for example, by providing a "regular and recurring rule," under which transaction costs incurred in transactions that occur on a regular and recurring basis in the routine operation of a taxpayer's trade or business are not required to be capitalized.

The proposed standards and rules described in this document will not alter the manner in which provisions of the law other than section 263(a) (e. g., sections 195, 263(g), 263(h), or 263A) apply to determine the correct tax treatment of an item. Moreover, these standards and rules will not address the treatment of costs other than those to acquire, create, or enhance intangible assets or benefits, such as costs to repair or improve tangible property. The IRS and Treasury Department are considering separate guidance to address these other costs.

The following discussion describes the specific expenditures to acquire, create, or enhance intangible assets or benefits for which the IRS and Treasury Department expect to require capitalization in the forthcoming notice of proposed rulemaking. The IRS and Treasury Department anticipate that other expenditures to acquire, create, or enhance intangible assets or benefits generally will not be subject to capitalization under section 263(a).

A. Amounts Paid to Acquire Intangible Property

1. Amounts paid to acquire financial interests.

Under the expected regulations, capitalization will be required for an amount paid to purchase, originate, or otherwise acquire a security, option, any other financial interest described in section 197(e)(1), or any evidence of indebtedness. For a discussion of related transaction costs, see section C of this document.

For example, a financial institution that acquires portfolios of loans from another person or originates loans to borrowers would be required to capitalize the amounts paid for the portfolios or the amounts loaned to borrowers.

2. Amounts paid to acquire intangible property from another person.

Under the expected regulations, capitalization will be required for an amount paid to another person to purchase or otherwise acquire intangible property from that person. For a discussion of related transaction costs see section C of this document.

For example, an amount paid to another person to acquire an amortizable   section 197 intangible from that person would be capitalized. Thus, a taxpayer that acquires a customer base from another person would be required to capitalize the amount paid to that person in exchange for the customer base. On the other hand, a taxpayer that incurs costs to create its own customer base through advertising or other expenditures that create customer goodwill would not be required to capitalize such costs under this rule.

B. Amounts Paid to Create or Enhance Certain Intangible Rights or Benefits

1. 12-month rule.

The IRS and Treasury Department expect to propose a 12-month rule applicable to expenditures paid to create or enhance certain intangible rights or benefits. Under the rule, capitalization under section 263(a) would not be required for an expenditure described in the following paragraphs 2 through 8 unless that expenditure created or enhanced intangible rights or benefits for the taxpayer that extend beyond the earlier of (i) 12 months after the first date on which the taxpayer realizes the rights or benefits attributable to the expenditure, or (ii) the end of the taxable year following the taxable year in which the expenditure is incurred.

The IRS and Treasury Department request comments on how the 12-month rule might apply to expenditures paid to create or enhance rights of indefinite duration and contracts subject to termination provisions. For example, comments are requested on whether costs to create contract rights that are terminable at will without substantial penalties would not be subject to capitalization as a result of the 12-month rule.

2. Prepaid items.

Subject to the 12-month rule, the IRS and Treasury Department expect to propose a rule that requires capitalization of an amount prepaid for goods, services, or other benefits (such as insurance) to be received in the future.

For example, a taxpayer that prepays the premium for a 3-year insurance policy would be required to capitalize such amount under the rule.

Similarly, a calendar year taxpayer that pays its insurance premium on December 1, 2002, for a 12-month policy beginning the following February would be required to capitalize the amount of the expenditure. The 12-month rule would not apply because the benefit attributable to the expenditure would extend beyond the end of the taxable year following the taxable year in which the expenditure was incurred. On the other hand, if the insurance contract had a term beginning on December 15, 2002, the taxpayer could deduct the premium expenditure under the 12-month rule because the benefit neither extends more than 12 months beyond December 15, 2002 (the first date the benefit is realized by the taxpayer) nor beyond the taxable year following the year the expenditure was incurred.

* * *

8. Defense or perfection of title to intangible property.

Subject to the 12-month rule, the IRS and Treasury Department expect to propose a rule that requires capitalization of amounts paid to defend or perfect title to intangible property.

For example, under the rule, if a taxpayer and another person both claim title to a particular trademark, the taxpayer must capitalize any amount paid to the other person for relinquishment of such claim. See, e.g., J.I. Case Company v. United States, 32 F.Supp. 754 (Ct. Cl. 1940).

C. Transaction Costs

The IRS and Treasury Department expect to propose a rule that requires a taxpayer to capitalize certain transaction costs that facilitate the taxpayer's acquisition, creation, or enhancement of intangible assets or benefits described above (regardless of whether a payment described in sections A or B of this document is made). In addition, this rule would require a taxpayer to capitalize transaction costs that facilitate the taxpayer's acquisition, creation, restructuring, or reorganization of a business entity, an applicable asset acquisition within the meaning of section 1060(c), or a transaction involving the acquisition of capital, including a stock issuance, borrowing, or recapitalization. However, this rule would not require capitalization of employee compensation (except for bonuses and commissions that are paid with respect to the transaction), fixed overhead (e.g., rent, utilities and depreciation), or costs that do not exceed a specified dollar amount, such as $5,000. The IRS and Treasury Department request comments on how expenditures should be aggregated for purposes of applying the de minimis exception, whether the de minimis exception should allow a deduction for the threshold amount where the aggregate transaction costs exceed the threshold amount, and whether there are certain expenditures for which the de minimis exception should not apply (e.g., commissions).

The IRS and Treasury Department are considering alternative approaches to minimize uncertainty and to ease the administrative burden of accounting for transaction costs. For example, the rules could allow a deduction for all employee compensation (including bonuses and commissions that are paid with respect to the transaction), be based on whether the transaction is regular or recurring, or follow the financial or regulatory accounting treatment of the transaction. The IRS and Treasury Department request comments on whether the recurring or nonrecurring nature of a transaction is an appropriate consideration in determining whether an expenditure to facilitate the transaction must be capitalized under section 263(a) and, if so, what criteria should be applied in distinguishing between recurring and nonrecurring transactions. In addition, the IRS and Treasury Department request comments on whether a taxpayer's treatment of transaction costs for financial or regulatory accounting purposes should be taken into account when developing simplifying assumptions.

For example, under the rule described above, a taxpayer would be required to capitalize legal fees in excess of the threshold dollar amount paid to its outside attorneys for services rendered in drafting a 3-year covenant not to compete because such costs facilitated the creation of the covenant not to compete. Similarly, the rule would require a taxpayer to capitalize legal fees in excess of the threshold dollar amount paid to its outside attorneys for services rendered in defending a trademark owned by the taxpayer.

Conversely, a taxpayer that originates a loan to a borrower in the course of its lending business would not be required to capitalize amounts paid to secure a credit history and property appraisal to facilitate the loan where the total amount paid with respect to that loan does not exceed the threshold dollar amount. The taxpayer also would not be required to capitalize the amount of salaries paid to employees or overhead costs of the taxpayer's loan origination department.

In addition, the rule would require a corporate taxpayer to capitalize legal fees in excess of the threshold dollar amount paid to its outside counsel to facilitate an acquisition of all of the taxpayer's outstanding stock by an acquirer. See, e.g., INDOPCO, Inc. v. Commissioner, 503 U.S. 79 (1992). However, the rule would not require capitalization of the portion of officers' salaries that is allocable to time spent by the officers negotiating the acquisition. Cf. Wells Fargo & Co. v. Commissioner, 224 F.3d 874 (8th Cir. 2000).

The rule also would not require capitalization of post-acquisition integration costs or severance payments made to employees as a result of an acquisition transaction because such costs do not facilitate the acquisition.

D. Other Items on Which Public Comment is Requested

* * *

3. Amortization periods.

Certain intangibles have readily ascertainable useful lives that can be determined with reasonable accuracy, while others do not. The IRS and Treasury Department expect to provide safe harbor recovery periods and methods for certain capitalized expenditures that do not have readily ascertainable useful lives. Comments are requested regarding whether guidance should provide one uniform period or multiple recovery periods and what the recovery periods and methods should be.

4. De minimis rules.

The IRS and Treasury Department request comments on whether there are types of expenditures other than those discussed above for which it would be appropriate to prescribe de minimis rules that would not require capitalization under section 263(a). If there are such categories or thresholds, comments are requested on how expenditures would be aggregated in applying these de minimis rules.

5. Costs of Software.

The IRS and Treasury Department request comments on what rules and principles should be used to distinguish acquired software from developed software and the administrability of those rules and principles. See Rev. Proc. 2000-50 (2000-2 C.B. 601).

***

Page 319:

See Bayles and Rich, "Repair or Capital Expenditure: The Tenth Circuit's General Plan of Betterment Rule," 1974 *Utah L. Rev.* 272 (1974).

Page 319:

The following is an OPTIONAL PROBLEM on capital expenditures v. repairs:

Landlord incurs the following expenses during the year on a ten unit apartment complex. Discuss whether each expenditure is currently deductible as a repair or is a capital expenditure:

(a) $350 for painting three rooms of apartment one.

(b) $1,000 for replacing the roof over apartment two which has suffered termite damage.

(c) $100 for plumber's bill to unclog a drain in apartment three.

(d) $250 for the replacement of a refrigerator in apartment four.

(e) $500 for patching the entire asphalt parking lot area.

(f) $750 for adding a carport to apartment six.

(g) $100 for newspaper advertisements.

(h) $200 for construction of a billboard to be placed on the apartment premises.

The ANSWERS to the above OPTIONAL PROBLEM are as follows:

(a).   year as a repair expense. Rose v. Haverty Furniture Co., 15 F.2d 345 (5th Cir. 1927). But where the painting is done as part of or incidental to a general reconditioning and overhauling project, it has been held that such costs are to be capitalized. Jones v. Comm'r, 242 F.2d 616 (5th Cir. 1957).

(b).   The cost of a new roof for the entire building is required to be capitalized as it adds to the value of the building and likely prolongs its life in the essential tax sense, Georgia Car & Locomotive Co., 2 B.T.A. 986 (1925), while the mere patching of a roof is a deductible repair anticipated in attaining expected life, Louise Kingsley, 11 B.T.A. 296 (1928).

Thus the issue here is whether the replacement of a portion of the roof over one apartment would extend the life of the entire building beyond that anticipated when initially constructed. Arguably, it would not and thus could be expensed as a current repair deduction. The reference in Reg. § 1.162-4 to adding to the value of the property is initially perplexing because any repair clearly does that; and still some may be expensed. But the thought is that, if the expenditure is of a kind that would have enhanced value when the item was new, it should be capitalized. Similarly, reference to appreciably prolonging life connotes extension of the asset's life beyond the point anticipated when constructed or acquired. Even so, the foregoing attempt to elaborate a little on these principles indicates how slippery they are to handle. The essentially factual nature of the inquiry makes previous cases of little use, except as a reading of many of them gives one a feel for this area.

The answer to the problem is certainly not clear, for the expenditure seems to have both repair and capital characteristics. In a similar situation, the expenses in repairing the side wall of a building which had been damaged by trucks were found to be essentially capital in nature in Automotive Bin Service Co., 12 T.C.M. 689 (1953), while the replacement of the rotten wood to mend deteriorated parts of a building to restore it to a sound condition were held to be a repair in Farmers Creamery Co. of Fredericksburg, Va., 14 T.C. 879 (1950).

(c). Plumbers' and electricians' bills for servicing previously existing assets are clearly for the purpose of keeping the property in efficient operating condition and do not add to its value or prolong its life. Thus the $100 can be deducted currently as a repair.

(d). The replacement of the refrigerator involves the addition of an asset which has a substantial useful life and the expenditure must be capitalized and depreciated.

(e). The $500 cost of patching the parking lot would likely be a repair. See Honigman v. Comm'r, 466 F.2d 69 (6th Cir. 1972), and Almac's Inc., 20 T.C.M. 56 (1961).

(f). The addition of a carport would materially add to the value of the property and would be a capital expenditure. See Herbert Shainberg, 33 T.C. 241 (1959).

(g). The cost of advertising in newspapers, radio, etc. would be a currently deductible expense. French Broad Ice Cream Co. v. U.S., 1957-2 USTC ¶ 9972 (E.D. Tenn. 1957); Rev. Rul. 92-80, 1992-2 C.B. 57.

(h). The expenditure for construction of a billboard probably should be capitalized since payments for assets that have greater than a one-year useful life normally constitute capital expenditures. For an interesting case in the capitalization area in which an advertising deduction argument was made, see Dana W. Brown, 29 T.C.M. 1126 (1970). The expenses of the president of a coffee company, incurred on a safari, were held to be nondeductible capital expenditures incurred to promote reputation and goodwill.

PROBLEM

Page 331:

1(a). Since Contaminator was aware that the building contained asbestos when Contaminator acquired the building, it is unlikely that the removal costs are deductible since the expenses would likely materially increase the value of the property over its value on acquisition. Reg. § 1.162-4. The expenditure should be equated to any other capital expenditure on the property.

1(b).   Section 198 would allow a deduction of this "qualified environmental remediation expenditure" (see § 198(b)(1)) since it is at a § 198(c) "qualified contaminated site." Note that Contaminator must elect to deduct the expenditure. § 198(a).

1(c).   This is a difficult and seemingly open issue. On the one hand, it is arguable that since Contaminator created the asbestos problem, the removal cost should be deductible as a repair following the rationale of Rev. Rul. 94-38, 1994-1 C.B. 35, holding that the removal of contaminated groundwater is a deductible expense. On the other hand, since the asbestos was in the building when Contaminator built the building, it is arguable that it may be distinguishable from *Rev. Rul. 94-38* in which case the cost of removal would be a capital expenditure materially increasing the value of the property and improving the status of the building.

1(d).   This is Contaminator's strongest case for deductibility because the costs merely restore the building to the status (a non-asbestos building) that Contaminator thought Contaminator originally acquired, and the removal costs do not materially enhance the value of the building over the amount Contaminator paid. Query whether Contaminator should have known of the asbestos and, if so, whether that would change the result.

1(e).   Even if the costs are deductible in (d), the *Norwest Corporation* case would disallow the deduction as the costs are incurred in conjunction with what constitutes a capital expenditure to the building. As *Norwest Corporation* makes clear, it would not matter whether the work was done by separate contractors. Query whether the result would be the same if the asbestos work was done in year one and the remodel in year two. The answer would probably depend on whether, in substance, the separate jobs constituted a single transaction.

Page 334:

> See Faura v. Comm'r, 73 T.C. 849 (1980), for a thorough discussion of the current deductibility of expenses incurred in the creation of works of art. In *Faura*, the taxpayer was permitted a § 162 deduction for expenses he incurred while writing two unpublished books.

Page 334:

> Rev. Rul. 99-23, 1999-1 C.B. 998, considers the types of expenditures that will qualify as investigatory costs that are eligible for amortization as start-up expenditures under § 195 when a taxpayer acquires the assets of an active trade or business.

PROBLEMS

Page 339:

1(a).   The expenses incurred in making a preliminary investigation into the development of industrial properties cannot be deducted under the provisions of § 162(a). Tycoon was not engaged in the business of developing industrial properties at the time the expenses were incurred. The expenses were not related to the conduct of the trade that he was then engaged in but were incurred preparatory to entering a new business. Hence, the expenses are not ordinary and necessary business expenses incurred in *carrying on* a trade or business. See *Morton Frank*. But such expenses may be amortized over a 60 month period if § 195 is elected, if Tycoon does enter the business of developing industrial properties and if the expenditure would have been allowed if paid or incurred in the operation of a business.

1(b).   The expenses incurred are deductible under the provisions of § 162(a). The industrial development of properties would be an extension of Tycoon's existing business of real estate development rather than the inception of a new pursuit. See York v. Comm'r, 261 F.2d 421 (4th Cir. 1958). If the expenses were not deductible under § 162 because this was considered a new trade or business they would be deductible under § 195.

1(c).   The expenses are not deductible under the provisions of § 162(a). The cost of investigating a prospective business for future operation is not deductible as a § 162 business expense if the taxpayer was not engaged in that trade or business at the time the expenditures were incurred. However § 195 may be applicable. See the answer to problem 1(a), above, and see Vincent W. Eckel, 33 T.C.M. 147 (1974), where a sporting goods proprietor was not allowed to write off expenses of an African safari. He was investigating a new business (instructing persons in techniques of big game hunting), not carrying on his existing business (retail gun sales).

1(d).   No. As the Text points out at page 335, a 1984 amendment to § 195 so clarifies the statute that all start-up expenditures must be capitalized. They are not currently deductible unless incurred in the expansion of an existing trade or business. See problem 1(b), above.

1(e).   Section 195(b)(2) allows Tycoon to deduct any deferred investigation expenses under § 165(c)(1) in the year of the disposition. If Tycoon had abandoned the transaction without entering the business, she might be entitled to a loss deduction under § 165(c)(2) (losses incurred in a transaction entered into for profit though not connected with a trade or business) for any *transactional* (but not investigatory) expenses. See Johan Domenie, 34 T.C.M. 469 (1975); Harris W. Seed, 52 T.C. 880 (1969); Rev. Rul. 77-254, 1977-2 C.B. 63; and problem 1(a) at page 475 of the Text.

2(a).   No. Spouse is not "carrying on" a trade or business at the time the expenses are incurred. The Code does not provide a deduction for expenses incurred by individuals in seeking their first jobs. Rev. Rul. 75-120, 1975-1 C.B. 55.

2(b).   No. Under the authority of *Rev. Rul. 75-120*, deductions for expenses incurred by individuals who are seeking their first jobs will be disallowed irrespective of success or failure. The Ruling revokes Rev. Rul. 60-223, 1960-1 C.B. 57, which improperly allowed a deduction in case of success.

A question might be raised as to the applicability of § 195 here, but Spouse's employee status does not seem to qualify for § 195 treatment. Although we have no concrete authority, the strong implication from a reading of the legislative history of § 195 which fails to mention employee status is that the section is inapplicable to employee status. See H.R. No. 96-1278, 96th Cong., 2d Sess. (1980), 1980-2 C.B. 709 at 711-714. It might also be argued that employee status fails the § 195(b) requirement of an "*active* trade or business."

2(c). Yes. In this area the Tax Court has made an exception to its assertion that pre-employment expenses are not deductible, and the Commissioner has acquiesced in this decision. In C.R. Hundley, Jr., 48 T.C. 339 (1967), acq., 1967-2 C.B. 2, services were rendered to a prospective employer prior to the taxpayer's being employed. Payment was contingent upon employment. When the taxpayer subsequently found employment, the pre-employment expenses were held deductible. The court's rationale for this holding was that, since the expenses were not due or incurred nor payable until the taxpayer was engaged in the business to which the expenses were related, they were incurred in carrying on the trade or business.

2(d). This is deductible under *Rev. Rul. 75-120* which properly holds that expenses incurred in seeking new employment in the employee's continuing trade or business are deductible whether successful or not. An issue might be raised whether a deduction is allowed if Spouse, while previously a secretary, had not been employed for 6 months, 12 months, 3 years, etc. The Ruling speaks of "substantial lack of continuity occurring between the time of past employment and the seeking of the new employment." Rev. Rul. 77-32, 1977-1 C.B. 38, involved an anesthesiologist who suspended practice indefinitely because of an increase in premiums for malpractice insurance coverage but incurred expenses to maintain professional competence and expertise. Since the expenses were in preparation for a return to practice only at some indefinite future date no deduction was allowed.

2(e). If Spouse had sought employment as a bank teller then, regardless of Agency's success, the thrust of *Rev. Rul. 75-120* would be to deny a deduction. Employment as a bank teller is a different, not a continuing trade or business.

What if Spouse had been looking for a secretarial job through Agency when they turned up the bank teller job which Spouse decided to take? Although there is no authority, it appears likely that a deduction would be allowed. It might be argued that the expenses are deductible for unsuccessful efforts to find another secretarial job!

PROBLEM

Page 354:

1(a). The principal alternatives are deductible compensation or nondeductible dividends. The basic issue raised by the problem is, of course, the "reasonableness" of the compensation paid to Employee. See Reg. § 1.162-7(b)(2) and (3) and the *Harolds Club* case at page 346 of the Text. If a substantial shareholder - employee of a corporation receives payments as compensation for services, to the extent the amount claimed as compensation is unreasonable the payments are constructive distributions to him in his capacity as a shareholder. This may be a matter of indifference to him; if the payments are determined to be dividends, the shareholder-employee would have income. Even if the payments do not constitute constructive dividends, the excess over the reasonable salary would be taxed to the employee under the broad interpretation of § 61(a) set forth in *Glenshaw Glass* at page 56 of the Text. See Reg. § 1.162-8 and Boston Drug Co., 2 B.T.A. 298 (1925). On the other hand, § 162(a)(1) allows a deduction for salaries or other compensation which are "reasonable." To the extent that compensation is determined to be unreasonable, it is not deductible by an employer corporation whether the excess is characterized as a dividend or not. Cf. Long Island Drug Co. v. Comm'r, 111 F.2d 593 (2d Cir. 1940). In addition, note that we reach the reasonableness issue only if the amounts are characterized as compensation.

1(b). The answer to this question depends upon the test employed to determine deductibility. In *Exacto Springs Corporation* at page 340 of the Text, the Seventh Circuit rejects the factors test historically adopted by other courts and substitutes an independent investor test. The independent investor test is described by the Second Circuit in Dexsil v. Comm'r, 147 F.3d 96 (2d Cir. 1998) at page 101 as follows:

> As noted, in this circuit the independent investor test is not a separate autonomous factor; rather, it provides a lens through which the entire analysis should be viewed. . . .Thus, if the company's earnings on equity, when

131

viewed in relation to such factors as the company's overall performance and levels of compensation, "remain at a level that would satisfy an independent investor, there is a strong indication that management is providing compensable services and that profits are not being siphoned out of the company disguised as salary."

Many circuits continue to employ the "factors" test to determine reasonableness that was used by the Tax Court in the *Exacto Springs Corporation* case. Under that test, the "reasonableness" of compensation for personal services is a question of fact. Among the factors generally considered in making a determination are: (1) the employee's qualifications; (2) the nature of employee's work; (3) the size and complexities of the business; (4) a comparison of salaries paid with the gross income and the net income of the payor; (5) the prevailing general economic conditions; (6) a comparison of salaries with distributions to stockholders; (7) the prevailing rates of compensation for comparable positions in comparable concerns; (8) the salary policy of the taxpayer to all employees; and (9) in the case of small corporations with a limited number of officers, the amount of compensation paid to the particular employee in previous years. No single factor is given decisive weight. Pepsi Cola Bottling Co. of Salina, Inc. v. Comm'r, 528 F.2d 176 (10th Cir. 1975). See also Van's Chevrolet, 26 T.C.M. 809 (1967), containing a list of several factors.

The *Exacto Springs Corporation* case is discussed at Friske and Smith, "The Status of the Independent Investor Test in Reasonable Compensation Determinations," 31 *Tax Adv*. 406 (June, 2000) (providing a chart relating to tests used in different courts); Barnard, "The Unreasonable Compensation Issue Raises From the Dead and Takes on the Independent Investor," 93 *J. Tax'n* 356 (2000). (also discussing cases subsequent to *Exacto Springs* and tests used in different circuits); and McClung and Weld, "Unreasonable Compensation and the Independent Investor Test," 79 *Taxes* 35 (2001) (providing a chart relating to the tests used in different courts).

1(c).   The Taxpayer in *Pepsi Cola Bottling Co.*, cited above, relied on Reg. § 1.162-7(b)(2) which provides generally that if contingent compensation is paid pursuant to a "free bargain" made before the services are rendered and solely for the purpose of securing the employee's services, it is allowable even though it proves to be greater than the amount that would ordinarily be paid. Both the Tax Court and the Fifth Circuit refused to apply this regulation to the taxpayer on the ground that there was no free bargain made solely to secure the employee's services, because the employee was the controlling shareholder of the corporation. See also the *Harold's Club* case at page 346 of the Text.

If Employee owned only 10 out of the 250 outstanding shares then Reg. § 1.162-7(b)(2) would appear to be applicable to allow the compensation deduction unless a "*Harold's Club*" situation existed. See, e.g., Kennedy v. Comm'r, 671 F.2d 167 (6th Cir. 1982), allowing a very high salary under the regulation.

Page 355:

In Kit v. U.S., 1976-2 USTC ¶ 9721 (D. Mont. 1976), taxpayers travelled around the country doing magic tricks for most of the year but for three months they ran the Goofy Shirt Shop in West Yellowstone, Montana, where they leased a trailer on an annual basis. The court allowed a deduction for their traveling expenses accepting West Yellowstone as their home and distinguishing *Rosenspan* where a taxpayer had no semblance of a home.

But compare In re Bechtelheimer, 1999-2 U.S.T.C. ¶ 50,781 (D. Fla. 1999) where taxpayers were crafters who went to craft shows around the country in their first mobile home and spent 35-40 days a year in Florida (where they had a second Florida mobile home, although they essentially lived in the first mobile home even while in Florida). The Court concluded that the Florida mobile home was only a potential dwelling used primarily for storage and denied a § 162 away from home deduction.

See also Henderson v. Comm'r, 143 F3d 497 (9th Cir. 1998), where a divided court held that the taxpayer was not "away from home" under § 162 (a)(2) when he kept his belongings at his parent's home and travelled on business to other locations during the year. Since he could not establish any business transaction to the parents' home and had no duplication of expenses, the court determined he was an itinerant taxpayer and denied a § 162 (a)(2) deduction.

Page 355:

> There had been disagreement whether Foreign Service members may deduct the costs of compulsory home leave. The Service said not, but the 4th, 9th, and D.C. Circuits allowed a deduction for the compulsory trips, concluding that they are primarily a business-related cost. Hitchcock v. Comm'r, 578 F.2d 972 (4th Cir. 1978); Stratton v. Comm'r, 448 F.2d 1030 (9th Cir. 1971); Teil v. Comm'r, 639 F.2d 805 (D.C. Cir. 1981). The Service has given up the fight and allows Foreign Service members to deduct substantiated home leave expenses. Rev. Rul. 82-2, 1982-1 C.B. 27.

Page 372:

> See Rev. Proc. 2000-9, 2000-1 C.B. ___, which provides rules under which the amount of § 162 meal and lodging expenses while away from home will be deemed substantiated under Reg. § 1.274-5 when a payor provides a per diem allowance under a reimbursement or expense arrangement.

PROBLEMS

Page 372:

1(a).   Expenses of commuting between taxpayer's residence and place of business, as well as meal costs even if incurred during working hours, are generally personal expenses for which no deduction is allowed. Reg. § 1.162-2(e) and § 1.262-1(b)(5). Although commuting expenses are in some sense connected with the taxpayer's business, no deduction is allowed under § 162(a) since such expenses are not required by the "exigencies of the business." Similarly, parking fees at one's business are nondeductible personal expenses. Cf. Russell Anderson, 60 T.C. 834 (1973) and § 132(a)(5), (f)(1)(C), (f)(2)(B) and (f)(5).

But see Pollei v. Comm'r, 877 F.2d 838 (10th Cir. 1989), where police captains were permitted to deduct expenses incurred as a result of using their own unmarked vehicles to travel between their residences and police headquarters because they were required to be on duty to and from headquarters.

1(b).   Transportation expense incurred in going from one business location to another within the same area are deductible under § 162(a) as ordinary and necessary business expenses. These expenses are distinguishable from commuting expenses of the type described in problem 1(a), above, in that they are directly attributable to the actual performance of the taxpayer's duties. The Service's standard mileage rate allowance for the business use of automobiles for 2002 is 36.5 cents per mile. Rev. Proc. 2001-54, 2001-2 C.B. ____. This amount is adjusted annually. The deduction for expenses of traveling from one business location to another is allowable whether the taxpayer has only one employer but two separate business locations, two separate employers, or is self-employed. See Rev. Rul. 55-109, 1955-1 C.B. 261.

If, however, Commuter goes from the City Court House to his residence at the end of the day, Rev. Rul. 76-453, 1976-2 C.B. 86 Example 8, states that the cost is not deductible. For now, the statement may be disregarded, as the Service has suspended Rev. Rul. 76-453, indefinitely. See Ann. 77-147, I.R.B. 1977-42, 45. Seemingly, such costs are still commuting costs, as Commuter probably goes to Court House on a regular basis and it is a regular place of business. Query whether in some situations, it would be a "temporary" work location allowing the expenses to be deductible under paragraph (2) of Rev. Rul. 99-7 at page 369 of the Text.

The cost of Commuter's meals is not deductible. He is not "away from home" under the *Correll* sleep or rest rule. See problem 1(c), below.

1(c).   As the *Correll* case (389 U.S. 299 (1967)) holds, unless a taxpayer is away from home in a situation in which sleep or rest is required, the taxpayer may not deduct any expense for meals. Thus Commuter may not deduct the cost of his meals, but he may deduct his transportation costs. *Correll* does not preclude a deduction for transportation costs that are an ordinary and necessary business expense even though a taxpayer is not "away from home" under § 162(a)(2). The same principles differentiate transportation and meals in the determination of deductible education expenses. See Cosimo Carlucci, 37 T.C. 695 (1962). Such transportation costs are not mere commuting expenses. See Rev. Rul. 99-7 paragraph (1) at page 371 of the Text.

2(a). Taxpayer may deduct her transportation and her lodging and 50% of her meals in Metro. She is engaged in a single business in two locations and the expenses are incurred "while away from home in the pursuit of a trade or business" under § 162(a)(2). As a result of § 274(n)(1) she may deduct only 50% of her meals. In addition, since she is in travel status if she dines alone or with family, but not with business people, she need not satisfy the § 274(a)(1)(A) "directly related to" or "associated with" tests which are considered later in the Text.

2(b). Taxpayer here incurs meal and lodging expenses that are (1) required by the exigencies of her business and (2) incident to necessary sleep or rest. To be deductible under § 162(a)(2), the expenses also must be incurred while "away from home." Since either City or Metro is taxpayer's "home," at least part of her meals and lodging expenses are deductible. The question is which of these two locations constitutes her tax home. The Commissioner, backed up by the Tax Court and some of the Circuit Courts of Appeal, has steadfastly maintained that a taxpayer's home for purposes of § 162(a)(2) is one's principal place of business. See, e.g., Rev. Rul. 75-432, 1975-2 C.B. 60. Some Circuits, see Chimento v. Comm'r, 438 F.2d 643 (3rd Cir. 1971) and the Second Circuit in *Rosenspan*, read the language of § 162(a)(2) more literally and have held that the principal place of residence of taxpayer is one's tax home. To date, the Supreme Court has been unwilling to resolve the split among the Courts of Appeal. See, e.g. Comm'r v. Stidger, 386 U.S. 287 (1967), and Comm'r v. Flowers, 326 U.S. 465 (1946). Under the *Rosenspan* approach, it seems that City would be Taxpayer's home. The crucial factors are that she spends more total time in City and that her family is located there.

Under the Commissioner's tax home concept, Taxpayer's principal place of business, City, would be her "home." Among the factors which have been considered relevant are where the taxpayer spends more of her time, engages in greater business activity, and derives the greater portion of her income. See Markey v. Comm'r, 490 F.2d 1249 (6th Cir. 1979), Ziporyn v. Comm'r, 73 TCM 2440 (1997), and Rev. Rul. 54-147, 1954-1 C.B. 51, 52. Based on these factors alone, it seems that Metro is the Taxpayer's home. However in a close case such as this, the location of the taxpayer's family has been considered and should result in City being deemed her home. Cf. Abe Brenner, 26 T.C.M. 1210 (1967). If so, Taxpayer's transportation, lodging in Metro,

136

and 50% of her costs of meals in Metro would be deductible.

2(c).   In this situation the courts in *Coerver* and *Foote* held that Taxpayer and her husband are separate taxpayers with separate businesses and different tax homes for § 162(a)(2) purposes. Consequently, Taxpayer's tax home is Metro and her meals and lodging there are not deductible because she is not "away from home." Her trips to City and meals and lodging in City are nondeductible personal expenses. The assumed permanent nature of both jobs differentiates this question from Six v. U.S., 450 F.2d 66 (2d Cir. 1971). If the hearth-is-home concept were applied to these facts, although Taxpayer arguably might be "away from home" while in Metro her meals and lodging expenses are not due to the exigencies of *her* business but to her *personal* decision to live in City. See the *Flowers* case. But see the concurring and dissenting opinions in Daly v. Comm'r, 662 F.2d 253 (4th Cir. 1981).

3(a).   Assuming the validity of the Commissioner's tax home concept, it is clear that Metro, the location of Burly's off-season permanent residence would not qualify as his tax home since he engages in no business activity there. Burly's principal post of duty and therefore his home is City, the location of the Stomper's franchise. Therefore, Burly is not "away from home" when he incurs meals and lodging expenses in City during the football season and thus no deduction would be allowed. Nor would a deduction for his living expenses in Metro be allowed, because he does not incur those expenses in pursuit of a trade or business.

3(b).   The added fact of Burly's insurance position in Metro changes the result and a deduction should be allowed. This is essentially the same issue that was raised in the *Andrews* case at page 363 of the Text in which the First Circuit allowed a deduction. See also *George R. Lanning*, 34 T.C.M. 1366 (1975), case involving a Sun Valley ski patrolman who worked summers at the casinos at Lake Tahoe and was permitted a deduction for his Tahoe expenses.

The issue is which of the taxpayer's two business locations constitutes the principal place of business. The three factors set forth in problem 2(b), above, must be considered in making this determination. It is the Commissioner's position that, if the taxpayer is an employee at both locations, the amount of income earned at each is the most important

137

consideration. Rev. Rul. 54-147, 1954-1 C.B. 51, 52. In other situations, the length of time spent is generally the most important factor. Rev. Rul. 63-82, 1963-1 C.B. 33. See also Markey v. Comm'r, 490 F.2d 1249 (6th Cir. 1974), Ziporyn v. Comm'r, 73 TCM 2440 (1997).

If Burly's principal place of business is Metro, he would be allowed to deduct the cost of 50% of his own meals and the cost of his lodging in City. However, if Burly's tax home is found to be City and he does not maintain his City apartment in the off-season, there is authority for disallowing in full the amount of any deduction for his living expenses in Metro under § 162(a)(2), since he incurred no duplicate living expenses. See U.S. v. Mathews, 332 F.2d 91 (9th Cir. 1964), and Steve L. Krase, 35 T.C.M. 272 (1976). Some courts espouse the theory that the taxpayer should not be allowed to deduct living expenses at one place if the taxpayer does not incur duplicate expenses at another. Whether duplication is required may depend upon the definition of "home" under § 162(a)(2). See problem 4(b), below.

4(a). This is an example of the *Peurifoy* doctrine which is discussed in the *Rosenspan* case. In Peurifoy v. Comm'r, 358 U.S. 59 (1958), the Supreme Court acknowledged that a deduction for transportation and meals and lodging is allowed if a taxpayer is employed at a location away from home for a "temporary" rather than an "indefinite" or "indeterminate" period of time and if the taxpayer retains a tie with the old place of business. As a rule of thumb a definite period of up to one year was deemed to be "temporary" and deductible, and that rule is now codified in the second to the last sentence of § 162(a). Here Temporary may deduct his expenses. Since Temporary has moved to Branch City for a definite nine month period and will thereafter return to City, his employment is "temporary" and his costs of transportation, lodging and 50% of his meals are deductible.

The Service has altered its prior position and now attempts to disallow the deduction of commuting expenses under § 162(a)(2) even when the taxpayer is "away from home." Dictum in a Tax Court Memorandum decision is supportive of disallowing such a deduction. Paolini v. Comm'r, 43 T.C.M. 513 (1982), aff'd by the 3rd Cir. in an unpublished opinion (1983).

An interesting application of the one-year temporary rule occurred in Mitchell v. Comm'r, 78 T.C.M. 355 (1999) where taxpayer, whose home was in Illinois, spent over 100 days a year in a temporary location in California in each of 5 consecutive years. The Commissioner asserted that this violated the one-year or the indefinite rule, but the Court concluded the work was on again, off again and was deductible. Cf. problems 2 and 3, above.

4(b).   In general, where the temporary time period exceeds 1 year, the second to the last sentence of § 162(a) disallows any deduction. However, where as here the time period realistically is expected to be less than one year, but at some point in time it is extended in excess of one year, expenses are deductible until the time period is extended. Thus, Temporary may deduct 8 months of expenses here. See Rev. Rul. 93-86, 1993-2 C.B. 71 Situation 3. Rev. Rul. 93-86 addresses three factual situations to determine whether a work assignment should be classified as either temporary or indefinite for purposes of § 162(a)(2). First, the Ruling holds that, if employment away from home in a single location is reasonably expected to last - and does in fact last - for one year or less, the employment is considered temporary so long as facts and circumstances do not indicate otherwise. Second, if the work assignment is realistically expected to last for more than one year and there is no realistic expectation that it will be a shorter period, the assignment will be considered indefinite, regardless of whether it actually exceeds a year. Finally, as here, if the assignment was initially expected to last one year or less, but later is expected to last for more than one year, then the employment will be considered temporary until the taxpayer's expectations changed, and indefinite thereafter. See also Notice 93-29, 1993-1 C.B. 311, providing further explanation of some aspects of the limitation.

4(c).   This problem hits directly at the question whether a deduction requires duplicate places of abode. If home connotes a residence, to be "away from home" a taxpayer ought to own or maintain a continuing residence in the area from which he or she is away, or so goes the questionable doctrine. Cavana v. Comm'r, 58 T.C.M. 1364 (1990). J.B. Stewart, 30 T.C.M. 1316 (1971); Berton N. Cross, 38 T.C.M. 234 (1979). Cf. Larry R. Adamson, 32 T.C.M. 484 (1973), disallowing the meals and lodging portion of education expenses not incurred "away from home." If home is defined as principal place of business, it is questionable whether residential duplication or significant contacts are required although they are present in all cases. See Charles G. Gustafson, 3 T.C. 998 (1944), nonacq., 1973-2 C.B. 4; but see Kenneth H. Hicks, 47 T.C. 71 (1966). The trend of recent cases seems to require duplication.

5(a).   Reg. § 1.162-2(a) states that "only such travelling expenses as are reasonable and necessary in the conduct of the taxpayer's business and directly attributable to it may be deducted." Thus the cost of lodging and 50% of meal costs for Monday to Wednesday are deductible, but the costs incurred on Thursday and Friday are not. The cost of transportation to and from Florida is deductible under Reg. § 1.162-2(b)(1), which provides that "if taxpayer travels to a destination and while at that destination engages in both business and personal activities, traveling expenses to and from such destination are deductible only if the trip is related primarily to the taxpayer's trade or business." Reg. § 1.162-2(b)(2) provides that the question whether the trip is primarily for business purposes depends on the facts and circumstances of each case but that the amount of time spent on each type of activity is an important factor. In this case since a majority of time was spent on business it is likely that Traveler's transportation expenses would be fully deductible.

5(b).   As a result of § 274(m)(3), Traveler may not deduct travel expenses for her spouse (or for that matter a dependent or any other person) unless:

(1)   the spouse is an employee of the person paying or reimbursing the expenses,

(2)   the travel of the spouse is for a bona fide business purpose (cf. Reg. § 1.162-2(c)), and

(3)   the spouse's expenses would otherwise be deductible by spouse.

If the requirements of § 274(m)(3) are met, Spouse's transportation expenses and Monday through Wednesday lodging and 50% of meals are deductible. The deduction denial is inapplicable to § 217 moving expenses.

5(c).   The question here depends on a factual determination of the primary purpose of Traveler's trip. Certainly a majority of the time was spent on pleasure. However, it is arguable that weekend days ought not be counted. This argument can be supported if a taxpayer shows that substantially cheaper air fares are permitted with a Saturday night stayover. If the primarily business test is met, then Traveler's transportation and Monday through Wednesday lodging and 50% of meals are deductible. If the test is not met and the trip is found to be primarily personal, her transportation costs would no longer be deductible. They cannot be brought within Reg. § 1.162-(b)(1) (last sentence), which provides that "expenses while at the destination which are properly allocable to the taxpayer's trade or business are deductible even though the travelling expenses to and from the destination are not deductible."

5(d).   If Traveler returns home on a cruise ship the primary purpose of the trip is still business and Traveler's costs are deductible. However under § 274(m)(1) the amount of Traveler's costs are limited to twice the highest Federal per diem for travel in the United States, times the number of days in transit. The 50% limit on meals is imposed prior to the above limitation.

5(e).   The result would be the same as in problem 5(a), above. Although Traveler's trip was outside the United States, the § 274(c) limitation would not apply because the travel did not exceed one week and the § 274(c)(2)(A) exception to § 274(c)(1) would apply.

5(f).   The § 274(c)(1) limitation would be applicable. Reg. § 1.274-4(d)(2)(v) sensibly classifies Saturday and Sunday as business days, even though business is not conducted on those days, if they are standby days in a work period. Thus six out of Traveler's nine days would be business days and two-thirds of her transportation costs would be deductible. Traveler's lodging and 50% of meals for all days except the final three days are also deductible.

5(g).   Congress seems to change its mind almost on a regular basis with regard to the deductibility of expenses to attend foreign conventions. Under § 274(h) no deduction is allowed to an individual attending a convention, seminar, or similar meeting outside the North American area (the U.S., its possessions, the Trust Territory of the Pacific Islands, Canada, Mexico, and certain Caribbean countries, and Bermuda) unless the taxpayer establishes that the meeting is "directly related" to the

141

active conduct of the taxpayer's trade or business and that it is "as reasonable" for the meeting to be held outside those areas as within. Among the factors to be considered in determining reasonableness are:

(1)   the purpose of the meeting and the activities taking place at the meeting

(2)   the purposes and activities of the sponsoring organizations or groups

(3)   the residences of the active members of the sponsoring organization and the places at which other meetings of the sponsoring organizations or groups have been or will be held.

Deductions claimed for expenses for conventions, etc., on cruise ships within or outside U.S. territorial waters are generally disallowed. If, however the cruise ship is registered in the U.S. and all ports of call are in the U.S. or its possessions, deductions up to $2,000 are allowed if the § 274(h)(5) reporting requirements are met. § 274(h)(2).

Traveler's convention is in Mexico, within the North American area, and is therefore deductible to the same extent as a normal business trip to Mexico. See § 274(c) and problems 5(e) and (f), above.

Page 385:

See Schoenfeld, "The Educational Expense Deduction: The Need for a Rational Approach," 27 *Vill. L. Rev.* 237 (1982).

Page 385:

Attempts to deduct expenses for an undergraduate college education are normally denied because the individual has yet to enter a trade or business and thus is not "carrying on." But if one attends college after entering a field, the expenses may be deductible if they relate to a *present* and do not qualify him for a *new* trade or business. In John D. Glasgow, 31 T.C.M. 310 (1972), aff'd per curiam, 1973-2 USTC ¶ 9773 (10th Cir. 1973), an ordained Baptist minister was allowed to deduct education expenses in attaining his college degree. The court viewed the issue as a question of subjective intent - i.e., did he intend to maintain and improve skills required of him in his employment. In this light, which is not in keeping with the current objective test of the regulations, there would seem to be many non-college graduates who could obtain a degree with the intent to improve their present skills, rather than to qualify for a new trade or business. Nevertheless the court said there were few situations in which undergraduate expenses would be deductible and that, in the case of the minister, the basic courses of a college education would be particularly helpful "in solving the wide-ranging problems peculiar to his calling." See, for example, Richard N. Warfsman, 31 T.C.M. 644 (1972), where a mechanic in the aerospace industry was denied a deduction for his bachelor's degree in mechanical engineering since it qualified him for a new trade or business.

Section 127 more liberally excludes the value of educational assistance without requiring the education to be business related. See page 115 of the Text; and see Mylan, "Current Tax Treatment of Education Costs," 32 *U. Fla. L. Rev.* 387 (1980).

Page 392:

As a result of § 117 (See § 117(c)), education expense reimbursements are often required to be included in an employee's gross income. However, if such payments are deductible as business expenses of the employee, they need not be reported on employee's return to the extent the expense equals the reimbursement, the employee accounts to his employer, and the education is job related. Compare Rev. Rul. 76-71, 1976-1 C.B. 308, with Rev. Rul. 76-352, 1976-2 C.B. 37, holding non job related payments are required to be included in income but may nevertheless be deductible if within Reg. § 1.162-5. Cf. Reg. § 1.162-17(b)(1). Payments made by the employee for books, tuition, etc. in excess of any reimbursements are deductible. Rev. Rul. 76-65, 1976-1 C.B. 46. See also Rev. Rul. 76-62, 1976-1 C.B. 12.

Education expenses that would be deductible under the rules of Reg. § 1.162-5 become nondeductible to the extent that they are reimbursed with tax exempt payments. See § 265(1). Manocchio v. Comm'r, 78 T.C. 989 (1982).

Page 392:

Are the costs of a bar review course and bar examination fees deductible expenses? Of course if the expense is incurred prior to any practicing then no deduction is allowed as taxpayer is not yet "carrying on." Cf. *Morton Frank* at page 332 of the Text. If one is both licensed to practice and practicing in another state, the "carrying on" requirement is met but the bar admission fee is a nondeductible capital expenditure. Arthur E. Ryman, Jr., 51 T.C. 799 (1969); Avery v. U.S., 419 F.Supp. 105 (N.D. Iowa 1976); and Sharon v. Comm'r, 591 F.2d 1273 (9th Cir. 1978), cert. den. 1979, reach that conclusion. Cf. Willard M. Christine, 33 T.C.M. 1110 (1974). It is likely that a bar review course should also be treated as a capital expenditure; there is authority that a bar review course is not a deductible education expense because it qualifies a taxpayer for a new trade or business. See the *Sharon* case, supra, so holding; and see Yarslaw Horodysky, 54 T.C. 490 (1970), and Rev. Rul. 75-412, 1975-2 C.B. 62, disallowing the expense of bar review courses of U.S. states to lawyers who were qualified to practice in foreign countries on the grounds that this qualified them for a new trade or business under Reg. § 1.162-5(b)(3)(i), and William B. Glenn, 62 T.C. 270 (1974), denying a public accountant a deduction for the cost of a review course to become a C.P.A. under the same regulation. All of the above occurred prior to the enactment of § 197. See Andrews, "Amortization of the Costs of Obtaining Additional Bar Admissions Under Section 197," 37 *Ariz. L. Rev.* 501 (1995) which suggests that such costs may be amortized over 15 years under § 197. And see Rev. Rul. 71-58, 1971-1 C.B. 55, holding that an employed teacher who meets the minimum education requirements for a permanent teaching certificate in one state may deduct costs incurred for prescribed education courses necessary to qualify as a teacher in another state.

PROBLEMS

Page 392:

1. Alice would not be allowed to deduct her law school expenses because they would qualify her for a new trade or business. See Reg. § 1.162-5(b)(3) and Anderson v. U.S., 1975-2 USTC ¶ 9578 (N.D. Cal. 1975).

    Barbara would, however, be allowed to deduct her expenses. Rev. Rul. 74-78, 1974-1 C.B. 44, permitted a dentist (already "carrying on" of course) to deduct expenses of orthodontic study as a change of duty within a trade or business. The ruling described the expenses as incurred "in connection with improving his skills as a dentist."

Cathy's expenses have long been denied. See Reg. § 1.162-5(b)(3) Ex. (1). It is possible her expenses would be deductible if she were admitted for special study only and not as a degree candidate, one who could not apply any academic credits earned toward a degree. There continue to be a large number of cases with taxpayers attempting to deduct the cost of education leading to the first degree in law, but the cases all deny such a deduction. The predominant basis for denial is the prohibition against qualification for a new trade or business. Reg. § 1.162-5(b)(3) has been upheld regardless of intent and regardless of whether or not the education improved or maintained the skills of one's employment. E.g. Melnik v. U.S., 1973-2 USTC ¶ 9521 (C.D. Cal. 1973), aff'd per curiam, 512 F.2d 1065 (9th Cir. 1975), cert. den., 425 U.S. 911 (1976) (I.R.S. agent); John K. Lunsford, 32 T.C.M. 64 (1973) (patent examiner); Philip R. Collings, 32 T.C.M. 890 (1973) (I.R.S. agent); Morton S. Taubman, 60 T.C. 814 (1973) (accountant); Rev. Rul. 72-450, 1972-2 C.B. 89 (marine officer).

The deductibility of Denise's expenses raises the toughest question here. Johnson v. U.S., 332 F. Supp. 906 (E.D. La. 1971), held that a lawyer's education in the specialized field of tax law qualified him for a new trade or business under Reg. § 1.162-5(b)(3). In Albert C. Ruehmann III, 30 T.C.M. 675 (1971), a lawyer was allowed a deduction for his expenses in acquiring an LL.M. degree but not in any specialized area. More recently the government has not contested the deductibility of education expenses incurred in acquiring an LL.M. in Taxation by lawyers already working in the tax field. See Larry R. Adamson, 32 T.C.M. 484 (1973); Alan E. Cobb, 35 T.C.M. 1480 (1976); and Ltr. Rul. 9112003 (1991) (allowing a lawyer who had practiced for 4 years and done some tax work to deduct LL.M. expenses). But see Goldenberg v. Comm'r, 65 T.C.M. 2338 (1993), where a licensed attorney who had been a CPA and an IRS appeals officer was not engaged in the practice of law and no deduction was allowed for his LL.M. in Taxation expenses. In view of the lenient attitude of the regulations on specialization in areas of teaching and psychiatry (see Reg. § 1.162-5(b)(3)(i) and (ii) Ex. (4)) and the lenient attitude toward dentists in *Rev. Rul. 74-78*, above, it would appear a like attitude should be taken toward lawyers. A word of caution, however. See Robinson v. Comm'r, 78 T.C. 550 (1982), where a licensed practical nurse was not allowed to deduct education costs of acquiring a degree to qualify as a registered nurse. Under state law separate licenses were required for these positions. And see Johnson v. Comm'r, 77 T.C. 876 (1981), disallowing an education expense deduction by holding a real estate broker to be in a trade or business different from a real estate agent. In addition, in Leonard T. Fielding, 57 T.C. 761 (1972), an education expense deduction was denied to a general medical practitioner for expenses in a three year program in psychiatry. Although the case was decided on a specialization rationale, it would have been properly decided as a "carrying on" case, because the taxpayer had never entered the actual practice of medicine before incurring the expenses. The same is true in the first *Johnson* case cited above.

2.   Denise's education expenses may qualify for a deduction since she is on a leave of absence from her firm and they are incurred while "away from home" within the meaning of § 162(a)(2). The question is the extent to which duplication is required. Cf. *Rosenspan* and *Andrews*. If deductible, her deduction would include transportation, lodging, 50% of meals, etc. Reg. § 1.162-5(e); § 274(n). Cf. the problems at page 372 of the Text. Of course if one is not "away from home" overnight within the *Correll* principle, meals (there would be no lodging) are not deductible. See Cosimo Carlucci, 37 T.C. 695 (1962).

3.   Carl is out of luck with respect to the deduction of his expenses. Section 274(m)(2) denies a deduction for travel as a form of education. Note the section does not preclude deductibility of travel to obtain education (see problem 2, above) or other travel that is necessary to engage in activities that give rise to deductible education.

4.   Although the statute does not specifically disallow a deduction here, the Conf. Comm. Rpt. of the 1986 Act states at pages II-31 to 32:

> The conferees also are concerned that some taxpayers may be claiming deductions under section 162 for travel and other costs of attending a convention, seminar, or similar meeting ("convention") at which each convention participant is furnished individually with video tapes of lectures, etc. on topics related to the

146

taxpayer's trade or business, to be viewed at the convenience of the participant, and at which no other significant business-related activities occur during the time allotted for the convention. In such situations, the taxpayer does not participate in activities normally conducted at a business-related convention, such as participating in meetings, discussions, workshops, lectures, or exhibits held during the day, and simply views the tapes at his or her own convenience. Because permitting deductions for travel, meal, or entertainment costs associated with such minimal business-related activities would allow taxpayers to treat expenditures that essentially are for vacation, recreation, or other personal purposes as business expenses, the conferees wish to make clear that no deduction is allowable under section 162 for travel or related costs of attending such a convention.

This clarification does not disallow deductions for the travel and other costs of attending a convention that involves activities otherwise deductible under present law which are related to the taxpayer's trade or business merely because the convention utilizes video-taped or televised materials where the participants must attend a convention session in person to view the video-taped materials, assuming that the generally applicable requirements for deducting expenses of attending a convention are satisfied. Also, this clarification does not disallow deductions for costs, other than travel, meal, or entertainment expenses, of renting or using business-related video tape materials.

Page 393:

In Flaig v. Comm'r, 47 T.C.M. 1361 (1984), the court agreed that a melee of 1000 guests enjoying food, drink, music and dancing at the taxpayer's annual birthday party was clearly entertainment, but the court found taxpayer's brief "chit-chat" with clients and the signing of a few documents over a number of years too insignificant to establish a direct relationship between the party expense and taxpayer's trade or business.

Page 395:

> In Moss v. Comm'r, 758 F.2d 211 (7th Cir. 1985), cert. den., 106 S.Ct. 382, the court refused to allow an attorney a deduction for his share of expenses incurred at daily meals eaten during luncheon meetings where office business was discussed. The court distinguished this situation from an occasional staff luncheon the cost of which it suggested would be deductible. See Wells v. Comm'r, 626 F.2d 868 (9th Cir. 1980) aff'g w/o opin. 36 T.C.M. 1698, 1699 (1977).

Page 400:

> Self-employed individuals (see § 401(c)(1)) may deduct a portion of the cost of medical care insurance (including qualified long-term care insurance subject to the § 213(d)(10) limits) paid during the year for the individual, the individual's spouse and dependents as a business expense under § 162(ℓ). The deductible portion is phased-in as follows:
>
> | | |
> |---|---|
> | 1997 | 40% |
> | 1998 | 45% |
> | 1999-2001 | 60% |
> | 2002 | 70% |
> | 2003 and thereafter | 100% |
>
> § 162(ℓ) is considered at page 565 of the Text.

PROBLEMS

Page 400:

1(a).   For business meals to be deductible, they must be "directly related to" or "associated with" the active conduct of a trade or business. § 274(a)(1). Here the directly-related-to requirement is met as a particular business matter is on the agenda and is discussed. Under § 274(k)(1)(A) the cost of the meals must not be lavish or extravagant. Query whether $100 is lavish or extravagant? What about two martinis with lunch? Does it matter if one is in Washington, D.C. versus Salina, Kansas? In addition, § 274(k)(1)(B) requires the presence of the taxpayer or the taxpayer's employee at the meal, a requirement which is met here. Finally, if the above requirements are met only 50% of the cost of meals (which includes taxes and tip) is deductible and Employee may deduct only $50 of the $100 if the $100 is otherwise deductible. It is premature to point out that this is an itemized deduction subject to the 2% floor of § 67(a).

1(b).   Not at all. This fails to satisfy either the directly related to or associated with requirements. But, see problem 1(c), below.

1(c).   This would violate the § 274(k)(1)(B) requirement and result in nondeductibility of the meals. This may not be such a bad consequence to Employee. If deductibility of a business meal is denied, can't it be argued that Employee has made a $25 gift to each client? If so, § 102(c) does not preclude deductibility and § 274(b)(1) would allow full deductibility if this were the only gift to each client for the year. Query: would we have to know the amount of each person's separate bill for lunch?

1(d).   Transportation costs are not subject to the limitations of § 274(k) which applies only to the costs of meals (or entertainment). The $15 cab fare is fully deductible.

1(e).   Section 274(e)(3) excludes reimbursed expenses from the rules of § 274(a), and § 274(k)(2) and § 274(n)(2)(A) exclude § 274(e)(3) reimbursements from their limitations. Thus Employee could fully deduct the reimbursements. Although it is premature, § 62(a)(2)(A) allows the deduction above the line and Reg. §§ 1.62-2 and 1.162-17(b)(1), seen at problem 1(c) on page 549 of the Text in Chapter 18, allows Employee to avoid this wash by a mere attachment on her return. Note, however, that to qualify for her deduction Employee's employer must meet the requirements of § 274(a), (k), and (n) and employer qualifies for only an $50 deduction.

2.   Businessperson may deduct only $75 of the $300 costs. Initially it should be pointed out that the expenses are "associated with" Businessperson's trade or business and the § 274(a)(1)(A) requirement is met. Section 274(l)(1)(A) limits deductibility for the cost of the ticket to the face amount of the ticket. In addition, § 274(n)(1)(B) allows only 50% of the otherwise deductible cost to be deductible. Thus only 50% of each $50 ticket or a total of $75 is deductible.

3.	Airline pilot may deduct $480 in expenses as follows:

(1)	The $250 cost of the uniform is deductible. Cf. Robert C. Fryers, 33 T.C.M. 403(1974).

(2)	The $30 cost of dry cleaning the uniform is a cost of maintaining the uniform which is also deductible.

(3)	The $100 in advertising is not deductible because it involves a new trade or business which he is not currently carrying on. Cf. Morton Frank at page 332 of the Text. If the ads were to find a new job as an airline pilot their costs would be deductible.

(4)	The $200 in union dues is generally deductible. But see § 162(e)(3).

(5)	The $50 in political contributions is nondeductible under § 162(e)(1)(B).

(6)	The $500 in gym fees is more personal than business and not deductible.

It should be added that all such deductions are itemized and subject to the 2% floor of § 67(a).

Page 422:

The Third Circuit agreed with *Simon* and found that a full-time professional musician was entitled to depreciation deductions on a 17th- century Ruggeri bass viol. Liddle v. Comm'r, 65 F.3d 329 (3d Cir. 1995). The Court rejected the Service's contention that the viol represented a work of art, noting that a "work of art" is a passive object that is displayed for admiration of its aesthetic qualities. By contrast, the viol was actively, regularly and routinely used by the taxpayer to produce income in his trade or business. The Court also denied the Service's contention that the property must have a determinable useful life in order to qualify for a § 168 deduction.

Writers disagree whether the *Simon* and *Liddle* results are correct. Compare Politia, "Fiddlers on the Tax: Depreciation of Antique

Instruments Invites Reexamination of Broader Tax Policy," 13 *Amer. J. Tax. Pol.* 87 (1996) (agreeing with the results in *Simon* and *Liddle*), with Dodge and Geier, "Simon says: A *Liddle* Night Music with Those Depreciation Deductions, Please," 66 *Tax Notes* 617 (1995) and Goetzl, "Depreciation of Antique Musical Instruments: Liddle v. Commissioner and Simon v. Commissioner," 49 *Tax Law.* 759 (1996).

PROBLEMS

Page 429:

1. No; as the *Beckley* case holds, if a business airplane is used as a transportation facility rather than a mere entertainment facility, § 274(a)(1)(B) is inapplicable. Cf. Reg. § 1.274-2(b)(1)(iii)(c).

    Rev. Rul. 72-111, 1972-1 C.B. 56, follows the holding in *Sharp* that an asset used for both business and personal purposes is divisible for tax purposes in determining gain or loss on a subsequent sale. Taxpayer purchased a new automobile and used it 75% for business purposes and 25% for personal purposes and sold it after 15 months at a loss. The Ruling sets forth the method of apportioning the loss on its sale between the business portion, on which the loss is deductible under § 165 (c)(1), and the personal portion on which the loss is nondeductible. Prefacing the computations is a comprehensive statement of the interrelationship of the applicable sections.

2(a). The *Idaho Power Company* case held that the trucks were a cost of acquiring the building and thus the amount of regular depreciation on the trucks during the construction of the building would not be currently deductible but would be added to the cost of the building. The basis of the trucks would be reduced by the same amount. In reaching its conclusion the Supreme Court found, in effect, that construction-related depreciation is like any other cost that cannot be expensed, such as wages. Capitalization of the depreciation leaves the do-it-yourself taxpayer on a parity with taxpayers who have such work done by others or who purchase a facility. The cost is an amount "paid out" within the meaning of § 263(a). Under § 161, § 263(a)'s capitalization provisions take precedence over § 167 and § 168. The Supreme Court decision in the *Idaho Power* case is discussed in case notes at 43 *Cinn. L. Rev.* 948 (1974) and 1975 *Wis. L. Rev.* 230.

2(b).   Maybe. Before 1976, there was no requirement that interest and taxes be capitalized. Section 266, allowing them to be capitalized if the taxpayer so elected, implied that they were currently deductible. However, this is an area of tax shelters that Congress acted on in 1976. See current § 263A, as the problem suggests, which requires that interest and taxes during the construction period be capitalized as they are paid or incurred and depreciated over the life of the property. See the discussion of § 263A at page 503 of the Text.

Page ___:

Pursuant to Rev. Proc. 2002-14, 2002-1 C.B. ___ Table 1, the depreciation limit for luxury cars placed in service in 2002, and taking into consideration the § 168(k) adjustment (see § 168(k)(2)(E)), is as follows:

Tax Year	Amount
1st tax year	$ 7,660 (3,060 + 4,600)
2nd tax year	4,900
3rd tax year	2,950
Each succeeding year	1,775

PROBLEMS

Page 439:

1(a).   If Depreciator elects under § 168(b)(5) to use the straight-line method the one-half year convention is applicable. § 168(d)(4)(A). The legislative history of § 168 states that the depreciation for the other 1/2 of the year is to be spread into the sixth year. Depreciator also elects out of § 168(k). Since the straight-line rate is 20% the results are as follows:

Year	% of Unadjusted Basis	Amount of Depreciation	§1016(a)(2) Adjusted Basis
1	10	$10,000	$90,000
2	20	20,000	70,000
3	20	20,000	50,000
4	20	20,000	30,000
5	20	20,000	10,000
6	10	10,000	0

When using the straight-line method, one-half of the first year's depreciation is in effect deducted in the sixth year. See Rev. Proc. 87-57, 1987-2 C.B. 687 at Table 8 on page 703. As seen in problem 1(b), below, the same reshuffling occurs when one switches from an accelerated to a straight-line method. See Sen. Rep. No. 99-313, 99th Cong., 2d Sess. 101 (1986).

1(b). Under the ACRS method the property is assigned a 5-year life and its salvage value is disregarded. See § 168(c) and(b)(4). Depreciator also elects current § 168(k). Depreciator would use the 200% declining balance method of depreciation with a switch to the straight-line method when it becomes preferable. Additionally, a "half-year convention" is used for the first year, regardless of the date on which the property is placed in service.

Depreciator would switch to the straight-line method in year 5 with one half of the straight-line amount deducted in year 6. See Rev. Proc. 87-57, 1987-2 C.B. 687 at Table 1 on page 696, and see Sen. Rep. No. 99-313, 99th Cong., 2d Sess. 101 (1986). Depreciator will have the following depreciation schedule:

Year	% of Adjusted Basis	Amount of Depreciation	§1016(a)(2) Adjusted Basis
1	20(40/2)	$ 20,000	$ 80,000
2	40	32,000	48,000
3	40	19,200	28,800
4	40	11,520	17,280
5	S.L.	11,520	5,760
6	S.L.	5,760	0
7	0	0	0

1(c).   The same schedule of depreciation as in Problem 1(b), above, applies, except that § 168(d)(4)(A) (parenthetical) allows only depreciation to the mid-point of the year (or mid-quarter if a mid-quarter convention is applicable) in the year of disposition, regardless of what point in the year the disposition of the property occurs.

Year	% of Adjusted Basis	Amount of Depreciation	§1016(a)(2) Adjusted Basis
1	20	$ 20,000	$ 80,000
2	40	32,000	48,000
3	40	19,200	28,800
4	40	11,520	17,280
5	½ S.L.	5,760	11,520

Thus her § 1016(a)(2) adjusted basis for purposes of measuring gain or loss is $11,520.

Although the § 168(d)(4)(A) result appears harsh, note that if the property is sold at a gain, the depreciation deduction combined with a recapture of the deduction would result in a wash.

1(d)   Under § 168(k) Depreciator would be allowed $30,000 of additional depreciation in year one and would reduce the adjusted basis of the property to $70,000 prior to applying the 200% declining balance method of depreciation under the regular ACRS rules. Depreciator will have the following depreciation schedule:

Year	% of Adjusted Basis	Amount of Depreciation	§1016(a)(2) Adjusted Basis
1 (§168(k))	30	$ 30,000	$ 70,000
(§168(a))	20	14,000	56,000
2	40	22,400	33,600
3	40	13,440	20,160
4	40	8,064	12,096
5	S.L.	8,064	4,032
6	S.L.	4,032	0

1(e). This problem shows the interrelationship of § 179 and the schedule in problem 1(d), above. This property qualifies under § 179(d)(1) for a § 179 election and, if the election under § 179(c) is made, the cost of the property up to a § 179(b) year 2003 maximum of $25,000 can be expensed in year one. The $25,000 limit is a per-taxpayer not a per-unit-of-property limit. The § 179 expense deduction requires a concurrent reduction in the basis of the property down to $75,000 prior to the computation of the depreciation under § 168. See footnote 44 at page 434 of the Text. Section 179 may be fully used only if Depreciator's total § 179 property put in service during the year has a cost which does not exceed $200,000. The $25,000 deduction amount is phased out dollar for dollar with no § 179 deduction if total cost equals or exceeds $225,000. In addition, a taxpayer's aggregate § 179 deductions in a year may not exceed the taxable income from taxpayer's active conduct of trades or businesses in a year.

Assuming § 179 is elected and fully used, § 168(k) may also be used (again with an immediate basis adjustment) and, once into § 168(a), the same percentages used in problems 1(b) and 1(d), above, apply to produce the following depreciation schedule:

Year	% of Adjusted Basis	Amount of Depreciation	§1016(a)(2) Adjusted Basis
1 (§ 179)		$ 25,000	$ 75,000
(§ 168(k))	30	22,500	52,500
(§ 168(a))	20	10,500	42,000
2	40	16,800	25,200
3	40	10,080	15,120
4	40	6,048	9,072
5	S.L.	6,048	3,024
6	S.L.	3,024	0

The answer is similar to problem 1(d), above, except that an additional $25,000 of the cost is expensed in the first year resulting in total depreciation of $58,000 in the first year. Note that the total depreciation over the 6 year period is the same, i.e., the full cost or unadjusted basis of the property.

1(f). If Depreciator elected to use the alternative depreciation system, she could not use § 168(k) (see § 168(k)(2)(C)(i)) and she would depreciate the equipment over a 6-year recovery period using the straight-line method. § 168(g). See Rev. Proc. 87-57, 1987-2 C.B. 687, Table 8 at page 703. The straight-line rate would be 16 2/3% and the results are as follows:

Year	% of Adjusted Basis	Amount of Depreciation	§1016(a)(2) Adjusted Basis
1	8 1/3	$ 8,333	$ 91,666
2	16 2/3	16,666	75,000
3	16 2/3	16,666	58,333
4	16 2/3	16,666	41,666
5	16 2/3	16,666	25,000
6	16 2/3	16,666	8,333
7	8 1/3	8,333	0

1(g). This problem requires an application of the anti-churning rules. Brother is a related party under I.R.C. (1954) § 168(e)(4)(D); § 267(b)(1) and (c)(4). Consequently § 168 (f)(5), applying I.R.C. (1954) § 168(e)(4) precludes use of the ACRS system as the property is no longer within § 168(f)(5). Depreciator is required to use § 167 depreciation under which the property will have a 6 year life and a $10,000 salvage value. Since the property is used, it may be depreciated under the 150% declining balance method, but not more rapidly. See Rev. Rul. 57-352, 1957-2 C.B. 150. In addition, § 179 is inapplicable. § 179(d)(2)(A).

Although the anti-churning rules are starting to show their age (perhaps they are almost over the hill), we chose to have the problem in the Text because the concept is one to which students should be introduced because it may be employed in the future if Congress liberalizes the depreciation rules. Note that it is irrelevant to the new § 168(k) 30% depreciation in the year that § 168(k) property is placed in service because that depreciation benefit only applies to new (as opposed to used) property. § 168(k)(2)(A)(ii).

Although the question does not require computations, if one desires to run through the numbers then the results under §167 are as follows:

Straight-Line Depreciation:

Year	% of Unadjusted Basis Less Salvage Value	Amount of Depreciation	§1016(a)(2) Adjusted Basis
1	16.67 (1/6)	$ 15,000	$ 85,000
2	16.67	15,000	70,000
3	16.67	15,000	55,000
4	16.67	15,000	40,000
5	16.67	15,000	25,000
6	16.67	15,000	10,000

150% Declining Balance Method:

Year	% of Adjusted Basis not Reduced by Salvage Value	Amount of Depreciation	§1016(a)(2) Adjusted Basis
1	25	$ 25,000	$ 75,000
2	25	18,750	56,250
3	25	14,062	42,188
4	25	10,547*	31,641
5	25	7,910	23,731
6	25	5,933	17,798

*   Depreciator would likely switch to the straight-line method and take $10,929 of depreciation in each of years 4-6. See now-repealed § 167(e)(1).

2(a).   Subject to the § 280F(a) luxury auto limits, Hi Roller would have the following amounts of depreciation:

Year	Amount of Depreciation
1	7,160 (see § 168(k)(2)(E)(i))
2	4,100
3	2,450
4	1,475
5	1,475
6	1,475
7	1,475
8	390
Total	$20,000

Note that Hi can continue to depreciate the car beyond year 6 until Hi writes off the $20,000 cost.

Note also that the first-year depreciation deduction reflects the $4,600 increase under § 168(k)(2)(E)(i).

2(b).   Subject to the § 280F(a) luxury auto limits adding now *Sharp* case principles, Hi Roller would have the following depreciation schedule:

Year	§ 280F Limitation	% of Business Use	Amount of Depreciation
1	$ 7,160	70%	$ 5,012
2	4,100	80%	3,280
3	2,450	70%	1,715
4	1,475	60%	885
5	1,475	60%	885
6	1,475	60%	885
7	1,475	60%	885
8	390	60%	234
Total	$20,000	Total	$13,781

2(c). If in year 4 Hi uses the automobile only 50% of the time for business, the year 4 depreciation is limited to $738(50% of $1,475). But in addition in year 4, § 280F(b)(2) requires a recapture of the excess depreciation taken over the depreciation that would have been allowed under the alternative depreciation system of § 168(g). The depreciation actually taken in years one through three was $10,007 (see problem 2(b), above). See § 168(k)(2)(E)(ii). Under the alternative depreciation system, Hi's $20,000 auto would be depreciable using the auto's $20,000 cost, a 5-year life and straight-line depreciation, but the depreciation in any year would be subject to the § 280F(a) dollar limitation. Cf. Temp. Reg. § 1.280(F)-3T(f) Example (8). See also the Conference Report 99-841, II-41 for the 1986 Act, reprinted at 1986-3 C.B. Vol. 4 at page 41.

Therefore the § 168(g) alternative depreciation system depreciation (subject to the § 280F(a) limitation) is:

Year	Alternative Depreciation	% Business Use	Depreciation
1	$2,000	70%	$1,400
2	$4,000	80%	3,200
3	$2,450*	70%	1,715
		Total	$6,315

* 3rd year limited by § 280F(a)(1)(A)(iii).

The recapture amount in year four is the excess of the first three years depreciation taken ($10,007) over $6,315, thus there is $3,692 of recapture under § 280F(b)(2).

Page 441:

> In Rev. Rul. 79-209, 1979-2 C.B. 97, taxpayer purchased a new duplex in days prior to ACRS. He lived in one unit and rented the other. The rental unit qualified under § 167(j)(2)(B) (now § 168(e)(2)(A)) as residential property. The Ruling held that the fair rental value of the portion of the premises used by the taxpayer as a residence, although not taxed, is included in rental income for purposes of the 80% test. Thus 100% of the use was residential and the entire unit that was rented qualified for § 167 (j)(2)(A) (now § 168(e)(2)(A)) accelerated depreciation.

PROBLEM

Page 443:

1(a). We assume the apartment building is rented exclusively for dwelling purposes and, therefore, 80% or more of the gross rental income is from dwelling units and the property is residential rental property. § 168(e)(2)(A). As such, it may be depreciated using only the straight-line method (§ 168(b)(3)(B) with a 27.5 year life (§ 168(c)) and no salvage value (§ 168(b)(4)). Thus the $100,000 building would be depreciated (other than in the year of acquisition when a mid-month conversion occurs) at a rate of $3,636 per year. Cf. Rev. Proc. 87-57, 1987-2 C.B 687 at Table 6 on page 701.

1(b). If the building were an office building it would be nonresidential real property under § 168(e)(2)(B), which is depreciated under the straight-line method using a 39 year life. § 168(c). Again, straight-line depreciation is required by § 168(b)(3)(A) and the property has no salvage value. § 168 (b)(4). Thus the $100,000 building would be depreciated in years after its first year (mid-month conversion) at a rate of $2,564 per year. See Rev. Proc. 87-57, 1987-2 C.B. 687 at Table 7 on page 702.

1(c). The results are the same as in (a) and (b), above. The anti-churning rules are inapplicable to both classes of real property. § 168(f)(5)(B)(i). The reason is that, since under current ACRS such property may be depreciated using only the straight-line method over longer lives than applicable under old ACRS or § 167, there is no depreciation advantage

160

to churning property. Additionally ACRS does not distinguish used from new property.

1(d).   Using the alternative depreciation system (see § 168(g)), both types of real-property would be assigned a 40 year recovery period under § 168(g)(2)(C)(iii) with the result that, using the straight-line method, there would be $2,500 of depreciation each year. This problem is added to provide a foundation for the alternative minimum tax. In the case of property placed in Service before 1999, the alternative depreciation system is employed to compute depreciation under the alternative minimum tax. See Chapter 27C, infra.

1(e).   The rehabilitation costs qualify for a 20% or $20,000 rehabilitation credit (§ 47(a)(2)) which reduces the adjusted basis by that amount prior to any depreciation of the property. § 50(c)(1). A subsequent year is used so as to avoid any issue under § 47(c)(1)(C)(i) requiring the rehabilitation cost to exceed the greater of the adjusted basis of the building or $5,000. This leaves $80,000 of cost to be depreciated over a 27.5 year or 39 year life, respectively, at annual amounts after the year of the improvement of $2,909 or $2,051 respectively. See § 47(c)(3).

1(f).   Here Depreciator qualifies for a 10% $10,000 rehabilitation credit (§ 47(a)(1)) which reduces the basis of the property to $90,000. § 50(c)(1). That basis can be depreciated using a 39 year life in the amount of $2,308 per year in subsequent years. See § 47(c).

Page 445:

A Court of Federal Claims case allowed a trade or business expense deduction for home office expenses of two investors who devoted a normal work week to their substantial investment activities. Moller v. U.S., 82-2 U.S.T.C. ¶ 9694 (Ct. Cls. 1982). The Court asserted that the case is distinguishable from *Higgins* but, of course, the only difference is the extent of *investment* activity. The case involved a deduction under § 280A(c)(1)(A), which allows a deduction only in the case of a "trade or business."

Page 448:

There is substantial litigation surrounding the issue whether a professional gambler who devotes a substantial amount of time to gambling activities is "carrying on a trade or business," if he is only betting on his own account. The cases generally involve a question related to whether gambling losses may be deducted above the line under § 62(a)(1). Even if gambling activities are a trade or business, § 165(d) limits the deductibility of such losses.

The Supreme Court held that gambling activities may qualify as a "trade or business" for purposes of § 162 depending on the "facts and circumstances" of the case. Comm'r v. Groetzinger, 480 U.S. 23, 107 S.Ct. 980 (1987), a case involving the alternative minimum tax. In upholding this "facts and circumstances" approach, the Court provided that a taxpayer does not have to "hold himself out to others as offering goods and services" in order to qualify as being engaged in a trade or business, thus failing to apply a test used by some circuits. The "goods and services" standard was expressly rejected. See prior use of that standard in Gajewski v. Comm'r, 723 F.2d 1062 (2d Cir. 1983), cert. den., 469 U.S. 818 (1984); Estate of Cull v. Comm'r, 746 F.2d 1148 (6th Cir. 1984), cert. den., 472 U.S. 1007 (1985); Novo v. U.S., 770 F.2d 1073 (3d Cir. 1985), aff'g without opinion 598 F.Supp. 440 (D. N.J. 1984). The Supreme Court noted that the following questions are relevant in determining whether there is a "trade or business": is it taxpayer's full-time activity, is taxpayer involved on a continual and regular basis, and is it intended as a livelihood source?

In Shiosaki v. Comm'r, 475 F.2d 770 (9th Cir. 1973), cert. den., 414 U.S. 830 (1973), taxpayer who was an engineer by profession took up crap shooting in Las Vegas. Over the years he was unsuccessful in his ventures at crap shooting and he properly deducted his gambling losses only to the extent of his gains. See § 165(d). However, he also attempted to deduct his travel and hotel expenses on his journeys to Las Vegas under § 212(1). Both the Tax Court and the Ninth Circuit denied the § 212(1) deductions.

Shiosaki is a man who apparently never says die; he again attempted to deduct his losses in a subsequent year, and of course he again "crapped out" at the Tax Court (James T. Shiosaki, 34 T.C.M. 127 (1975)), after overcoming the Commissioner's unsuccessful motion for summary judgment. James T. Shiosaki, 61 T.C. 861 (1974).

The § 165(d) limit on gambling losses in effect treats gambling losses as personal expenses except to the extent of gains. If a person is a big winner on a horse race, proof of losses in the same year may be difficult. See William H. Green, 31 T.C.M. 592 (1972), where the court applied the *Cohan* principle on some claimed losses but did not allow all the claimed losses, because "several of the losing tickets submitted unmistakably bore heel marks". In Walter Irwin Myers, 35 T.C.M. 823 (1976), the court estimated gambling losses as falling somewhere between the taxpayer's and the Commissioner's allegations of losses. See also Anothony J. Saitta, 34 T.C.M. 753 (1975), disallowing all claimed losses and refusing to apply *Cohan*.

Page 448:

In Wassenaar v. Comm'r, 72 T.C. 1195 (1979), the Tax Court denied taxpayer a § 212(3) deduction for the costs of acquiring an LL.M. degree at New York University. The opinion indicates the expenses were not ordinary and necessary and that it strained the Court's credulity to conclude that such expenses were reasonable or bore any reasonable relationship to the preparation of his return. 72 T.C. 1195 (1979).

PROBLEMS

Page 465:

1(a).   The question why Speculator would want to deduct the commissions instead of permitting them merely to reduce her gain is somewhat premature but provides an opportunity to lay a foundation for both timing and characterization of income which is discussed in Chapters 19 and 21 and following. If Speculator is allowed a deduction it would be an ordinary deduction while the increased gain on the stock (in the amount of the deduction) would be a capital gain possibly receiving some preferential treatment. See Chapter 21B of the Text.

The *Spreckels* case indicates that commissions paid as a selling expense on the sale of stock merely reduce the amount realized and are in effect to be treated the same as commissions paid in purchasing stock. Reliance on the regulations and the case of Helvering v. Winmill, 305 U.S. 79 (1938), were a disappointing substitute for free analysis. Nevertheless, the treatment is settled. Thus, on the sale of her stock, Speculator would have an amount realized of $3,940, an adjusted basis of $3,050, and an $890 gain. The *Spreckels* opinion does indicate that commissions paid by a dealer in securities as a selling expense may be treated as ordinary and necessary business expenses because of "practical considerations of accounting convenience which make it ... difficult for such dealers in many instances to set commissions off against the proceeds of individual sales." 315 U.S. at 629. Reg. § 1.263(a)-2(e) and see Reg. § 1.212-1(g).

1(b).   The *Spreckels* principle again applies and Speculator has an adjusted basis in the stock of $3,050 and an amount realized of $2,455, resulting in a $595 loss on the sale. That loss is deductible under § 165(c)(2) because, although under *Higgins* the investment activity is not a trade or business, nevertheless the loss occurs in a "transaction entered into for profit."

1(c).   No. This problem illustrates the fact that a § 212 deduction is subject to the same "ordinary and necessary" requirement that is present under § 162. Thus, while the expenditure might be "appropriate and helpful" (see Welch v. Helvering), nevertheless it would be extraordinary for such a minute shareholding to incur such substantial cost in proportion to her investment. Cf. Rev. Rul. 56-511, 1956-2 C.B. 170, and Rev. Rul. 84-113, 1984-2 C.B. 60. What result if she spent $5 cab fare to go to New York City from Brooklyn to attend the meeting? (Of course one-tenth of one percent of AT&T would not be insubstantial; we

164

should have put a low dollar value on her holding.)

1(d).   Here Speculator's expenses would be deductible under § 212(1) and (2) as ordinary and necessary expenses if she could show a legitimate investment interest in attending the meeting. Stranaham v. Comm'r, 43 T.C.M. 883 (1982). Cf. J.C. Hilton, 30 T.C.M. 444 (1971). However, attendance merely to determine whether to make further investments in the company should be questioned. See Rev. Rul. 56-511, 1956-2 C.B. 170.

1(e).   Deduction of § 212 expenses allocable to conventions, seminars, or similar meetings are disallowed by § 274(h)(7).

1(f).   Again, deductibility turns on whether the expenses meet the ordinary and necessary test. In J.C. Hilton, 30 T.C.M. 444 (1971), taxpayer, a 25% corporate shareholder, was allowed to deduct expenses incurred in investigating a corporation's financial affairs; however, the investigation centered principally around salary and rent arrearages owed taxpayer by Corporation rather than taxpayer's investment in the corporation. In Charles W. Nichols, 22 T.C.M. 698 (1963), taxpayer was a majority shareholder of a European company. He and his family journeyed to Europe for a month (with two weeks spent on a vacation to Scandanavia) to study why Corporation was operating at a loss. A § 212(2) deduction was disallowed as the expenses were not ordinary. The same result was reached in William R. Kinney, 66 T.C. 122 (1976). Cf. Surasky v. U.S., in the Text at page 452 and Graham v. Comm'r, 326 F.2d 878 (4th Cir. 1964). Again the "ordinary and necessary" question is a factual question and more facts should be known in order to determine deductibility.

2(a).   In general, Payor Spouse's attorneys' fees incurred in getting a divorce are personal expenses and are not deductible. U.S. v. Gilmore, 372 U.S. 39 (1963). However, under Carpenter v. U.S., 338 F.2d 366 (Ct. Cls. 1964), cited in the *Fleischman* case, to the extent that the legal fees are related to the *tax aspects* of the divorce, they are deductible under § 212(3).

In Rev. Rul. 72-545, 1972-2 C.B. 179, discussed in comments on problem 3, below, the Commissioner attempts to require a fairly strong showing of the allocation of the legal costs to tax advice. See also Hall

v. U.S., 1978-1 U.S.T.C. ¶ 9126 (Ct. Cls. 1977), in which the then Claims Court adopted a similar position. However, the *Merians* case, discussed along with the Ruling, seems to be more lenient than the Ruling and invokes the *Cohan* principle allowing reasonable estimation of the amount.

Compare Dolese v. U.S., 605 F.2d 1146 (10th Cir. 1979), cert. den., 445 U.S. 961 (1980), where some of a corporation's legal expenses were held deductible when a corporation, joined in a divorce action brought by the spouse alleged that the shareholder was dissipating the company's assets. The court held the expenses, to the extent that they were incurred to resist actions that interfered with business activities, arose out of the corporation's business activities and were deductible.

2(b).   As in the situation with respect to Payor Spouse, Payee Spouse may deduct attorneys' fees in a divorce situation, to the extent that they are attributable to tax advice. *Carpenter*. Further, in Ruth K. Wild, 42 T.C. 706 (1973), the Court properly held that a payee spouse may also deduct attorneys' fees that are incurred to negotiate that spouse's alimony payments. These fees are deductible because the alimony is income to Payee Spouse under § 71 and the attorneys' fees are therefore § 212(1) expenses incurred "for the production or collection of income." Cf. Jimmie T. Jernigan, 34 T.C.M. 615 (1975), where husband and wife, as a part of a divorce and property settlement, split wife's $75,000 attorneys' fees, with wife paying $50,000 of such fees asserted by both to be completely allocable to production of alimony. Wife was allowed a $50,000 § 212(1) deduction over the Commissioner's objection. But see Enid P. Mirsky, 56 T.C. 664 (1971), and Helen Kellner, 35 T.C.M. 326 (1976), where wife was denied a § 212(1) deduction because she failed to carry the burden of establishing the portion of attorneys' fees allocable to alimony payments.

See also Jane U. Elliott, 40 T.C. 304 (1963), acq. 1964-1 C.B. (Part 1) 4, where it is similarly held that a wife may deduct attorneys' fees incurred in recovering Husband's alimony arrearages as expenses incurred "for the ... collection of income" under § 212(1).

2(c).   Payor Spouse cannot deduct the payment of Payee Spouse's attorneys' fees. The only section possibly allowing a deduction is § 215(a), but for it to apply the attorneys' fees must be included in Payee Spouse's income as alimony under § 71 and the requirements of § 71(b)(1)(D) are not met here. See Ribera v. Comm'r, 73 TCM 1807 (1997).

3.   Rev. Rul. 72-545, 1972-2 C.B. 179, discusses whether a § 212(3) deduction would be allowed in various situations involving legal fees for tax advice. The Ruling states:

> Section 1.212-1(l) of the regulation provides, in part, that expenses paid or incurred by a taxpayer for tax counsel or expenses paid or incurred in connection with the preparation of his tax returns or in connection with any proceedings involved in determining the extent of tax liability are deductible. In order for an expense to be deductible under Section 212(3) of the Code it must relate solely to tax counsel. . . . If such expense is incurred in connection with an activity that is not solely concerned with tax matters, the expense for tax counsel must be properly allocated and substantiated . . .

In Sidney Merians, 60 T.C. 187 (1973), the court allowed a deduction for a part of legal expenses incurred by a taxpayer for estate planning services. The majority treated only one issue - that of allocation of legal services between tax and nontax considerations. Perhaps at variance with the requirement of a reasonable method of allocation expressed in *Rev. Rul. 72-545*, the Court invoked the *Cohan* principle to allow a deduction under § 212(3) for 20% of the total legal fee. The bill for legal services did not include a breakdown of services rendered "nor did the attorney's testimony provide such information." See also Howard C. Goldaper, 36 T.C.M. 1381 (1977), reaching a similar result. The Claims Court took a tougher position, more along the lines of the ruling, in Hall v. U.S., 1978-1 U.S.T.C. ¶ 9126 (Ct. Cls. 1977).

Another question raised here, not treated by the majority in *Merians* but considered in the numerous concurring and dissenting opinions, is the scope of § 212(3) itself. At least two judges (Sterret, J., concurring, and Whithey, J., dissenting) chose to construe § 212(3) as being limited to "actual contested tax liability . . . [precluding] any expenses incident to a determination of tax liability prior to the period it becomes due or contested" (Withey, J., dissenting) and "to the preparation of . . . tax returns [gift tax returns in this case]." (Sterret, J., concurring). But these very restrictive views are opposed by a formidable amount of history and practice. Those two judges did state that the cost of other legal advice might be deducted under § 212(2). The *Merians* case is discussed in Grisham, "Deductibility of Legal Expenses for Federal Income Tax Purposes," 26 *U.S.C. Tax Inst.* 875 (1974) and Allington, "Deductibility of Estate Planning Fees," 60 *A.B.A.J.* 482 (1974).

PROBLEMS

Page 475:

1(a). No. The opinion in the *Frank* case deals with these issues, but that portion of the opinion was omitted from the Text in Chapter 14 because it did not relate to § 162. The omitted portion of the opinion is presented below:

> Neither are the travel and legal expenses incurred by the petitioners in their attempt to find and purchase a business deductible under section § 23(a)(2), Internal Revenue Code, [§ 212] which allows the deduction of expenses incurred in the production or collection of income or in the management, conservation or maintenance of property held for the production of income. There is a basic distinction between allowing deductions for the expense of producing or collecting income, in which one has an existent interest or right and expenses incurred in an attempt to obtain income by the creation of some new interest. *Marion A. Burt Beck*, 15 T.C. 642, aff'd 194 F.2d 537. *Stella Elkins Tyler*, 6 T.C. 135. The expenses here involved are of the latter classification. The traveling costs were incurred in an endeavor to acquire a business which might, in the future, prove productive of income. It might reasonably be said that petitioner was engaged in the active search of employment as newspaper owners, but that cannot be regarded as a business. It is much like the situation obtaining in *Mort L. Bixler*, 5 B.T.A. 1181, or like that found in *McDonald v. Commissioner*, 323 U.S. 57, where it was held that a Pennsylvania court of common pleas judge seeking reelection could not deduct under

168

section 23(a)(2) expenses of such campaign. The Supreme Court said ". . . his campaign contributions were not expenses incurred in being a judge but in trying to be a judge for the next ten years."

The petitioners contend finally that the expenses in question must be allowed as deductions as nonbusiness losses under section 23(e)(2), Internal Revenue Code, [§ 165(c)(2).] This subsection of the Code provides a deduction for losses incurred in transactions entered into for profit. The only transaction entered into for profit by the petitioners, as disclosed by the facts, was the purchase of a newspaper in Canton, Ohio. Other possible transactions were investigated and rejected or otherwise not entered into. It cannot be said that the petitioners entered into a transaction every time they visited a new city and examined a new business property. Nor can we hold that petitioners entered into such transactions and then abandoned them, as they here contend. Rather they refused to enter into such transactions after the preliminary investigation. If the general search for a suitable business property itself be considered as a transaction entered into for profit, no abandonment of such project occurred in the taxable year so as to enable deduction of these expenses as losses. Travel and legal expenses, such as were incurred here by petitioners, are not deductible as losses. *Robert Lyons Hague*, 24 B.T.A. 288; Cf. *Charles T. Parker*, 1 T.C. 709. The cases cited by the petitioners concern instances where transactions were actually entered into and the losses where then sustained upon abandonment. We cannot find this situation here.

1(b). Yes. Although the capital expenditures would not be deductible as "expenses" under §§ 162 or 212, nevertheless the expenditures were made after entering the transaction and would constitute a loss either incurred in a trade or business, or more likely in a "transaction entered into for profit" even though the trade or business was not yet being carried on. These facts are well within the *Domenie* case which allowed a deduction under § 165(c)(2) for expenditures made after a meeting of the minds with respect to acquisition of a business in preparing to consummate the business. The deduction was allowed when the transaction was abandoned. As announced in *Rev. Rul. 77-254*, the Service agrees with this result. It is arguable that the $1,000 of attorney's fees that Frank paid in unsuccessful negotiations to purchase a newspaper in Wilmington, Delaware (see page 332 of the Text) ought to have been deductible by Frank under the rationale of *Domenie* and the Ruling.

1(c).   The remainder of his unamortized § 195 expenditures would be deductible under § 165(c)(1) as "a loss incurred in a trade or business." See § 195(b)(2).

2(a).   The question whether § 212(2), § 167(a)(2) and § 168(c)(1)(B) apply depends upon whether the property is "held for the production of income" as considered in the *Lowry* case. That case, as distinguished from *Horrmann*, makes it clear that it is not necessary for the property to be put up for rent in order for the sections to apply. Whether the sections apply depends upon the taxpayers' intent as determined by several surrounding facts and circumstances. The court will look at how long the property was held as a personal residence and whether the taxpayer occupied the residence between the abandonment of the property and the ultimate disposition of it and it will overlook the fact that no rental offers are made. However, where the property is not offered for rent, as in this problem, the principal factor relied on by the court in *Lowry* is whether taxpayer intended to obtain a post-conversion profit on the property by holding it for appreciation subsequent to the time the taxpayer abandoned it as a residence. And it does not matter that prior to such conversion the property had declined in value. This is one of those unfortunate questions of the *intent* of the taxpayer after looking at the facts and circumstances.

There is language in the *Lowry* opinion that the taxpayers must be seeking to sell the property at a price in excess of their "investment" (i.e., adjusted cost basis). The concurring opinions in the *Newcombe* case cited in *Lowry* both attack that requirement and would require only that the property be held for post-conversion appreciation in value (not necessarily for a price in excess of its adjusted basis). The courts have not definitively solved this discrepancy as yet, but we think the concurring opinions argue for the better result. See Erck, "And You

Thought Moving Was Bad - Try Deducting Depreciation and Maintenance Expenses on Your Unsold Residence," 26 *U. of Fla. L. Rev.* 587 (1974).

The case of Hulet P. Smith, 26 T.C.M. 149 (1967), aff'd per curiam, 387 F.2d 804 (9th Cir. 1968), which the *Lowry* case cites, is more lenient in allowing deductions under such circumstances. In *Smith*, taxpayers merely moved out of their old residence, acquired a new residence, and put the old residence up for sale but not rent. They sold it after three years. The court found that during that period the property was "held for the production of income" under §§ 167(a)(2) and 212(1), seemingly because it was simply abandoned and put up for sale; and the court did not appear to be concerned about whether the taxpayer intended to obtain a post-conversion profit on the property.

But the more recent cases are not following the *Smith* case and have looked to the *Lowry* and *Newcombe* factors to determine whether the property was "held for the production of income." Several more recent cases, following *Newcombe*, have concluded that taxpayers who merely put their homes up for sale were not attempting to reap a post-conversion appreciation profit on the property such as would support a deduction for expenses. Lewis v. U.S., 1973-1 USTC ¶ 9254 (S.D. Ohio 1973); Raymond L. Opper, 31 T.C.M. 485 (1972); Paul M. Butler, Jr., 29 T.C.M. 880 (1970); Edward C. Quinn, 65 T.C. 523 (1975); and Ida Meredith, 65 T.C. 34 (1975), also holding that the *Horrmann* rental test requires a bona fide effort to rent.

Three problems arise with respect to the deductions here. First, as pointed out above, if the post-conversion appreciation that is being sought must be appreciation over taxpayer's cost basis in the property (so as to produce some gross income) then the taxpayers here will fail, because their sales price of $170,000 is less than their adjusted basis in the property of $180,000 (even though it exceeds the conversion value of $160,000). This should not be the result; the test ought merely to be post-conversion appreciation.

The second problem arises out of the fact that the property was immediately put up for sale. In *Newcombe*, the court states that:

The placing of property on the market for immediate

sale, at or shortly after the time of its abandonment as a residence, will ordinarily be strong evidence that a taxpayer is not holding the property for post-conversion appreciation in value.

In another case, citing *Newcombe*, it was held that where taxpayers inherited property, lived in it for years, and then placed it for immediate sale but not for rent, and subsequently reduced their sale price prior to sale, the property was not "held for the production of income." Charles D. Mayes, 30 T.C.M. 363 (1971). *Lowry*, of course, did not allow an immediate offer for sale to alter its conclusion.

The third problem is that if Homeowners lived in the residence more than 14 days of the year (§ 280A(d)(1)(A)) no deduction other than interest, taxes, etc., could be allowed in the year of conversion under the general limitation of § 280A(a). See § 280A(b). The exception of § 280A(d)(4) would be inapplicable because the property was not put up for rent. This limitation would be inapplicable for years after the year of conversion when no personal use is made of the property.

If the property is found to be "held for the production of income" then depreciation deductions will be allowed under §§ 167(a)(2) and 168(c)(1)(B) (see Reg. § 1.167(g)-1) and maintenance expenses will be allowed under § 212(2). There are several types of maintenance expenses which are deductible such as repairs to the property, gardening expenses, utilities expenses, and other noncapital maintenance expenditures.

As the *Horrmann* case points out, even if the property here were found to be "held for the production of income," if it were subsequently sold at a post-conversion loss the loss would not be deductible, because there was no rental of the property and no § 165(c)(2) "transaction entered into for profit." See also Louis F. McAuley, 35 T.C.M. 1236 (1976). Compare the factual difference (actual rental) in problem 2(b), below. However, there may be an exception to this rule in an inheritance situation. See the *Assman* and *Crawford* cases cited in *Horrmann* at page 469 of the Text and H.V. Watkins, 32 T.C.M. 809 (1973).

Although a residence was actually rented, a case denied a loss deduction on its sale. Henry B. Dawson, Jr., 31 T.C.M. 5 (1972). No conversion of a residence to rental property was found since the rental of the home to the purchasers was an interim measure only, as evidenced by the fact that the purported rental agreement and the purpose of the rental period was only to allow the purchaser time to obtain financing. Thus the loss on the sale was denied to the owners since there was "no transaction entered into for profit."

2(b)(1). Homeowners would have a deductible loss of $5,000 on the subsequent sale of residence. Their original basis for the building was its cost of $170,000 and, after taking depreciation of $10,000 based on the property's fair market value which was lower than its basis at the date of conversion (Reg. § 1.167(g)-1), they would appear to have a $160,000 adjusted basis for the building and a $170,000 adjusted basis for the entire property (including the land). Nevertheless, they would have only a $5,000 deductible loss on the sale, because Reg. § 1.165-9(b)(2) properly provides that, if the fair market value of the property is less than the taxpayers' basis at the date of conversion, the fair market value of the property, after making adjustments for post-conversion depreciation, is the adjusted basis of the property for determining loss. On these facts, Homeowner's adjusted basis would be $140,000 ($150,000 less $10,000 of depreciation) for the building plus $10,000 for land, or $150,000 and as Homeowners' amount realized is $145,000, they would have a $5,000 loss on the sale.

Students are inclined to view any sale of a residence as a "heads-I-win, tails-you-lose" proposition, and in a sense it is. However, it reflects deliberate congressional policy to tax gain, taking account of adjusted basis, no matter how fortuitously it arises (*Cesarini*) and, with some exceptions (§ 165(c)(3)), to disallow deduction for losses that are personal in nature.

A Revenue Ruling suggests an interesting additional problem here. Taxpayer transferred his residence with a basis of $30,000 and worth $20,000 to an unrelated individual in exchange for an annuity worth $20,000. Although it might be argued that the purchase of the annuity with loss property might be a "transaction entered into for profit," it was held that taxpayer in substance sold the residence at a loss and purchased the annuity with the amount realized on the sale. Anticipated profit on the annuity acquired was properly viewed as not bringing the disposition of the residence within the ambit of a "transaction entered into for profit." Thus, taxpayer had a nondeductible loss on the sale and $20,000 cost basis in the annuity. Rev. Rul. 71-492, 1971-2 C.B. 127.

2(b)(2). If Homeowner sold the property at a gain, the Reg. § 1.165-9(b)(2) *loss* rule on basis would not be applicable. Thus their cost basis in the land and building of $180,000, reduced under § 1016(a)(2) by the $10,000 of depreciation, gives them an adjusted basis for determining gain of $170,000. On a sale of $175,000, they have a $5,000 gain. It is premature to worry about characterization of the gain.

2(b)(3). If Homeowners sell the property for $165,000, they recognize neither gain nor loss. Their basis for determining gain is $170,000 (thus they have no gain) and their basis for determining loss is $150,000 (and they have no loss). Compare this neither-gain-nor-loss situation with problem 1(b)(3) at page 128 of the Text involving a similar result in the § 1015 area and Reg. § 1.1015-1(a)(2) Example.

2(c). Even if Homeowners met the two-year ownership and use as a principal residence requirements of § 121(a), the $5,000 gain does not exceed the $10,000 of depreciation allowed on the property, and the entire $5,000 gain would have to be recognized as a result of § 121(d)(6). It is premature to discuss the character of such gain. Although straight-line depreciation was taken, it is arguable that the property was held as depreciable property for less than one year and the gain is $1,250 ordinary income to the extent of the depreciation allowed. It is also unclear if §1250 does not apply, whether the gain is §1231 gain or LTLG. Assuming, even if it is §1231 gain that it becomes LTLG, then to the extent of the depreciation taken on the property, the gain is taxed at a 25% rate. § 1 (h)(1)(D).

Chapter 16.   Deductions Not Limited to Business or Profit-Seeking Activities

Page 477:

Congress seems to have recognized, as pointed out in the Surrey comment, that there is an "upside down" result at variance with usual expenditure policies under our tax deduction system. At least in some instances Congress has accepted the principle that the use of credits is more equitable than the use of deductions. See Chapter 27B, infra.

The cause of the upside down result, steeply graduated tax rates, has been substantially reduced by the current rate structure. For example, a single taxpayer earning in excess of $215,000 of taxable income in 1981 could expect Uncle Sam to pick up the tab for $70 of every $100 he spent on mortgage interest while a taxpayer earning only $5,000 of taxable income would effectively be reimbursed for only $14 of every $100 spent on mortgage interest. In 2002, the same two taxpayers would "receive" $35 or $38.60 and $10, respectively. Thus, while the distortion persists on these facts, its impact has been substantially reduced.

A question that can also be raised in this Chapter is whether the tax law seems to promote home ownership over home rental by means of deductions for taxes and interest paid, respectively, on residences and residential mortgages. The tax law seems to favor home ownership, and one can question whether this inequality of treatment is fair. Should some part of rental payments be deductible by a renter? Should interest and tax deductions on the purchase and ownership of a principal residence be reduced or denied? Congress says NO. In the alternative, it can be argued that one has the freedom to rent or buy and that the interest and tax deductions allowed a purchaser are one of the factors to be considered in making the decision to rent or buy. See Harmelink and Krause, "Reduction of Tax Inequity to Renters of Dwellings: A Recommendation," 51 *Taxes* 204 (1973). Cf. Rev. Rul. 79-180, 1979-1 C.B. 95.

Page 478:

See Turnier, "Evaluating Personal Deductions in an Income Tax-the Ideal," 66 *Cornell L. Rev.* 262 (1981), and Turnier, "Personal Deductions and Tax Reform: The High Road and the Low Road" 31 *Vill. L. Rev.* 1703 (1986), discussing the role of personal deductions in our income tax system.

Page 502:

A restriction on the deduction of interest also occurs under § 265(a)(1). An illustration of the restriction appears in Rev. Rul. 83-3, 1983-1 C.B. 72, which states that a minister's mortgage interest payments and real property taxes allocated to tax-free housing allowances under § 107 are nondeductible under § 265(a)(1). In 1986 Congress reversed the holding of the ruling in their enactment of § 265(a)(6).

PROBLEMS

Page 504:

1(a). Since Lender made an interest-free demand loan as a gift to Borrower, § 7872(a) requires the amount of interest which would have been payable on the loan at the applicable Federal rate (foregone interest) be treated as transferred from the Lender to the Borrower as a gift and then retransferred from the Borrower to the Lender as interest, both transfers occurring on the last day of the calendar year. See § 7872(a)(1) and (2) and (e). Essentially, Lender is deemed to have funded the Borrower's interest payment.

As given, the amount of the foregone interest for the first year is $10,250, the principal amount of the loan multiplied by the applicable Federal rate of 10% compounded semiannually. Lender is deemed to have made a gift to Borrower of $10,250 on December 31. Similarly, on the last day of the year, Borrower is likely treated as paying $10,250 in interest to Lender, which interest is likely deductible by Borrower as qualified residence interest under § 163(h) (cf. § 63) and Lender is likely treated as receiving the same amount as interest income. If so, is this artificial restructuring realistic? Where is the financial gain to Lender, a normal characteristic of income?

The reason we stated merely that Borrower *likely* makes an interest payment to Lender is that § 7872(d) provides with respect to a gift loan between a borrower and a lender where their total loans do not exceed $100,000, the amount retransferred from a borrower to a lender shall not exceed the borrower's net investment income and that, if Borrower's net investment income does not exceed $1,000, no amount is deemed retransferred. § 7872(d)(1)(E)(ii). The term net investment income is defined in § 163(d)(4) (see reference in § 7872(d)(1)(E)(i)) and is essentially net income from non-business, profit-seeking activities. Thus if Borrower's net investment income equals or exceeds $10,250 and this is Borrower's only gift loan, Borrower is deemed to pay $10,250 of interest to Lender who then has $10,250 of gross income, and Borrower has a $10,250 deduction. If Borrower's net investment income is less than $10,250 but in excess of $1,000, that amount of net investment income is deemed paid by Borrower to Lender. Finally, if Borrower's net investment income is less than $1,000 no interest is deemed paid by Borrower to Lender. § 7872(d)(1)(E)(ii). In these last two cases see § 7872(d)(1)(B) which disregards the net investment income exception if one of the principal purposes of the loan is tax avoidance. The authors' antipathy for "principal purpose" legislation extends to this.

In addition, if Borrower has a small interest deduction as a result of § 7872(d), then the interest deduction may not be taken in lieu of the standard deduction. See § 63(e) and Chapter 18F.

1(b).   Section 7872 also applies to compensation-related loans between an employer and an employee or an independent contractor and the person who hired the independent contractor. § 7872(c)(1)(B). Since the loan is an interest-free demand loan, generally the same rules that apply to a gift loan are applicable to this compensation related loan. § 7872(a). Therefore, the answer is the same as in problem, (a), above, except that the $10,250 is constructively transferred from Lender (employer) to Borrower (employee) as compensation instead of as a gift. The employer will have a § 162 deduction for the compensation deemed paid and the employee will have to include that amount in gross income. § 61(a)(1). Additionally, $10,250 interest is constructively paid by Borrower to Lender which generates an interest deduction for Borrower and interest income to Lender. Note that in this demand compensation loan situation if the compensation is deductible by

Lender (§ 162) and if the interest is deductible by Borrower (§ 163(a) and (h)) then the overall effect to both parties is a wash. Much ado about nothing? Not quite. Cf. § 63.

1(c).   Corporation-Shareholder loans are also subject to the provisions of § 7872. § 7872 (c)(1)(C). When a corporation makes an interest-free loan to its shareholder it is deemed to have paid a dividend to the shareholder on the last day of the year assuming it has sufficient Earnings and Profits. Sufficient Earnings and Profits would likely be generated by Borrower's deemed repayment of interest. (See next paragraph.) § 7872(a)(1)(A) and (a)(2). The shareholder, on the same day, retransfers to the corporation, as interest, an amount equivalent to the deemed dividend payment. § 7872(a)(1) (B) and (a)(2). Thus the answer here is that Lender (corporation) constructively pays a nondeductible $10,250 dividend to Borrower (shareholder) which is included in Borrower's gross income.

In addition, Borrower makes an interest payment of $10,250 to Lender which is deductible by Borrower (§ 163(h)) and is gross income to Lender. Cf. § 63.

2(a).   The purpose of this problem is to demonstrate some of the § 7872 exceptions (i.e. how to make interest free loans without § 7872 consequences). There are no tax consequences to Mother or Daughter here. Section 7872 is inapplicable because § 7872(c)(2)(A) creates a de minimis exception in these circumstances.

2(b).   The exception above is inapplicable here because the proceeds of the loan are used to purchase income-producing assets. See § 7872(c)(2)(B). As a result, Mother makes a gift of $1,025 in the year (see § 7872(a)(1) and (2) and (e); but see § 2503(b)) and Daughter makes a $1,025 interest payment to Mother, which is included in Mother's gross income and is likely deductible by Daughter under § 163. See problem 1(a), above, and see § 163(d).

2(c).   First, Mother makes a gift to Daughter of $10,250. See § 7872(a)(1) and (2) and (e). Cf. §2503(b). The issue then becomes whether there is a retransfer of $10,250 of interest from Daughter to Mother. Since Daughter has $20,000 of net investment income (§ 7872(d)(1)(E)), there is a retransfer of interest and § 7872(d)(1)(A) is inapplicable.

Mother has $10,250 of interest income and Daughter may have a $10,250 § 163 interest deduction. See problem 1(a), above.

2(d). Again, Mother makes a $10,250 gift to Daughter. Assuming the loan does not have the avoidance of Federal tax as one of its principle purposes (see § 7872(d)(1)(B)), there is no retransfer of interest by Daughter to Mother. Since Daughter's net investment income does not exceed $1,000 it is treated as equaling zero for purposes of § 7872(d)(1)(A) (see § 7872(d)(2)(E)(ii)), and the amount of interest retransfer is also zero.

3(a). Taxpayers may deduct 100% of the interest paid or accrued on the loan. Under § 163(h)(2)(D), a taxpayer may deduct "qualified residence interest" in full. That term is defined, in § 163(h)(3)(A)(i), to include interest paid on any "acquisition indebtedness" which, in turn, is defined as any debt that is secured by a qualified residence and is used to acquire such residence. § 163(h)(3)(B). As Taxpayers have incurred the mortgage to purchase a qualified residence (their principal residence) and the proceeds are, in fact, used for such purpose, Taxpayers may deduct interest paid on the mortgage in full.

3(b). Taxpayers may deduct 100% of the interest paid on the total indebtedness secured by their residence. The outstanding principal on the 1998 loan still qualifies as acquisition indebtedness for the reasons stated in problem 3(a), above. In addition, the $100,000 loan qualifies as acquisition indebtedness, because it is secured by a qualified residence and the proceeds from the loan will be used to substantially improve a qualified residence. § 163(h)(3)(B). Therefore, interest paid on this loan may also be fully deducted as qualified residence interest.

3(c). Taxpayers may deduct 100% of the interest paid on the remaining balance of the 1998 loan ($200,000), because this debt qualifies as acquisition indebtedness. § 163(h)(3)(B). In addition, Taxpayers may deduct 100% of the interest paid on the $100,000 loan. The $100,000 loan does not qualify as acquisition indebtedness because the proceeds are not used to acquire, construct, or substantially improve a qualified residence. However, the loan can be classified as home equity debt, the interest on which is fully deductible. According to § 163(h)(3)(C)(i), "home equity indebtedness" is defined as any debt that is secured by a qualified residence the amount of which does not exceed the fair market

179

value of the residence, reduced by any acquisition debt outstanding on the residence. Additionally, home equity debt is subject to a $100,000 limitation. § 163(h)(3)(C)(ii). The fair market value of Taxpayers' residence is $400,000 and the outstanding acquisition debt on the residence is $200,000. Therefore, Taxpayers may borrow up to $100,000 against the equity they have built up in their home and still fully deduct interest attributable to such loan as interest paid on home equity indebtedness. Query: Was it wise for Congress to provide an incentive to Taxpayers to place their home at risk in order to buy a Ferrari? What is behind this, anyway?

3(d).   The home has a fair market value of $500,000. The amount left to be paid off on the original 1998 loan is $50,000. The 2010 loan is for $200,000. Taxpayers may deduct only 75% of the interest paid or accrued on the 2010 refinancing loan. Under § 163(h)(3)(B) (flush language), the amount of debt resulting from a refinancing, that is classified as acquisition indebtedness, can not exceed the remaining principal of the acquisition debt immediately prior to refinancing. Since the remaining principal of the 1998 loan in 2010 is $50,000, only $50,000 of the $200,000 debt resulting from the refinancing will be classified as acquisition indebtedness. However, under § 163(h)(3)(C)(ii), up to $100,000 of the debt resulting from refinancing, can be classified as home equity indebtedness; and interest attributable to this portion is fully deductible. Thus $150,000 of the $200,000 qualifies under § 163(h)(3) and a total of 75% of the interest is deductible. If the remaining balance of the 1998 loan which was refinanced was $100,000 (rather than $50,000), Taxpayers would be allowed to deduct 100% of the interest on the mortgage resulting from the refinancing ($100,000 of acquisition debt and $100,000 of home equity debt).

3(e).   Under § 163(h)(2)(D), Taxpayers are allowed a deduction for qualified residence interest. Under § 163(h)(4)(A) the term "qualified residence" is defined as a taxpayer's principal residence (under § 121) and, if an election is made, one other residence used by the taxpayer within the meaning of § 280(A)(d)(1). In order to "use" a residence within the meaning of § 280A(d)(1), if a taxpayer rents out a residence, the taxpayer must use it for personal purposes for the greater of 14 days of each year of 10% of the number of days the taxpayer rents out the residence. Since Taxpayers clearly use the Florida home for the requisite number of days each year (45 days), the vacation home will be treated as a qualified residence, if Taxpayers elect it to be so treated. As the proceeds of the $950,000 loan are used to purchase the qualified residence, the debt is potentially classifiable as acquisition indebtedness. However, under § 163(h)(3)(B)(ii), the maximum amount of debt that may be treated by Taxpayers as acquisition indebtedness with respect to post-October 13, 1987, property is $1,000,000. When the $950,000 loan secured by the Florida residence is added to the $250,000 loan already outstanding on Taxpayers' principal residence, it becomes apparent that Taxpayers have exceeded the $1,000,000 limitation by $200,000. The House Report on the Revenue Act of 1987 suggests that, where a taxpayer exceeds the dollar limitation on acquisition debt, the excess to be disallowed will be subtracted from the debt which is incurred by the taxpayer last in chronological order. H. Rep. No. 100-391, 100th Cong., 1st Sess., 1033 (1987). Compare Temp. Reg. § 1.163-10T. Therefore, $200,000 of the $950,000 loan will not qualify as acquisition indebtedness. However, $100,000 of this disallowed amount will qualify as home equity indebtedness, capable of generating fully deductible qualified residence interest. In total, Taxpayers will be able fully to deduct interest attributable to the $250,000 loan as interest paid on acquisition debt, fully to deduct interest attributable to $750,000 of the $950,000 debt as interest paid on acquisition debt, and fully to deduct interest attributable to $100,000 of the $950,000 debt as interest paid on home equity debt. Thus only the interest on $100,000 of the mortgage on the Florida home is nondeductible personal interest.

3(f). This problem is intended to illustrate the "grandfathering" rule of § 163(h)(3)(D)(i). Under this rule, any indebtedness incurred on or before October 13, 1987, is grandfathered into the new scheme of deductibility by being treated as acquisition indebtedness, regardless of the use made of the proceeds of the grandfathered debt. Therefore, the entire $250,000 principal of the 1985 loan is classified as acquisition debt and interest paid on it is fully deductible qualified residence interest. Note that, unlike true acquisition debt, grandfathered debt is not subject to the $1,000,000 limitation normally applicable to acquisition debt. § 163(h)(3)(D)(i)(II). However, this dollar limitation itself is reduced by the amount of grandfathered debt and thereby reduces the amount of post-October 13, 1987, debt which may be treated as acquisition debt. § 163(h)(3)(D)(ii). Like other acquisition indebtedness, grandfathered debt may be refinanced but, the amount of the debt resulting from such refinancing that is treated as acquisition indebtedness cannot exceed the outstanding principal of the grandfathered debt immediately prior to the refinancing. § 163(h)(3)(D)(iii). As the outstanding principal of the 1985 loan in 1998 is $175,000, only $175,000 of the 1998 refinancing loan is treated as acquisition debt. As the remaining $125,000 of the refinancing loan does not exceed the residence's fair market value less the outstanding acquisition indebtedness, it is classified as home equity indebtedness, subject to the $100,000 ceiling of § 163(h)(3)(C)(ii). (The fact that the proceeds are used to finance education costs is no longer relevant.) Therefore, interest paid on $275,000 of the $300,000 refinancing loan will be fully deductible, while the interest on the remaining $25,000 of the loan is nondeductible personal interest.

4(a)   Since T's modified adjusted gross income does not exceed $50,000, no phase-out occurs. § 221(b)(2). However, the maximum deductible interest on qualified education loans in 2002 is $2,500. § 221(b)(1). Thus, $2,500 of T's $3,000 interest payment is deductible. Although premature, the deduction is an above-the-line deduction. § 62(a)(17).

4(b)   Only $1,250 of T's $3,000 interest payment is deductible. As in problem 4(a), above, the ceiling for 2002 is $2,500. § 221(b)(1). However, ½ (the ratio of $7,500 ($57,500 less $50,000) to $15,000) of the potential $2,500 deduction or $1,250 is phased out under § 221(b)(2)(B).

4(c)   No interest deduction is allowed, because in the case of a joint return, the deduction is fully phased out as T and Spouse's modified adjusted gross income exceeds $130,000. § 221(b)(2)(B).

4(d)   Since there are no limitations on the time period of § 221 interest payments and since the phase out is inapplicable because modified adjusted gross income is only $80,000 (§ 221(b)(2)(B)), a $2,500 deduction is allowed in 2003. Although T and Spouse pay a 10% $300 penalty to the lender, they are in a higher than 10% income tax bracket and the deferral to and deduction in 2003 save them after-tax dollars.

If the interest payment were only $2,000 with a $200 flat 10% penalty, the penalty of $200 is not interest and is not deductible under § 221. Cf. Rev. Rul. 60-127, 1960-1 C.B. 84.

5(a).   Under § 163(d), Investor can deduct investment interest only to the extent she has net investment income during the taxable year. § 163(d)(1). Net investment income is the excess of investment income over investment expenses. § 163(d)(4)(A). Here, Investor has $80,000 in investment income, made up of $60,000 gain from the sale of investment property which does not qualify for § 1(h) treatment (see § 163(d)(4)(B) and § 1(h)(3)) and $20,000 income from investment property and she has $10,000 in investment expenses. Thus, she has $70,000 in net investment income and can deduct investment interest only to that extent. Since she has incurred $100,000 in investment interest, she will be able to deduct only $70,000 of such investment interest in the current tax year. However, she has a $30,000 carryover of the investment interest into the succeeding tax year. § 163(d)(2).

5(b).   Section 265(a)(2) forecloses a deduction for interest on debt incurred to purchase or carry tax-exempt obligations. Therefore, Investor will get no deduction for investment interest in this, or any succeeding year.

5(c).   The issue here is whether there is the necessary connection between the loan and the tax-exempt interest. Will the fact that Investor purchased 50% stock and 50% tax-exempt bonds with the loan proceeds be enough to allow some investment interest deduction? Under Rev. Proc. 72-18, 1972-1 C.B. 740 at 743, if a fractional part of the indebtedness is directly traceable to the holding of a certain tax-exempt obligation, then the same fractional part of the interest incurred on the debt will be disallowed. Since 50% of Investor's indebtedness was incurred for the purpose of purchasing tax-exempt obligations, then 50% of her total investment interest or $50,000 is nondeductible as a result of § 265(a)(2). The § 163(d) limitation will not limit the deductibility of the other $50,000 of investment interest. Under § 163(d)(3)(A) "investment interest" is limited to deductible interest and since Investor has $70,000 in net investment income (see problem 3(a), above), § 163(d) imposes no limitation on the deductibility of her $50,000 of deductible interest.

PROBLEMS

Page 509:

1(a).   Not deductible. The 1986 legislation repealed the previously allowed deduction for general sales taxes. Cf. problem 2 and the last sentence of § 164(a) for deductibility of such taxes if paid in carrying on a trade or business or in a § 212 activity.

1(b).   Deductible. State real property taxes are deductible under § 164(a)(1). Section 164(d)(1) requires that the tax be apportioned between A and B according to the portion of the year that each owns the property. This allocation rule applies whether or not A and B actually apportion the tax. Therefore, A and B are allowed a deduction of $500 each. This is an exception to the general principle that only the person on whom the obligation falls may claim the deduction.

1(c).   Deductible. A state income tax is specifically made deductible by § 164(a)(3).

1(d).   Not deductible. Section 164 does not provide a deduction for any Federal taxes, and § 275(a)(1) expresses a negative rule, not subject to exception.

1(e).   Not deductible. Now repealed § 164(a)(5) allowed a deduction for state and local taxes on the sale of gasoline, diesel fuel, and other motor fuels. The Revenue Act of 1978 repealed § 164(a)(5) during the energy crisis. Cf. problem 2 and the flush language of § 164(a).

2(a).   Deductible. The tax would constitute an ordinary and necessary business expense, and the deduction gets perhaps unnecessary support from the flush language of § 164(a).

2(b).   Nondeductible. In *Nichols*, the Tax Court relied on McDonald v. Comm'r, 323 U.S. 57 (1944), to hold that the amount was not deductible because the taxpayer was not "*carrying on* a trade or business or an activity described in § 212...." (Emphasis added.) The court assumed without deciding that the fee might be a state tax, but not one listed in § 164(a).

3(a).   Father would not be allowed a § 164(a)(2) tax deduction because he was not liable for the obligation. See the payment of the mother's taxes in *Cramer* case in the Text. To allow Father a deduction would be to allow an assignment of a deduction, just as inappropriate as an assignment of income. Cf. Uslu v. Comm'r, 74 TCM 1376 (1997) (interest deduction on mortgage on residence allowed to equitable not legal title holder of residence).

3(b).   The issue then becomes whether Son is allowed a deduction. The terms of § 164 imply a requirement that payment be made by the Son. Here, we find that, in substance there is an indirect payment by Father for Son which is also a gift by Father to Son. If Father gave the money to Son who then paid his obligation, Son would receive a § 164 deduction. It would seem that a difference in form here should not operate to deny Son a deduction since no policy underlying the allowance of tax deductions is violated by looking at the substance of the transaction and allowing Son a deduction. This is in the nature of an *Old Colony Trust* concept in a gift rather than a compensation situation. The *Cramer* case agrees, stating that there is a gift to mother and implying a deduction for mother in that case.

4(a).   Dr. Medic may deduct both amounts X and Y. Amount X is the employee's contribution made by way of amounts withheld from his salary. Although such payments are not deductible under § 164, they are properly viewed as a part of the employer's salary expense deductible under § 162. See John Calamaras, 19 T.C.M. 1045 (1960), opinion item 10. Amount X should be viewed as additional salary paid by Dr. Medic to Charles and then paid by Charles as tax. As to amount Y, the second sentence of § 164(a) would not support a deduction even though the expense was incurred in Dr. Medic's trade or business, because that clause applies only to "state and local, and foreign taxes." Again, however, the employer's payment should be viewed as a § 162 expense; § 275(a)(1)(A) does not preclude a deduction because it does not concern itself with § 3111 which imposes the F.I.C.A. exaction on employers. Cf. Rev. Rul. 74-70, 1974-1 C.B. 116, discussing the timing of an employer's deduction of his § 3111 tax liability.

4(b).   Charles's indirect payment of the tax is nondeductible. Section 275(a)(1)(A) disallows his deduction of the § 3101 tax.

5. Section 164(c)(1) would deny Woodman a deduction under § 164 when the City of Oz builds a road in front of Woodman's property and taxes him for a part of the cost. The reason for the rule is that the payment is for a capital expenditure that increases the value of Woodman's property and the amount is added to the basis of his property. Of course, if the expenditure were for a mere repair to the road or if it were an interest payment on a previous assessment, then a deduction would be allowed. See the last clause of § 164(c)(1) and see Erie H. Rose, 31 T.C.M. 142 (1972).

Chapter 17.   Restrictions on Deductions

Page 514:

See August, "Navigating the At-Risk Waters After the Tax Reform Act of 1984," 63 *Taxes* No. 2, 83 (1985) and Cash, "The Application of the At-Risk Rules to Limited Liability Companies" 14 *Va. Tax Rev.* 483 (1994).

PROBLEMS

Page 517:

1(a).   Taxpayer's losses would be fully deductible under these facts. Since Taxpayer gave his personal note he is personally liable for the $400,000 obligation; and in year one he is "at risk" both to that extent (see § 465(b)(1)(B) and (b)(2)(A)) and to the extent of his cash contributions of $100,000 and may deduct the $80,000 loss. In year two he is "at risk" to the extent of his remaining $420,000 basis plus his $50,000 cash contribution and he may again deduct his $80,000 loss, with a remaining basis and "at risk" amount of $390,000 at the beginning of year three.

1(b).   In this problem, although Taxpayer has the same basis for his interest under *Crane* principles, nevertheless § 465(b)(2) and (4) provide that he is not "at risk" to the extent of the nonrecourse financing. Thus, since he has made $100,000 of cash contributions and is "at risk" to that extent (§ 465(b)(1)(A)) in year one, his $80,000 loss for that year is fully deductible. In year two he is "at risk" to the extent of $70,000 (his "at risk" amount) and $70,000 of his $80,000 loss may be deducted for that year. The $10,000 disallowed loss is carried over and treated as a deduction allocable to his farming activity in the succeeding year under § 465(a)(2).

Note that real estate used in farming is part of the farming activity fully subject to the "at risk" rules. House Report on the Rev. Act of 1978. H.R. No. 95-1445 page 71 at 1978-3 Vol. 1 C.B. 245. Compare problem 2, below.

1(c).   This problem illustrates the recapture rule of § 465(e). While Taxpayer properly deducted his full $80,000 loss in year two (based on the facts of problem (a), above), the conversion of his personal liability to nonrecourse financing in year three (when he breaks even) results in a situation where his total deducted losses over the years ($160,000) exceed his total amounts "at risk" ($150,000). In effect he has a $10,000 negative "at risk" balance at the end of year three; and § 465(e)(1)(A) requires a recapture of the $10,000 amount as ordinary income. He is allowed a $10,000 carry over deduction to year four under § 465(e)(1)(B).

1(d).   The $10,000 payment of principal increases Taxpayer's "at risk" amount to a total of $160,000 with the result that the full $80,000 loss in year two (along with the $80,000 in year one) is deductible. Naturally there is no carryover of deductions to year three. This assumes Taxpayer's payment is made with funds outside the activity. It should be pointed out that if there is a payment of principal on a recourse loan, there is no increase in the at-risk balance.

1(e).   In this situation in year three, Taxpayer may use his $10,000 carryover from year two when he becomes "at risk" to the extent of the $10,000 payment of principal on his loan. Again, it is assumed that the payment is made with funds outside the activity.

2(a).   Vestor is considered at risk with respect to the entire $200,000 nonrecourse loan because the loan is for a real estate activity and is "qualified nonrecourse financing." § 465(b) (6)(A). Qualified nonrecourse financing is defined in § 465(b)(6)(B). One of its main requirements is that the loan is from a "qualified person" as defined in § 49(a)(1)(D)(iv). Here we have a qualified person who is actively and regularly engaged in the business of lending money and is an unrelated lender and in addition, although not explicitly set forth in the facts, the lender is not a person from whom Vestor acquired the property (i.e., the seller), and is not a person who receives a fee for Vestor's investment in the property (i.e., the promoter of the activity). See § 49(a)(1)(D)(iv)(I) - (III).

2(b).   Vestor is not considered at risk with respect to any of the $200,000 nonrecourse loan because the lender is a person from whom Vestor acquired the property (i.e., the seller). § 465(b)(6)(B)(ii) and § 49 (a)(1)(D)(iv)(II).

2(c). Vestor is not considered at risk with respect to any of the $200,000 nonrecourse loan because the lender is related to Vestor. § 49(a)(1)(D)(iv)(I) and (v). Section 465(b)(6)(D)(ii) provides an exception if all other requirements are met even though the parties are related. Here the exception is not satisfied because the terms of the nonrecourse financing are *not* commercially reasonable and *not* on substantially the same terms as loans involving unrelated persons. § 465(b)(6)(D)(ii).

2(d). Vestor is considered at risk with respect to the entire $200,000 nonrecourse loan. Even though the lender is related to Vestor, the terms of the nonrecourse financing are commercially reasonable and on substantially the same terms as loans involving unrelated persons. § 465(b)(6)(D)(ii). Thus the related exception applies and all the other requirements of § 465(b)(6)(B) are met.

Page 519:

Fn. 7. An illustration of § 183's denial of a deduction occurred in the case of Maurice C. Dreicer. Dreicer v. Comm'r, 78 T.C. 642 (1982). Maurice, accompanied by his full-time amanuensis, Brigette Kimmick, travelled the globe doing research on a book tentatively entitled "My 27 Year Search for the Perfect Steak - Still Looking"!! His previous book, the "Diner's Companion," netted $643 in royalties. The Tax Court denied his claimed deductions of roughly $25,000 per year using § 183. Similarly, a mechanic who engaged in drag racing but failed to win in any of the years in issue was found to be without profit motive. Franz v. Comm'r, 48 T.C.M. 1196 (1984).

Page 520:

See Mulligan, "Tax Implications of the Rental Use of a Vacation Home: I.R.C. Section 280A," 88 *Dickinson L. Rev.* 109 (1983); and Lawyer, "Vacation Homes, Section 280A and Bolton v. Commissioner: The Right Result For the Wrong Reasons," 1985 *Duke Law J.* 793.

Page 522:

Note that, although the effect of the § 280A(d)(4) "qualified rental period" rule is to waive the § 280A(c)(5) limitations, the § 280A(e) limitations are still applicable.

Page 523:

The Service has issued Rev. Rul. 94-24, 1994-1 C.B. 87, in response to the *Soliman* case. Under the Ruling, the Service will first apply the "relative importance" test, comparing the activities performed at each taxpayer's principal place of business for purposes of § 280A(c)(1)(A). If the "relative importance" test reveals no definitive answer, then the Service will apply the "time" test comparing the amount of time spent at each location. The Ruling addresses four specific situations in which the issue arises. First, a plumber's home office will not qualify as his principal place of business because the nature of his business requires him to make service calls to customers - activities which are deemed more important than the administrative functions carried out at the home office. Second, a teacher's home office will also not qualify because the essence of her trade requires her to meet with students at the school. Third, a writer who uses her home office for writing will meet the "relative importance" test even though she conducts research and other activities away from the office because of the relative importance of the writing conducted at home. Finally, a retailer of costume jewelry who markets his products at various craft fairs, consignment shops and through catalog orders filled from the home office must meet the "time" test in order to have home office quality because the relative importance test would not yield a definitive result - since the essential activity of his trade or business, sells to customers, is performed at various locations including the home office. See also Notice 93-12, 1993 - 1 C.B. 298, where the Service issued a response to the *Soliman* case and promised that proposed regulations would soon be written to reflect the decision. The Notice applies the two part test adopted by the *Soliman* decision to provide three additional examples to illustrate the application of the rule. The first example involves essentially the *Soliman* facts and the second and third examples both involve salespeople who use their homes to some extent in business.

Rev. Rul. 94-24 and Notice 93-12 were both issued prior to the 1997 liberalization of the principal place of business requirement under §

190

280A(c)(1) flush language. As a result of the legislative change, the results in Situation 1 of Rev. Rul. 94-24 and Examples 1 and 2 of Notice 93-12 are reversed and those home office expenses are now deductible. The § 280A(c)(1) flush language legislative change is discussed in Fleischman, "Home Office Deduction Rules Eased Next Year," 26 *Tax'n For Law.* 277 (1998).

Page 523:

See also Popou v. Comm'r, 246 F 3d 1190 (9th Cir. 2001), where the court allowed a professional violinist to deduct a portion of her home used exclusively for musical practice. The court concluded that the "relative importance" test of *Soliman* was inconclusive as to deductibility, but concluded that under the relative time test the expenses were deductible.

Page 523:

The *Soliman* case is discussed in Rosen, "The Home Office Deduction Game: Will Soliman v. Commissioner Return the Taxpayer to Square One?" 12 *Virg. Tax. Rev.* 141 (1992); Megaard and Megaard, "Supreme Court Narrows Home Office Deductions in Soliman" 78 *J. Tax'n* 132 (1993).

PROBLEMS

Page 525:

1(a). T's deductions are subject to the limitations of § 280A. T personally uses the property for 30 days and that exceeds the greater of 14 days or 10% of the 90 rental days (9 days); consequently § 280A applies. See § 280A(d)(1). If § 280A applies, § 183 does not apply. § 280A(f)(3)(A). Thus, § 183 is inapplicable. Since the property is rented for more than 14 days during the year,the § 280A(g) exception to §§ 183 and 280A is inapplicable.

1(b). The ceilings for deductions of T's expenses are computed as follows:

(1) Gross rental income $3,000

(2)	Less deductible portion of interest and taxes allocable to rental use 90/365 of $2,000 (rounded)	$ 500
(3)	§ 280A(c)(5) limit on deductions for items other than interest and taxes	$2,500
(4)	Portion allocable under § 280A(e) to expenses other than depreciation (3/4 of $1,600)	$1,200
(5)	Maximum depreciation deduction	$1,300
(6)	Portion allocable under § 280A(e) to depreciation deduction, 3/4 of $2,000 = $1,500 but limited by § 280A(c)(5) to:	$1,300

Thus T may deduct $1,200 of expenses and $1,300 of depreciation. Further $200 of depreciation expense is carried over as a deduction in the succeeding year. § 280A(c)(5), flush language.

1(c). All the property taxes and interest expenses are deductible so that total deductions are $2,000 plus $2,500 or $4,500. The problem assumes that the interest is qualified residence interest under § 163(h)(3). Therefore, all the interest along with all of the taxes are deductible because such expenses could be deducted regardless of the extent of the personal use of the property. See § 280A(b) and Chapter 16. If the interest was not qualified residence interest, the portion not attributable to the rental use would be nondeductible.

1(d). Since T uses the property no more than two weeks it is not "used as a residence," § 280A(d)(1), and § 280A is inapplicable. See § 280A(d)(1)(A). Nevertheless § 183 may be applicable. The question is whether the activity is engaged in for profit within that section. If § 183 is applicable, then the results are as follows:

(1)	Gross rental income	$3,000
(2)	Less taxes (See Reg. § 1.183-1(d) Assume taxes = $1000	$1,000

The issue here is whether the interest is deductible to any extent. Since T rents the property and does not use the residence for at least 14 days, the residence is not a qualified residence under § 163(h)(4) (A)(i)(II) and the interest is personal interest under § 163. Since § 183 applies, the residence is also not a valid investment activity and the interest is not deductible as investment interest.

(3)	§ 183(b) limit on rental expenses other than taxes	$2,000
(4)	Portion allocable under § 280A(e) to expenses (including interest) other than depreciation (3/4 of $2600) or	$1,950
(5)	Depreciation (3/4 of depreciation of $2000 or $1500) but limited to	$ 50

If §183 is inapplicable, then the portion of this interest allocable to the investment property becomes investment interest and deductions are not limited to gross income. The taxes are fully deductible ($1,000) plus 3/4 of the interest, expenses and depreciation or 3/4 of $1,000 + 3,600 ($4,600) = $3,450 or total deduction of $4,450.

2.   Taxpayer cannot deduct any of the utilities or depreciation. The limitation on his home office deductions is the $2,000 gross income less the $1,600 business deductions not allocable to use of the home and the $400 mortgage interest and taxes. The disallowed deductions for the utilities expense and depreciation are carried forward to subsequent taxable years. § 280A(c)(5).

3.   Yes, Widow's deductions related to the rooms are limited by § 280A. Prop. Reg. § 1.280A-1(c) states that a single structure may contain more than one dwelling unit. For example, each apartment in an apartment building is a separate dwelling unit. However, to be considered a separate dwelling unit, the unit must provide basic living accommodations such as sleeping space, toilet, and cooking facilities. Assuming that none of the three rooms provides all of the necessary basic living accommodations, they are part of Widow's dwelling unit rather than separate dwelling units. Thus, since Widow uses the

dwelling unit as her residence, her deductions related to the rooms are limited by § 280A.

Page 532:

> Fn. 68. Recall that publicly traded partnerships (PTPs) are generally treated as corporations under § 7704(a). See page 277 of the Text. However, both existing PTPs (see 1987 Act § 10211(c)) and PTPs with at least 90 percent of their gross income made up of "qualifying income" (see § 7704(c)) continue to be treated as partnerships. PTPs that are treated as partnerships are subject to a special rule under the passive activity loss limitations of § 469.
>
> Section 469(k) provides that each PTP that is treated as a partnership will be treated separately under § 469 with the result that gains and losses (and generally credits) of a PTP may not be netted against the partners' other passive activity gains and losses or another PTP's gains and losses. Losses from a PTP must be carried forward. They may be used against subsequent gains from the same PTP or they may be used upon the disposition of the PTP or the activity of the PTP which gave rise to the loss. (See § 469(b) and (g).)
>
> In addition, § 469(k) provides that the $25,000 active participation in real estate exception of § 469(i) is inapplicable to PTPs. This is no big deal because interests in most PTPs will be limited partnership interests which are already precluded from taking advantage of § 469(i). See § 469(i)(6)(C).
>
> Note finally that portfolio income of a PTP should be classified as passive income that is not subject to the § 469 rules. § 469(e).

PROBLEMS

Page 537:

1(a). The $200,000 of taxable income from Lawyer's practice is not income from a passive activity. § 469(c)(1). The same applies for the $10,000 dividends and interest. § 469(e) (1)(A)(i)(I). None of Lawyer's $210,000 nonpassive income can be reduced by the partnership loss because the partnership is a passive activity; thus none of the $50,000

194

loss is currently deductible. § 469(c)(1) and (h)(2). See also § 469(a) and (d). The $50,000 partnership loss is carried forward to the next taxable year. § 469(b).

1(b). The $30,000 gain from the windmill power tax shelter is aggregated with the $50,000 loss from the movie partnership to produce a $20,000 passive activity loss which is not currently deductible. § 469(a)(1)(A) and (d)(1). This passive activity loss may be carried forward. Lawyer's taxable income is therefore $210,000.

1(c). The $50,000 passive activity loss carried forward under § 469(b) is aggregated with the $90,000 gain from the passive activity in the succeeding year with the result that the net passive activity income in the succeeding year is $40,000. Cf. § 469(d). Thus, Lawyer's taxable income is $250,000 in the succeeding year ($200,000 + 10,000 + 40,000).

1(d). Lawyer's sale of her movie limited partnership interest releases the $50,000 loss from the partnership. § 469(g). The $50,000 loss is allowable against income in the following order: First, against income or gain from the movie limited partnership for the taxable year (including any gain recognized on the disposition); second, against net income or gain for the taxable year from all other passive activities; and the remainder, against any other income or gain. § 469(g)(1)(A). However, the limitation on the deductibility of capital losses is applied before determination of the amount of losses allowable upon the disposition under the passive loss rules. §§ 469(g)(1)(C) and 1211. Who said the income tax law couldn't be made simple?

1(e). None of the $50,000 partnership loss can offset any of Lawyer's $210,000 nonpassive taxable income. For the $25,000 rental real estate exemption to apply, Lawyer must actively participate in the activity. § 469(i)(1). Active participation can not exist with respect to a limited partnership interest. § 469(i)(6)(C). Since Lawyer does not actively participate in the rental real estate activity, the $25,000 exemption is unavailable and none of the $50,000 partnership loss can offset Lawyer's $210,000 of nonpassive income. Compare the result in problem 1(g), below. The $50,000 disallowed partnership loss is carried forward. § 469(b).

1(f).   None of the $50,000 partnership loss can offset any of Lawyer's $210,000 nonpassive income. The $25,000 rental exemption is applicable but, because Lawyer's adjusted gross income exceeds $150,000, the exemption is reduced to zero. § 469(i)(3)(A). The $50,000 disallowed partnership loss is carried forward. § 469(b).

1(g). $10,000 of the $50,000 partnership loss is not treated as a loss from a passive activity. § 469(i). The $25,000 exemption is reduced by $15,000 (50% of the excess of the $120,000 law practice income and the $10,000 dividends and interest over $100,000) to $10,000. § 469(i)(3)(A). Thus, Lawyer's taxable income is $120,000 ($120,000 law practice income plus $10,000 dividends and interest less $10,000 partnership loss). $40,000 of the partnership loss is carried forward. §469(b).

2(a).   The issue here is whether grocer materially participates in the grocery business. If there is material participation the § 469 rules are inapplicable. See § 469(c)(1)(B); see also § 469(a) and (d). Material participation requires regular, continuous and substantial involvement by the taxpayer in the activity. § 469(h)(1). Grocer satisfies the 500 hour first test of Temp. Reg. § 1.469-5T(a)(1). Thus, the entire $50,000 loss is not subject to § 469 and is currently deductible by Grocer.

2(b).   Grocer probably does not materially participate in the grocery business because his involvement is not regular and continuous and probably not substantial. The Senate Report states that an intermittent role in management, while relevant, does not establish material participation in the absence of regular, continuous and substantial involvement in operations. S. Rep. No.99-313, 99th Cong., 2d Sess. 734 (1986). However, the issue of material participation can not be conclusively established without a detailed examination of the facts and circumstances. See Temp. Reg. § 1.469-5T(a)(7) and (b)(2)(ii). In addition, Grocer might satisfy one of the regulations' mechanical tests. See, e.g., Temp. Reg. § 1.469-5T(a)(3). See also Temp. Reg. § 1.469-5T(b)(2)(iii). If Grocer does not materially participate, none of the $50,000 loss is currently deductible unless there is passive activity income. The disallowed loss is carried forward to subsequent years. § 469(b).

2(c).   The fact that Grocer is retired and may have no other business interests is not conclusive in determining material participation. In addition, the activities of agents are not attributed to a taxpayer. S. Rep. No. 99-313, 99th Cong., 2d Sess. 735 (1986). Thus, Grocer does not appear to meet any of the tests of Temp. Reg. § 1.469-5T(a) or to have materially participated in the grocery store activity. None of the $50,000 loss is currently deductible unless there is passive activity income. The disallowed loss is carried forward to subsequent years. § 469(b).

2(d).   When Grocer begins to manage the grocery business on a full-time basis in the succeeding year, he begins to materially participate in the business. Temp Reg. § 1.469-5T(a)(1) would be met. See also Temp. Reg. § 1.469-5T(a)(7) and (b)(2)(ii). Previously suspended losses, unlike passive activity losses generally, are allowed against income from the activity after it ceases to be a passive activity with respect to the taxpayer. § 469(f)(1) and (3). Thus, $60,000 of Grocer's succeeding year active grocery store income can be offset by the $50,000 suspended loss from current year.

3(a).   All rental activities are passive activities. § 469(c)(2). However, since the activity is rental real estate, the $25,000 exemption is available if the active participation standard is met. § 469(i). The active participation standard can be satisfied without regular, continuous, and substantial involvement in operations so long as the taxpayer participates, e.g. in the making of management decisions, in a significant and bona fide sense. S. Rep. No. 99-313, 99th Cong., 2d Sess. 737 (1986). The Senate Report states that under facts similar to these facts, the taxpayer will generally be considered to have met the active participation standard. Id. at 738. Thus, the entire $8,000 loss is deductible by Eileen since her year two adjusted gross income does not exceed the § 469(i)(3) phase-out exemption amount.

3(b).   The shopping mall is a rental real estate activity and therefore is a passive activity. § 469(c)(2). The Senate Report states that under facts similar to these facts, the taxpayer has not met the active participation standard. S. Rep. No. 99-313, 99th Cong., 2d Sess. 738 (1986). The reasoning is apparently that there has been no significant and bona fide participation in the activity by the taxpayer. Thus, the $25,000 exemption can not be applied to any of the shopping mall loss and therefore none of the $3,000 shopping mall loss is deductible by Eileen.

The $3000 loss will be carried over under § 469(b). As explained in part (a), above, however, Eileen's $8,000 loss from the apartment is deductible.

4.   Julia is given substantial flexibility with respect to her Town Y catering business under the § 469 activity rules. She may group her catering businesses in Town X and Town Y and they would be treated as an appropriate economic unit; if so, she would meet the material participation requirement (see Reg. § 1.469-5T(a)) as to both catering businesses. Reg. § 1.469-4(c). In the alternative, Julia could treat the two catering businesses as separate activities; if she did so she does not materially participate in the Town Y business. See Reg. § 1.469-4(c)(3) Example 1. If the later alternative were chosen, income from the Town Y passive activity would be reduced by losses from the real estate limited partnership which would not be subject to the § 469(i) exception due to § 469(i)(6)(C). However, if the Town Y activity generated losses, Julia would prefer to group the catering activities so as to deduct the Town Y losses and not subject them to the § 469 limits.

Julia's principal problem is that once she determines whether to group her catering activities, no regrouping is allowed. Reg. § 1.469-4(e). Whatever grouping she decides on for material participation purposes also controls for the purposes of freeing up losses on disposition under § 469(g).

Seemingly, Julia intends to profit from the Town Y business and if the Town Y business generates profits she should not group it with the Town X business. If she separates them, Town Y is a passive activity and its profits would allow deductibility of the real estate losses. If the Town Y business were unprofitable, Julia would likely dispose of it after a short period anyway and she could then deduct Town Y losses (which would have been non deductible under § 469) on disposition of the Town Y business. § 469(g).

5(a).   Dentist's net income from passive activities is $15,000 ($35,000 income less $20,000 loss). Dentist's income tax liability allocable to this passive income is $4,500 ($15,000 x 30%). Dentist's passive activity credit is therefore $2,500 (excess of $7,000 credit over the $4,500 tax liability allocable to passive activities). § 469(d) (2). Section 469(a) disallows use of the $2,500 passive activity credit in the current year. It is carried forward under § 469(b).

5(b).   Dentist's share of the rental real estate activity loss is $20,000. Since Dentist actively participates in the rental real estate activity, the § 469(i) exemption is available. The $20,000 rental real estate activity loss must be netted with the $15,000 income from other passive activities to determine the amount eligible for the rental real estate exemption. Conf. Rep. No. 99-841, 99th Cong., 2d Sess. II-141 (1986). The net amount eligible for the exemption is $5,000. The full $5,000 net amount is currently deductible. The amount of the rental real estate exemption is reduced by 50% of the excess of Dentist's AGI over $100,000. § 469(i)(3). AGI for purposes of the rental real estate exemption is determined without regard to passive losses. § 469(i)(3)(D). Thus, Dentist's AGI for purposes of determining the reduction in the exemption is $110,000 and the exemption is reduced by $5,000 (50% x $10,000) to $20,000. Since the rental real estate exemption of $20,000 exceeds the amount eligible for the exemption of $5,000, $5,000 can be offset against income from nonpassive activities.

As a result of the above, Dentist has a passive activity credit of $7,000 because there is no income from passive activities. § 469(d)(2). The passive activity credit may not be used in the current year but is carried forward to the next taxable year. § 469(b).

6(a).   Doctor's sale of his interest to an unrelated third party releases the passive activity carryover losses of $60,000. § 469(g). The $60,000 loss is allowable against income in the following order: First, against income from the passive activity for the taxable year (including any gain recognized on the disposition); Second, against net income or gain for the taxable year from all other passive activities; and the remainder against any other income or gain. § 469(g)(1).

6(b).   Doctor's sale of his partnership interest still releases the $60,000 of suspended losses. Selling the partnership interest at a loss does not affect the release of suspended losses. See problem 6(a), above, for the order of allowance under § 469(g)(1).

6(c).   The basis of Doctor's partnership interest is potentially increased by the $60,000 passive activity carryover loss to $110,000. § 469(j)(6)(A).

Thus if the son subsequently sells the interest for a price in excess of $110,000, he may use the full $110,000 basis. Note, however, that the son's basis for determining loss on a subsequent sale cannot exceed $100,000, the fair market value at the date of gift. § 1015(a) and S. Rep. No. 99-313, 99th Cong., 2d Sess. 726, footnote 12 (1986). Losses potentially used to increase basis are not then allowed as a deduction (see § 469(j)(6)(B)); thus,it is possible no benefit may ultimately be derived from $10,000 of passive activity loss carryovers.

6(d).   Doctor's son is a related party within § 267(b). Accordingly, the $60,000 suspended loss is not triggered when Doctor sells the partnership interest to his son. However, if Doctor's son sells the entire interest in a taxable transaction to an unrelated party, Doctor's entire $60,000 passive activity carryover loss is released and available to offset Doctor's active income. § 469(g)(1)(B).

6(e).   The $60,000 suspended losses are deductible on the final return of Doctor only to the extent they exceed the "step-up" in the basis of the partnership interest. § 469(g)(2). Since there is a $50,000 step-up in basis of the partnership interest ($100,000 - $50,000), only $10,000 of the suspended losses are deductible on Doctor's final return ($60,000-$50,000).

Page 540:

In Pittsburgh Milk Co., 26 T.C. 707 (1956), it was held that an illegal rebate to customers at the time of a sale of milk resulted in a reduction of the gross sales price and not an expense currently nondeductible under § 162(c)(2). Similar results were reached in Dixie Dairies Corporation v. Comm'r, 74 T.C. 476 (1980), also involving milk sales, Haas Bros., Inc. v. Comm'r 73 T.C. 1217 (1980), and Sobel Wholesale Liquors v. Comm'r, 630 F.2d 670, (9th Cir. 1980), both involving illegal liquor rebates. Although the Commissioner initially fought these results (see Rev. Rul. 77-244, 1977-2 C.B. 58), his position is now in line with them. See Rev. Rul. 82-149, 1982-2 C.B. 56.

Legal kickbacks shown to be a part of a long established practice in the industry are deductible. Raymond Bertolini Trucking Co. v. Comm'r, 736 F.2d 1120 (6th Cir. 1984).

Page 547:

The following is a more detailed description of Section 86 with a PROBLEM involving Section 86. They may be duplicated and distributed to students.

EXPLANATION OF SECTION 86

Adjusted gross income serves as a part of the measuring device for computing the portion of social security benefits[1] which must be included in gross income under Section 86.[2] In general, as a taxpayer's adjusted gross income (as modified) and one half of the social security benefits received exceed certain base amounts, up to 85 percent of the social security benefits are included in gross income. Computation of the amount of social security benefits included in gross income is essentially a three step process. The first step is to compute an amount equal to the sum of the taxpayer's "modified adjusted gross income" plus one-half of social security benefits received in the year.[3] "Modified adjusted gross income" is an individual's adjusted gross income for the year not including the social security benefits increased by the amount of certain exclusions[4] from gross income including the

---

[1] The term "social security benefit" includes monthly benefits received under Title II of the Social Security Act or tier 1 railroad retirement benefits. I.R.C § 86(d)(1).

[2] The provision is applicable to benefits received after 1993. Prior to 1994, only the first two steps applied imposing a 50% ceiling on the gross income inclusion of social security benefits.

[3] I.R.C. § 86(b)(1)(A). Technically, the computation can be seen as a two step process depending whether the excess of the step one amount exceeds the base amount (step two) or the adjusted base amount (step three).

[4] I.R.C. § 86(b)(2)(A). The concept of modified adjusted gross income disregards the exclusions of I.R.C. §§ 135, 137, 221, 222, 911, 931 and 933, thus including those statutory exclusions in a modified gross

amount of the taxpayer's tax-exempt interest.[5]

The first step amount is then measured against threshold amounts known as "the base amount" and "the adjusted base amount.[6] The base amount is $32,000 for married individuals filing a joint return, zero for married individuals filing separately who reside together during the taxable year, and $25,000 for all other individuals.[7] The adjusted base amount is $44,000 for married taxpayers filing a joint return, zero for married taxpayers filing separately who reside together during the year, and $34,000 for all other individuals.[8] If the step one amount is less than the base amount, then none of the social security benefits are included in gross income. If the step one amount exceeds the base amount and is less than the adjusted base amount, then under the second step, the amount required to be included in gross income is one-half of the *lesser* of (1) the total social security benefits received during the taxable year or (2) the excess of the step one amount over the base amount.[9] Under this computation, a maximum of 50 percent of the social security benefits are included in gross income. In the alternative, if the step one amount exceeds the adjusted base amount, a separate third step computation is made.[10] Under this third step, the amount included in gross income is the *lesser* of (1) the sum of 85% of the excess of the step one amount over the adjusted base amount *plus* the *lesser* of (a) the step two amount or (b) one-half of the excess of the

------

income.

[5] I.R.C. § 86(b)(2)(B).

[6] I.R.C. §§ 86(c)(1) and (c)(2).

[7] I.R.C. § 86(c)(1). Congress provides a zero base amount for married individuals in order to prevent couples whose incomes are relatively equal from substantially reducing benefits subject to tax by filing separate returns. H.Rep. No. 98-25, 98th Cong., 1st Sess., 25 (1983).

[8] I.R.C. § 86(c)(2).

[9] I.R.C. § 86(a)(1).

[10] I.R.C. § 86(a)(2).

adjusted base amount over the base amount[11] or (2) 85% of the social security benefits received during the year.[12] As a result if the third step applies, a maximum of 85 percent of a taxpayer's social security benefits may be included in gross income.[13]

To illustrate this complicated computation, assume married taxpayers filing a joint return have $100,000 of modified adjusted gross income and $30,000 of social security benefits. Their step one amount is $115,000 ($100,000 plus one half of the social security benefits of $15,000).[14] Since the step one amount of $115,000 exceeds their adjusted base amount of $44,000, step three applies. Under step three, the taxpayers' inclusion in gross income is $25,500, computed as follows.[15] It is the *lesser* of:

(1) The total of:
      85% of $71,000 (the excess of the step one
      amount of $115,000 over the adjusted base
      amount of $44,000) $60,350
    Plus the lesser of:
      (a) The step two amount: ½ of the *lesser* of
          $30,000 (the social security benefits) or
          $83,000 (the excess of the $115,000 step one

---

[11] The one half of the adjusted base amount over the base amount will be $6,000 for marrieds filing a joint return ½ of $44,000 less $32,000), zero for married individuals filing separately who resides together during the taxable year, and $4,500 for all other individuals (½ of $34,000 less $25,000).

[12] I.R.C. § 86(a)(2).

[13] Taxpayers who receive lump sum social security benefit payments which are attributable to prior years may make a special election to limit the amount of tax in the current year to the amount of tax that would have been paid had the benefits been received in the prior years. I.R.C. § 86(e). Cf. I.R.C. § 1341.

[14] I.R.C. § 86(b)(1)(A).

[15] I.R.C. § 86(a)(2).

amount over the $32,000 base amount) $15,000
(b) ½ of the $44,000 adjusted base
     amount less the $32,000 base   6,000
                                                   $ 6,000
                                               $66,350

(2) 85% of the social security benefits (85% of $30,000) $25,500

Thus $25,500 of taxpayers' social security benefits are included in taxpayers' gross income.

PROBLEM

Retired, a single individual, receives $40,000 of social security benefits in the current year when his adjusted gross income (not including the social security benefits) is $30,000 and he has $10,000 of tax exempt interest. He has no § 86(b)(2)(A) deductions of exclusions. What is the amount, if any, of Retired's gross income inclusion under § 86?

ANSWER TO PROBLEM

Retired has $26,600 of § 86 gross income computed below. The first step is to compute the combination of the modified adjusted gross income plus ½ of the social security benefits. The sum of Retired's modified adjusted gross income of $40,000 ($30,000 of adjusted gross income plus $10,000 of tax exempt interest computed under § 86(b)(2)) plus one-half of his social security benefits of $20,000 is $60,000.

As the $60,000 step one amount exceeds the $34,000 adjusted base amount (§ 86(c)(2)(A)), step three (§ 86(a)(2)) applies. Under step three, the amount of social security benefits included in gross income is the *lesser* of:

(1) The sum of 85% of $26,000 ($60,000-$34,000) $22,100
plus the *lesser* of:

    (a) the step two amount of $17,500 ½ of the
       lesser of (1) the $40,000 of social security
       benefits or (2) the $60,000 step one amount

204

less the $25,000 base amount or $35,000)

<table>
<tr><td>(b) ½ of $34,000 less $25,000 or $4,500</td><td></td><td><u>4,500</u></td></tr>
<tr><td></td><td>Total</td><td>$26,600</td></tr>
<tr><td style="text-align:center">or</td><td></td><td></td></tr>
<tr><td>(2) 85% of $40,000</td><td></td><td>$34,000</td></tr>
</table>

Thus $26,600 of social security benefits, the lesser amount, is included in Retired's gross income under § 86. This computation illustrates that 85% of the social security benefits are not always included in gross income.

PROBLEM

Page 548:

1(a). The cost of Employee's uniform allowed as a deduction under § 162 (see page 398 of the Text) would potentially be deductible only as an itemized expense under § 63(d) because it is an unreimbursed employee's expense not specifically listed under § 62(a). Under § 63 itemized deductions are deductible only if an election is made under § 63(e) to itemize. But discussion of those concepts should be postponed until section E of this Chapter.

Students often tend to read § 62 as authorizing deductions. It should be emphasized that another Code section must be found which allows the deduction; § 62 merely determines whether the deduction so authorized is "above or below the line," i.e. one claimed in *arriving at* adjusted gross income, or a part of itemized deductions under § 63(d). An easy way to stress the point is first to require the student to identify the Code section allowing the deduction and then to determine whether the deduction is within § 62(a).

1(b). Employee Salesman's entertainment expenses would potentially be deductible only as itemized expenses under § 63(d) for the same reasons as in problem 1(a), above.

1(c)(1). As this is a reimbursed employee's expense, it would be deductible from gross income under § 62(a)(2)(A). Note that Reg. § 1.162-17(b)(1) broadly provides an exclusion from gross income for the reimbursement and a disallowance of a deduction for the expenses, where the reimbursement equals the expenses and the employee must account to the employer. Reg. § 1.62-2 adds detail to Reg. § 1.162-17 and overrides Reg. § 1.162-17 to the extent the two regulations are inconsistent. See Reg. § 1.162-17(e)(3). See also § 62(a)(2)(A). The problem uses a cf. cite to Reg. § 1.162-17(b)(1) because the intent of the problem is to simply convey the concept of a wash to students, not to drag them through all the statutory and regulatory requirements at this point. For those of you who want to provide more detail, read on.

Under Reg. § 1.162-2(c), amounts received from an accountable plan are excluded from an employee's gross income and are exempt from withholding. An accountable plan is an arrangement that (1) reimburses an employee for expenses deductible under sections 161 through 197 that the employee incurs in connection with his or her services as an employee, (2) requires the employee to substantiate each expense, and (3) requires the employee to return any excess reimbursement to the employer. Reg. §§ 1.62-2(c)(2)(i), (d), and (f). The expenses must be timely and properly substantiated. As a rule, the expenses are substantiated within a reasonable time if the employee substantiates an expense to the employer within 60 days of incurring the expense. Reg. § 1.62-2(g)(2)(i). The employee must substantiate expenses governed by § 274(d) with sufficient detail to satisfy Reg. § 1.274-5T and substantiate other expenses with detail sufficient to enable the employer "to identify the specific nature of each expense and to conclude that the expense is attributable to the [employer's] business activities." Reg. § 1.62-2(e)(3).

Employer can deduct the § 162 expense above the line under § 62(a)(1); but Employer is limited to deduction of only 50% of the amount of such entertainment expenses by § 274(n)(1).

1(c)(2). The excess is included in the employee's gross income. See Reg. § 1.162-17(b)(2). In addition, it is reported on the employee's Form W-2, and subject to withholding, unless the employee received the excess under an accountable plan and returns it within a reasonable time (generally 120 days). Reg. §§ 1.62-2(c), (g)(2), and (h)(2). The balance - i.e., the amount of reimbursement - is excluded from the employee's gross income and exempt from withholding, so long as the reimbursements are paid under an accountable plan. Reg. § 1.62-

2(c)(2)(i), (c)(4), and (h)(1).

1(c)(3). The reimbursements, to the extent they are from an accountable plan, are excluded from income and exempt from withholding. Reg. § 1.62-2(c)(2)(i) and (h)(1). Reg. § 1.162-17(b)(3) allows an employee a deduction for the deficiency, with added requirement that she file a statement setting forth such particulars as the nature of her occupation and the exact nature and amount of expenditures for entertainment expenses. Although premature, note that the excess is an itemized deduction subject to the § 67(a) 2% of adjusted gross income floor. See Reg. § 1.62-1T(e)(3); see Chapter 18F.

1(d). Employer's entertainment expenses would be deductible from gross income under § 62(a)(1) allowing an "above the line" deduction for all trade or business expenses incurred by an employer, or at least incurred by one other than in the capacity as an employee. Again, the deduction is limited to only 50% of the expenses. § 274(n)(1).

1(e). If Employee deducted the expenses under § 162 because of the limitations of § 222(b), Employee's educational expenses would be deductible only as an itemized expense under § 63(d), because they are not specifically listed under § 62(a). If Employee deducted the expenses under § 222, they would be above-the-line deductions under § 62(a)(18).

1(f). All expenses mentioned here are personal expenses of Employee. Nevertheless, they are made deductible by §§ 213, 170, 164 and 163, respectively. None, however, falls within § 62(a) and consequently none is deductible unless Employee itemizes her deductions. § 63(e). If so, under § 67(b) the deductions are not subject to the 2% floor.

1(g). The difference here from problem 1(f), above, is that the payments for taxes and interest now relate to income producing property. Under § 62(a)(1) or (4) deductions otherwise allowed (here by §§ 163 and 164) attributable to property used in a trade or business or held for the production of rent may be claimed in arriving at adjusted gross income. The medical expenses and charitable contributions remain potentially deductible, however, generally only as itemized deductions.

1(h). Employee's stock loss is allowed as a deduction under § 165(c)(2) and it would be deductible from gross income under § 62(a)(3).

1(i).   Employee's $1,000 of interest on student loans is deductible under § 221 and is deductible from gross income under § 62(a)(17).

1(j).   Employer's state income taxes would be potentially deductible only if itemized under § 63(d). Douglas H. Tanner, 45 T.C. 145 (1965), aff'd per curiam, 363 F.2d 36 (4th Cir. 1966). The *Tanner* case upheld Reg. § 1.62-1(d), relying upon the legislative history of § 62 in which both the Senate and House reports specifically stated that state income taxes on business profits are not within § 62(a) [§ 22(n) of the 1939 Code], because they may be a consequence of but are not directly incurred in carrying on a trade or business. See page 546 of the Text and H. Rep. No. 1365, 78th Cong., 2d Sess., p. 23 (1944).

1(k).   Under Rev. Rul. 92-29, 1992-1 C.B. 20, $150 of the deduction (allowed by § 212(3) or § 162) is directly related to his sole proprietorship business and is deductible under §62(a)(1). The remaining $250 (allowed by § 212(3)) is an itemized deduction and is subject to the 2% floor limitation under § 67.

1(ℓ).   The alimony deduction under § 215(a) is taken from gross income under § 62(a)(10). T.R.A. 1976 elevated the § 215(a) deduction above the line. However, the § 215(a) deduction does not seem to be within the common thread of § 62(a) deductions whose purpose is to make more equivalent the tax lot of taxpayers whose incomes are derived from varying sources. The Joint Committee report on the enactment of § 62(a)(10) stated that the deduction should be above the line (and not itemized) because it involves the splitting of income or assignment of income.

1(m).   The § 217 moving expense deduction is now deductible above the line. § 62(a)(15). Cf. § 132(a)(6).

1(n) $250 of the cost of the materials is deductible under § 162 and is deductible above the line. § 62(a)(2)(D). The remaining $100 is also deductible under § 162 and is an itemized deduction subject to the 2% floor limitation under § 67. This benefit to teachers applies only to deductions allowed in the years 2002 and 2003. § 62(a)(2)(D).

Page 549:

It might be advisable to point out to students that assigned regulation §§ 1.217-2(b)(2),(3),(4),and (8) are now somewhat outdated as a result of the 1993 legislative changes.

PROBLEMS

Page 553:

1(a).   The distance requirement of § 217(c)(1)(A) requires that Lawyer's new principal place of work (Town Y) be at least 50 miles farther from his former residence (Suburb) than was his old principal place of work (Town X). Since it was 10 miles from Suburb to Town X, in order for Lawyer to meet the distance requirement Town Y must be at least 60 miles from Suburb.

1(b).   Section 217(c)(1)(B) provides that if a taxpayer has no former principal place of work then his new principal place of work must be at least 50 miles from his former residence. Thus if Lawyer had not previously been employed, Town Y need only be 50 miles from Suburb in order to meet the distance requirement. This problem also illustrates that one need not have been previously employed in order for § 217 to apply. Cf. Rev. Rul. 78-174, 1978-1 C.B. 77, holding that an employee who was temporarily out of work after working for a long period of time must meet the § 217(c)(1)(A) as opposed to (B) requirement.

1(c).   If Lawyer is a sole practitioner he is a "self-employed individual" under § 217(f)(1), and the § 217(c)(2)(B) time requirements must be satisfied. Under those requirements, he must be employed during the 24 month period immediately following his arrival in Town Y for at least 78 weeks and at least 39 weeks of that employment time must occur during the first 12 month period immediately following his arrival.

1(d).   The requirement would be the same as in problem 1(c), above, because as a partner in the firm, Lawyer would be a "self-employed individual." See § 217(f)(2).

1(e).   If Lawyer is an associate he is an employee rather than self-employed, and § 217(c)(2)(A) requires only that he be a full-time employee during at least 39 weeks of the 12 month period immediately following his arrival in Town Y.

1(f).   Assuming the necessary distance and time requirements are met, Lawyer will be allowed a total § 217 deduction of $650 made up of the following amounts:

(1)   § 217(b)(1)(A): $400
(2)   § 217(b)(1)(B): $250

Lawyer's total § 217 deduction: $650

The $200 of meals expenses are nondeductible. § 217(b)(1) flush language. Section 217 became an operative part of the Code in 1964. Students may well be asked to ponder the congressional reason for enacting § 217. Moving expenses are not substantially different from commuting expenses, at least when taxpayer moves to a job with a new employer. Both involve getting *to* the work. Nevertheless the expense of moving is considered sufficiently related to the earning activity to warrant a deduction. In the light of the mobility of our labor force and the frequency and current cost of such moves this seems reasonable. But if so, how far has Congress gone and how far should it go in bringing peripheral personal-type expenditures within the area of deduction? Might Congress ultimately decide to allow a deduction for commuting expenses? Their failure to do so may simply be the incredible cost to federal revenues.

1(g).   If both Lawyer and Spouse commence work in Town Y and assuming they file a joint return, there is no difference in the above result. In addition if *either* satisfies the time requirement, the § 217 deduction becomes available.

1(h).   If Lawyer's firm reimburses him for $850 of his expenses, only $200 will be included within his gross income. § 132(a)(6) excludes $650 of the reimbursement (the amount deductible under § 217 for the year). See § 132(g). This amount would be a wash if included in income because it would be deductible under § 62(a)(15) and thus the exclusion is appropriate. Note there is no exclusion if a § 217 deduction were taken for the expenses in a prior year. The excess $200 of reimbursement is included in lawyer's gross income.

2.	Tardy's moving expenses, presumably all incurred and paid in 1998, are deductible for *that* year. § 217(a). The year of deduction is not determined by when the 39 week or 78 week tests of § 217 are met. Reg. § 1.217-2(d)(2)(i),(ii). Consequently, the Commissioner's disallowance of the deduction for 1999 is correct. If, as is usually the case with an individual, Tardy was a calendar year taxpayer, her 1998 return was due on April 15, 1999. When on April 10, 2002 she received the deficiency notice she still had five days within which to file a refund claim for 1998, properly claiming the § 217 deduction for that year. If Tardy filed her 1998 return early the 3-year period for filing a refund claim, § 6511(a) nevertheless runs from the date the return was due, April 15, 1999. § 6513(a). The Tax Court took this all into account in the *Meadows* case and, somewhat regretfully, denied the deduction for the later year when the time had passed for seeking a refund for the earlier year.

3.	In *Seth Keener* the taxpayer sold his residence at a loss for which his employer reimbursed him in accordance with their agreement. The reimbursement was properly treated as compensation, taxable as ordinary income. See also Ritter v. U.S., 393 F.2d 823 (Ct. Cls. 1968), cert. den., 393 U.S. 844 (1968). The matter should be treated just the same if the employer purchases the employee's house for more than it will bring. In effect, Employer has reimbursed Ms. Keen for a *personal* loss and the reimbursement is income subject to tax. See Thomas L. Karsten, 34 T.C.M. 868(1975). Nothing in § 217 alters this.

	In the view of the above, Employer would be able to deduct his $5000 loss on the house as an ordinary and necessary business expense of compensation for services rendered.

4.	Professor Bionic can get no help from § 217. The travel expense deduction of § 162(a)(2) and the moving expense deduction of § 217 are mutually exclusive. See Reg. § 1.217-2(c)(3)(iii). As Bionic was temporarily away from home, Peurifoy v. Comm'r, 358 U.S. 59 (1958), he could properly claim travel expenses under § 162, but he had not incurred moving expenses (going or coming) to get to a new place of work. *Alvin L. Goldman.* See also Wassinaar v. Comm'r, 72 T.C. 1195 (1979), in which taxpayer graduated from Wayne State Law School in Detroit, attended N.Y.U.'s graduate tax program, and returned to Detroit to enter practice. The Tax Court denied him a § 212(3) deduction and a § 217 deduction. The § 217 deduction for his expenses incurred in moving from New York to Detroit was not allowed because, even before his departure to Detroit, his principal residence was Detroit. See Reg. § 1.217-2(b)(8).

In a Ruling involving a situation similar to the *Goldman* case, it was held that a new Congressman is allowed a § 217 moving expense deduction for the costs incurred in moving from his home state to Washington, D.C. and in the same year he may deduct living expenses in Washington, D.C. up to $3000 under § 162(a). Rev. Rul. 73-468, 1973-2 C.B. 77. Of course the same expenses are not deductible under both sections. The Ruling concluded that the dual deductions did not violate Reg. § 1.217-2(c)(3)(iii) stating:

> A new Member of Congress claiming deduction under sections 162(a) and 217 will not be maintaining an inconsistent position within the meaning of section 1.217-2(c)(3)(iii) of the regulation when his tax "home", by virtue of and for purposes of section 162(a), is a place other than Washington, D.C., while his new principal place of work is factually determined to be Washington, D.C. for purposes of section 217.

Page 560:

A broad summary of deductible medical expenses is found in I.R.S. Publication 502 (1999). The list of unusual types of medical expenses continues to grow and keep up with the times, but with some limitations. Additional costs above the cost of normal foods of chemically uncontaminated foods, are deductible on a joint return by taxpayer and spouse who suffer severe allergic reactions to commercially processed foods. Theron G. Randolph, 67 T.C. 481 (1976). The extra cost of equipment that displays substitutes for the audio portion of television programs as subtitles on the television screen is a deductible medical expense for hearing-impaired persons. Rev. Rul. 80-340, 1980-2 C.B. 581. In Letter Ruling 8033038 (1980) a person with a severe hearing problem was allowed to deduct the cost of maintaining a cat that was registered as a hearing aid animal. In TSV v. Comm'r, 40 TCM 1277 (1980), the cost of a Navajo healing ceremony performed by a medicine man was allowed as a deductible medical expense. In Letter Ruling 8919009 (1989) fees incurred for a child-birth preparation class were allowed as a medical expense. Instruction given to pregnant women for the purpose of preparing them for an active role in the process of child birth is directly related to, if not a necessary component of, obstetrical care, which as specifically included in the definition of medical care for purposes of § 213. But in Letter Ruling 8021004 (1980) a mother was not allowed to deduct the cost of deprogramming her son who had been a member of a religious cult. Articles discussing special applications of the medical expense deduction are Self, "Abortion to Aging: Problems of Definitions in the Medical Expense Tax Deduction," 58 *Boston U.L. Rev.* 165 (1978), and Maule, "Federal Tax Consequences of Surrogate Motherhood," 60 *Taxes* 656 (1982).

Page 562:

Two interesting (not necessarily novel) medical expenses cases are considered below:

(1) Polyak v. Comm'r, 94 T.C. 337 (1990). Mrs. Polyak had heart disease and associated lung problems. She lived with her husband in Michigan. Cold weather created health problems for her. Her doctors advised her to move to a warmer climate in the winter. During the tax year in issue, she lived in Florida for 5 months in a trailer at a campground. She saw her Florida doctor twice during the 5 months. The Tax Court:

> (a) Disallowed a § 213(d)(2) deduction for the campground rental fees she paid because her move to Florida was not essential to medical care provided by a physician in a hospital. See § 213(d)(2)(A).

> (b) Disallowed a deduction for the cost of installing a telephone in the trailer. The taxpayer installed the telephone to quickly contact the doctor if necessary. The court relied on *Bilder* for the proposition that personal living expenses incidental to medical treatment are not within § 213 except the transportation expenses expressly allowed by § 213(d)(1)(B).

> (c) Disallowed a deduction for an air conditioner installed in

the trailer. Although the primary purpose of the air conditioner was for Mrs. P's medical care, the court found that Mrs. P did not meet the burden of proving that the air conditioner was detachable or that the increase in value to the trailer was less than the cost of the air conditioner. The court cited *Gerard* and Reg. § 1.213-1(e)(1)(iii).

(2) Urbauer v. Comm'r, 63 T.C.M. 2492 (1992). The taxpayers' teenage son became addicted to drugs and experienced severe behavioral problems. The taxpayers sent their son to a private school which treated his emotional needs as well as educated him. The school required its students to maintain a personal cash account to provide for expenses other than tuition, room, board and therapy. The taxpayers traveled to and from the school to participate in therapy sessions with their son. During these trips, the taxpayers incurred expenses for hotels, rental cars, meals and movies. The school required the taxpayers to place telephone calls to the school for the purpose of participating in certain therapy sessions with their son. The taxpayers bought clothing, toiletries and jewelry for their son's use while at school. The court:

> (a) Allowed the tuition, room, board and therapy expenses.

> (b) Allowed the cost of maintaining the personal cash account because it was required by the school and was incidental to the school's treatment program.

> (c) Allowed the airfare and rental car expense, and the telephone expenses, incurred so that the taxpayers could participate in therapy sessions.

> (d) Disallowed the hotel expense because the taxpayers failed to prove that the therapy sessions were conducted by a physician as required by § 213(d)(2)(A).

> (e) Disallowed the expenses for meals, citing *Bilder*.

> (f) Disallowed the expenses for clothing, toiletries, jewelry and movies.

Page 563:

In Rev. Rul. 2002-19, 2002-16 I.R.B. 778, the IRS considers the deductibility of the costs of a weight-loss program as expenses for medical care. In the ruling, one taxpayer is diagnosed by a physician as obese but does not suffer from any other specific disease. A second taxpayer is not obese but suffers from hypertension and is directed by a physician to lose weight as treatment for hypertension. Both taxpayers pay fees for a weight-loss program, receive diet information, and purchase reduced-calorie diet foods. None of the costs are compensated by insurance or otherwise. The ruling concludes that obesity is a disease and the costs of the obese taxpayer's weight-loss program is an amount paid for medical care. The other taxpayer's participation in the weight-loss program is also medical care for hypertension. Thus, both taxpayers could deduct the costs of participating in the program.

Rev. Rul. 2002-19 distinguishes Rev. Rul. 79-151, 1979-1 C.B. 116, which holds that participation in a weight-loss program to improve appearance, general health and sense of well-being, and not to cure a specific disease, may not be deducted under § 213. In Rev. Rul. 2002-19 neither taxpayer was allowed to deduct any portion of the cost of purchasing reduced-calorie diet food because those foods were substitutes for food the taxpayers would normally consume and satisfy general nutritional requirements.

Page 564:

In Weaver v. Comm'r, 49 TCM 249 (1984), the court held that a taxpayer may deduct out of pocket medical expenses even though he failed to seek reimbursement from his medical insurance. The IRS argued that the situation was analogous to that under § 162 where a taxpayer is denied a deduction for failure to claim reimbursement from his employer for business expenses. The court rejected this argument finding the language of § 213(a) parallels that of § 165 which limits deductions to those not compensated by insurance or otherwise. At the time § 165 did not preclude a deduction for failure to claim reimbursement. Miller v. Comm'r, 733 F.2d 399 (6th Cir.1984). But see § 165(h)(4)(E) added in the 1986 Act. Query whether the *Weaver* court would reach the opposite result today or whether a statutory amendment (a la § 165 (h)(4)(E) is required to alter the *Weaver* result.

Page 565:

The 1996 Health Insurance Portability and Accountability Act added a new (and not surprisingly complex) experimental plan now known as an Archer Medical Savings Account (MSA). Employees of small businesses and self-employed individuals who purchase "high deductible" medical insurance policies may use the premium savings resulting from the high deductible aspect of the insurance to fund an MSA. MSAs are discussed in the Manual for page 674 of the Text.

PROBLEMS

Page 565:

1(a). Homeowner's medical expense deduction is $2,120, as computed below. There are some preliminary hurdles here:

(1) May Homeowner take account of medical care expenses for Daughter? Yes, § 213 allows it. As the facts state, Daughter is a "dependent," as defined in § 152. She bears a § 152(a)(1) relationship to taxpayer who provides over one-half of her support. (Note, while not significant here, § 152 depends only on relationship and support.) Even if Daughter had $5000 of dividend income and was not a student, she could be a dependent for purposes of § 213, though not qualifying for the dependency exemption under § 151. See part E of this Chapter.

(2) May a capital expenditure be a medical "expense"? Yes, this is no longer controversial. See Reg. § 1.213-1(e)(1)(iii) and *Raymond Gerard*, at page 554 of the Text. However, an expenditure of this type is limited to the amount by which the expenditure exceeds the increase in value of the house, here $2000. See also Ferris v. Commissioner, 582 F.2d 1112 (7th Cir. 1978), involving a "luxurious" swimming pool added to taxpayer's home for medical reasons. The court disallowed the part of the expense related to the luxury features concluding that only the minimum reasonable cost of a functionally adequate pool and housing structure reduced by the value it added to the

216

home qualified as a medical expense. In addition, if the taxpayer purchases a new house that has a pool, no part of the purchase price may be treated as a medical expense. Lerew v. Comm'r, 44 T.C.M. 918 (1982); Robbins v. Comm'r, 44 T.C.M. 1254 (1982). Furthermore, if year-round swimming facilities are otherwise available to the taxpayer, then the addition of a pool may not be treated as a medical expense. Evanoff v. Comm'r, 44 T.C.M. 1394 (1982).

(3)   The prescription medicine is fully treated as a medical expense. In addition, the accident and health insurance is also a medical expense.

Thus Homeowner's total expenses for medical care are:

Medicine		$ 320
Doctor bills		400
Insurance		300
Air conditioning less	$4,100	
increase in value	2,100	
Net for air conditioning		2,000
Total expenses		$3,020
Less 7-½% of AGI		900
Total § 213 deduction		$2,120

1(b).   In a business setting we would allocate the $2,000 deductible expenditure for the air conditioner over the 5 years of the equipment's life. That might seem sensible here; but note that neither § 167, § 168, nor any other section provides for it. Therefore we pretend a long-time asset represents an "expense," which is better than a denial of any deduction. Congress could change this (add § 167(a)(3) property acquired for medical care as defined in § 213(d)(1) but limit the depreciation deduction to the amount that it and other medical expenses in the year of acquisition exceed 7-1/2% of taxpayer's adjusted gross income." See also § 168(a).) Recall however that the $2,000 deductible expenditure did not purchase an asset worth $2,000. At the end of the year Homeowner's home has no additional value as a result of *this* $2,000 of expense.

1(c).   Expenditures for "operation and maintenance" of the air conditioning

217

system are now deductible, Reg. § 1.213-1(e)(1)(iii), although that was once controversial. The cost of electricity is clearly an expenditure for operation. And here George M. Cohan's ghost (Cohan v. Comm'r, 39 F.2d 540 (2d Cir. 1930)) supports a reasonable estimate. As the system will not work at all unless maintained and fed electricity, it would seem inappropriate to allocate these expenditures in part to mere personal expense and in part to medical care. But cf. Fausner v. Comm'r, 413 U.S. 838 (1973).

2.   It may be possible to say that hotel and 50% of meal expenses away from home are not expenses for medical care, (Comm'r v. Bilder, 369 U.S. 499 (1962)) and that, if they are not incurred for business reasons, they are not § 162 expenses. However, if a business trip is extended by illness, additional expenses incurred which are normally personal should be viewed as costs of carrying on business and deductible under § 162. Cf. Kelly v. Comm'r, 440 F.2d 307 (7th Cir. 1971).

3.   Wobbly probably can but Sickly cannot deduct the payments. It is medical expenses "paid or incurred" in the taxable year which may be deducted. Thus a mere deposit against expected future medical expenses is not deductible, as *Bassett* holds. Cf. Weary v. U.S., 510 F.2d (10th Cir. 1975), cert. den., 423 U.S. 838 (1975), holding depreciation on an automobile does not constitute an "amount paid." On the other hand, an advance payment for promised medical care may be deducted. *Rev. Rul. 75-302* so holds as to lump sum life care payments to a retirement home. Estate of Helen Smith v. Comm'r, 79 T.C. 313 (1983), reaches the same result.

PROBLEMS

Page 567:

1(a)   Since Student's adjusted gross income computation disregards § 222 (§ 222(b)(2)(C)) and Student's adjusted gross income does not exceed $65,000 (§ 222(b)(2)(A)(i)) and since the year is 2003 when the limit on § 222 deductions is $3,000 (§ 222(b)(2)(A)(i)), Student may deduct $3,000 of the $10,000 payment. The deduction is an above-the-line deduction. § 62(a)(18). Student should consider whether a § 25A credit is preferable to the deduction. See problem 2, below.

1(b)   While Student potentially could be allowed a $3,000 deduction as in problem 1(a), above, since $8,000 of Student's $10,000 tuition was funded by a scholarship that was excluded from gross income, Student's tuition is reduced by the excluded amount to $2,000. §§ 222(d)(1), 25A(g)(2). As Student directly incurred only $2,000 of tuition, a limitation of the deduction to $2,000 is appropriate.

1(c)   Since Spouses have $140,000 of adjusted gross income prior to consideration of § 222 and since that amount exceeds the 2003 ceiling of $130,000, Spouses are allowed no deduction. § 222(b)(2)(A)(i), (ii).

1(d)   If the year is 2004, Spouses are not allowed to deduct the maximum $4,000 amount because, as in problem 1(c) above, they exceed the $130,000 adjusted gross income ceiling. § 222(b)(2)(B)(i). However, since their adjusted gross income prior to consideration of § 222 is $140,000, they may take a $2,000 deduction in 2004. § 222(b)(2)(B)(ii).

2   The issue whether to take a deduction or use the credit for qualified tuition and related expenses depends upon a number of factors including the amount of one's tuition and related expenses, one's adjusted gross income (or modified adjusted gross income), one's taxable income and tax bracket, and the year involved. Since Student's adjusted gross income (and we assume modified adjusted gross income) does not exceed the § 25A $40,000 or the § 222 $65,000 floors on phased-out amounts and since the year is 2003, the potential Lifetime Learning credit is 20% of $10,000 or $2,000 (§ 25A(c)(1)) and the potential deduction is $3,000 (§ 222(b)(2)(A)(i) and see problem 1(a), above). The issue is whether Student is better off with a $2,000 credit or a $3,000 deduction. In 2003, assuming Student otherwise has $30,000 of taxable income, under § 1(c), Student will be in a 27% bracket and the deduction would save 27% of $3,000 or $810 in taxes, while a $2,000 credit would save $2,000 in taxes. Thus, in these circumstances, Student should elect to use the credit.

        Some additional factors should be emphasized. The phase-out occurs at higher levels for the deduction that the credit, with the result that in some situations where a taxpayer has an adjusted gross income (and, we assume a modified adjusted gross income) of between $50,000 and $65,000 or $80,000 (depending on the year) for a single taxpayer (or between $100,000 and $130,000 or $160,000 for married taxpayers filing jointly), no credit (but only a deduction) would be available. In the alternative, if the tuition or related expenses amount were lower ($3,000 rather that $10,000) the credit amount would be only $600 versus a $3,000 deduction with the deduction producing a more beneficial tax result.

Page 568:

Adjusted for inflation, the exemption amount for the year 2002 is $3,000. See Rev. Proc. 2001-59, 2001-2 C.B.___.)

Page 569:

A general discussion of the dependency exemption appears in an article by Krawchick, "Who Is a Dependent? Whose Dependent? What Is Support?" at 29 *N.Y. Inst. on Fed. Tax* 1343 (1971).

Page 569:

For some light reading in this area, see Robertson, "Fritz and Marilyn and Mike and Suzanne," 51 *Taxes* 268 (1973), discussing possible tax consequences on the highly unusual baseball wife trade of Fritz Peterson and Mike Kekich. See also Vetter, "I.R.C. § 152(b)(5) and Victorian Morality in Contemporary Life," 13 *Yale L. Pol'y. Rev.* 115 (1995).

Page 569:

Amounts spent on a dependent's health insurance premiums are includable in a § 152 support computation but health insurance proceeds may not be included. McGuire v. Commissioner, 77 T.C. 765 (1981); Rev. Rul. 64-223, 1964-2 C.B. 50.

PROBLEMS

Page 571:

1(a).   T has two personal exemptions. T is allowed a personal exemption as the taxpayer under § 151(b). T is also allowed a personal exemption for

H under § 151(b), because under § 7703(a) (see § 153(4)), the determination of marital status is made as of the close of T's taxable year (December 31) and:

(1)   T and H do not file a joint return;

(2)   H has no gross income for the calendar year in which the taxable year of T begins because the $50 of tax exempt interest is excluded from gross income by § 103(a); and

(3)   H is not the dependent of another taxpayer.

1(b).   As the wedding present is excluded from gross income by § 102, the answer here is the same as for problem 1(a), above.

1(c).   T has only a single personal exemption. T is not allowed a personal exemption for H because H has $50 of gross income from the sale of bonds and therefore H does not meet the second requirement of § 151(b). Note that H need not file a return. § 6012(a).

1(d).   No, H is not a dependent of T for purposes of § 151(c) as H does not meet the relationship requirement of § 152(a). See especially the parenthetical clause in § 152(a)(9).

1(e).   Two personal exemptions are allowed. As a joint return is filed, each spouse is a "taxpayer" under § 151(b), and each is allowed a personal exemption. Reg. § 1.151-1(b).

2(a).   A dependency exemption may be claimed for Brother-in-law X, who is supported by T and who has little gross income. See § 152(a)(8).

2(b)(1). Although T's wife's death might raise a question about the § 152(a)(8) relationship, it is logical to treat and there is authority to treat the relationship as unaffected by her death. Once a Boy Scout, always a Boy Scout. Reg. § 1.152-2(d); cf. Steele v. Suwalski, 75 F.2d 885 (7th Cir. 1935). Imagine the brother-in-law might be supported by and continue to be supported by T. Would it be fair to terminate the exemption if he did not live with T to satisfy § 152(a)(9)?

2(b)(2). There is good reason further to treat X as T's brother-in-law, even if the relationship of T and Wife is terminated by their divorce. The result should be the same as in problem 2(b)(1), above. The *Steele* case is again some authority. But see Brotherhood of Locomotive Firemen and Enginemen v. Hogan, 5 F. Supp. 598 (D.C. Minn. 1934).

2(c).   A wife's sister's husband is not an anything-in-law and fails to meet the relationship requirement of § 152(a). Rev. Rul. 71-72, 1971-1 C.B. 49.

2(d).   No relationship is required under § 152(a)(9) if the potential dependent uses the taxpayer's home as a principal household. X would probably qualify for a dependency deduction here. But note § 152(b)(5).

2(e).   X qualifies here. His gross income ($2,000) is not *less than* the $2,000 exemption amount, so he violates § 151(c)(1)(A). Further he is a child of the taxpayer but he does not meet the under-19 test, even though his birthday is in January, as he will be considered 19 on December 31st. Cf. Reg. § 1.151-1(c)(2). But as he is a full-time student and has not attained the age of 24 at the close of the tax year, he fits within § 151(c)(1)(B).

2(f).   This problem involves the interrelationship of two code sections. § 151(d)(2) provides that if a dependency exemption for an individual (X here) is allowable to another taxpayer, then the individual's exemption amount is zero. § 151(c)(2) disallows a taxpayer (T here) a dependency exemption for any dependent who has made a joint return with his spouse for the year. X is married as of the close of the year and thus may file a joint return. See §§ 6013(a) and 7703(a)(1). X and X's spouse may each claim a personal exemption. Reg. § 1.151-1(b). Since they have done so, the married dependent rule of § 151(c)(2) clearly forecloses T's deduction here. Students should be cautioned about this for their own personal reasons. Joint filing by married students defeats a dependency deduction by one of their parents, which could have a greater tax saving for the family.

2(g).   When have taxpayers filed a joint return? Despite the language of § 151(c)(2) if their purpose was merely to secure a refund in a situation in which no return would normally be required to be filed, as here, the deduction by a parent who paid one-half their support may be allowed. *Rev. Rul. 65-34* and Martino v. Comm'r, 71 T.C. 456 (1978).

2(h). Since support paid by X is paid out of gifts received by him, the support requirement of § 152(a) is not met by T. No exemption.

2(i). Under § 152(d), support in the form of a scholarship is disregarded in applying the support test of § 152(a) to a parent or step parent. It should be noted that neither the gift in problem 2(h), above, nor the scholarship here is gross income. §§ 102 and 117, respectively. Here by special rule the exemption can be claimed.

3. This problem involves the application of a multiple support agreement under § 152(c), the subject of an exception to the usual support requirements. Tracking the statute:

   (1)   On the facts no one person contributed over half of X's support.

   (2)   Either T or A or B could have claimed X had he paid over half of X's support and, together, they did pay more than half. (25% + 20% +10% equals 55%.)

   (3)   T and A contributed more than 10% of X's support.

   (4)   If the other files a written declaration that he will not claim X, either T or A may do so.

4(a). W is entitled to the dependency exemption because she is the custodial parent. § 152(e)(1). This is true even though H actually provided the majority of the child's support. This hard-and-fast rule was added by the Tax Reform Act of 1984 to help clarify the controversy as to which parent is entitled to the dependency exemption. Prior to this, Congress felt, the rules were "subjective" and presented difficulties in "proof and substantiation." Thus, it enacted this more objective approach in order to keep the Service out of many disputes in which little tax revenue is at stake. H. Rep. No. 98-482, 98th Cong., 2d Sess. 1498-99 (1984).

4(b). Section 152(e)(2) provides that the non-custodial parent is entitled to the dependency deduction if the custodial parent signs a waiver and the non-custodial parent attaches the waiver to his or her return. Thus, if H attaches W's waiver to his return for the current year, he is entitled to the deduction.

4(c).   W is entitled to the dependency exemption because she is the custodial parent. Under § 152(e)(1) the parent who has custody of the child for the greater portion of the calendar year is deemed to be the custodial parent and is entitled to the dependency exemption.   The term "custody", as used in the statute, refers to legal, not physical, custody over the dependent. See Reg. § 1.152-4(b). The terms of the most recent divorce, custody, or separate maintenance decree dictate who has legal custody and only in the event that such decree is inconclusive or of uncertain validity will physical custody determine which parent has custody over the child. Reg. § 1.152-4(b). Since W had legal custody of H, Jr. for the greater portion of the calendar year, she is entitled to the dependency exemption even though Grandpa had physical custody for nine months out of the year. See Wells v Comm'r, 52 TCM 833, 835 (1986) (wife, who was awarded legal custody of children, deemed to be custodial parent even though both dependents lived away at college.)

4(d).   H would be entitled to the deduction because he is the custodial parent. See Reg. § 1.152-4(b). A divorce decree is not necessary if both spouse's live apart at all times during the last 6 months of the calendar year. § 152(e)(1)(A)(iii).

5(a).   This divorce decree would not be governed by § 152(e)(4) because it is silent as to who is entitled to the deduction. Hence, one would have to fall back on the principles of § 152(e)(1) which give the deduction to the custodial parent, Mr. Kramer.

5(b).   Once again, Mr. Kramer is entitled to the deduction under the general rule of § 152(e)(1). Section 152(e)(4) would not apply because, even though it is a "qualified pre-1985 instrument," the non-custodial parent must provide at least $600 for the support of the child in order to get the deduction. § 152(e)(4)(A)(ii).

5(c).   Ms. Kramer is entitled to the deduction because she now has fulfilled all of the requirements of § 152(e)(4).

Page 573:

   See Kaplow, "The Standard Deduction and Floors in the Income Tax," 50 *Tax L. Rev.* 1 (1994).

Page 574:

Adjusted for inflation, the standard deduction amounts for the year 2002 are as follows:

Filing Status	Standard Deduction
Marrieds filing jointly and surviving spouses	$7,850
Heads of households	6,900
Unmarried individuals	4,700
Marrieds filing separately	3,925

See Rev. Proc. 2001-59, 2001-2 C.B. ___.

PROBLEMS

Page 583:

1(a). Taxpayer's taxable income for the current year is $14,900. Taxpayer is allowed a § 151(a) exemption deduction of $2,000. Taxpayer's basic standard deduction is $3,000 (§ 63(c)(2)(C)). Taxpayer's total deductible itemized deductions are determined under § 67. The itemized deductions of $1,500 for interest and taxes are deductible in full (see § 67(b)(1) and (2) but the remaining miscellaneous itemized deductions of $2,000 for unreimbursed travel, tax preparation fees, and bar association fees are subject to the 2% floor of § 67(a) and they are therefore deductible only to the extent of $2,000 less (2% of $20,000) $400 or $1,600. Thus Taxpayer's total itemized deductions are $3,100 and since that amount exceeds the standard deduction of $3,000, Taxpayer will make a § 63(e) election to itemize. Computationally Taxpayer's taxable income is determined as follows:

Adjusted gross income:	$20,000
Less the total itemized deductions:	3,100
Less the personal exemption:	2,000
Equals taxable income of:	$14,900

1(b). Taxpayer's taxable income is $14,250. If Taxpayer's 65th birthday is January 1, of the succeeding year, Taxpayer is treated as reaching age

225

65 on December 31, of the current year. (See Reg. § 1.151-1(c)(2) and problem 2(e) on page 556 of the Text) and Taxpayer qualifies for an additional standard deduction of $750. § 63(f)(1)(A) and (f)(3). When added to the $3,000 basic standard deduction, § 63(f)(1) and (f)(2)(C), Taxpayer's total standard deduction for the year of $3,750 exceeds Taxpayer's deductible itemized deductions of $3,100 as determined in 1(a), above.

Computationally:	
Adjusted gross income:	$20,000
Less the total standard deduction:	3,750
Less the personal exemption:	2,000
Equals taxable income of:	$14,250

1(c). If Taxpayers are a married couple filing a joint return their taxable income is $11,000. They each qualify for a personal exemption so their total personal exemptions are $4,000. Reg. § 1.151-1(b). Their basic standard deduction is $5,000 under § 63(c)(2)(A)(i) and, since that amount exceeds deductible itemized deductions of $3,100, they would not elect to itemize. Computationally:

Adjusted gross income:	$20,000
Less the standard deduction:	5,000
Less the personal exemptions:	4,000
Equals taxable income of:	$11,000

1(d). Taxpayers' taxable income is $9,900. This problem differs from 1(c), above, in that Taxpayers have an additional $3,000 of itemized interest deductions and total deductible itemized deductions of $6,100 which exceed their $5,000 standard deduction. Thus they will elect to itemize under § 63(e) with the following computational result:

Adjusted gross income:	$20,000
Less total itemized deductions:	6,100
Less the personal exemptions:	4,000
Equals taxable income of:	$ 9,900

2(a). T's taxable income for the year is $3,500. First, since T is properly claimed as a dependent of T's parent, T may claim no personal exemption. § 151(d)(2). In addition T's standard deduction is limited by § 63(c)(5) to the greater of T's earned income plus $250, or $500; here $500. Thus T's taxable income is $4,000 less $500 or $3,500.

2(b). T's taxable income here is $2,750. Again T is denied a personal exemption by § 151(d)(2). Now T's standard deduction is limited to the $1,000 earned income plus $250 under § 63(c)(5). Thus T's taxable income is $4,000 less $1,250 or $2,750.

2(c). T's taxable income is $1,000. T is again denied a personal exemption by § 151(d)(2). T's basic standard deduction of $3,000 is potentially limited under § 63(c)(5) but since T's earned income of $4,000 exceeds the basic standard deduction, T may fully deduct the $3,000 standard deduction. Thus T has taxable income of $4,000 less $3,000 or $1,000.

2(d). The results are the same as in (a) - (c), above. If a dependency exemption is "*allowable*" to X (not necessarily allowed), the § 151(d)(2) and the § 63(c)(5) limitations apply.

3. B should use the standard deduction as B has no itemized deductions and use of the standard deduction would reduce B's taxable income and tax liability.

If A uses the standard deduction, A's standard deduction is $3,000 and § 63(b) precludes deduction of A's $4,000 itemized deduction. Since A's itemized deduction exceeds S's standard deduction, A would elect to itemize.

If A's $4,000 deduction were attributable to deductible alimony, A could take an above the line deduction of $4,000 under § 62(a)(10) and additionally could utilize the standard deduction of $3,000.

4. Section 63(c)(6)(A) prohibits use of the standard deduction on a separate return by one spouse if the other spouse itemizes deductions. The reason for this rule is that without it one spouse could pay and deduct all the itemized expenses while the other spouse could elect the standard deduction and they would receive a double benefit. This would be a distortion. As the standard deduction is intended to replace itemized deductions, such intra-family tailoring could defeat its purpose.

5.	Under § 7703(b) if an individual (1) is married; (2) files a separate return; (3) maintains as a home a household which for more than one-half of the year is the principal abode of a son, daughter, stepson, or stepdaughter for whom the individual is entitled to a dependency exemption (§ 151(c)); and (4) furnishes over one-half of the cost of maintaining such household; and if the individual's spouse is not a member of such household, then such individual is considered not married for purposes of the standard deduction limitations on married persons. In this problem, Wife meets the § 7703(b) requirements and she may take a $3,000 standard deduction because she is not subject to the maximum $2,500 limitation of § 63 (c)(2)(D). Since Husband does not meet the § 7703(b) requirements he is still treated as married and is subject to the § 63(c)(2)(D) $2,500 ceiling for his standard deduction. Thus Congress has recognized the phenomenon of the unilateral marriage.

6.	If Z had total itemized deductions including Father's medical expenses in excess of Z's standard deduction, Z would wish to deduct those expenses. A taxpayer may deduct another's medical expenses only if the other is a spouse or a dependent. In determining who is a dependent, § 213 adopts the § 152(c) multiple support rule. Thus, it may have been a mistake for X to claim Father as a dependent, possibly depriving Z of $2,000 in medical expense deductions.

PART FIVE: THE YEAR OF INCLUSION OR DEDUCTION

Chapter 19.   Fundamental Timing Principles

Page 586:

> Fn.4. Commissioner approval is required for a change in a taxpayer's accounting period in order to avoid a substantial distortion of a taxpayer's income of a type suggested in Reg. § 1.442-1(b)(1). One facet of the problem is dealt with by the statutory requirement of annualization if a return is filed for a short period.   § 443(b).

Page 599:

> In 1998, Congress enacted § 451(h) which provides that a qualified prize winner (lottery, jackpot, etc.) who has an option to take the prize as an annuity or in a lump sum not later than 60 days after becoming entitled to the prize is not treated as constructively receiving the lump sum in the year of the prize, and the qualified prize winner may either be taxed on the receipt of the lump sum or on annuity payments, depending upon the option the taxpayer elects.

Page 599:

> Kay Starr was appearing at a Hotel in Las Vegas at a $19,000 weekly salary. Her salary for the week ending December 30, 1970, was paid by a check dated December 30, but the check was not deposited in Kay's account until January 7, 1971, and was reported as part of her 1971 income. Her manager had dated the deposit slip December 30, 1970. The Tax Court concluded that Kay failed to disprove the correctness of the Commissioner's determination that she constructively received (i.e. had unrestricted access to) the $19,000 in 1970 since no one was quite sure what happened when. Kay Starr, 35 T.C.M. 1291 (1976).

Page 599:

> In Miele v. Comm'r, 72 T.C. 284 (1979), calendar year, cash method law partners received money in a trustee account for prepaid fees which, under state law, could be transferred to the firm's general

account only as the fees were earned. Any excess, amounts not ultimately earned, had to be refunded. The taxpayer made transfers only four times per year with no transfers in November or December. The Tax Court properly held that amounts received by the trustee account were owned by the client until the fees were earned but that fees earned in November and December of a year were constructively received in that year even if not transferred until the next.

Page 603:

In Hradesky v. Comm'r, 540 F.2d 821 (5th Cir. 1976), a cash method taxpayer paid real estate taxes into an escrow account set up by the holder of his mortgage in year one as required under his mortgage agreement. The mortgage holder did not pay the tax to the state until year two. The Fifth Circuit held that the taxpayer got no deduction until year two when payment was made to the taxing authority, stating at page 824:

> . . . [In] the absence of any indication in the record by taxpayer that his prepayment of taxes to the mortgagee represented actually assessed rather than estimated taxes, that such taxes were actually due in the tax year in question, or that a firm commitment on the part of the mortgagee to pay the taxing unit within 1966 existed, the Tax Court's finding under the clearly erroneous rule is adequately supported by the evidence.

Page 605:

In Rev. Rul. 78-173, 1978-1 C.B. 73, the taxpayer's parent paid the taxpayer's medical expenses in return for his negotiable promissory note to pay the parent in the succeeding year. The Ruling, citing William J. Granan, 55 T.C. 753 (1971), which was also relied on in *Rev. Rul. 78-38* and *Rev. Rul. 78-39*, allowed the taxpayer to deduct the expenses for the year of the parent's payment rather than the year in which his note was paid. Cf. Rev. Rul. 80-335, 1980-2 C.B. 170. After all, the result would not seem surprising if the taxpayer borrowed the money at the bank and paid his expenses, which is analogous to the parent's payment here.

With certain limitations, § 461(g)(2) allows a deduction for the prepayment of interest in the form of points, even though other prepaid interest must be amortized under § 461(g)(1). The result in the *Cathcart* case is not affected by § 461(g)(2) which was enacted since it was decided. In *Cathcart*, the court holds that under the form of the transaction no payment of the points had been made; payment will occur only as the principal of the mortgage is paid off. The § 461(g)(2) exception for points (a form of prepaid interest) requires a payment of those points which had not occurred in *Cathcart*. See also Schubel v. Comm'r, 77 T.C. 701 (1981). Settled doctrine here seems to exalt form over substance. For example, had Cathcart borrowed the points money from another lender and paid it to Southern Federal, his economic situation would be much the same, but he would be allowed a current deduction for the points "paid." Cf. William J. Granan, 55 T.C. 753 (1971).

The Tax Court has held § 461(g)(1) applicable even though a prepaid interest payment is nonrefundable. Zidanic v. Comm'r, 79 T.C. 651 (1982).

In Huntsman v. Comm'r, 905 F.2d 1182 (8th Cir. 1990) the Eighth Circuit reversed the Tax Court and held that points incurred in connection with a refinancing of a short term acquisition loan to finance the purchase of a principal residence were currently deductible under § 461(g)(2). The Eighth Circuit rejected the Tax Court's holding that the points must be amortized over the term of the refinanced loan under § 461(g) because, in the view of the Tax Court, § 461(g)(2) required the indebtedness to be "directly related" to the purchase or improvement of the taxpayer's residence. In reversing the Tax Court, the Eighth Circuit held that the statutory language of § 461(g)(2) only requires the indebtedness to be "in connection with" the purchase or improvement of the taxpayer's residence. Because the statutory language "in connection with" is broader than "directly related to", the Eighth Circuit concluded that a refinancing of a short term acquisition loan and a home improvement loan met the statutory requirements of § 461(g)(2). The court indicated that it would not have reached the same result if taxpayer had paid the points to refinance permanent financing of the principal residence in order to obtain a lower interest rate, which is consistent with the result reached in Rev. Rul. 87-22 with respect to 80 percent of the points paid.

See Tierney, "Pointing the Way Through Section 461(g): The Deductibility of Points Paid in Connection with the Acquisition or Improvement of a Principal Residence," 71 *Neb. L. Rev.* 1095 (1992), for a discussion of § 461(g)(2).

PROBLEMS

Page 614:

1(a).   Under the *Kahler* case, checks are generally to be treated as cash for federal tax purposes. Debtor has a deduction in year one when the check is mailed. *Rev. Rul. 54-465.* Nevertheless, Lender has no income until actual or constructive receipt. Here the check is neither actually nor constructively received until year two. See Reg. §§ 1.446-1(c)(1)(i) and 1.451-2.

1(b).   Since the check is the equivalent of cash, Lender has income (*Kahler*) and Debtor a deduction for year one (*Rev. Rul. 54-465*).

1(c).   Lender has $25,000 of income in year one because Lender has received the cash (even though prepaid) and Lender has it as of right with no restrictions on its use. See the *North American Oil* case.

Debtor cannot claim a full deduction in year one. Prior uncertainty is now answered by the amortization treatment required by § 461(g)(1). Thus Debtor may deduct only $5,000 in year one. Cf. Comm'r v. Boylston Market Association at page 603 of the Text, and compare Zaninovich v. Comm'r, cited at page 605 of the Text. Both cases involve prepayment of deductible items other than interest, which is specifically covered by statute.

1(d).   Lender has prepaid income in year one as in problem 1(c), above. The result appears the same as in problem 1(c), above, to Debtor also. Section 461(g) made one exception ("points" on a principal residence) for prepayments. However, Congress might well reconsider if we view this case as very much like the § 461(g)(2) exception. Should there be a new § 461(g)(3)? (This is how the Code "grows.")

1(e).   Lender has income and Debtor a deduction of $10,000 in year two. Lender has no income until the payment is made (here year two), and Debtor no deduction until payment (again, year two). Note that Debtor may defer payments and thus bunch Debtor's deductions.

1(f).   This is an example of constructive receipt (see Reg. § 1.451-2) of income by Lender who has income in year one.

As the *Vander Poel* case at page 610 of the Text points out there is no doctrine of constructive payment and Debtor would not have a deduction until year two. The point seems settled, but the weak rationale of the court is that deductions are matters of legislative grace to be strictly interpreted and thus there is no deduction until payment.

1(g).   Seemingly Lender has no income until year two because Debtor's note is a mere evidence of indebtedness under *Williams v. Commissioner* and not the equivalency of cash under *Cowden*, and thus Lender would have $5,050 of income in year two. Cf. Lawrence B. Woodman, 36 T.C.M. 121 (1977), a situation where taxpayer unsuccessfully asserted that a note had cash equivalence in the year of receipt so as to preclude income on payment of the note. See Rev. Rul. 76-135, 1976-1 C.B. 114, where taxpayer immediately discounted the note at a local bank and was held to have income in year one, and see Chapter 24B2.

Debtor has a $5,050 deduction in year two when the payment is made regardless of the result to Lender. See *Rev. Rul. 76-135*, supra.

2(a).   Since no payment is received in year one and there is no constructive receipt in year one, Lawyer has no income in that year. At the end of year one Lawyer holds a receivable for services with a zero basis and presumably a $1,000 value. Similarly Client, having made no payment, has no tax consequences in year one.

In year two Lawyer collects on the receivable and has $1,000 of income (in excess of the zero basis for the receivable). Since Client's attorney's fees result in a deductible expense they are deductible when paid in year two. If personal expenses they would, of course, be nondeductible.

2(b).   Lawyer is paid and has income in year one. The tax consequences to Client are considered in the Credit Card Payment Note at page 612 of the Text. That Note points out there are three possible times when the payment may be deemed made:

(1)   at the time of the signing of the credit card chit;

(2)   at the time the credit card company pays the taxpayer's bill; or

(3)   at the time the taxpayer pays the credit card company

Despite an earlier contrary indication in Rev. Rul. 71-216, 1971-1 C.B. 96, the Treasury has adopted the position taken in the Note as it appeared in an earlier edition. Two rulings, Rev. Rul. 78-38 1978-1 C.B. 68, and Rev. Rul. 78-39, 1978-1 C.B. 73, agree the deduction occurs when the credit card charge is made and, under that rationale, the first possibility applies and the deduction would occur in November of year one. Cf. *Rev. Rul. 78-173*, discussed in the Manual for page 605 of the Text.

2(c).   Under the (Sugar) *Ray Robinson* case, 44 T.C. 20 (1965), Lawyer may arrange, prior to rendering services, when Lawyer will receive payment for those services. And if Lawyer is bound in by the contract Lawyer has no constructive receipt of all the income in year one. Thus Lawyer has $500 of income in year one and $500 of income in year two. Similarly, Client has a $500 deduction in each year.

2(d).   It seems pretty clear that Client's check was set apart so that Lawyer could have drawn upon it during year one.   As the check is the equivalent of cash, Lawyer has income in year one. The fact that Lawyer was ill and had no one to pick up the check makes no difference. See the *Loose* case cited in the problem. See, however, Beatrice Davis, 37 T.C.M. 42 (1978), where a check sent by certified mail could not be delivered when attempted on December 31, 1974, as the payee was not home, was not constructively received in 1974. The Court in *Davis* distinguished *Loose* on the basis that taxpayer had no knowledge or expectation that the income would be available to her in 1974. See Rev. Rul. 76-3, 1976-1 C.B. 114, reaching a result contrary to *Davis*.

Client would have a hard time asserting she had paid attorney in year one so as to support a deduction in that year. As previously noted under *Vander Poel* there is no doctrine of constructive payment, and at the end of year one Client has given neither cash nor its equivalent either to Lawyer or to one who might be considered Lawyer's agent. Cf. Baker v. Comm'r, 81 F.2d 741 (3rd Cir. 1936).

Page 629:

Compare Barnett Banks of Florida, Inc. and Subsidiaries v. Comm'r, 106 T.C. 103 (1996) (Rev. Proc. 70-21 applied) with Signet Bank Corp. v. Comm'r, 106 T.C. 117 (1996) (Rev. Proc. 70-21 not applied). In the Barnett Bank case, taxpayers issued annual credit cards which could be canceled at any time but required a pro rata refund to cardholders. The arrangement was held to be a services arrangement under which although the services were contingent, they were substantially ratable over the period. The *Barnett Bank* case distinguished the *Signet Bank* case which did not fall within Rev. Proc. 70-21 because the membership fee was nonrefundable and was paid in consideration for the card and for the establishment of the cardholder's limit and was not for services over a 12-month period.

Page 630:

In the Charles Schwab Corporation and Includable Subsidiaries v. Comm'r, 107 T.C. 282 (1996), the Tax Court concluded that an accrual method discount securities brokerage firm had to accrue brokerage commissions on the trade date (the day a trade occurs) rather than the settlement date (the day that payment is made from buyer to seller and the certificates are transferred from seller to buyer) because the "all events test" was satisfied on the trade date.

Page 631:

In Thor Power Tool Co. v. Comm'r, 439 U.S. 522 (1979), the Supreme Court disapproved a write-down of excess inventory to scrap value under the lower of cost or market method of valuation. The taxpayer, instead of offering the merchandise for sale at prices below replacement cost, continued to sell the written down inventory at original prices, and the Court concluded therefore that the taxpayer's accounting method did not clearly reflect income.

Page 631:

Under Rev. Proc. 92-98, 1992-2 C.B. 512, the Service, using § 446 discretionary power, provides special accounting rules that are available for sellers of durable goods (automobiles, household appliances etc.) when they sell multi-year warranty contracts and immediately pay a third party to cover the warranties. Normally an accrual method taxpayer would include the amount of the contract as income in the year it was sold, but would have to spread the deduction of the cost of the insurance over the life of the contract. Because of the obvious mismatching of income and deductions, the IRS allows manufacturers, wholesalers and retailers of durable consumer goods to spread the income from the contracts over the life of the contract. To receive this treatment the taxpayer must qualify and change to the Service Warranty Income Method (S.W.I.M.) of accounting. Under S.W.I.M., the taxpayer includes the difference between the price received for the warranty and the price paid for insurance as gross income in the year of sale. The remainder of the warranty contract is reduced to its present cash value and treated as installments over the life of the contract (not to exceed six years). Each year the taxpayer includes the amount of the annual payment and deducts the cost of the insurance attributable to that year.

PROBLEMS

Page 642:

1.   Under the accrual method of accounting Lawyer would include the $1,000 for the services in year one. Reg. §§ 1.446-(1)(c)(1)(ii) and 1.451-1(a). Note, however, § 448(d)(5) which in some circumstances would justify exclusion of the income. Assuming the $1,000 had been included in income in year one, at the end of year one, Lawyer holds a receivable with a basis and value of $1,000.

Similarly, all events have occurred to determine the fact of Client's liability and the amount, $1,000, can be determined with reasonable accuracy. § 461(h)(4). Economic performance occurred at the time Lawyer performed the services in year one. § 461 (h)(2)(A)(i). Therefore, if Client's attorney's fees are deductible expenses, they are deductible in year one.

236

Although cash flows in year two, under the accrual method Lawyer merely recovers basis and Client pays off the acknowledged liability and neither has any tax consequences in that year as a result of the payment.

2(a).   The government would argue, probably successfully, that interest prepaid to Lender, even though Lender is an accrual method taxpayer, should be included in gross income in the year of the prepayment. This is in keeping with the *New Capital Hotel Co.* case at page 620 of the Text. The prepayment would not fall within the government's limited two year deferral exceptions for prepaid services in *Rev. Proc. 70-21* discussed at page 629 of the Text. The Procedure is perhaps questionably made specifically inapplicable to prepaid rents and interest. Additionally, this prepayment extends beyond the end of the succeeding year.

The *Artnell* and the *Morgan Guaranty* cases raise a question as to how prepaid interest should be treated. Although both cases involved a prepayment for only a two-year period, theoretically the doctrine these cases applied might allow deferral of recognition of income in any situation in which purchased benefits relate to performance at specific future times. Arguably, Lender should be allowed to defer recognition of the prepaid interest received in year one for years two through five, and then the prepaid interest should be accounted for ratably over those later years.

Although Debtor prepaid the interest, Debtor would not be allowed a deduction until the year in which the liability for the interest accrues, i.e., until the all events test and the economic performance requirements are met. § 461(h). The Conference Committee Report for the Tax Reform Act of 1984 stated that in the case of interest, "economic performance occurs with the passage of time (that is, as the borrower uses, and the lender forgoes use of, the lender's money) rather than as payments are made." H. Rep. No. 98-861, 98th Cong., 2d Sess. 875 (1984). (Recall that § 461(g) specifies similar timing for *cash* method taxpayers.) Thus Debtor would have a $5,000 deduction in each of the five years. Unless *Artnell* and *Morgan Guaranty* foretell a change, under these facts both Lender and Debtor are treated the same whether they are on the cash or the accrual method.

2(b). For purposes of reporting income, the same issue as in problem 2(a), above, once again arises: whether inclusion of the $10,000 interest (*New Capital Hotel Co.*) or partial deferral of the prepaid interest (*Artnell* and *Morgan Guaranty*) should be allowed. Even though in problem 2(a), above, the full five year prepayment may be included in income in the first year, a payment spanning only a two year period might be partially deferred to the next year. Allowing a deferral of prepaid interest over a two year period was, of course, the result in the *Morgan Guaranty* case. Therefore Lender's recognition of $5,000 interest income may be deferred to year two. Note that *Rev. Proc. 70-21* cannot be used by Lender here because interest payments are excluded from that Procedure.

Debtor is required to deduct each year's $5,000 of interest as it accrues. § 461(h) and see problem 2(a), above. If deferral of the interest income is not allowed, Lender and Debtor are treated the same whether they are on the cash or the accrual method.

2(c). Lender's right to the $5,000 interest for year one became fixed and certain on December 31, and the $5,000 would be included in income in year one regardless of when paid. *Spring City Foundry Co.*

Debtor would be allowed a $5,000 deduction in year one since all events have occurred to determine the fact of Debtor's liability and the amount, $5,000, can be determined with reasonable accuracy. § 461(h)(4). See also *Rev. Rul. 57-463*. Additionally, the economic performance test, as set out in problem 2(a), above, was met in year one. Acceleration of the deduction under the accrual method (as compared with the cash method) provides a more realistic annual net income figure for Debtor, because the interest expense for year one is not a proper charge against income for the next year in which the interest was paid.

2(d). Under the rationale of *Spring City Foundry* an obligee cannot defer recognition of income just because an economic contingency raises a question whether a debt will ever be paid. The equalizer is that, if the debt becomes worthless in a subsequent year, the obligee will be allowed a bad debt deduction under § 166. See Chapter 23A and Rev. Rul. 80-361, 1980-2 C.B. 164. Nevertheless, "for interest income to be accruable, there must be a reasonable expectancy at the time of accrual, of receiving the interest." Kenneth P. Harrington, 31 T.C.M. 888, 893 (1972). Therefore, in this case, depending upon when Debtor's financial condition became serious, Lender may not be required to accrue the full year's interest.

In general, a deduction is allowed an accrual basis taxpayer when the taxpayer has satisfied the "all events" test and the "economic performance" test, even though an economic contingency raises a question whether payment will ever be made. Nevertheless whether a debtor may accrue interest (as opposed to other deductions) and be allowed a § 163 deduction when the debtor has neither the intention nor the means of paying it, is unsettled. The Tax Court's general rule is that " . . . deductions for accrued interest are proper where it cannot be categorically said at the time [the] deductions were claimed that the interest would not be paid, even though the course of conduct of the parties indicated that the likelihood of payment of any part of the disallowed portion was extremely doubtful." Edward L. Cohen, 21 T.C. 855, 857 (1954), citing D. J. Jorden, 11 T.C. 914, 925 (1948). See also, Fahs v. Martin, 224 F.2d 387 (5th Cir. 1955); Zimmerman Steel Co. v. Comm'r, 130 F.2d 1011 (8th Cir. 1942); Rev. Rul. 70-367, 1970-2 C.B. 37, generally allowing an interest deduction even though an economic contingency existed.

2(e).   This problem involves a legal contingency as opposed to an economic contingency. In general, accrual does not occur until a legal contingency is finally determined. See *Rev. Rul. 70-151* at page 617 of the Text and *Rev. Rul. 57-463* at page 634 of the Text; U.S. v. Consolidated Edison Co. of N.Y., 366 U.S. 380 (1961). Thus Lender has no income and Debtor has no deduction in year one. Tax consequences occur to both Lender and Debtor when the legal dispute is finally determined. According to the *Fifth Avenue Coach Line* case, 281 F.2d 556 (2d Cir. 1960), cert. den., 366 U.S. 964 (1961): (1) if appeal from a decision is taken then a contest is not finally determined until the appeal is finally determined or (2) if no appeal is taken then the contest ends when the right of appeal ends (see *Rev. Rul. 70-151*) or when there is clear evidence of a formal acquiescence to the lower court decision.

2(f).   *The North American Oil* claim of right doctrine applies and Lender has income in year one even though Lender may be required to return it.

With respect to Debtor, § 461(f), overriding the *Consolidated Edison* rule, provides an exception to the legal contingency rule. Section 461(f) permits Debtor to deduct the interest in the year when the cash payment is made. The four requirements for application of § 461(f) are specifically enumerated in the subparts of that provision and are met under the facts of this problem. Note that § 461(f) was amended by the Tax Reform Act of 1984 so as to require that economic performance occur before a taxpayer is allowed a deduction thereunder. § 461(f)(4). See also Reg. § 1.461-2(a)(1). If Debtor claimed the deduction under § 461(f), and it is subsequently determined that the interest was not due and Debtor then receives a refund, Debtor must report the refund as income in the year of recovery, except as provided in § 111, which is accorded broader scope than its precise language would suggest. See Southwestern Illinois Coal Corp. v. U.S., 491 F.2d 1337 (7th Cir. 1974), and Chapter 20B, infra.

3.   The first issue is whether Accrue may postpone recognition of income under the *Artnell* and *Morgan Guaranty* cases, using the rationale that, as the services are to be rendered at specific times in the future, deferral does not distort income. If such a postponement is deemed clearly to reflect income in year one Accrue would have $12,000 of income ($10 per month per student or 100 times $120) and $4,800 of expenses ($4 per month times 12 per student times 100) with a net result of $7,200 of taxable income in year one. In year two Accrue would again have $7,200 of net taxable income and one-half that amount for the 6 months of year three, or $3,600.

However, Accrue may not be allowed to defer the income. *Rev. Proc. 70-21*, promulgated after *Artnell*, but before *Morgan Guaranty*, would preclude Accrue from doing so because of the time span of the prepayment, which extends to services performed beyond the year after the year of payment. Query whether the Commissioner may properly draw a "clearly-reflect-income" line at this point? If deferral is not allowed, Accrue has $30,000 of income in year one except to the extent that § 448(d)(5) permits non-inclusion.

If the income cannot be deferred, the issue then becomes whether Accrue may establish a reserve for estimated expenses, taking a $12,000 deduction for actual expenses and charging $7,200 to the reserve in year one. Although there may have been some doubt before the enactment of § 461(h), § 461(h)(2)(B) makes it clear that where the liability of the taxpayer requires the taxpayer to provide services to another (the dance students), economic performance occurs and the deduction ripens *only* as the taxpayer provides the services. Accrue would not be permitted to establish a reserve for estimated expenses. This would result in Accrue having $30,000 of income and $4,800 of deductions, for a taxable income of $25,200 in year one. While likely, the expected result can certainly be seen as unsatisfactory when on these transactions taxable income for year one is compared with results for the next two years:

Year Two: expenses of $4,800 with a net loss of $4,800

Year Three: expenses of $2,400 with a net loss of $2,400

4(a).   As to Mr. Carpet Cleaner it will include the $3,000 in its gross income for year two, the year in which it receives the money. § 451(a) and Reg. § 1.451-1(c)(1)(i).

With respect to Widget Corporation, the issue is for what year it may take a deduction for the $3,000 of carpet cleaning expense. The "all events" test of § 461(h)(4), applicable to accrual method taxpayers, appears to be met in year one, i.e., all the events have occurred which determine the fact of the liability, and the amount of the liability is determinable with reasonably accuracy. However, § 461(h)(1), the "economic performance" test, provides that the all events test is not considered to be met at any time earlier than when economic performance with respect to the item occurs. Section 461(h)(2)(A)(i) provides that if the liability of the taxpayer, Widget, arises out of the providing of services to the taxpayer by another person, Mr. Carpet Cleaner, economic performance occurs as the person provides the services. In this case, economic performance occurs when Mr. Carpet Cleaner provides the services to Widget in year two. Consequently, Widget will not be allowed to deduct the $3,000 until year two.

4(b).   Mr. Carpet Cleaner is a cash method taxpayer, and it must include the $3,000 in its gross income for the year in which it is received, year one.

As to Widget, the result is the same as it is in problem 4(a), above, i.e., no deduction is allowed until year two. This is so even though Widget *pays* the $3,000 in year one. Section 461(h) makes it clear that no deduction is allowed to an accrual method taxpayer until economic performance occurs, which in this case, as determined in problem 4(a), above, is when the services are provided to Widget in year two. § 461(h)(2)(A)(i).

Note that Reg. §1.461-4(d)(6)(ii) provides a special rule that does not apply on these facts because the carpet cleaning is not expected to be done within 3 ½ months of payment. Under the regulation, a taxpayer is permitted to treat services or property as provided to the taxpayer as the taxpayer makes payment to the person providing the services or property if the taxpayer can reasonably expect the person to provide the services or property within 3 ½ months after the date of payment.

4(c).   Mr. Carpet Cleaner is a cash method taxpayer and will include the $3,000 in its income in the year of receipt, year two, unless the doctrine of constructive receipt requires its inclusion in year one. There are no facts to indicate the application of the doctrine of constructive receipt here.

Widget, though not paying the $3,000 until year two, will be allowed to deduct the expense in year one. The economic performance test is met in year one because the services are provided to Widget in year one, § 461(h)(2)(A)(i), and as discussed in problem 4(a), above, the other facets of the all events test are also met in year one.

4(d).   The issue in this problem is whether the recurring item exception to the economic performance test applies so as to allow Widget to take the $3,000 deduction in year one, rather than in year two when economic performance actually occurs. § 461(h)(3). There are four requirements that must be met before this exception will apply. The first requirement is that the all events test must otherwise be met during the taxable year. § 461(h)(3)(A)(i). As discussed in problem 4(a), above, the all events test is satisfied in year one.

Second, under § 461(h)(3)(A)(ii), economic performance must occur with respect to the item within the shorter of a "reasonable period" after the close of the taxable year or 8 1/2 months after the close of the taxable year. Reg. § 1.461-5(b)(1)(ii) requires that economic performance occur on or before the earlier of: (1) timely filing (including extensions) of a return for the year or (2) the 15th day of the 9th month after the close of the year. Since economic performance occurs on February 1, year two, one month after the close of the taxable year, the reasonable period test is met.

The third requirement is that the item be recurring in nature and that the taxpayer consistently treat the expense as incurred in the year the all events test is otherwise met. § 461(h)(3)A)(iii). Since Widget incurs approximately $3,000 of carpet cleaning expense every ten months, it is "recurring in nature." See Reg. § 1.461-5(b)(3). Though the facts do not state whether Widget consistently treats the item as incurred in the year the all events test is met, it is a safe bet that prior to the enactment of the economic performance test Widget did treat the item that way and that it will continue to do so if permissible under § 461(h).

The last requirement, set forth in § 461(h)(3)(A)(iv), is that *either* the item not be "material," *or* that the accrual of the item in the year the all events test is otherwise met results in a more accurate match against income than accruing the item in the year the economic performance test is met. The Conference Committee Report provides that in determining whether an item is "material," the size of the item both in absolute terms and in relative terms when compared to the taxpayer's income and other expenses is taken into account. H. Rep. No. 861, 98th Cong., 2d Sess. 873, 874 (1984). See Reg. § 1.461-5(b)(4). Thus, by comparing the $3,000 carpet cleaning expense with the $2,000,000 of income and $1,500,000 of "other expenses," it becomes apparent that the $3,000 of expense is not a material item. The exception of § 461(h)(3)(A) will apply so as to permit Widget to accrue the $3,000 of office supplies expense in year one, rather than defer its deductibility to year two.

4(e).   Since economic performance does not occur until October 1, year two, nine months after the close of the taxable year in which the all events test was otherwise met, the recurring item exception to the economic performance test, as discussed in problem 4(d), above, would not apply, and Widget would not be allowed to deduct the $3,000 until year two. The reason that the recurring item exception is not met is found in § 461(h)(3)(A)(ii), which requires that economic performance occur with respect to the item within the *shorter* of a reasonable period after the close of the taxable period or within eight and one-half months after the

243

close of the taxable year. See Reg. § 1.461-5(b)(1)(ii). Since economic performance here does not occur until nine months after the close of the taxable year, the recurring item exception is inapplicable and Widget therefore will not be allowed a deduction until year two.

PROBLEMS

Page 646:

1(a).   A would be allowed a $500 deduction in year one, whereas B would not have to include the $500 in gross income until year two. Under the accrual method of accounting, an expense is deductible in the year in which the two-prong "all events" and "economic performance" tests are met. The all events test is set forth in § 461(h)(4), which provides that an accrual method taxpayer may take a deduction for the year in which all the events have occurred which fix the liability, and the amount of the deduction can be determined with reasonable accuracy. Both of these requirements were met at the time A purchased the supplies, in year one. Additionally, economic performance occurred at the time A received the supplies from B, in year one. § 461(h)(2)(A)(ii). B, assuming that there is no constructive receipt, would include the $500 in income in the year it is actually received, year two. § 451(a) and Reg. § 1.451-1(a).

1(b).   B would again include the $500 in gross income in year two, but A would not be allowed a $500 deduction until year two. A is not allowed to deduct the $500 in year one, even though both the all events test and the economic performance test are met in year one, due to the application of § 267(a)(2).

Section 267(a)(2) provides, in effect, that no deduction is allowed to an accrual method payor until the amount is included in the cash method payee's gross income, if the payor and payee are related. Section 267(b)(1) provides that related persons include "members of a family," which § 267(c)(4) indicates includes ancestors and lineal descendants. Father and daughter are related and consequently the father cannot deduct the $500 until the daughter includes that amount in her gross income in year two. In an earlier edition we called attention to an overly harsh result where, in an earlier form, the statute permanently disallowed (did not merely defer) the deduction in this setting.

244

1(c).   In this situation, § 267(a)(2) is not applicable. It applies only where the related parties are an *accrual* method payor and a *cash* method payee. Thus, the *cash* method payor, A, would not receive a deduction until year two, the year in which the $500 was actually paid. § 461(a) and Reg. § 1.461-1(a)(1). The *accrual* method payee, B, would include the $500 in gross income in year one, the year in which all the events have occurred which fix the right to receive the income and the year in which the amount, $500, is determinable with reasonable accuracy. Reg. § 1.451-1(a).

2(a).   Section 267(a)(2) would apply. The issue in the situations presented in this problem is whether the accrual method payor, X Corporation, and the cash method payee, B, are related taxpayers within the meaning of § 267(b). This series of problems presents a relatively in-depth application of a set of attribution rules which are typical of other sets of attribution rules found throughout the Code.

Section 267(b)(2) provides that an individual and a corporation are related if that individual owns, directly or indirectly, *more* than 50 percent in value of the outstanding stock of the corporation. Since B owns 60 percent of the stock of X, B and X Corporation are related and therefore the rules of § 267(a)(2) apply.

2(b).   Section 267(a)(2) would again apply. The issue is whether B owns more than 50 percent in value of stock of X Corporation. Initially, it appears that B owns only 40 percent of the X Corporation stock. However, § 267(c)(2) provides that an individual is considered as owning the stock owned by a family member, which is defined in § 267(c)(4) as including an individual's spouse. Thus, under the so-called attribution rules of § 267(c), B is treated as owning the 15 shares of X Corporation stock owned by B's spouse. This means B "owns" 55 percent of the outstanding stock of X Corporation and consequently § 267(a)(2) is applicable. § 267(b)(2).

2(c).   Section 267(a)(2) is applicable to this situation. B owns 20 shares and, by attribution, the 15 shares held by B's spouse (see problem 2(b), above). Additionally, § 267(c)(1) provides that stock owned by or for a partnership is considered being owned proportionately by its partners. Since B has a 50 percent interest in the B and Z partnership, B constructively owns 50 percent of the shares of X Corporation held by the partnership, or 20 shares. Thus, B owns, directly and indirectly, 55 percent of the X Corporation stock, making B and X Corporation related parties within the meaning of § 267(b)(2). (As will be seen in problem 2(d), below, B will also be deemed to own the other 20 shares of X Corporation stock owned by the B and Z partnership via § 267(c)(1) and § 267(c)(3). B therefore is deemed to own 75 percent of the X Corporation stock.)

2(d).   Section 267(a)(2) would again be applicable to the situation presented. B actually owns 20 shares of X Corporation stock; B constructively owns the 15 shares of X Corporation owned by B's spouse § 267(c)(2); and B constructively owns 10 shares of the X Corporation stock held by the B and Z partnership by application of § 267(c)(1). In addition, under § 267(c)(3), B will be deemed to own the 10 shares of X Corporation stock attributed to Z under § 267(c)(1). Section 267(c)(3) specifically provides that an individual, B, owning any stock in a corporation, X, is considered as owning the stock owned, directly or indirectly, by B's partner, Z. Since, under § 267(c)(1), Z constructively owns 50 percent of the stock of X Corporation held by the B and Z partnership, B is deemed to own those 10 shares via § 267(c)(3). Thus B owns, actually and constructively, 55 percent of the shares of X Corporation. Section 267(c)(5) does not preclude such attribution.

2(e).   Section 267(a)(2) would not apply. The issue is again whether B and X Corporation are related within the meaning of § 267(b)(2), i.e., whether B owns more than 50 percent in value of the stock of X Corporation. Again, B actually owns 20 shares of X Corporation. B constructively owns the 15 shares held by B's spouse by application of § 267(c)(2). B also constructively owns the 10 shares of X Corporation attributed from the partnership to B's spouse under § 267(c)(1), by applying § 267(c)(2). Though the other 10 shares of X Corporation held by the partnership can be attributed to Z under § 267(c)(1) and then to S, B's spouse, under § 267(c)(3), they could not again be attributed to B under § 267(c)(2) because of the attribution cut-off rules of § 267(c)(5). Section 267(c)(5) provides, in part, that stock constructively owned by an individual by reason of the application of § 267(c)(3), i.e., the 10 shares of stock attributed from the partnership to Z to S, is not treated as owned by S for purposes of applying § 267(c)(2) to make another, B, the constructive owner of such stock. Thus, B owns only 45 percent in value of the X Corporation stock, and therefore B and X are not related parties within the meaning of § 267(b)(2) and § 267(a)(2) is inapplicable.

2(f).   The provisions of § 267(a)(2) would not apply to the situation presented. B actually owns 30 shares of X Corporation stock. B constructively owns 15 shares of X Corporation stock held by B's spouse via § 267(c)(2). The 10 shares held by S's brother would be attributed to S under the family attribution rules of § 267(c)(2) since family includes brothers and sisters under § 267(c)(4). However, those 10 shares cannot again be reattributed from S to B under § 267(c)(2) because § 267(c)(5) prohibits double family attribution, i.e., stock which a person owns because of § 267(c)(2) cannot be attributed to another person by again applying § 267(c)(2). Thus, B owns directly or constructively 45 shares, but B falls short of the "more than 50 percent" benchmark set forth in § 267(b)(2), and § 267(a)(2) does not apply.

Page 651:

> The question posed in this Note is considered in problem 2 at page 656 of the Text.

PROBLEMS

Page 656:

1(a). Section 1341 is applicable if the following three requirements are met:

> (1) An amount was included in the taxpayer's gross income in a prior taxable year because it appeared the taxpayer had an unrestricted right to it;
>
> (2) a deduction is allowable for the current year because it is established after the close of the prior year that the taxpayer did not have an unrestricted right to all or a portion of the amount and
>
> (3) the amount of the deduction exceeds $3,000.
>
> Note as well § 1341(b)(2), which makes § 1341 inapplicable if the amount included in gross income in the prior year resulted from the sale of stock in trade or inventory of the taxpayer.
>
> With regard to the paragraph (2) test, see Rev. Rul. 65-254, 1965-2 C.B. 20; and see problem 2(c), below. Once its requirements are met the operative rules of § 1341 provide that liability for the year is the lesser of the § 1341(a)(4) amount or the § 1341(a)(5) amount.

1(b). If § 1341 is applicable, the taxpayer is allowed to follow the *Lewis* result taking a deduction in the subsequent year (§ 1341(a)(4) or, if it results in a *lesser* amount under § 1341(a)(5), the taxpayer is required to compute tax liability for the current year without the deduction but reduced by the decrease in tax liability which would have occurred if the returned item had not been included in gross income in the prior year. Note that both computations are simply computations of tax for the *current* year.

1(c).   The result under § 1341(a)(4) is identical to the *Lewis* result. If § 1341(a)(5) results in a lower tax liability for the subsequent year, then §1341 is more helpful to the taxpayer than the *Lewis* case. Section 1341(a)(5) comes into play only when the taxpayer's top increment of income was taxed at a higher rate in the prior year than it will be in the current year. Actual rates for the years involved are taken into consideration. See Chapter 27A, infra.

2(a).   In Rev. Rul. 72-78, 1972-1 C.B. 45, the Commissioner acknowledges that under the facts of this problem, § 1341 is applicable because the following § 1341(a)(1)-(3) requirements are met:

   (1)   the prepaid commissions were included in Payer's gross income in a prior year because it appeared Payer had an unrestricted right to them;

   (2)   a deduction is allowable for the current year because it was established after the close of the prior year that Payer did not have an unrestricted right to a portion of such commissions; and

   (3)   the amount of the deduction exceeds $3,000.

Note, as well, § 1341(b)(2) is inapplicable.

2(b).   No. For § 1341 to apply § 1341(a)(1) requires that the item was previously included in gross income because it appeared the taxpayer had an "unrestricted right" to it. No such right appears in the case of embezzlement. Bernard A. Yerkie, 67 T.C. 388 (1976); McKinney v. U.S., 574 F.2d 1240 (5th Cir. 1978); Rev. Rul. 65-254, 1965-2 C.B. 50.

In Buff v. Comm'r, 496 F.2d 847 (2d Cir. 1974), a cash method taxpayer acknowledged his obligation to repay embezzled funds in the year of the embezzlement when he executed a confession of judgment. The Tax Court held that the acknowledgement converted the embezzlement to a loan, which was not taxable. The Second Circuit properly reversed, stating there was instant income at the time of the taking with no bona fide intent to repay, regardless of what subsequently happened in the year or a later year. Naturally no deduction would be allowed (if any is allowed under § 162 or § 165) until repayment was made, not merely for a confession of judgment. As noted in this problem, when repayment is made, § 1341 is inapplicable, if initially the receipt did not appear rightful.

2(c). No. Under Pike v. Comm'r, 44 T.C. 787 (1965), and Blanton v. Comm'r, 46 T.C. 527 (1966), aff'd per curiam, 379 F.2d 558 (5th Cir. 1967), taxpayer did have an unrestricted right to the commission under § 1341(a)(1) but the § 1341(a)(2) "established" requirement is not met.

2(d). A question might be initially raised whether § 1341(b)(2) would preclude use of § 1341 in this situation. Although Employer would be unable to use § 1341 because of § 1341(b)(2), nevertheless it should not disallow Payer's use. See Reg. § 1.1341-1(f). The merchandise is not "stock in trade of . . . [Payer] or property held by [Payer] . . ."

This is an attempt to present about as close a question as is possible whether § 1341 applies. Clearly § 1341(a)(3) is met. With respect to § 1341(a)(1) and (a)(2) it is also clear that a $10,000 deduction is allowable for year two. But the problems are whether the $10,000 was included in gross income for year one because it "appeared" Payer had an unrestricted right to the $10,000 and whether it was "established" after the close of year one that Payer did not *in year one* have an unrestricted right to the $10,000.

Under *Van Cleave* the subsequent occurrence of an event would not preclude a determination that the taxpayer had an "appearance" of an unrestricted right to the compensation when he received it. In other words the court rejected the Commissioner's argument that Van Cleave had an unrestricted right to the compensation in the year he received it because the right became restricted only upon the occurrence of a subsequent event.

The only subsequent event of consequence, in *Van Cleave*, was the Commissioner's determination that the compensation was excessive and therefore not deductible by the employer. The taxpayer had an *appearance* of an unrestricted right to the full amount of compensation in the year of receipt, not an unrestricted right, since a subsequent event might indicate the taxpayer did not have the right to the income. A subsequent event such as a customer returning merchandise for

250

whatever reason, would not preclude meeting the § 1341(a)(1) requirement.

The court in *Van Cleave* did not address whether the requirement of § 1341(a)(2) was met. Was it "established" after the close of year one that the taxpayer did not *in year one* have an unrestricted right to the $10,000? It was the subsequent occurrence of an event which established in *Van Cleave* that the taxpayer did not have a right to the compensation when he received it. But the case was remanded to the district court to see if the other requirements of § 1341 were met.

Based upon the *Pike* and *Blanton* decisions, it is not enough that it was established after year one that Payer had to repay the money. The question, as generally indicated in *Pike* (as well as in *Blanton*), is whether the repayment is required because of circumstances that existed in the year of receipt. (But see Rev. Rul. 72-78, 1972-1 C.B. 45, where § 1341 was applied when an apparent right in one year was upset because something *failed* to happen in a later year.) This approach sensibly reads together paragraphs (1) and (2) of § 1341(a) to indicate that the taxpayer's right to the payment must have been only apparent in that year and not then a real right.

Probably more facts are needed to answer this problem than are stated. Suppose for example in the problem that the contract was rescinded because the customer did not like the goods, and in order to generate business goodwill the employer simply agreed to take them back in the following year. Admittedly, it is unlikely that Payer who had earned the commission would have to repay it under such circumstances. Nevertheless, if that was his agreement with his employer, Payer could claim the deduction only in year two and no benefit under § 1341, because the obligation to repay arose out of circumstances that developed in year two (Cf. *Van Cleave*). In other words, Payer could not establish having an unrestricted right to the commission in the year of the sale.

On the other hand, suppose that, through a breach of an implied warranty or the failure of some other condition of the contract not involving any impropriety on the part of Payer (see Rev. Rul. 65-254, 1965-2 C.B. 50), the contract was voidable from its inception and again Payer had to repay the commission. In this instance it only appeared

251

that Payer had a right to the commission in the year of sale and, when Payer was later required to return the commission, §1341 would allow the deduction-tax reduction alternatives.

The difference between the results under these two assumptions is what is hinted at in the two questions at the end of the Note that precedes these problems. With regard to those two questions we are tempted to say: "Don't call us; we'll call you." The story comes to mind of the illegitimate litigant in the probate court who, when told by the judge, regretfully, that the employee was a technical bastard, told his honor that his attorney had said the same thing about the judge. The question is how much statutory nitpickery should go on here? If employee agrees with employer that the employee is to receive only "reasonable" salary within § 162(a), a required repayment later would rest on the determination that at the very time of payment the employee had only an apparent right to the amount found to be excessive. Invoking § 1341 would require subsequent establishment that, at the very time of receipt, employee "did not have an unrestricted right" to such amount. On the other hand, if employee agreed only to repay amounts *determined to be excessive*, it could be argued, in a hair-splitting fashion, that employee did have an unrestricted right to the amounts received at all times until there was later determination. Thus § 1341 would not apply. Actually the two cases are too close to justify different results and perhaps the Ruling should be viewed as too technical so that both arrangements could be considered within § 1341, seemingly consistent with its broad objective.

Page 657:

See Carter, "Donative Transfers of Expensed Property and the Fundamental Inconsistency Rule of Hillsboro," 58 *Tenn. L. Rev.* 151 (1991).

Page 657:

The *Sullivan* case has been followed in Rosen v. Comm'r, 611 F.2d 942 (1st Cir. 1980), with the First Circuit stating at page 944:

> Thus the rationale of the rule is that if the
> Rosens received a tax deduction in the year in

which the conveyance was made and thereafter the property was returned to them, they were subject to taxation to the extent of the value of the property returned, up to the amount of the charitable deduction previously taken.

PROBLEMS

Page 660:

1(a).   In the general words of § 111(a), gross income does not include income attributable to a recovery of an amount deducted in a prior year to the extent such amount did not reduce the amount of tax imposed in the deduction year. Here, in year one, the excess $3,000 of deduction did not reduce taxes as it did not further reduce taxable income (disregarding any consideration of § 172 which is appropriate under these facts). As a result, the $2,000 recovery is excluded from gross income.

1(b).   Under the rationale of problem 1(a), above, the $4,000 recovery would result in $3,000 of exclusion under § 111(a) and $1,000 of § 61 gross income.

1(c).   With the resurrection of the standard deduction and the death knell to the zero bracket amount, Rev. Rul. 56-447, 1956-2 C.B. 102, which had been declared obsolete by Rev. Rul. 79-15, 1979-1 C.B. 80, should also be resurrected. The Ruling appropriately takes the position that if a taxpayer uses the standard deduction foregoing itemized deductions in a prior year, any subsequent recovery of such itemized deductions are excluded from income by § 111(a). That aspect of the ruling was affirmed in Rev. Rul. 79-15, supra at page 82 which states:

> if a taxpayer did not itemize deductions for the year in which the state tax was paid, no amount of a subsequent refund attributable to that tax is includible in the taxpayer's gross income for the year in which the refund is received ...

Although there has been an amendment to the language of § 111 since the Ruling, its holding should still be intact.

2.   While the courts generally have upheld the integrity of the taxable year (*Lewis* and *Sullivan*), Congress in enacting § 111 and § 1341 have mixed a little equity with the integrity. And § 1341 is more equitable (really more favorable) than § 111. It gives Lewis even more than he wanted (i.e. the bigger saving of reducing the prior year's tax *or* a deduction in the current year.) On the other hand, § 111 provides a very limited tax benefit concept (an exclusion only to the extent there was no prior tax benefit). Perhaps in § 111 Congress should have required a recomputation of the prior year's taxable income without the deduction and have required inclusion in the later year's tax an amount based on the difference between the tax paid and the higher tax without the deduction. A parallel approach in § 1341, allowing only the § 1341(a)(5) (not the § 1341(a)(4) alternative) computation would seem equitable, if less favorable at times, to the taxpayer.

Page 672:

Fns. 38-42. See Kaplan, "Retirement Funding and the Curious Evalution of Individual Retirement Accounts," 7 *Elder L.J.* 283 (1999).

Page 674:

The following excerpt which considers Medical Savings Accounts may be reproduced and distributed to students:

Archer Medical Savings Accounts. In 1996 Congress used concepts similar to those that they employ for Qualified Plans, H.R. 10 Plans, and IRAs to enact an experimental program known as a Medical Savings Account (MSA), which in the year 2000 were retitled "Archer Medical Savings Account" in honor of former House Ways and Means Committee Chairman Bill Archer. With Coverdell Education Savings Accounts and Roth IRAs, need we say more about the trend mentioned at page 673 of the Text in conjunction with Roth IRAs? The idea behind MSAs is to allow an individual to purchase medical insurance at a low premium cost but with a high deductible amount and to self-insure by using an MSA trust to pay the deductible amount when medical expenses are incurred.[1] An MSA trust is similar to a deferred compensation arrangement except that it is used to pay uninsured

---

[1] I.R.C. §§ 106(b), 220.

medical expenses of an individual and the individual's spouse and dependents rather than to make retirement payments.[2] Under the MSA program, an initial group limited to a maximum of 750,000 individuals who are either self-employed or employees of small businesses having 50 or fewer employees are allowed to use an MSA trust between the years 1997 and 2002.[3] At the heart of the MSA mechanism is the requirement that such individuals have a health insurance plan with a "high deductible" amount which in the case of "self-only" coverage requires the individual to pay the first $1500 to $2250 of expenses (with a maximum of $3000 of out-of-pocket expenses) and in the case of "family coverage" requires payment of the first $3000 to $4500 of expenses (with a maximum of $5500 of out-of-pocket expenses).[4]

The amount which may be contributed to an MSA trust each month is limited to 1/12 of 65% of the deductible amount under the insurance plan for self-only coverage and 75% for family coverage.[5] MSA trusts are similar to deferred compensation arrangements in several ways. If an employer makes such contributions, they are both deductible by the employer and excluded from the employee's gross income.[6] If an employee or self-employed person makes such contributions, they are deductible by the person[7] as an above-the-line deduction.[8] Income earned on the MSA trust fund is generally excluded from gross income.[9] Unlike deferred compensation arrangements,

---

[2] I.R.C. §§ 220(d), 106(b)(6).

[3] I.R.C. § 220(c)(1), (c)(4), (i), (j).

[4] I.R.C. § 220(c)(2). These amounts are adjusted for inflation.
I.R.C. § 220(g).

[5] I.R.C. §§ 220(b)(2), 106(b)(1).

[6] I.R.C. 106(b)(1), (3).

[7] I.R.C. § 220(a). No deduction is allowed if the amount is excluded under I.R.C. § 106(b). I.R.C. § 220(b)(5).

[8] I.R.C. § 62(a)(16).

[9] I.R.C. § 220(e)(1).

distributions from an MSA trust are excluded from the recipient's gross income to the extent that they are used to pay unreimbursed medical expenses under the high deductible plan.[10] Other distributions from an MSA trust are not only included in gross income but also are subject to an additional 15 percent tax,[11] although the additional tax is not applicable to payments made to an individual who is over 65, disabled, or dies.[12]

---

[10] I.R.C. § 220(d)(2), (f)(1). This includes payments to an individual's surviving spouse. I.R.C. § 220(f)(8). Such amounts shall not qualify as deductible medical expenses under I.R.C. § 213. I.R.C. § 220(f)(6).

[11] I.R.C. § 220(f)(2), (4)(A).

[12] I.R.C. § 220(f)(4)(B), (C).

PART SIX: THE CHARACTERIZATION OF INCOME AND DEDUCTIONS •

Chapter 21. Capital Gains and Losses

Page 683:

> Fn 16: Other articles discussing capital gains and losses include: Mayhall, "Capital Gains Taxation - The First One Hundred Years," 41 *La. L. Rev.* 81 (1980), providing a history of capital gains taxation and the rationale for preferential treatment; Katsoris, "In Defense of Capital Gains," 42 *Fordham L. Rev.* 1 (1973), suggesting that the capital gains tax be put on a sliding scale so that gains on property held for long periods of time would be taxed at lower rates than gains on property held for shorter periods; Foulis, "The Impact of Inflation on Capital Gains," 59 *ABAJ* 855 (1973); and Note, "Inflation and the Federal Income Tax," 82 *Yale L. J.* 716 (1973).

PROBLEMS

Page 694:

1(a). T's net capital gain would be $35,000. T has LTCGs of $15,000 and $20,000 or a total of $35,000 and no LTCLs resulting in a NLTCG (§ 1222(7)) of $35,000. Since T has zero NSTCLs (§ 1222(6)), T has a NCG under § 1222(11) of $35,000.

1(b). T's net capital gain is made up of:
   (1)   a $15,000 collectible gain (see § 1(h)(6)(A)) which is taxed at a 28% rate under § 1(h)(1)(E); and
   (2)   a $20,000 adjusted net capital gain (see § 1(h)(4)) which is taxed at 20% rate under § 1(h)(1)(C).

1(c). T's tax liability for the year is $23,200, computed below. Although we wouldn't expect students to plug in all the numbers, we are doing so in case a question comes up in class.

   1(h)(1)(A): a § 1(c) 30% tax on $50,000, the *greater* of: $15,000
   (i) $50,000, TI less NCG, $85,000 - $35,000
   or

(ii) zero, the *lesser* of:
      (I) zero (under our assumed facts)
         or
      (II) $65,000, TI $85,000 - ANCG $20,000

1(h)(1)(B): a 10% tax on zero $20,000 ANCG "as does not exceed" (up to) zero (zero TI taxed at 15% less $65,000, which is TI ($85,000) less ANCG ($20,000))	0
1(h)(1)(C): a 20% tax on $20,000 (ANCG $20,000 less (B) amount of zero)	4,000
1(h)(1)(D): (there is no unrecaptured § 1250 gain)	0
1(h)(1)(E): a 28% tax on $15,000 TI $85,000 less 70,000 (the amounts taxed in (A)-(D) $50,000 plus $20,000)	4,200
Tax Liability	$23,200

1(d). The ANCG stock would now be taxed at an 18% rate (§ 1(h)(1)(C), 1(h)(2)(B), 1(h)(9)). Thus, T's tax liability would be $22,800, computed as follows:

§ 1(h)(1)(A):	$15,000
§ 1(h)(1)(B):	0
§ 1(h)(1)(C): 18% of $20,000	3,600
§ 1(h)(1)(D):	0
§ 1(h)(1)(E): 28% of $15,000	4,200
Tax Liability	$22,800

2(a). In this situation, Taxpayer has a $5,000 NCG under § 1222(11). Taxpayer has a $10,000 LTCG (§ 1222(3)) less a $5,000 LTCL (§ 1222(4)) which results in a $5,000 NLTCG (§ 1222(7)) and since Taxpayer has no NSTCL, there is a $5,000 NCG.

The NCG is taxed at a 20% rate under § 1(h)(1) which nets within each class leaving only the 20% gain to be taxed. Taxpayer's tax liability on the gain is $1,000.

If we assume Taxpayer has $50,000 of ordinary income taxed at a flat 30% rate, Taxpayer's tax liability is $16,000, computed below.

Taxpayer has a zero 28% rate gain because the $5,000 collectible gain under § 1(h)(5)(A)(i) is reduced by the $5,000 collectible loss under § 1(h)(5)(B)(i) leaving the $5,000 of adjusted net capital gain as defined in § 1(h)(4), $5,000 reduced by zero (the sum of the unrecaptured § 1250 gain and 28% rate gain). Under § 1(h)(1)(C) that gain is taxed at a 20% rate. Tracking the statute, Taxpayer's tax liability is:

§ 1(h)(1)(A): a § 1(c) tax on $50,000	$15,000
§ 1(h)(1)(B): 10% of zero	0
§ 1(h)(1)(C): 20% of $5,000	1,000
§ 1(h)(1)(D): no unrecognized § 1250 gain	0
§ 1(h)(1)(E): 28% of zero	0
Tax Liability	$16,000

2(b)   Again, Taxpayer has a $5,000 § 1222(11) NCG. Since gains and losses are first netted within each class, the 20% loss wipes out the 20% gain leaving the $5,000 28% gain to be taxed at a 28% rate. See § 1(h)(4),(5).

Making the same assumptions as in problem 2(a), above, Taxpayer's tax liability will be $16,400, the total of $15,000 of tax on ordinary income and $1,400 of tax on the NCG (28% of $5,000).

2(c).   If Taxpayer's loss was a STCL (rather than a collectible loss), the results would be the same as in problem 2(a), above. There would still be a $5,000 NCG under § 1222(11), the excess of a $10,000 NLTCG less a $5,000 NSTCL. Under § 1(h)(5)(A)(i), the $5,000 collectible gain is reduced by the NSTCL (see § 1(h)(5)(B)(ii)), resulting in a zero 28% rate gain and leaving only the $5,000 stock gain which is taxed at a 20% rate under § 1(h)(1)(C). Making the same assumptions as in problem 2(a), above, Taxpayer's tax liability would again be $16,000.

259

3.   *Additional Problem.* Although we did not publish this problem in the Text, one may want to assign it:

Single Taxpayer simply "invests" for a living and has no salary, but Single has (1) a gain of $10,000 from the sale of stock held for less than 1 year; (2) a gain of $15,000 on a "collectible" held for 2 years; and (3) a gain of $20,000 on stock held for 15 months. Disregarding any deductions (including the standard deduction and personal exemption), what is Single's tax liability in the year 2002?

Answer. This problem requires students to actually track the statute. If you're brave enough to assign it, the answer is $7,155 of tax liability, computed as follows:

1(h)(1)(A): a § 1(c) tax on *$25,000*, the *greater* of: $3,450
    (i) $10,000, $45,000 (TI) less $35,000 (NCG)
    or
    (ii) $25,000, the *lesser* of:
        (I) $27,950 (§ 1(c))
        or
        (II) $25,000, TI $45,000 - ANCG $20,000

1(h)(1)(B): 10% of $2,950   295
    $20,000 ANCG "as does not exceed" (up to)
    $2,950 ($27,950) (§ 1(c)) less $25,000)
    (TI $45,000 less ANCG $20,000)

1(h)(1)(C): 20% of $17,050   3,410
    ANCG $20,000 less the $2,950 (B) amount

1(h)(1)(D): no unrecaptured § 1250 gain   0

1(h)(1)(E): 28% of zero   0
    TI $45,000 less $45,000 (the sum of the (A)-(D)
    amounts, $25,000 plus $2,950 plus $17,050)   _____

Tax Liability $7,155

Note that Single's STLG of $10,000 which is taxed as ordinary income and $15,000 of net capital gain that would ordinarily be taxed at 28%

is taxed at § 1(c) ordinary income rates, $2,950 of ANCG is taxed at 10%, and the remaining $17,050 of ANCG is taxed at 20%.

Page 699:

The Code would be simplified if the rule were that individuals, like corporations, were permitted to deduct capital losses only to the extent of capital gains. There would be no § 1211(b) excess computation and, more importantly, the § 1212(b) computation would be substantially simplified. The suggested simplification would, of course, be at the expense of the § 1211(b) maximum $3,000 reduction of ordinary income. This involves a question of tax simplification at the expense of a small economic benefit to taxpayers. *Query*: Which is the better of the two?

Page 699:

If one feels compelled to illustrate § 1212(b)(2)(A)(ii) and (B), try out the following problem: Assume a taxpayer has $1,000 of taxable income prior to a $2,000 § 151 personal exemption and consideration of capital losses in a year in which he has LTLG: $2,000; LTCL: $10,000; STCG: $2,000; and STCL: $4,000. Determine his § 1211(b) excess and his § 1212(b) carryover.

Answer: Under § 1211(b) his excess amount is $3,000, the lesser of $3,000 or $10,000. Under § 1212(b)(2)(B) his adjusted taxable income is taxable income [$4,000] plus $5,000 (the $3,000 § 1211(b) amount plus the $2,000 § 151 amount) or $1,000. Under § 1212(b)(2)(A) there is $1,000 of constructive STCG (the lesser of $3,000 or $1,000). Now applying § 1212(b)(1)(A), there is a $1,000 STCL carryover ($4,000 STCL less $3,000 STCG) and an $8,0000 LTCL carryover ($8,000 NLTCL less no NSTCG).

PROBLEM

Page 699:

1.   Losses are deductible under § 165(a) if, in the case of an individual, they meet an origin test imposed by § 165(c). Here we deal with losses

261

that are deductible because, presumably, they arose in transactions entered into for profit within the scope of § 165(c)(2).

The deduction of losses from the sale or exchange of capital assets is further restricted by § 1211. Under § 1211(b), non-corporate capital losses are deductible to the extent of capital gains plus the lesser of two amounts described in § 1211(b)(1) and (2). Here, the taxpayer may deduct capital losses of $2,400 from ordinary income under § 1211(b)(2). The § 1211(b) amount is the lesser of:

§ 1211(b)(1):	$3,000
§ 1211(b)(2): (the excess of $7,000 of capital losses over $4,600 of capital gains)	2,400

The taxpayer's "net capital loss" under § 1222(10) is zero, so there will be no capital loss carryover. The taxpayer's "net capital loss" is defined in § 1222(10) as the excess of capital losses over the sum allowed under § 1211. Here, capital losses total $7,000 ($6,000 plus $1,000), and the amount allowed under § 1211 also equals $7,000 ($4,600 (gains) plus $2,400 (§ 1211(b) amount)). Thus, there is no "excess", and no "net capital loss" under § 1222(10). Consequently, § 1212(b) does not apply, and there will be no capital loss carryover. Because of the amendment to § 1211(b) in the '86 Act, the above conclusion will always be reached in cases where § 1211(b)(2) sets the limit on additional capital loss deductions.

Even if § 1212(b) applied, when one plugs in the numbers, the end result is that there is no carryover. Section 1212(b)(2)(A)(i) would construct $2400 of STCG resulting in a NSTCG of $4,000, with the end result that under § 1212(b)(1)(B) there would be no LTCL carryover.

2.   Under § 1211(b) Taxpayer may deduct capital losses to the extent of gains ($4,000) plus additional losses of $3,000 from ordinary income. He has a "net capital loss" under § 1222(10) of $7,000, and a LTCL carryover of $7,000 computed under § 1212(b).

The § 1211(b) amount is $3,000, the lesser of:

§ 1211(b)(1):	$ 3,000
§ 1211(b)(2) (the excess of capital losses of	

$14,000 over capital gains of $4,000): $10,000

Since there is a "net capital loss," the § 1212(b) computation must be made and the carryover is computed as follows:

§ 1212(b)(1)(A): $ 0

The $3,000 constructive short-term capital gain causes a net short-term capital gain, of $1,000; thus there is no excess NSTCL.

§ 1212(b)(1)(B): $ 7,000

The $3,000 constructive short-term capital gain causes a $1,000 NSTCG. Thus, under § 1212(b)(1)(B), NLTCL of $8,000 less NSTCG of $1,000 results in a LTCL carryover of $7,000.

The result is explained by pointing out that to "pay for" the $3,000 of reduction of ordinary income, the statute first uses the NSTCL (here $2,000) and that the remaining $1,000 comes out of NLTCL leaving only $7,000 of LTCL to be carried over.

One may want to take the carryover discussion a bit further. As pointed out in the Text, the LTCL carryovers are treated as a loss from capital assets whose gains would be taxed at a 28% rate (see § 1(h)(5)(A)(ii)(IV)). Such losses first wipe out the 28% rate gains and then work their way down the § 1(h) rate scale.

Page 705:

The Tax Court reversed its position on characterization consequences when a taxpayer who owns property primarily for sale to customers in the ordinary course of business receives a condemnation notice and subsequently disposes of the property. In prior cases, it had held there could be an alteration of intent between the time of the notice and the sale. See e.g., Tri-S Corp. v. Comm'r, 48 T.C. 316 (1967), aff'd on other grounds, 400 F.2d 862 (10th Cir. 1968). The Tax Court now treats the notice as a constructive sale and holds that characterization is to be determined with respect to the purpose for which the property is held at the time of notice. Daugherty v. Comm'r, 78 T.C. 623 (1982).

Page 707:

> Section 1236 does not expressly foreclose reclassification of securities originally classified by dealers as investments if they are sold at a gain, because that reclassification would produce ordinary income; and that situation does not present a possibility of dealers manipulating their taxes.

Page 717:

> The rhetorical question regarding the § 1001(e)(3) exception can be answered in the affirmative for the reason that the exception allows 100% use of basis.

PROBLEMS

Page 717:

1. Agent has $50,000 of ordinary income. Although Agent might argue that she has made a sale of property (her contract) to Company which should have long term capital gain consequences, nevertheless it seems settled that Agent has ordinary income, because the only thing she relinquished was her right to receive income for future services. Homer S. Deal, 32 T.C.M. 216 (1973). Even if Agent's contract constituted property and a capital asset it would seem that there has been no transfer of the contract, only its extinction which is not a sale. Cf. Galvin Hudson at page 735 of the Text; but see § 1241 regarding certain other cancellations considered in problem 3, below.

2. The character of the gain in the *Stranahan* case is ordinary. The taxpayer sold only the right to income and not the underlying property as well. Cf. *Hort*.

3(a). L has $200,000 of ordinary income. L is selling only the right to rental income without also selling the income producing property and under the *Hort* case, L would have ordinary income even though the sale is to a third party. See also Comm'r v. P.G. Lake, Inc., 356 U.S. 260 (1958).

3(b). L has $20,000 of ordinary income. This *is* the *Hort* case. See also Reg. § 1.61-8(b).

264

3(c).   T probably has $20,000 of LTCG. Section 1241 makes it clear that such a transaction is to be treated as an exchange. As regards T, T has exchanged property, T's leasehold interest. Unless T is in the business of selling lease agreements, T's gain is capital gain. What § 1241 principally does is preclude the possible contention by the Government that the lease was merely extinguished rather than exchanged. Cf. *Galvin Hudson* at page 735 of the Text. Even before § 1241 an exchange result was sometimes recognized on these facts, e.g., Comm'r v. Golonsky, 200 F.2d 72 (3rd Cir. 1952), cert. den., 345 U.S. 939 (1953), where the taxpayer transferred his entire interest in underlying property or a coterminous portion thereof.

3(d).   T has a $10,000 LTCG. This situation is in substance the *Metropolitan Building Company* case. In that case T transferred the interest in the lease to L (rather than to S as in the problem), but that factual difference and the fact that this is only one of two parcels (i.e. an underlying portion of T's interest) would not affect the result.

3(e).   T has $1,200 of ordinary income each month. T continues to own some vestiges of the underlying property (a reversion in case of S's default) and consequently T's sublease, even though a coterminous portion, is a mere carve-out of less than T's entire property interest.

4(a).   B has a $10,000 LTCG. As B originally purchased the income interest and B has a $50,000 cost basis remaining in it, B's gain is $10,000. The gain is LTCG. Bell's Estate v. Comm'r, 137 F.2d 454 (8th Cir. 1943). McAllister v. Comm'r, 157 F.2d 235 (2d Cir. 1946), cert. den., 330 U.S. 826 (1947), reaches the same LTCG result. The Commissioner has indicated he will follow the *McAllister* case. Rev. Rul. 72-243, 1972-1 C.B. 233.

4(b).   B has a $2,500 LTCG. B would have a $12,500 basis in this 1/4 of the purchased interest and B would have a $2,500 gain, which would be LTCG. The theory here is the same as in the assignment of income cases determining who is taxed on the income. Since B sold a coterminous portion of B's entire underlying interests B would have a LTCG. See *Blair* at page 259 of the Text.

4(c).   B has a $60,000 LTCG. Since B acquired the interest by gift, § 1001(e)(1) applies and B has no basis in the interest sold. See the Note at page 715 of the Text. The LTCG character of B's gain is based on the same rationale as used in problem 4(a), above.

4(d).   B has a $10,000 LTCG. Although B inherited the interest, § 1001(e)(3) creates an exception to § 1001(e)(1) where, as here, the entire interest in the property (that of both B and R) is sold; and B's basis of $50,000 determined under the uniform basis provisions of Reg. § 1.1014-5, is accorded full recognition. The character of B's gain is the same as in problem 4(a), above.

4(e).   R has a $50,000 LTCG. A remainder interest is "property" for purposes of § 1221. The sale of such an interest results in capital gain. It is assumed that R has a sufficient holding period for the capital gain to be long term. Cf. § 1223(2) and § 1223(11). R's adjusted basis of $100,000 may be taken into account in computing R's realized gain. Section 1001(e) is not applicable since a remainder interest does not constitute a "term interest".

Page 718:

For a number of years, the *Corn Products* doctrine was substantially expanded beyond its original facts. See, for example, Becker Warburg Paribas Group, Inc. v. United States, 514 F. Supp. 1273 (N.D. Ill. 1981) (investment and securities corporation sustained ordinary loss on sale of stock exchange seat (traditionally, a capital asset) because the seat was used to generate ordinary income in the everyday course of business); Chemplast, Inc. v. Comm'r, 60 T.C. 623 (1973), aff'd. in an unpublished opinion (3rd Cir. 1974) (ordinary loss on loans to newly-formed corporation to acquire services of research scientist because formation and funding was integrally related to creditor's business); and cf. Wallace L. Hirsch, 30 T.C.M. 1008 (1971) (ordinary loss on stock purchased as a condition of employee retaining employment). In more recent years, prior to *Arkansas Best*, the courts had begun to restrict the expansion of the doctrine. See, for example, Pollack v. Comm'r, 69 T.C. 142 (1977) (*Corn Products* was inapplicable to the sale of a partnership interest (i.e., it did not override § 741) even though the interest was acquired to secure a source of business supply); W. W. Windle Co., 65 T.C. 694 (1976), (court refused to expand *Corn Products* to situation where an acquisition of stock, although motivated primarily by need to acquire captive customer, was also motivated by substantial investment purposes). The problem below considers the *Corn Products* doctrine after *Arkansas Best*.

Page 723:

> The *Arkansas Best* case is discussed in Tolman, "The *Arkansas Best* Decision: Taking *Corn Products* Off the Taxpayer Menu," 8 *Virg. Tax Rev.* 705 (1989); Kleinbard and Greenberg," Business Hedges after *Arkansas Best*," 43 *Tax L. Rev.* 393 (1988); O'Neill, "Arkansas Best Corp. v. Commissioner -- The Demise of the Corn Products Doctrine? 35 *Wayne L. R.* 1481 (1989).

PROBLEM

Page 730:

> Prior to the Supreme Court's *Arkansas Best* decision narrowly interpreting the *Corn Products* case to simply be a broad interpretation of § 1221(1), case law in effect wrote in a judicial exception to § 1221: the *Corn Products* doctrine. Under the exception, if the acquisition and disposition of property were essentially business motivated, any gain or loss on the property was ordinary gain or loss. See, i.e. Mansfield Journal v. Comm'r, 274 F.2d 284 (6th Cir. 1960); Western Wire and Liquor Co., 18 T.C. 1090 (1952), acq. 1958-1 C.B. 6. See also W. W. Windle Co., 65 T.C. 694 (1976). Under this broad interpretation of *Corn Products*, T would have a $50,000 ordinary loss.

> As a result of the *Arkansas Best* case, the result will be $50,000 of long-term capital loss. The *Arkansas Best* case has limited *Corn Products* to a situation where a broad interpretation is given to the § 1221(1) inventory exception. In effect, the Supreme Court has overruled many of the prior *Corn Products* cases.

> Section 1221(a)(7) will not change the result here. The purchase of the Corporation X stock would not be a hedging transaction as defined in § 1221(b)(2).

Page 730:

The *Kenan* case involved characterization of a gain on satisfaction of a pecuniary bequest. Recent legislation under § 1239 generally makes § 1239 applicable to a transfer from an estate to a beneficiary of the estate if the property is depreciable by the beneficiary. See page 769. However, § 1239 is inapplicable to a pecuniary bequest from an estate to a beneficiary of an estate. § 1239(b)(3). Cf. § 267(b)(13).

Page 740:

Section 1234A is inapplicable to foreign currency to the extent that § 988(a)(1)(A) provides ordinary gain or loss treatment.

PROBLEM

Page 741:

1. This problem provides a simple illustration of the *Kenan* and *Hudson* dichotomy and also provides a review of the measurement of gain or loss as previously seen in Chapter 6. Creditor has a $1,000 gain, measured by the difference between Creditor's amount realized (the $5,000 value of General Motors stock) and $4,000 (cost basis and adjusted basis) in the note. Debtor has a $3,000 gain measured by the difference between the relief of a $5,000 obligation (cf. the *Old Colony Trust* and *Crane* cases) and $2,000 (cost basis and adjusted basis) in the General Motors stock.

    The next step is to characterize the gains above. The first issue is whether the note and stock are capital assets to Creditor and Debtor, respectively. If in either case they are not, then the gain to the taxpayer is ordinary income. We are told that Creditor's note was purchased as an investment and thus assume that it is not held in Creditor's trade or business; in addition we will assume Debtor is not a dealer and the stock is a capital asset to Debtor. Cf. § 1236.

    The issue then becomes whether the requisite sale or exchange is present. Here the result seems somewhat bizarre. Debtor has an exchange under the *Kenan* case because the stock which Debtor transfers is not extinguished on the transfer; but Creditor does not have

268

an exchange under the *Galvin Hudson* case because the note which Debtor transfers is extinguished in the transaction and the amendments made to § 1271(b) are not yet in effect with respect to an obligation issued by an individual prior to June 8, 1997 or purchased by a creditor prior to June 9, 1997. Students should be alerted to the effective dates (which are applicable here) and that Debtor would have had an exchange if the note had been purchased by Creditor after June 8, 1997.

Thus Creditor has $1,000 of ordinary income and Debtor has a $3,000 long-term capital gain. Some students will be troubled by this difference in result to the taxpayers. However, Creditor could have converted the gain to capital gain by selling the note to a third party prior to its collection.

Page 741:

The Tax Court applied the *Arrowsmith* doctrine to payment of a settlement of a violation of § 12(1) of the Securities Act of 1933, characterizing the payment as a LTCL. Paul H. Smith, 67 T.C. 570 (1976). The Court did not however retreat from its non-application of *Arrowsmith* to voluntary payments of alleged § 16(b) violations; it merely concluded that the relationship of taxpayer's capital gain to alleged § 12(1) violation payments was "more direct" than a capital gain is to alleged § 16(b) violation payments.

Page 755:

A popular offbeat investment device has been the commodity tax straddle. The Economic Recovery Tax Act of 1981 and the Tax Reform Act of 1984 added several code sections designed to prevent the tax avoidance aspects of straddles. The Senate Finance Committee (Sen. Rep. No. 97-144, 97th Cong., 1st Sess. p. 146, 1981-2 C.B. 469) explains the basic theory of the commodity tax straddle as follows:

> Simple commodity tax straddles generally are used to defer tax on short-term capital gain from one tax year to the next tax year and, in many cases, to convert short-term capital gain realized in the first year into preferentially taxed long-term capital gain in a later year. . . . A simple

commodity tax straddle is constructed by taking equal long and short positions in futures contracts in the same commodity with different delivery dates. The two positions, called "legs," are expected to move in opposite directions but with approximately equal absolute changes. Thus, for example, if one leg of a straddle in future contracts increases $500 in value, the other leg can be expected to decrease in value by about the same amount. By maintaining balanced positions, the risks of the transaction are minimized.

The taxpayer can then sell the leg that has decreased in value and realize a loss, while holding the other leg in order to postpone recognition of the gain. The Senate Report discusses further tax avoidance possibilities. (*Id.* at 155-56 and at 474.)

The Tax Reform Act of 1984 (Act 101-108, P.L. No. 98-369, 98 Stat. 678 (1984)) generally continued the statutory scheme enacted by ERTA, and additionally expanded the coverage of these tax straddle rules.

Two code sections govern the treatment of gain or loss on commodities futures and related transactions. Section 1256 applies to "§ 1256 contracts" which are regulated futures contracts, foreign currency contracts, nonequity options and dealer equity options. § 1256(b). Each § 1256 contract held by the taxpayer at the close of the taxable year is treated as sold for its fair market value on the last business day of the year. Forty percent of the gain or loss from the sale of a contract is treated as short-term gain or loss; the other sixty percent is treated as long-term gain or loss, regardless of holding period. § 1256(a)(3). Special rules govern the carryback and carryover of losses on § 1256 contracts. § 1212(c).

These rules are expressly inapplicable to "hedging transactions" - transactions entered into in the normal course of the taxpayer's trade or business primarily to reduce the risk of price changes, interest rate changes, or currency fluctuations. §§ 1256(e)(1),(2); 1221(b)(2). Gain or loss on a "hedging transaction" which is timely identified as such is treated as ordinary income or loss as the case may be. See § 1221(a)(7) at page 729 of the Text.

Section 1092 limits the recognition of loss on "positions" that are part of straddles. A "position" is an interest, including a futures or forward contract or option, in actively-traded personal property other than stock. § 1092(d). A "straddle" means offsetting positions with respect to actively traded personal property. § 1092(c), (d)(1). Positions are offsetting if there is a substantial diminution of the taxpayer's risk of loss from one position because of one or more other positions that he holds. § 1092(c)(2). The section also provides that in several situations positions are presumed to be offsetting. § 1092(c)(3). Under § 1092, the loss from any position may be taken into account for any taxable year only to the extent that the loss exceeds the unrecognized gain with respect to any offsetting positions. § 1092(a)(1). "Unrecognized gain" is the amount of gain a taxpayer would take into account if the taxpayer sold a position for its fair market value on the last business day of the taxable year, i.e., the amount of gain which has been realized but not recognized as of the close of the taxable year. § 1092(a)(3)(A). Disallowed losses are carried forward to the next year and are subject to the same loss disallowance rules in that year. § 1092 (a)(1)(B).

If all of the offsetting positions in a straddle are § 1256 contracts, then § 1092 does not apply to the straddle. § 1256(a)(4). However, a taxpayer may elect to have only § 1092 apply to a clearly identified "mixed straddle," a straddle in which at least one but not all positions are § 1256 contracts. § 1256(d). See § 1256(d)(4).

Section 1092 provides a special rule under which any loss with respect to an "identified straddle" is treated as sustained no earlier than the day that disposition of all positions is effected. § 1092(a)(2)(A). An identified straddle is one in which all of the original positions are acquired on the same day. Also, all of the positions must be either disposed of on the same day or held through the close of the taxable year, § 1092(a)(2)(B), and thus considered disposed of on the last day.

Section 1092, like § 1256, does not apply to hedging transactions. § 1092(e).

In short, the "marked to market" rule of § 1256(a) requires that "§ 1256 contracts" held by a taxpayer at the close of the year be treated as sold for their fair market value, with the resulting gain or loss being characterized as 40 percent short-term capital gain or loss, and the remaining 60 percent as long-term capital gain or loss. On the other hand, straddles involving actively traded personal property are not subject to the "marked to market" rule of § 1256(a), but instead, losses from any position are allowed under § 1092(a) only to the extent that such losses exceed the unrecognized gains of the taxpayer on offsetting positions.

After 1986, the maximum tax rate on these contracts will equal the maximum tax rate for the particular year.

PROBLEMS

Page 755:

1(a). $1,000 LTCG from an asset held more than 12 months. Under *Rev. Rul. 66-7* the more than 12-month holding period is met. The requirement is satisfied because both January 16, 2002 and January 16, 2003 are counted. As a result, T potentially would pay tax on the gain at a 20% rate. § 1(h)(1)(C).

1(b). $1,000 STCG. There is a sale of a capital asset, but under *Rev. Rul. 66-7* the holding period is measured from the day after acquisition, March 1, 2003 to February 29, 2004 does not exceed 12 months. Thus, the property not having been held for more than 12 months is a STCG.

1(c). $1,000 LTCG from an asset held more than 12 months. Where the taxpayer cannot actually identify which block of stock was sold, Reg. §§ 1.1223-1(i) and 1.1012-1(c) provide a first-in, first-out rule and therefore the February 10, 2002 to February 15, 2003 holding period is more than 12 months. "Adequate identification" is discussed in *Rev. Rul. 72-415*, 1972-2 C.B. 463, which should be consulted on facts such as these if, for example, T had a loss on one block of stock.

1(d).   Probably $1,000 LTCG from an asset held more than 12 months in 1999. T's "trade dates" which govern the holding period are December 29, 2002 and December 30, 2003. That is more than 12 months and T has LTCG that potentially will be taxed at a 20% rate. § 1(h)(1)(C). Even though T is a cash method taxpayer, the Treasury takes the position that T's gain is included in income on December 30, 2003, the "trade date." Rev. Rul. 93-84, 1993-2 C.B. 225. See § 453(k)(2)(A) providing that § 453 is inapplicable to such sales of stock and precluding the possibility of having the choice of including the gain in either 2003 or 2004. Note that the above result is consistent with the result suggested in the Senate Report cited in footnote 2 on page 752 of the Text, and seemingly is based on an equivalency of cash argument. Arguably there is no income until 2004 when cash flows. Cf. Rev. Rul. 82-227, 1982-2 C.B. 89, allowing a choice but published prior to the enactment of § 453(k)(2)(A).

1(e). $500 LTCL from an asset held for more than 12 months in 2003. Again T has long term consequences measured by T's "trade dates." However, T's loss is treated as realized and therefore deductible in the year in which the 2003 "trade date" falls. *Rev. Rul. 70-344*, 1970-2 C.B. 50. See also Rev. Rul. 93-84 and the Senate Report cited in problem 1(d), above.

1(f). $3,000 LTCG from an asset held for more than 12 months. T's gain is measured by the difference between T's $6,000 amount realized and T's $3,000 § 1015 transferred basis, assuming no § 1015(d) adjustment for gift tax. Section 1223(2) provides for tacking holding periods when there is a transferred basis under § 1015. Although T has actually held the shares for less than 12 months, the permitted tacking makes T's gain long-term and as the stock is held for more than 12 months the gain potentially is taxed at a 20% rate. § 1(h)(1)(C).

1(g). $10,000 LTCG from an asset held for more than 12 months. Under § 1014 the stock is allowed $50,000 "stepped up" basis. And T has a $10,000 gain on the sale for $60,000. Section 1223(11) applies to result in more than 12 month gain consequences.

1(h). $10,000 LTCG from an asset held for more than 12 months. This problem applies the rationale as in problem 1(g), above, a § 1014 "stepped up" basis and a § 1223(11) holding period with the gain potentially taxed at a 20% rate. § 1(h)(1)(C).

2(a).   Although this problem is posed for the purpose of raising a holding period issue, nevertheless a tougher measurement of gain issue is also present. Tacker's prior treatment of the base payment will determine her basis in her option rights. If she deducted the full $10,000 each year she has zero basis in her option rights. If she deducted only $9,000, she has a $25,000 basis in her option rights. It is not likely that she might fall somewhere in between (i.e. $9,500 deduction and $12,500 basis). We will assume she deducted only $9,000. Her gain here would then be $50,000, $300,000 less her $250,000 basis. In part (b), she would have the same $50,000 gain, $75,000 less $25,000. If Tacker exercises the option and sells the property, she would like to tack to her brief period of ownership the time she has held the property as lessee. But the time of possession as lessee is not a part of her holding period and cannot be tacked. See Footnote 8 in the immediately preceding part of the Text and the discussion in the cases there cited. Cf. Vernon Molbreak, 61 T.C. 382 (1973). Tacker has a STCG on the transaction.

2(b).   The sale of the option is obviously the answer for Tacker. She needs no tacking here. The option that she sells *has* been held for 25 years. She has the same amount of gain. See also § 1234 characterizing the gain on sale of the option with reference to the property to which the option relates. Thus, the gain would be LTCG which in the absence of other capital gains or losses potentially would be taxed at 20% depending upon Tacker's other income. § 1(h).

Perhaps it should be stated that, upon exercise and sale of the property, the period the option is held may not be tacked.

3.   The problem allocates $250,000 of the purchase price to the land. Of the remaining $350,000, the amount received for the house, the *Paul* case requires that the proceeds be allocated between the portion of the construction completed more than 12 months prior to the sale, and the portion completed within one year prior to the date of sale.

In this problem, the land gain of $50,000 and the gain on 50% of the house or $25,000 would be a LTCG from an asset held greater than 12 months. The other 50% of the house gain, $25,000, would be STCG.

A similar issue is raised in the context of the application of § 1231 and its holding period requirements in *Rev. Rul. 75-524*, 1975-2 C.B. 342.

Page 751:

> The principle of the *Paul* case (illustrated in problem 3 at page 756 of the Text) that a building can be partitioned for short- and long-term holding periods is also applicable under § 1231. See Rev. Rul. 75-524, 1975-2 C.B. 342.

PROBLEMS

Page 768:

1(a).   The first parcel of land is used in Hotchpot's trade or business and has been held long term; it is within § 1231(a)(3)(A)(i). The $10,000 gain on its sale is included in the § 1231 main hotchpot. If the land were not pulled into § 1231, it would have resulted in ordinary income under § 1221(2).

A compulsory conversion by *condemnation* is not one of the types of involuntary conversions that fall within the subhotchpot. Thus the loss on the second parcel of land is also in the main hotchpot as a compulsory conversion of a capital asset held long term.

Therefore Hotchpot has:

> Land #1: $10,000 § 1231(a) main hotchpot gain
> Land #2: $ 2,000 § 1231(a) main hotchpot loss

Since gains in the main hotchpot exceed losses in the main hotchpot all gains and losses are long-term capital gains and losses. § 1231(a)(1). Hotchpot has a $10,000 LTCG and a $2,000 LTCL. Note that further characterization is required for purposes of § 1(h) and that the $10,000 LTCG is from an adjusted net capital gain held for 4 years and the $2,000 LTCL is from an adjusted net capital gain held for 3 years.

1(b).   The result is similar to 1(a), above. Since Hotchpot inherited the parcels of land, their bases are determined under § 1014 and Hotchpot's holding period is greater than 12 months under § 1223(11). Since the holding period is greater than one year the land meets the § 1231 time requirements for property used in a trade or business. See § 1231(b)(1). One purpose of this problem is to emphasize that unless property has been held long term, at least artificially as here, it will not fall within § 1231.

Therefore Hotchpot has:

Land #1:	$4,000 § 1231(a) main hotchpot gain
Land #2:	$2,000 § 1231(a) main hotchpot loss

Since gains in the main hotchpot exceed losses in the main hotchpot, all gains and losses are long-term capital gains and losses. § 1231(a)(1). Hotchpot has a $4,000 LTCG and a $2,000 LTCL. Note that further characterization is required for purposes of § 1(h) and that the $4,000 gain and the $2,000 loss will be netted against each other and potentially be taxed under § 1(h)(1)(C).

1(c).   The $10,000 gain on the building is a § 1231(a) main hotchpot gain. It results from the sale of property used in a trade or business as defined in § 1231(b)(1).

The car destruction will result in a § 1231(a)(4)(C)(i) involuntary conversion loss of $2,000. The amount of the loss is the $8,000 change in value resulting from the fire, but only $6,000 (the car's adjusted basis) may be taken into account. See Reg. § 1.165-7(b)(1). The $6,000 is then reduced by the $4,000 of insurance proceeds. § 165(a). The issue here is the character of that $2,000 loss.

The involuntary conversion of property used in a trade or business falls into the § 1231(a)(4)(C) subhotchpot. Since there is only a $2,000 loss and no gain from involuntary conversion, the § 1231(a) main hotchpot will not apply to characterize the loss. The loss is therefore ordinary; it fails to meet the sale or exchange requirement for capital loss characterization. The $10,000 gain on the building is the only item in the § 1231(a) main hotchpot and it becomes a LTCG.

Thus Hotchpot has:

Building:	§ 1231(a) main hotchpot LTCG of $10,000

Car: Ordinary loss of $2,000

Although premature here, it should probably be pointed out that the gain on the building may fall into more than one category of gain under § 1(h). See § 1(h)(1)(C) and (D) and Chapter 22E2, infra.

1(d).   As seen in problem 1(c), above, Hotchpot has a $10,000 main hotchpot gain and a $2,000 subhotchpot loss. In addition, he has a $4,000 subhotchpot gain resulting from the involuntary conversion of his painting by fire. § 1231(a)(4)(C)(ii). The investment painting is a capital asset which he has held long term, but it was not the subject of a sale or exchange as is necessary for capital gain treatment. See § 1222 and § 1033. Since this gain ($4,000) exceeds the amount of the car loss which is also in the subhotchpot ($2,000), both are transferred into the main hotchpot and combined with the $10,000 building gain. Since total gains in the main hotchpot ($14,000) exceed total losses ($2,000), they are all given LTCG or LTCL treatment.

Therefore Hotchpot has:

Building: $10,000 LTCG (§ 1231(a)(1))
Car: 2,000 LTCL (§ 1231(a)(1))
Painting: 4,000 LTCG (§ 1231(a)(1))

Again, it should be recognized that the different gain assets are subject to different classifications for purposes of § 1(h). See § 1(h)(1)(C), (D), and (E).

1(e).   As seen in problem 1(d), above, Hotchpot has a $10,000 § 1231 main hotchpot gain, a $2,000 § 1231 subhotchpot loss and a $4,000 § 1231 subhotchpot gain. Additionally the sale of the land constitutes a loss on the sale of property used for several years in his trade or business and is a $20,000 main hotchpot loss. § 1231(a)(3)(B) and (b)(1).

As seen in problem 1(d), above, since subhotchpot gains exceed subhotchpot losses both are transferred to the main hotchpot. In the main hotchpot, total losses ($22,000) exceed gains ($14,000); therefore all losses and gains are ordinary. § 1231(a)(2).

Thus Hotchpot has:

Building:	$10,000 ordinary gain (§ 1231(a)(2))
Car:	$2,000 ordinary loss (§ 1231(a)(2))
Painting:	$4,000 ordinary gain (§ 1231(a)(2))
Land:	$20,000 ordinary loss (§ 1231(a)(2))

The net result is an $8,000 ordinary loss, reducing taxable income to that extent.

1(f). No. If the Commissioner successfully argued that the land in problem 1(e), above, had been held as an investment, its sale would have resulted in a $20,000 LTCL, outside of § 1231. The § 1231 outcome, as determined in problem 1(d), above, from the building, car and painting, was a $12,000 LTCG. Netting the two, Hotchpot has $8,000 NLTCL for the year and, assuming no other capital gains and losses he would likely have a $3,000 § 1211 (b) ordinary deduction and a $5,000 § 1212 LTCL carryover. He could hardly prefer that result to the $8,000 net ordinary loss deduction allowed in problem 1(e), above.

1(g). Section § 1231(c) requires any net § 1231 gain to be recharacterized as ordinary income to the extent of any non-recaptured net § 1231 losses for the five most recent preceding years. Consequently, the $8,000 aggregate loss from three and four years ago will serve to recharacterize $8,000 worth of net § 1231 gain from LTCG to ordinary income. The remaining $4,000 net LTCG (see problem 1(d), above) will remain LTCG.

Therefore Hotchpot has:

| $8,000 ordinary income | (§ 1231(c)) |
| $4,000 LTCG | (§ 1231(a)(1)) |

Again with § 1(h) in the back of one's mind, an additional issue arises as to which of the gains is recharacterized: the building (see § 1(h)(1)(C), (D)) or the painting (see § 1(h)(1)(E)) and part of the building? Congress left a gap in the statute under § 1231(c) that the Treasury has filled in (see § 1(h)(10)) by providing that the gains which would be taxed at the highest rates are recharacterized first. Thus the painting is first reconverted, then 25% gain on the building, and finally any 20% gain on the building. See Notice 97-59, 1997 - 2 C.B. 309.

1(h).   The $14,000 aggregate § 1231 loss from two, three and four years ago will serve to recharacterize up to a total of $14,000 worth of net § 1231 gain from LTCG to ordinary income. Since in problem 1(d), above, Hotchpot has only a $12,000 net § 1231 gain, all of this will be recharacterized as ordinary income. The remaining $2,000 ($14,000 - $12,000) of non-recaptured § 1231 loss will continue to be available to recharacterize future net § 1231 gains. The legislative history indicates that losses will be deemed recaptured in the order in which they arose (first in-first out). Consequently, the $2,000 non-recaptured § 1231 loss remains from two years ago.

Therefore Hotchpot has:

$12,000 ordinary income   (§ 1231(c))

1(i).   If, one year ago Hotchpot had a $10,000 net § 1231 gain, then $10,000 of the $14,000 aggregate net § 1231 loss from two, three and four years ago will have been used to recharacterize this $10,000 net § 1231 gain to ordinary income. As a result, only $4,000 ($14,000 - $10,000) remains as non-recaptured net § 1231 loss. This remaining $4,000 will cause $4,000 of Hotchpot's $12,000 net § 1231 gain in the current year (from problem 1(d), above) to be recharacterized as ordinary income. The remaining $8,000 ($12,000 - $4,000) will continue to be characterized as LTCG.

Therefore Hotchpot has:

$4,000 ordinary income   (§ 1231(c))
$8,000 LTCG   (§ 1231(a)(1))

Again, a question arises as to which of the LTCGs is recaptured. See 1(g), above, which indicates that the gain which would be taxed at the highest rate under § 1(h) is the painting whose $4,000 gain would be converted to ordinary income.

2.   *Rev. Rul. 75-538* holds that depreciation may not be allowed on such cars and that the gain on their sale is ordinary, not § 1231 gain, because in both instances the cars are held primarily for sale in the ordinary course of taxpayer's business and are not used in business. The ruling does recognize that this is a straight factual question but presumes that

such autos are primarily held for sale forcing a taxpayer to overcome that presumption. The same approach is taken to other items held only for temporary business use.

3(a).   As the case of *Williams v. McGowan* points out, an amount paid for an unincorporated sole proprietorship must be specifically allocated among the various property interests sold in accordance with their respective values. A separate computation of gain or loss and characterization must be made with respect to each. On her sale Merchant has the following consequences:

Inventory: $8,000 ordinary income. § 1221(1).

Goodwill: Since the goodwill was generated by Merchant, it was not subject to § 197 amortization, it is a capital asset and the $20,000 gain is a LTCG which is also an adjusted net capital gain for purposes of § 1(h). Arguably, some of the goodwill was created in the year of the sale in which case to that extent there would be some STCG. The facts assume, however, that all assets have been held more than one year.

If the goodwill had been acquired on the acquisition of a trade or business and amortized under § 197 (given the number of years involved, a computational impossibility here!), the gain would be § 1231 MHPG. Note that § 1245 would override § 1231 if it were not assumed out of the problem. See § 1245(a).

With the enactment of § 197, the goodwill - covenant not to compete dichotomy has taken an interesting turn. Prior to the enactment of § 197, goodwill was always a capital asset to the seller but was not amortizable by the buyer, and a covenant not to compete was ordinary income (from services) to the seller and amortizable by the buyer. The courts were generally willing to abide by any allocation between goodwill and a covenant not to compete in the contract, because there was a self-policing principle at work because the parties were dealing at arm's length with conflicting tax interests,

Dock B. Bennett, 29 T.C.M. 1230 (1970), aff'd per curiam, 450 F.2d 959 (6th Cir. 1971). See also Hamlin's Trust v. Comm'r, 209 F.2d 761 (10th Cir. 1954). But see Throndson v. Comm'r, 457 F. 2d 1022 9th Cir. 1972), where an agreement was disregarded by the court because the seller was unaware of the allocation. When the contract failed to state whether or to what extent a payment is for goodwill or a covenant not to compete, litigation occurred. See Ernest Stewart, 30 T.C.M. 485 (1971), aff'd sub nom. Dixie Finance Co., Inc. v. U.S., 474F.2d 501 (5th Cir. 1973), and Harry A. Kinney, 58 T.C. 1038 (1972). Some of those disputes alleviated with the enactment of § 1060 in the 1986 Act which adopted the § 338(b)(5) residual method of allocation of the sale and purchase price when there is an applicable asset acquisition. The section also includes a reporting requirement. § 1060(b).

After the enactment of § 197, goodwill is amortizable under § 197 and so the goodwill - covenant not to compete dichotomy is much less significant especially to the buyer. If goodwill is a LTCG to the seller, the seller will prefer an allocation to goodwill and the buyer being able to amortize both goodwill and a covenant not to compete over a 15 year period will not care what designation is made.

Land: $10,000 § 1231 main hotchpot loss.

Building: $5,000 § 1231 main hotchpot gain. Note that § 1250 might override if it were not assumed out of the problem. Cf. § 1(h)(1)(C) and (D).

Machinery &
Equipment: $2,000 § 1231 main hotchpot gain. Note that § 1245 might override if it were not assumed out of the problem.

Covenant not

to compete: $10,000 ordinary income. This is in essence a payment for future services, even though for agreed inaction. See Rodney B. Horton, 13 T.C. 143 (1949).

Again if in the netting for purposes of § 1231, the assets are treated as LTCGs and LTCLs, further classification may have to be made for purposes of § 1(h).

3(b).   Merchant would have a $20,000 LTCG on the sale of the stock of the incorporated business. For purposes of § 1(h), this would be an adjusted net capital gain. This problem is intended to illustrate that the form in which a business is operated may alter one's tax consequences, especially on a sale of the business. In addition, the instructor should mention § 741 and § 751 of subchapter K. Those sections deal with the sale of a partnership interest and adopt a modified entity approach which reaches a result somewhere between the nonentity (sole proprietorship) and complete entity (corporate) results reached above.

While Merchant would have a LTCG on the stock sale, the $10,000 received for the covenant not to compete is separate from the sale of the stock and is again in the nature of compensation for services and ordinary income. Est. of Mildred K. Hyde, 42 B.T.A. 738 (1940). The same result is reached with respect to a covenant not to compete sold in conjunction with a partnership interest. Barran v. Comm'r, 334 F.2d 58 (5th Cir. 1964).

PROBLEM

Page 774:

1(a).   Depreciator has a $40,000 § 1231 main hotchpot gain on the sale of the building (note no § 1250 gain because of straight-line depreciation) and a $20,000 § 1231 main hotchpot gain on the sale of the land. Attribution to Depreciator of the stock of Spouse and Son (See § 267(c)(2) and (4) results in only 40% of the stock being treated as held by Depreciator. This does not meet the more than 50% in value requirement of § 1239(c)(1)(A), and § 1239 is inapplicable. Although premature, note that if Depreciator's § 1231 gains become LTCGs, they must be separated for purposes of reclassification under § 1(h). See, e.g., § 1(h)(1)(C) and (D).

1(b). Depreciator has a $40,000 § 1239 gain on the sale of the building and a $20,000 § 1231 main hotchpot gain on the sale of the land. Section 1239 is applicable to the sale of the building because the sale was between Depreciator, a person, and Redepreciation, a "controlled entity," here a corporation owned more than 50% in value by such person, § 1239(b)(1) and (c)(1)(A) and (c)(2), and § 267(c)(2) and (4) and, as the building is to be used in Redepreciation's business, it is depreciable to the corporation.

Since the land is not depreciable by Redepreciation and assuming it has been held long term its gain remains in the § 1231 main hotchpot and is not characterized by § 1239. Cf. § 1(h).

1(c). The result will be the same as in either problem 1(a) or 1(b), above. *Spouse's* brother's stock would not be attributed to Depreciator because of the preclusion against double attribution in § 267(c)(5). Thus only 50% of the stock would be owned by Depreciator as a result of attribution. This raises a "*Parker*" issue whether "more than 50 percent of the *value* of the outstanding stock" is owned by Depreciator. If only 50% of the value is owned then the result is the same as in 1(a), above; if more than 50% of the value is owned, the 1(b) result is reached.

1(d). The result would be the same as in problem 1(b), above, $40,000 of § 1239 ordinary income and 20,000 of § 1231 main hotchpot gain. This problem illustrates that § 1239 is applicable to sales between commonly controlled entities as well as between owners and controlled entities. Section 1239(a) applies to sales between related persons and § 1239(b)(1) defines related persons as a person and *all* controlled entities of such persons. Since Depreciator controls both Other Corporation (100% ownership) and Redepreciation Corporation (see problem 1(b), above which employs the § 267(c) rules other than paragraph (c) thereof (§ 1239 (c)(2))), this is a sale between such controlled entities.

1(e). The result is the same as in problem 1(b), above. Section 1239(b)(2) makes § 1239 applicable to sales between a taxpayer and a trust in which the taxpayer or taxpayer's spouse is a beneficiary, unless the beneficiary is a remote contingent beneficiary as defined in § 318(a)(3)(B)(i).

One should point out that the 1997 legislation added § 1239(b)(3) which makes § 1239 applicable to sales between an estate and a beneficiary of the estate (other than a sale or exchange in satisfaction of a pecuniary bequest). Cf. § 267(b)(13) adding a similar provision to the § 267 loss disallowance rule discussed in Chapter 25A.

1(f).   We again reach the same result as in problem 1(b), above. This problem emphasizes that § 1239 applies if the property is depreciable in the hands of the transferee even though not in the hands of the transferor. The property is not required to have been the subject of depreciation deductions by the seller for § 1239 to apply. Thus, in this and other circumstances, § 1239 produces ordinary income where § 1245 and § 1250 would not.

1(g).   The purpose of § 1239 is to deny LTCG treatment to a sale or exchange of property that immediately qualifies for ordinary depreciation deductions when it is continued to be held in substance by the same person. § 1239(b)(1) and (2). The need for § 1239 is diminished by the various recapture provisions. Note, however, that § 1239 classifies as ordinary *all* gain on the property, not just post-1961 depreciation as in the case of § 1245 property or just "additional depreciation" as in the case of § 1250 property.

PROBLEMS

Page 781:

1(a).   Regardless of when in 1996 the property was purchased, in 2002 § 1016(a)(2) would give it a zero adjusted basis, and Recap's gain would be $30,000. Tracking the statute, the entire gain of $30,000 would be § 1245 ordinary income. This is § 1245 property under § 1245 (a)(3). Applying § 1245(a), the lesser of:

(A)   the § 1245(a)(1)(A) "recomputed basis" as defined in § 1245(a)(2)(A), of $100,000, or

(B)   the § 1245(a)(1)(B)(i) amount realized of $30,000

exceeds Recap's zero adjusted basis by $30,000, and that amount is § 1245 ordinary income. Where the amount realized is the lower of the alternative figures, as here, the entire gain is subject to recapture.

1(b).   The result is the same if Recap had elected to use § 179, because amounts expensed under § 179 are treated as amortization taken for purposes of § 1245 recapture. See § 1245(a)(2)(C). Cf. § 179(d)(10) relating to a conversion of § 179 property prior to the end of its recovery period.

1(c).   Recap would have a $30,000 § 1231(a) main hotchpot gain. Recap's adjusted basis would still be zero under § 1016(a)(2), because Recap would be required to reduce basis by the amount of depreciation "allowable." See page 410 of the Text. If no depreciation deduction is claimed and no accelerated method is elected, the amount of reduction in basis is determined under the straight-line method. Cf. Reg. § 1.1016-3(a)(2). Thus at the end of 2002, Recap would have a zero basis in the property. However, in contrast, recomputed basis under § 1245(a)(2)(B) does not include depreciation "allowable" in excess of the amount actually "allowed," if the taxpayer can prove by adequate records that the amount actually allowed was less than the amount allowable. Assuming Recap can do so, in this problem Recap's "recomputed basis" is zero, the same as Recap adjusted basis, and Recap has no § 1245(a) gain. Accordingly Recap's full $30,000 gain is a § 1231 main hotchpot gain. Depreciation is a kind of ongoing cost that always affects basis for purposes of gain or loss and which is not broadly susceptible to taxpayer manipulation. Recapture, however, involves retribution; and it is inappropriate to "punish" a taxpayer when the taxpayer has in no way made improper charges against income.

In all likelihood, Recap would be better off having actually taken the depreciation. Thus Recap would want to claim depreciation for the two prior years in which depreciation could have been taken (now there would be no depreciation in the current year, 2002) by means of a refund claim. Years prior to that would be closed by the statute of limitations. See Chapter 28C, infra. For a case in which the refund years were closed and the taxpayer got burned because the mitigation of limitations provisions would not open up the closed years, see Gardiner v. U.S., 391 F. Supp. 1202 (C.D. Utah 1975).

1(d). If Recap sells the property to Spouse, Recap has the same $30,000 of § 1245 realized gain. But the interrelationship of § 1041(b)(1) and § 1245(b)(1) allows Recap not to recognize that gain. Recap's adjusted basis and holding period along with the § 1245 taint carries over to Spouse.

1(e). Recap's gain is $110,000 of which $100,000 is ordinary income under § 1245 and the remaining $10,000 is a § 1231(a) main hotchpot gain.

Applying § 1245(a), the lesser of:

(A) the § 1245(a)(2)(A) "recomputed basis" of $100,000 or

(B) the "amount realized" of $110,000

exceeds Recap's zero adjusted basis by $100,000, which is ordinary income. Recap's remaining $10,000 gain, unaffected by § 1245, goes into the § 1231(a) main hotchpot.

After working problems 1(a) and (1)(c), the student should be able to extract an easy rule of thumb with respect to the general rule of § 1245: It recaptures as ordinary income any gain otherwise required to be recognized to the extent that post-1961 depreciation or amortization was actually allowed on the property. This general rule is subject to the usual weaknesses of generalizations. For one thing, it assumes that if depreciation allowed was less than depreciation allowable the taxpayer could establish that fact with sufficient evidence.

1(f). This problem illustrates the interrelationship of a sale of § 1245 property with some § 1231 gain and other § 1231 transactions. The consequences of the sale of the § 1245 property would be the same as in problem 1(c), above, $100,000 of § 1245 ordinary income and a $10,000 § 1231 main hotchpot gain.

Additionally Recap has an $11,000 main hotchpot loss on the sale of the land. Consequently since loss ($11,000) exceeds gain ($10,000) in the main hotchpot, both the gain and the loss are characterized as ordinary.

Therefore Recap has:

Sale of Equipment: $100,000 ordinary income (§ 1245)
                                  $10,000 ordinary income (§ 1231(a))

Sale of Land: $11,000 ordinary loss (§ 1231(a))

1(g).   If the land was sold for $15,000 the gain in the main hotchpot ($10,000) would exceed the loss ($5,000) and they would be characterized as LTCG and LTCL, respectively. The results to Recap would be:

Sale of Equipment: $100,000 ordinary income (§ 1245)
                                  $10,000 LTCG (§ 1231(a))

Sale of Land: $5,000 LTCL (§ 1231(a))

The gain would be an adjusted net capital gain under § 1(h). See § 1(h)(4).

2.   The statute does sanction assignment of "fruit" here as a gift either under § 102 (and § 1015) or § 1041. Although a disposition occurs which would trigger § 1245(a) into recognizing the § 1245 gain "notwithstanding any other provision of this subtitle," nevertheless § 1245(b)(1) puts a halt to such recognition. Note that the nonrecognition occurs because of an exception within § 1245 itself. However that does not mean that the § 1245 gain disappears, because the property takes a carryover basis to the donee and, regardless of whether it continues to be depreciable, it is still § 1245 property on the donee's disposition of it. (See § 1245(a)(3) ". . . property which is or *has been* property of a character subject to the allowance for depreciation . . .") Under the definition of recomputed basis in § 1245(a)(2)(A) depreciation which was taken by a donor is added back because of the language" . . . adjustments . . . reflected in such adjusted basis on account of deductions. . . allowed . . . to the taxpayer or *to any other person* . . ." While § 1245(b)(1) does not require a donor to recapture the gain, nevertheless it carries over to the donee who may recognize it. Thus

the statute sanctions assignment of such gain but not its recharac-terization. Note, however, that § 1014 and § 1245(b)(2) permit avoidance of all recapture at death.

PROBLEMS

Page 783:

1. Real property placed in service after 1986 must be depreciated by way of the straight-line method. § 168(b)(3). If such property is held for more than one year, § 1250 is inapplicable because the § 1250(b)(1) additional depreciation would be zero as there is no excess depreciation over straight-line depreciation and under § 1250(a)(1)(A), the 100% applicable percentage of zero is zero. If such property is not held for an excess of one year, the full amount of straight-line depreciation is recaptured to the extent of the gain on the property. Thus, here, where the property is held for less than one year, § 1250 operates identically to § 1245.

2. Owner would have a gain of $260,000 on the building, the difference between the $550,000 amount realized and the $290,000 of adjusted basis. The adjusted basis is equal to the acquisition basis of $390,000 reduced by $100,000 of depreciation ($10,000 per year for 10 years). The gain on the land would be $50,000, the difference between the $150,000 amount realized and the $100,000 adjusted basis.

    The gain would be characterized as a LTCG under § 1231 where gains exceed losses. Since there are no other capital gains or losses, Owner has a $310,000 LTCG and net capital gain, $260,000 from the building and $50,000 from the land.

    Since Owner has $100,000 of ordinary income, that income fills up the 10% and 15% brackets and the issue is the rate of tax on the NCGs. Turning to § 1(h)(7), Owner has $100,000 of unrecaptured § 1250 gain which is taxed at a 25% rate under § 1(h)(1)(D). Note the § 1(h)(1)(D)(ii) amount would be zero: (I) the sum of $100,000 plus $310,000 less (II) taxable income of $410,000.

The remaining $160,000 gain on the building and the $50,000 gain on the land would be adjusted net capital gain taxed at a 20% rate. § 1(h)(1)(C).

3. Owner has a gain on the building of $143,000, the difference between the amount realized of $150,000 less the adjusted basis of $7,000. Owner has a gain on the land of $75,000 ($125,000 amount realized less the adjusted basis of $50,000).

The building is § 1250 property. §1250(c). In characterizing the gain, under § 1250(a)(1), 100% is the applicable percentage, § 1250(a)(1)(B)(v), which applies to the *lower* of the:

(i)   additional depreciation ($93,000 less $90,000) or $3,000 or

(ii)   gain $143,000

This results in $3,000 of § 1250 gain.

The remaining $140,000 gain on the building and the $75,000 gain on the land would be characterized as LTCG under the § 1231 main hotchpot and Owner would have a $215,000 NCG for the year.

When Owner enters § 1(h), there is $90,000 of unrecaptured § 1250 gain under § 1(h)(7)(A) (the amount of capital gain which would be § 1250 gain if § 1250(b)(1) included all depreciation, i.e., $93,000 less the gain otherwise characterized as ordinary income, $3,000). That gain would be taxed at a 25% rate under § 1(h)(1)(D). Owner's remaining $125,000 of ANCG would be taxed at a 20% rate under § 1(h)(1)(C).

Page 784:

The following excerpt from a prior edition of the Text discusses other recapture provisions and may be reproduced and distributed to students:

RECAPTURE PROVISIONS

Congress has extended the recapture concept, applying it to assumed past overcharges arising out of deductions other than the depreciation (or related amortization) deduction. Section 1252, which

290

bears a direct relationship to Section 175 and now repealed Section 182, presents a somewhat simpler recapture rule. Section 175 permits expenditures for soil and water conservation and to prevent soil erosion to be expensed, not merely charged to capital account. Section 182 sometimes accorded similar treatment to expenditures made for the purpose of clearing farm land. Thus, as explained by the Staff of the Joint Committee (General Explanation of the Tax Reform Act of 1969, Staff of the Joint Comm. on Int.Rev.Tax, 95 (1970):

> The current deduction allowed for soil and water conservation expenditures and land clearing expenditures with respect to farmland, combined with the capital gains treatment allowed under prior law on the sale of the farm land permitted high-income taxpayers to convert ordinary income into capital gains. These taxpayers could purchase farm land, deduct these expenditures from their high-bracket nonfarm income, and then receive capital gain treatment on the sale of the farm land.

Under Section 1252, if farm land is sold and it has been held for less than 10 years and has been the subject of deductions from ordinary income under Sections 175 or 182, gain on the sale to the extent of such deductions may be recaptured as ordinary income. I.R.C. § 1252(a)(1). If the land has been held for only five years or less, the amount of the Section 175 and 182 deductions fixes the amount of the gain subject to ordinary income treatment. [I.R.C. § 1252(a)(1), (3)]. If a sale takes place in the sixth year only 80% of the amount of such deductions is recaptured; and there are corresponding 20% reductions in each succeeding year so that, in effect, Section 1252 becomes inapplicable to land held for more than 10 years. I.R.C. § 1252(a)(3).

Section 1254, added by the Tax Reform Act of 1976 and expanded by the 1986 tax legislation taxes as ordinary income some gain on the disposition of oil, gas and mineral property. I.R.C. § 1254(a)(3). Section 1254 recaptures two types of deductions with respect to property placed in service after 1986. First, to the extent that prior depletion deductions resulted in a reduction of the adjusted basis of such property, gain on the sale of the property is recaptured as ordinary income. I.R.C. § 1254(a)(1)(A)(ii). In addition, if intangible drilling and development expenditures on the property, normally capital expenditures, have been expensed (currently deducted) as permitted by Sections 263(c), 616, or 617, the amount of the deductions are also recaptured as ordinary income to the extent of the gain on such property. I.R.C. § 1254(a)(1)(A)(i). Total recapture under both recapture rules cannot exceed the gain on the property. I.R.C. § 1254(a)(1)(B).

Another recapture provision, Section 1255, was added by the Revenue Act of 1978. Under that Act, Congress also added Section 126, which excludes from gross income certain payments received under a number of Federal and state cost-sharing conservation programs. Under Section 1255, if property acquired, improved, or otherwise modified with Section 126 excluded grants is disposed of within 10 years of receipt of the grant, the amount of the grant is potentially recaptured as ordinary income. I.R.C. § 1255(a)(1). The amount of recapture is phased out by being reduced by 10 percent per year for each year after the first 10 years; thus there is no recapture on dispositions of property 20 years after receipt of the grant. I.R.C. § 1255(a)(3). The recapture gain cannot exceed the gain on the property. I.R.C. § 1255(a)(1)(B). Both Sections 1254 and 1255 adopt a form that will appear familiar from prior study of Sections 1245 and 1250.

In 1986, Congress added Section 1257 to the growing list of recapture provisions. Congress was concerned about the environmental impact of the conversion of the nation's wetlands and erodible lands to farming uses and wished to discourage such conversions. General Explanation of the Tax Reform Act of 1986, Staff of the Joint Comm. on Int. Rev. Tax, 189 (1987). As a result, it provided that any gain on the disposition of converted wetland (see I.R.C. § 1257(c)(1)) or highly erodible cropland (see I.R.C. § 1257(c)(2)) is treated as ordinary income. The recapture treatment is patterned after Section 1245. See I.R.C. § 1257(a) last sentence and (d). In addition, any loss recognized on the disposition of such property is long-term capital loss. I.R.C. § 1257(b).

Chapter 23.   Deductions Affected by Characterization Principles

Page 785:

> A pawnshop owner loaned money without collateral and at usurious interest rates, both of which violated state law. When loans were not repaid he attempted to deduct them under § 166. The Tax Court held that the debts were "void" under state law and consequently not "debts" for purposes of § 166. However, the court concluded that, while § 165 and § 166 are mutually exclusive, since there was no § 166 "debt" the amount of the loans was allowable as a business loss under §165. Herbert E. Tharp, 31 T.C.M. 22 (1972).

Page 791:

> The two ways in which a business debt may be accorded different treatment from a nonbusiness debt when uncollectibility looms are:
>
> (1)   Partially worthless business bad debts may be deducted; (§ 166(a)(2)) and
>
> (2)   Business bad debts are characterized as ordinary deductions while nonbusiness bad debts are characterized as short term capital losses. (§ 166(d)).

Page 793:

> Fn. 15. In order to protect his job, employee guaranteed a loan obtained by an officer of his corporation. When the officer failed to repay the loan, employee was liable. Employee was unable to collect from the officer and he was allowed a business bad debt deduction. Rev. Rul 71-561, 1971-2 C.B. 128. See also Wallace L. Hirsch, 30 T.C.M. 1008 (1971), reaching a similar result.

Page 794:

> Fn. 20. The *Generes* case has created a substantial amount of litigation. Most cases have held debts to be nonbusiness bad debts in view of the *Generes* dominant motive test. See, for example, French v. U.S., 487 F.2d 1246 (1st Cir. 1973); Estate of Byers v. Comm'r, 472 F.2d 590

(6th Cir. 1973); Kelson v. U.S., 503 F.2d 1291 (10th Cir. 1974); Robert E. Imel, 61 T.C. 318 (1973), acq. 1974-1 C.B. 2. But see the *Haslam* case at page 794 of the Text; Bowers v. Comm'r, 678 F.2d 509 (4th Cir. 1982); and Estate of Allen v. Comm'r, 44 T.C.M. 9 (1982).

PROBLEMS

Page 798:

1(a). To answer this problem one must know whether Lawyer is an accrual or cash method taxpayer. If Lawyer is an accrual method taxpayer, Lawyer has previously included the receivable in income, has a $1000 basis for it, and is allowed a bad debt deduction to the extent of his $1000 basis (§ 166(b)).

Note, however, § 448(d)(5) which provides that an accrual method taxpayer is not required to accrue income from the performance of services to the extent that on the basis of experience the income is not expected to be collected. This rule operates like a reserve for bad debts for an accrual method taxpayer receiving income from the performance of services. If, in fact, an amount excluded from income by § 448(d)(5) is subsequently recovered it constitutes gross income on its recovery.

If Lawyer is a cash method taxpayer, Lawyer has not included the fee within gross income and Lawyer has no basis for it. Under § 166(b) the amount of Lawyer's loss is zero.

If Lawyer is allowed a $1,000 bad debt deduction, Lawyer's deduction will be characterized as ordinary since it is a business bad debt. Compare § 166(a) and § 166(d).

1(b). Lawyer's use of a bad debt deduction is not foreclosed because § 6511(d)(1) provides a special seven year statute of limitations period for refund claims related to § 166 bad debts and § 165(g) worthless securities. The seven year limitations period is an exception to the general three year limitations period under § 6511(a). See Chapter 28C. Therefore Lawyer may file a timely claim for refund for year two.

1(c). If Lawyer was allowed a deduction in year six, recovery of the $1000 will constitute gross income unless some or all of it is excluded under

§ 111. See Chapter 20B. Under § 111 Lawyer is allowed to exclude from gross income the amount of the prior bad debt deduction which did not result in a reduction in a tax liability in the prior year (for which Lawyer received no tax benefit). The character of Lawyer's income would be ordinary income under the *Arrowsmith* rationale, because in year six Lawyer would have deducted the bad debt as an ordinary deduction for a business bad debt. See Merchants National Bank of Mobile v. Comm'r, 199 F.2d 657 (5th Cir. 1952).

If Lawyer had not been allowed a deduction in year six (because Lawyer was a cash method taxpayer), Lawyer would have $1000 of ordinary income in year seven when the payment is made. In effect Lawyer is simply receiving the account receivable which, had it been received in the ordinary course of business, would have generated $1,000 of ordinary income.

2(a).   This problem deals not only with the bad debt area, but incorporates as well a review of the mechanics of capital gains and losses and of § 1231. An instructor wishing to cover only bad debts is advised to disregard the specific questions asked and merely ask students the amount and character of deduction generated by items (1) through (4) of problem 2.

The bottom line is that these transactions would reduce Cher's taxable income by $3,000 to $37,000. We get there by noting that, in addition to Cher's taxable income of $40,000, she has:

(1)   A $5,000 LTCL on worthless stock held for two years. See §§ 165(g)(1), 165(g)(2)(A), and 166(e). Since the "note" represents an equity interest in the corporation, it is stock and a "worthless security." Cf. Raymond v. U.S., 511 F.2d 185 (6th Cir. 1975). If it were a bona fide "note" it would still have generated a $5000 LTCL under § 165(g)(1) if it had either interest coupons or was registered. § 165(g)(2)(C).

If it was not registered or did not have interest coupons, it would have generated a $5,000 STCL under § 166(d).

(2)   Again this is a $3,000 LTCL on worthless stock held for three years. See §§ 165(g)(1), 165(g)(2)(A), and 166(e).

(3)   This is a $2,600 STCL under § 166(d). Loans made on an intra-family basis or between friends are subjected to close scrutiny to determine whether a bona fide debt was created at the time of the transfer. In determining whether the parties intended a loan or gift, courts generally look to whether at the time of the transfer a repayment date was set, interest rates were set, and there was any written evidence of indebtedness. Cf. Carolyn C. Marltee, 35 T.C.M 456 (1976).

(4)   Cher has a $4,000 LTCG on the bonds. This is a § 1231 subhotchpot gain and assuming no other subhotchpot trans-actions it is thrown into the main hotchpot. Assuming no other trans-actions in the main hotchpot, gain exceeds loss and it is a LTCG from bonds held for four years.

Netting capital gains and losses Cher would have a NLTCL of $4,000 and a NSTCL of $2,600. Under § 1211(b), she would be allowed to deduct capital losses of $7,000 (equal to capital gains of $4,000 plus a § 1211(b) amount of $3,000). The § 1211(b) amount fixing deductible capital losses in excess of capital gains is the lesser of:

§1211(b)(1): $ 3,000 or
§1211(b)(2): $ 6,600

Obviously the limiting figure, which is determinative here, is $3,000.

2(b).   In addition, under § 1212(b), Cher would have a $3,600 LTCL carryover. The § 1212(b) carryover is computed as follows:

§ 1212(b)(1)(A): no short-term carryover.

§ 1212(b)(2) creates an additional $3,000 STCG, which soaks up the $2,600 STCL leaving no NSTCL in excess of NLTCG.

§ 1212(b)(1)(B): $3,600 long-term carryover.

§ 1212(b)(2) creates an additional $3,000 STCG.

Then under § 1212(b)(1)(B) her NLTCL $4,000 less her recomputed NSTCG $400 ($3,000 - $2,600) yields a $3,600 LTCL carryover.

2(c).   Cher's taxable income for the current year is $44,000. Under these facts we add a $10,600 LTCG to our already recognized $8,000 LTCL, $4,000 LTCG, and $2,600 STCL. This results in a net capital gain of $4,000 ($10,600 + $4,000 - $8,000 - $2,600). Under § 1(h) the LTCGs all arise from an adjusted net capital gain. The computation of her taxable income is as follows:

Gross Income	
(as adjusted $60,000 + $4,000):	$64,000
Other § 62 and § 63 deductions:	-$20,000
Taxable Income:	$44,000

2(d).   Cher must include a $2,600 in gross income in the following year. In the prior year Cher had a $2,600 STCL deduction under § 166(d) for Mooney's bad debt (see item (3), above), which resulted in a tax benefit in the form of a deduction of the full amount. Consequently, upon recovery of the debt, Cher must include the full amount of the recovery in her gross income. There would be no exclusion under § 111.

Characterizing the income is not an easy task. The recovery may be ordinary income. The *Arrowsmith* doctrine might apply to characterize the recovery as a STCG. But query whether *Arrowsmith* applies to a loss followed by a gain situation? If *Arrowsmith* applies, we feel, without firm authority, we should go a step further in determining the *Arrowsmith* consequences; since the STCL in the prior year actually wiped out LTCG, then on recovery of the bad debt it can be argued that she should have LTCG. Note an additional indirect preference of characterizing a gain as capital gain is potentially to allow current deductibility of a greater amount of capital losses under § 1211. See also *Skelley Oil*. Life is like that: long on issues and short on solutions.

Page 799:

With Rev. Rul. 83-104, compare Rev. Rul. 80-77, 1980-1 C.B. 56, quoted in full below:

        FACTS

Situation 1: A tornado destroys several homes in a town. The local chapter of the American National Red Cross provides food and temporary shelter to a taxpayer whose home was destroyed. The taxpayer, motivated by gratitude, makes a contribution of 5x dollars to the local chapter of the American National Red Cross.

Situation 2: A taxpayer owns a home in an area served by a volunteer fire department. No state or local taxes are used to support the fire department. The taxpayer makes a contribution of 5x dollars to the volunteer fire department's annual fund drive.

Situation 3: The taxpayer's daughter is a member of a local unit of the Girl Scouts of America. The taxpayer makes a contribution of 5x dollars to the Girl Scouts of America.

Situation 4: The taxpayer has a dependent parent who is a resident of a home for the elderly which is a member organization of a combined charity fund. The taxpayer makes an unrestricted contribution of 5x dollars to the combined charity fund that distributes the contributions to the member organizations according to a formula.

HOLDING

In each of the four situations, the taxpayer is allowed a charitable contribution deduction under section 170 of the Code, subject to the percentage limitations of section 170(b)(1).

Page 803:

As *Rev. Rul. 67-246* points out, a quid-pro-quo § 170 charitable deduction is allowed only to the extent of the excess of the amount paid over the consideration received. Similarly it is often correctly stated that a charitable contribution presupposes a *gift* and that: "If a payment proceeds primarily from the incentive of anticipated benefit to the payor

298

beyond the satisfaction which flows from the performance of a generous act, it is not a gift." Harold Dejong, 36 T.C. 896 at 899 (1961), and *Rev. Rul. 71-112*. Thus where taxpayer conveyed an easement to a city to widen a street, it was held that he made no charitable contribution because the transfer "was made in the expectation of the receipt of specific direct economic benefits in the form of additional utility and value which may be realized through the commercial development of the remainder of [his] land." Larry G. Sutton, 57 T.C. 239 (1971). The *Sutton* case was followed in Charles O. Grinsdale, 59 T.C. 566 (1973). See also Harold E. Wolfe, 54 T.C. 1707 (1970).

The *Dejong* rationale was also relied on in a Ruling to deny a charitable deduction on the repayment of student loans to a charitable institution. There was no binding legal obligation of repayment, because the debtor incurred the obligation when he was a minor and the contract was therefore voidable. Nevertheless, the Ruling held that the payment was not a voluntary payment and was in fact made because of the consideration for the contract and the benefits previously conferred. Rev. Rul. 71-269, 1971-1 C.B. 93. See also Winters v. Comm'r, 468 F.2d 778 (2d Cir. 1972).

The above result does not always work to a taxpayer's disadvantage, however. Some transfers made by a business to a charitable organization, which do not qualify for § 170, may still qualify under § 162 and the deduction is therefore not foreclosed by § 162(b) or restricted by the § 170 limitations.

Page 808:

Fn 7. A parent of a murder victim contributed money to the local police department to be used as a reward for information leading to the conviction of the killers and to be used for other public purposes if no one could claim the reward. The Service allowed a § 170 deduction for the donation under § 170(c)(1) because the donation was for an exclusively public purpose. Rev. Rul. 81-307, 1981-2 C.B. 78. See also Sampson v. Comm'r, 43 T.C.M. 1408 (1982), allowing a deduction for a similar contribution to a municipality for information leading to drug arrests.

Page 809:

Fn. 16. In Davis v. U.S., 495 U.S. 472, 110 S. Ct. 2014 (1990), the Supreme Court denied a charitable deduction to taxpayers who transferred funds to their sons' personal accounts and claimed a § 170 deduction because the sons were missionaries of the Church of Latter-day Saints. The court held that the contributions were neither "to" or "for the use of" the church. See Leavitt, "When is a Gift to Mr. Minister not a Gift to the Church? The Impact of Davis v. United States in Charitable Giving," 66 *Tulane L. Rev.* 245 (1991).

Page 811:

Fn 35. The Service has applied § 170(e)(1)(A) to reduce the amount of a charitable contribution deduction in several situations:

(1)   Where a taxpayer raised ornamental plants as a hobby and after holding them long term donated large numbers of them to various charities. Rev. Rul. 79-256, 1979-2 C.B. 105, situation 1.

(2)   Where a taxpayer, not a dealer in art, purchased a substantial part of the total limited edition of a particular lithograph print, held the prints more than a year and then donated them to various art museums. Rev. Rul. 79-256, *supra* situation 2.

(3)   Where a taxpayer purchased books at a volume discount, warehoused them over one year and then donated them to various charities. Rev. Rul. 79-419, 1979-2 C.B. 107.

Page 817:

In Rev. Rul. 72-542, 1972-2 C.B. 37, a pari-mutuel race track corporation held a "Charity Day" and donated gross receipts to a charity. The corporation asserted in accordance with Reg. § 1.61-2(c) that none of the amount given should be included in its gross income or deducted by it. Under the rationale of *Horst*, the Treasury ruled that, since the corporation was the promoter of the event, it was not a mere agent of the charity, and the proceeds belonged to it and must be included in its gross income. The ruling distinguished Rev. Rul. 68-

503, 1968-2 C.B. 44, where services are rendered at an event promoted by a charity. Also, the corporation could not deduct the contribution as a § 162 business expense since there was no reasonable expectation of return. The corporation could take a charitable deduction, limited of course to 5% (now 10%) of its contribution base.

Page 818:

> Fn 115. In Rev. Rul. 79-249, 1979-2 C.B. 104, donors made contributions to a building fund. The contributions were to be returned to donors if sufficient funds were not raised and any excess donations were to be retained by the charity. The Ruling stated, questionably, that no deduction was allowable for a contribution until sufficient contributions were received to meet the construction costs. See Reg. § 1.170A-1(e).

PROBLEMS

Page 819:

1(a).   Under § 170(b)(1)(A)(ii) T would be allowed a deduction of up to $75,000 (50% of T's contribution base). Section 170(d)(1)(A) would allow T a $25,000 carryover into the succeeding 5 years. The carryover would be treated as a § 170(b)(1)(A) contribution qualifying for the 50% limitation possibly affected, however, by other contributions in those years.

1(b).   Under § 170(b)(1)(B), T has a $45,000 deduction. It is an amount equal to the *lesser* of:

§ 170(b)(1)(B)(i) 30% x $150,000 = $45,000
or
§ 170(b)(1)(B)(ii) $75,000 - 0 = $75,000

The $55,000 that is not deductible is a carryover into each of the succeeding 5 years. The carryover would be treated in a manner consistent with the provisions of § 170(d)(1)(A) as a § 170(b)(1)(B) contribution subject to the 30% limitation and possibly affected by other actual contributions made in the succeeding years.

1(c).   T would be allowed a $60,000 § 170(b)(1)(A) deduction and, under § 170(b)(1)(B)(ii), T would be allowed an additional $15,000 deduction. The § 170(b)(1)(B) contribution is deductible to the extent of the lesser of:

(i)   30% of the contribution base, $45,000
or
(ii)   the excess of 50% of the contribution base less the § 170(b)(1)(A) amount ($75,000 - $60,000), $15,000.

Since the § 170(b)(1)(A) amount does not exceed 50% of the contribution base, there is no carryover under § 170(d)(1)(A). Since the aggregate contributions exceed the § 170(b)(1)(B) limitation the $25,000 excess ($40,000 less $15,000) would be a carryover into each of the succeeding 5 years. § 170(b)(1)(B) and (d)(1)(A).

1(d).   T would be allowed a $20,000 §170(b)(1)(A) deduction and, under § 170(b)(1)(B)(i), T would be allowed an additional $45,000 deduction. The § 170(b)(1)(B) contribution is deductible to the extent of the lesser of (i) $45,000 or (ii) $75,000 - $20,000 or $55,000. Since the § 170(b)(1)(A) amount does not exceed 50% of the contribution base, there is no carryover of any § 170(b)(1)(A) contribution, but the amount ($35,000) by which the aggregate contributions exceed the § 170(b)(1)(B) limitation will be a § 170(b)(1)(B) contribution carryover into the succeeding 5 years.

Compare the results with problem 1(c), above, noting that the same dollar amount of contributions generates a different amount of current deductions depending upon the recipient of the contributions.

1(e).   T would likely not be entitled to any charitable deduction. Tuition, even though paid to a charitable institution, is clearly not deductible as a quid pro quo is received. The issue involved is the Sponsor's Club $10,000 contribution. If T joined the Club in order for daughter to be admitted or as insurance that she would be admitted, a quid pro quo has been received and no deduction is allowed. See Rev. Rul. 71-112, 1971-1 C.B. 93. If daughter would have been admitted regardless, then a deduction appears allowable. Cf. Rev. Rul. 83-104 at page 799 of the Text.

302

2(a).   This problem deals with both the § 170(b) limitations on charitable contributions seen in problem 1, above, and the § 170(e) determination of the amount of a contribution that is "taken into account" which must be considered prior to § 170(b). T would be allowed a $70,000 deduction. Under § 170(e)(1)(A) the amount taken into account is reduced from $90,000 by $20,000 (the property's potential gain that is not LTCG) to $70,000, which amount is then fully deductible within the § 170(b)(1)(A) 50% limit.

2(b).   T would be allowed a $60,000 deduction. The amount of T's contribution which is taken into account is $70,000, as in problem 2(a), above; however that amount is subject to the maximum 30% limitation on gifts to private foundations under § 170(b)(1)(B)(i). In addition, the excess $10,000 contribution would be a contribution carryover into the succeeding 5 years. §§ 170(b)(1)(B) and (d)(1)(A).

2(c).   T would be allowed a $60,000 deduction. In addition T has a $30,000 carryover gift of appreciated capital gain property. This gift of appreciated property does not come within § 170(e)(1)(A) or (B)(i) or (ii), but a gift of capital gain property as defined by § 170(b)(1)(C)(iv) is subject to the 30% limitation imposed by § 170(b)(1)(C)(i); T may deduct $60,000 (30% of T's $200,000 contribution base). The unused $30,000 contribution is allowed a five year carryover under § 170(b)(1)(C)(ii). In the alternative, T could make a § 170(b)(1)(C)(iii) election. See problem 2(f), below.

2(d).   T would be allowed a $70,000 deduction. If the stock had been held only five months then T's gain on its sale would have been a $20,000 STCG. Since it would not have been a LTCG, § 170(e)(1)(A) would reduce the amount of the $90,000 contribution to be taken into account by $20,000 - the amount which would not have been a LTCG had the property been sold at the time of the contribution. The $70,000 contribution is within the § 170(b)(1)(A) 50% of contribution base limitation and the result here is identical to the result in problem 2(a), above.

2(e).   If T had given LTCG stock with an adjusted basis of $70,000 and a fair market value of $90,000 to a public charity, § 170(e)(1)(B) would not have applied to reduce the amount of the gift to be taken into account. See problem 2(d), above. However, the deduction would have been reduced by the 30% limitation of § 170(b)(1)(C)(i) to $60,000 with a (ii) carryover of the $30,000 excess. Using the § 170(b)(1)(C)(iii) election the appreciated capital gain property would be treated as though it fell within § 170(e)(1)(B) where the amount of the contribution to be accorded recognition would be reduced by the LTCG; but the gift would not be subject to the § 170(b)(1)(C)(i) 30% limitation. If the election were made, the amount of the contribution would be $70,000 ($90,000 less $20,000) which would be fully deductible within the § 170(b)(1)(A) 50% limitation. There would be no carryover. By making the election under these facts, T would relinquish a $30,000 appreciated capital gain property carryover in return for a $10,000 additional deduction in the current year.

T is more likely to make the (iii) election as the adjusted basis of the property approaches its fair market value. If T's basis in the property were $86,000 and T made a § 170(b)(1)(C)(iii) election the amount of his contribution under § 170(e)(1)(B) would be $86,000. The contribution would not be subject to the 30% limitation, and T would not be allowed any § 170(b)(1)(C)(ii) carryover. Thus T could get a $86,000 deduction in the current year, giving up only a negligible carryover, as compared with a $60,000 deduction and $30,000 carryover if no election were made.

2(f).   T would be allowed a $60,000 deduction. The amount of T's contribution would be reduced to $80,000 under § 170(e)(1)(A), subtracting the $10,000 amount of potential recapture. Doubt about the impact of § 170(e)(1)(A) on § 1231 property is dispelled by § 170(e)(1), last sentence. However, as the property is also appreciated LTCG or § 1231 property which is not within § 170(e)(1)(B), § 170(b)(1)(C)(i) limits T's deduction in the current year to $60,000 (30% of T's $200,000 contribution base) with a $20,000 § 170(b)(1)(C)(ii) carryover. If T elects under § 170(b)(1)(C)(iii), T will be allowed a $70,000 deduction in the current year with no carryover.   § 170(e)(1)(B) would require a $10,000 reduction, the potential $10,000 hotchpot gain, *after* reduction for the § 1250 ordinary income.

After working these problems the student should see that on gifts of appreciated property the amount of the charitable contribution is reduced by the amount of the potential gain in the property that is neither LTCG nor § 1231 gain. Further, if the property is appreciated

304

LTCG or § 1231 property the amount of the contribution is reduced by the appreciation if the gift is to a tainted private foundation (except for qualified appreciated stock, see § 170(e)(5)) or is a gift of tangible personal property unrelated to the recipient charity's purpose or function. These reductions in the amount taken into account are mandatory. Any remaining appreciated property to a public charity is subject only to the 30% limitation with a 5 year carryover of the excess, unless a § 170(b)(1)(C)(iii) election is made; the election carries with it a required § 170(e)(1)(B) reduction. Any remaining LTCG or § 1231 appreciated property for the use of a public charity or to or for a private charity is subject to the maximum 20% § 170(b)(1)(D)(i) limitation.

2(g).   T would be allowed a $40,000 deduction. If T gave the LTCG stock to Private Foundation, § 170(e)(1)(B)(ii) would let T take into account only the amount of the contribution reduced by T's LTCG of $20,000 or $70,000. However, under § 170(b)(1)(D)(i) T would be allowed a deduction of only 20% of T's $200,000 contribution base or only $40,000. T would be permitted a carryover of $30,000.

2(h).   If qualified appreciated stock is contributed and § 170(e)(5)(A) applies, § 170(e)(5)(A) makes the § 170(e)(1)(B)(ii) reduction inapplicable. Section 170(b)(1)(D)(i) would apply to limit the amount contributed to 20% of the contribution base or $40,000 with a $50,000 § 170(b)(1)(D)(ii) carryover to the 5 succeeding taxable years. See § 170(d)(1)(A).

3(a).   Publius will not be allowed a charitable contribution for the gift. Although the papers have a $100,000 value, it is assumed Publius has a zero basis for them. If he sold the papers he would have a $100,000 gain that would be ordinary income because the papers do not constitute a capital asset. See § 1221(3). Therefore under § 170(e)(1)(A) the amount of his contribution to be taken into account would be the $100,000 fair market value less $100,000 (potential ordinary income) or zero. See Morrison v. Comm'r, 71 T.C. 683 (1979) aff'd per curiam, 611 F.2d 98 (5th Cir. 1980), holding that a Congressman's cost of holding office did not create a basis in his papers, etc. and consequently he had no charitable contribution for them when he contributed them to a university. The result with respect to the papers would have been different prior to the 1969 amendments. See Bernard Goss, 59 T.C. 594 (1973), acq. 1974-2 C.B. 2.

The Revenue Act of 1978 added § 1231(b)(1)(D) providing U.S. government publications received from the government for a price less than that at which they are offered to the general public, held by a taxpayer described in § 1221(5), are not § 1231 property. Thus gains on the sale of such publications result in ordinary income and the publications are subject to a § 170(e)(1)(A) reduction on a contribution to charity.

3(b).   Reg. § 1.170A-1(g) provides that the value of services rendered to a charity does not qualify as a charitable deduction. The result is rational in the sense that Publius has no basis (or tax cost) for his services, and consequently he should not be allowed a deduction. The regulation does add: "However, unreimbursed expenditures made incident to the rendition of services to an organization contributions to which are deductible may constitute a deductible contribution." Reg. § 1.170A-1(g) goes on to add: "Reasonable expenditures for meals and lodging necessarily incurred while away from home in the course of performing donated services. . . . are deductible. For the purposes of this paragraph, the phrase 'while away from home' has the same meaning as that phrase is used for purposes of Section 162 and the regulations thereunder." Note as well the § 274(n) 50% limit on the deductibility of meals. Under § 170(i) a taxpayer who uses his or her car in the current year in performing charitable services is allowed a 14 cents per mile charitable deduction. However, § 170(j) denies a charitable deduction for travelling expenses (including meals and lodging) while away from home unless there is no significant element of personal pleasure, recreation or vacation in such travel.

In Travis Smith, 60 T.C. 988 (1973) acq. 1974-2 C.B. 4, under the predecessor regulation to Reg. § 1.170A-1(g), taxpayer was allowed to deduct his out-of-pocket expenses incurred in an evangelistic trip to spread the gospel. The Court concluded the trip was on behalf of the taxpayer's church and not personally motivated. And in McCollum v. Comm'r, 37 T.C.M. 1817 (1978), taxpayer's whole family volunteered for the National Ski Patrol and, although they could not deduct the value of their services, they could deduct out-of-pocket expenses for transportation, meals, lodging, special uniforms, equipment and repairs, lift tickets, etc. But the above cases were prior to the enactment of § 170(j); see problem 3(e), below. And see Rev. Rul. 80-45, 1980-1 C.B. 54. But see Grey B. (Miller) Tate, 59 T.C. 543 (1973), where under the prior regulation no deduction was allowed.

3(c).   The Ruling cited, which allows no deduction, is probably wrong. Seemingly blood is property. Green v. Comm'r, 74 T.C. 1224 (1980). The blood's donation may be an accommodation but it is not a service, as the Ruling holds. See United States v. Garber, 607 F.2d 92 (5th Cir. 1979), and Lary v. United States, 787 F.2d 1538 (11 Cir. 1986), neither concluding whether blood is services or property because such a determination was unnecessary in reaching their decisions. Assuming blood is property, nothing in § 1221 removes blood from the definition of a capital asset. (Although if such "donations" were made regularly and were taxpayer's main source of income, there is questionable authority that the blood would be excluded from capital asset status by § 1221(1).) No doubt blood has a zero basis; consequently its sale in our case for $100 would yield a $100 capital gain. Regrettably, Publius would have the burden of proving that it was held long-term. If Publius met the challenge, a $100 deduction should be allowed, subject to the 30 percent rule of § 170(b)(1)(C) since the contribution would escape the proscriptions of § 170(e)(1)(B). If not, § 170(e)(1)(A) would reduce the contribution to zero. This problem demonstrates that a simple factual situation can generate several complex tax issues.

3(d).   No, Publius will not be allowed a deduction for the use of his property since mere permission to use is not payment. He is donating a mere partial interest in the property, and § 170(f)(2)(B) and § 170(f)(3)(A) disallow a deduction for the use of property. See Rev. Rul. 70-477, 1970-2 C.B. 62. If Publius leases an office in his building to the charity but requires it to pay no rent, there would still be no deduction. A deduction for an income interest in property is allowed only if it is in the form of a guaranteed annuity or fixed percent of income interest. The theory here is that to allow a deduction would result in a double benefit to the taxpayer because nothing would be included in his income but he would also be allowed a deduction. The same theory applies to a gift of the use of tangible property. Compare a gift of an undivided portion of one's property.

3(e).   Although such expenses were deductible in McCollum v. Comm'r, 37 T.C.M. 1817 (1978) (see problem 3(b), above), their deductibility would seemingly be precluded by § 170(j).

3(f).   Although this advertising tactic, which is commonly being used, is appealing, Publius may have some problems. First, since the gift of property has a claimed value in excess of $5,000, Publius must obtain a formal qualified appraisal by an independent appraiser and attach it to his return. Reg. § 1.170A-13(c). Second, Publius may deduct only the fair market value, the appraiser's value for the car, no matter what Charity advertises. Although it is unlikely, if the fair market value of Publius's car exceeds its adjusted basis, Publius must deal with § 170(e)(1)(A) and (B)(i).

4(a).   This is a part-gift, part-sale to a charity, subject to the special rule of § 1011(b). Under that section the amount realized on the sale ($60,000) may be offset by an amount that bears the same ratio to the taxpayer's basis ($60,000) as the amount realized bears to the fair market value of the property ($80,000). Thus, the basis for the sale is $45,000 ($60,000/$80,000 x $60,000) and, on the sale, Planner would have a $15,000 LTCG ($60,000 - $45,000) from stock held for 4 years.

These same principles would apply if the property had been subject to a mortgage liability of $60,000 and Planner gave the property subject to the mortgage to the charity. See Guest v. Comm'r, 77 T.C. 9 (1981); Hodgdon v. Comm'r, 98 T.C. 424 (1992).

4(b).   The amount of Planner's charitable contribution would be $20,000. This is a gift of appreciated capital gain property to a public charity and there would be no mandatory § 170(e)(1)(B) adjustment. However, § 170(b)(1)(C)(i) would limit the amount of Planner's contribution taken into account to 30% of her contribution base of $65,000 ($50,000 plus her $15,000 gain on the sale) or to $19,500 with a $500 carryover under clause (ii). If Planner made a clause (iii) election with respect to this gift, she would still be allowed only a $15,000 current deduction and no carryover. The § 170(e)(1)(B) reduction would be the potential gain on the $20,000 gift. This is $5,000 ($20,000 F.M.V. less remaining basis, $15,000). Thus Planner would not make the (iii) election.

4(c).   The theory behind this part-gift, part-sale to charity is that Planner is selling three-fourths and donating one-fourth of her property. On the sale of three-fourths of her property she would have a $60,000 amount realized, a $45,000 adjusted basis and she would recognize a $15,000 gain. Under the part-gift, part-sale proportion theory that gain would be $7,500 of § 1250 gain (3/4 of the $10,000 § 1250 gain) and $7,500 (the balance) of § 1231 gain. Reg. § 1.1011-2(c) Ex. 7. If the $7,500 of § 1231 gain becomes LTCG and if taxpayer has a NCG, some of the

$7,500 will potentially be taxed at a 25% rate as unrecaptured § 1250 gain and the remainder at 20% as unadjusted net capital gain. See § 1(h)(1)(C) and (D). There are insufficient facts given to provide a more specific answer.

There is a gift of the remaining $20,000 worth of property which has a $15,000 adjusted basis and on sale would result in $2,500 of § 1250 gain and $2,500 of § 1231 gain. Under § 170(e)(1)(A) the amount of Planner's donation would be subject to a mandatory reduction by the amount of the § 1250 gain on the gift portion of the property ($2,500) to $17,500. Again § 170(b)(1)(C)(i) would limit Planner's deduction to 30% of Planner's now $65,000 contribution base or to $19,500. Thus, the $17,500 would be currently deductible in its entirety.

5.   Investor should make use of her gains and losses. First, as discovered in Chapter 21C, Investor can use $3,000 of excess capital losses to shelter or wipe out $3,000 of ordinary income. § 1211(b). Thus, Investor should take that amount of net losses each year. If Investor wants to continue the investment in the loss investment, she can reinvest in it, although this can be done only outside the 30 day § 1091 wash sale time period considered in Chapter 25B. A safe investor would likely duplicate the investment more than 30 days before the loss is incurred just in case the investment should increase in value during the 61 day period.

Second, as seen in this section, when Investor makes other than minimal charitable gifts, Investor should give Investor's most appreciated long-term investments and avoid the LTCG on the investments, although this will trigger the § 170(b)(1)(C)(i) 30% ceiling. Again, if Investor does not want to part with the investment, Investor should reinvest (no 30 day period on a gain) in the investment. Although this requires Investor to part with the amount of cash she would have given to charities (disregarding stock commissions), she effectively gets a step-up in basis in the investment.

Page 822:

With Rev. Rul. 63-232, compare Rev. Rul. 79-174, 1979-1 C.B. 99, where a massive southern pine beetle attack on ornamental pine trees destroyed the trees within a matter of days and a § 165(c)(3) loss was allowed. The Ruling distinguished Rev. Rul. 57-599, 1957-2 C.B. 142, holding that the death of a tree as a result of disease is not a deductible casualty loss. See also Coleman v. Comm'r, 76 T.C. 580 (1981), and Maher v. Comm'r, 76 T.C. 593 (1981), denying casualty losses to diseased trees, and Ruecke v. Comm'r, 41 T.C.M. 1587 (1981), allowing a casualty loss deduction where a drought destroyed plants over a three to four month period.

Page 822:

The Service has denied a casualty loss in an arson-for-profit situation. Rev. Rul. 81-24, 1981-1 C.B. 79. Taxpayer burned down a building he owned in order to collect insurance proceeds, and he was convicted of arson. Taxpayer was unable to collect insurance and attempted to deduct the loss as a § 165(c) casualty loss. The Service disallowed the deduction because its allowance would frustrate public policy. See page 540 of the Text. See also Raymond Mazzei, 61 T.C. 497 (1970), and Rev. Rul. 77-126, 1977-1 C.B. 47, both holding that the public policy doctrine codifications under § 162 are not exclusive.

Page 824:

Two taxpayers were unsuccessful in deducting casualty losses in a situation like *Pulvers* where there was a downward fluctuation in valuation but there was no physical damage to their property. The taxpayers were both Brentwood neighbors of O.J. and Nicole Simpson who claimed that their property declined in value as a result of the events surrounding Nicole's murder and O.J.'s trial, including media and gawkers. Chamales v. Comm'r, 79 TCM 1428 (2000); Caan v. United States, 99-1 USTC ¶ 50,349 (D.C. Ca. 1999).

Page 825:

Rev. Rul. 72-112, 1972-1 C.B. 60, includes ransom within the concept of theft loss stating:

> Thus, to qualify as a "theft" loss within the meaning of section 165(c)(3) of the Code, the taxpayer needs only to prove that his loss resulted from a taking of property that is illegal

310

under the law of the state where it occurred and that the taking was done with criminal intent.

In Florida, where larceny cannot generally be asserted against a co-owner of property, wife could not claim a theft loss when her husband withdrew funds from their joint checking account. Alice Dandeneau, 30 T.C.M. 542 (1971), aff'd per curiam, 456 F.2d 799 (5th Cir. 1972).

The *Cohan* principle was used in determining the amount of theft losses in Norman A. Pharr, 30 T.C.M. 118, aff'd 1972-1 USTC ¶ 9272 (2d Cir. 1972), and Arthur Willis, 32 T.C.M. 182 (1973), aff'd per curiam, 496 F.2d 1198 (9th Cir. 1974).

PROBLEM

Page 827:

1(a).   If an occurrence within the concept of a casualty (sudden, unexpected, etc.) causes a loss of property, the loss will be deductible. The case and ruling cited so indicate. As a matter of fact, in the problem there *was* physical damage to property, the ring, which would seem to bring this matter within routine casualty concepts. The case would be closer if when the car door slammed on her right hand Mrs. Prone made a wild gesture with her left hand which caused a ring to fly from her finger and be lost. Compare Keenan v. Bowers, 91 F. Supp 771 (D.S.C. 1950), which involved an equally tragic situation in which a deduction was denied because it lacked "suddenness."

1(b).   Following the case of White v. Comm'r, 48 T.C. 430 (1967), the Service has stated in Rev. Rul. 72-592, 1972-2 C.B. 101, that under certain circumstances property that has been accidentally and irretrievably lost may give rise to a casualty loss deduction under § 165(c)(3). Should the unexplainable disappearance of the brooch in *Mary Frances Allen* lead to a deduction in spite of the inability to prove there was a theft?

In *White*, the Court noted that the wife "did not just misplace, mislay, or lose her ring. If she had merely dropped it in the leaves or the gravel driveway we would be faced with that situation, but the evidence before us paints a far different picture of the casualty loss claimed here."

311

White, supra at 433. In agreeing with the *White* case, Rev. Rul. 72-592, supra, emphasizes that an accidental loss of property qualifies for a § 165(c)(3) deduction only if the loss also qualifies as a "casualty" under existing criteria. Thus, "the loss must result from some event that is (1) identifiable, (2) damaging to property, and (3) sudden, unexpected, and unusual in nature." 1972-2 CB 101.

The position taken by the Service and the above-quoted dictum from *White* support the conclusion that the loss of the brooch in *Mary Frances Allen* does not give rise to a casualty deduction. The loss did not occur as the result of an identified event which was sudden and rather unexpected and caused damage to the brooch. Rather, the loss was unexplainable and no event was identified. The loss was more similar to an accidental misplacement or loss referred to in the *White* dictum for which neither the Service nor the courts have allowed a deduction.

Page 830:

This distinction occurs because, in the case of business or profit-making property, the asset or its adjusted basis represents a business expenditure which has been completely dissipated.

Page 830:

If casualty loss property involves business property or property involved in a transaction entered into for profit, a separate loss computation must be made for each identifiable property damaged or destroyed. Reg. § 1.165-7(b)(2)(i). Thus, where a hurricane destroyed a citrus grove, the ripening fruit and the trees were separate property and no loss was allowed for the zero basis ripening fruit where the costs of growing the fruit had properly been deducted. Rev. Rul. 68-351, 1968-2 C.B. 80. No such separation occurs on personal use property. Reg. § 1.165-7(b)(2)(ii). See, for example, Allen Huss, 32 TCM 977 (1973), where ornamental trees on residential property were destroyed in a storm and the trees were treated as an integral part of the property and no separate basis was allocated to the trees and other properties in determining the personal casualty loss.

312

PROBLEMS

Page 831:

1(a). Sleepy's personal casualty loss is equal to $5900. The amount of the casualty loss is determined by the lesser of her adjusted basis in the car of $10,000 or its change in fair market value as a result of the accident, $7,000. Reg. § 1.165-7(b)(1). The loss amount is then reduced by any reimbursement such as insurance (in this case $1,000, leaving $6,000). Since this is a personal asset and the loss is claimed under § 165(c)(3), the § 165(h)(1) $100 floor comes into play reducing the personal casualty loss on the car to $5900. § 165(h)(3)(B).

1(b). Sleepy's personal casualty gain is equal to $10,000 which is the difference between the $20,000 received from the insurance company and Sleepy's $10,000 basis in the vase. Like the car, the vase is not depreciable.

1(c). Since the personal casualty gain, $10,000, exceeds the personal casualty loss, $5,900, the gain is treated as a gain from the sale or exchange of a capital asset (§ 165(h)(2)(B)(i)) and the loss is treated as a loss from the sale or exchange of a capital asset. § 165(h)(2)(B)(ii). Both the gain and the loss are long-term from the sale of a capital asset held more than 12 months.

1(d). The $5,900 loss is fully deductible since § 165(h)(2)(B) imposes no restrictions. Cf. §§ 165(f), 1211(b) and 1212(b).

1(e). Since capital losses are generally deductible from capital gains, § 1211(b), the capital loss, here, is not an itemized deduction. The effect of § 165(h)(2)(B) in treating such gains or losses as capital is to bring them into the overall capital gain and loss netting which, as seen is Chapter 21, in essence allows the losses to the extent they are deductible to be deducted above the line. Cf. § 62(a)(3).

1(f). If Sleepy recovers only $12,000 in insurance for the vase then the personal casualty gain will be $2,000. See problem 2(b), above. In that case, the personal casualty loss, $5,900, exceeds the casualty gain of $2,000 by $3,900. Lacking a sale or exchange the gain and loss are both characterized as ordinary. Cf. § 165(h)(2)(B). The deductibility

of the loss is limited to the extent of the gain or $2000, §
165(h)(2)(A)(i), plus the amount of the excess that exceeds 10% of
AGI. The excess gain, $3900, exceeds 10% of adjusted gross income,
$3000, by $900. § 165 (h)(2)(A)(ii). Thus a total of $2,900 is
deductible. Section 165(h)(4)(A), for purposes of determining AGI,
treats the loss as deductible to the extent of the gain under § 62(a).
However, any excess loss is allowed only as an itemized deduction.
Thus the $900 is an itemized deduction. See § 63(d). It is not subject
to the 2% floor. § 67(b)(3).

This whole process bears some similarity to the § 1231 subhotchpot
process. If personal casualty gains exceed such losses, all are capital
gains and losses. If losses exceed gains, all are ordinary. However §
165(h) then goes further both limiting the amount of deductibility of
excess losses under § 165(h)(2)(A)(ii) and dropping any deductible
excesses below the line into "itemized" status.

1(g).   None. Section 165(h)(4)(E) denies a loss to the extent that a taxpayer
        could but did not seek insurance recovery. The statute reverses the
        result under prior case law. See Miller v. Comm'r, 733 F.2d 399 (6th
        Cir. 1984). Thus the tax results to Sleepy are the same as if she had
        recovered the insurance, and her loss is not increased by the
        unrecovered insurance.

2.   Shaky's possible deductible loss is limited to the amount of his property
        damage. Rev. Rul. 59-360, 1959-2 C.B. 75. Cf. § 165(k). But, as that
        loss is fully "compensated for by insurance," no deduction is allowable
        under § 165(a).

        Of the $1,200 received for the family's meals and lodging expenses,
        $800 (the excess of actual living expenses ($1,800) over normal living
        expenses ($1,000)) is excluded from gross income by §123 and the
        balance, $400, is gross income for lack of any exclusionary rule
        applicable to it, *Glenshaw Glass*; Reg. §1.123-1(a)(4); and see Sen.
        Rep. 91-552, 91st Cong., 1st Sess. (1969), 1969-3 C.B. 423, 596.

Chapter 24.   The Interrelationship of Timing and Characterization

PROBLEMS

Page 850:

1(a).   Seller would report as income in each year the ratio of the "gross profit" to the "total contract price," § 453(c), times the amount paid by Buyer. The gain reported in each year has the character determined by the original sale. Seller would have a $1,600 LTCG from the sale of a capital asset held for 4 years, in the year of the sale ($8,000/$10,000 x $2,000) and in each of the succeeding four years. Even though the payments extend over more than 5 years from the acquisition of the property, the holding period is measured from the date of the sale, i.e., 4 years. Cf. § 1(h)(2).

The appropriate working of § 453 becomes instantly clear when cash transactions and installment sales are compared, as follows:

1.   Assume a cash sale for $10,000:

Amount realized	$10,000
Adjusted basis	2,000
Gain on Sale:	$ 8,000

2.   Sale on the *installment* method:

Year	Include in Income		Exclude from Income
1	$1,600		$ 400
2-5	$1,600/year x 4 = 6,400	$400/year x 4 =	1,600
	Gain on sale $8,000	Adjusted basis	$2,000

Acceleration of payments will make no difference, except in timing, as the ratio applies to whatever payments are received during the year. There is some analogy to the § 72 and § 101 treatment of annuities and life insurance proceeds paid as annuities, as all involve the tax aspect

315

of pro rata recovery of capital.

1(b). The results to Seller under § 453 would be the same regardless of whether Seller is a cash or accrual method taxpayer. It is probably not worth adding that for a short period from mid 1999 to the end of 2000, the installment method was unavailable to accrual method taxpayers.

1(c) If Seller has $3,000 of § 1245 recapture gain on the property's disposition, that amount is required to be recaptured in the year of disposition under § 453(i); and it is recaptured in full even though other gain is accorded installment treatment. The $3,000 recaptured amount is added to the property's adjusted basis prior to computing the § 453 gain. Thus the gross profit ($5,000), total contract price ($10,000) ratio is 50%; and of each actual payment of $2,000 Seller would in addition recognize 50%, or $1,000 as § 1231 main hotchpot gain. The effect of § 453(i) here is to accelerate the taxation of the recapture portion of Seller's $8,000 gain, taxing $3,000 immediately and permitting only the excess $5,000 to qualify for installment treatment.

1(d). These facts bring the rules of § 453(g) and § 1239 into play. The requirements of § 1239 are met and the gain is ordinary income. Under § 453(g)(1), all payments to be received are deemed received in the year of the disposition (see § 453(f)(7)) unless, under § 453(g)(2), Seller establishes that the disposition did not have as one of its principal purposes the avoidance of the Federal income tax law. Assuming § 453(g)(1) applies, Seller would realize $10,000 and have an $8,000 ordinary gain in the year of the sale. As stated in the legislative history S. Rep. No. 96-1000, 96th Cong., 2d Sess. (1980), 1980-2 C.B. 494, 503:

> In general, this rule is intended to deter transactions which are structured in such a way as to give the related purchaser the benefit of depreciation deductions (measured from a stepped-up basis) prior to the time the seller is required to include in income the corresponding gain on the sale.

1(e). Seller would have a total gain of $8,000 all of which would be § 1231 gain. Using the same figures as in 1(b), above, there would be a $1,600 § 1231 gain in each of the 5 years. Since there are no other § 1231 gains or losses and no "look-backs" under § 1231(c), all the gains will be LTCG.

When the $1,600 LTCGs make their way into § 1(h), $5,000 of the gains will be § 1(h)(1)(D) 25% gains as unrecaptured Section 1250 gains and $3,000 of the gains will be § 1(h)(1)(C) 20% gains as adjusted net capital gains. Reg. § 1.453-12(a) requires the full amount of 25% gains to be recognized prior to recognition of the 20% gains. Thus Seller will have $1,600 of 25% gains in years 1-3, $200 of 25% gains and $1,400 of 20% gains in year 4, and $1,600 of 20% gains in year 5. See Reg. § 1.453-1(d) Example 1.

1(f).   The payments in the year of sale include the amount of the mortgage only to the extent that it exceeds the basis of the property. Reg. § 1.453-4(c). See also Reg. § 15A.453-1(b)(3)(i). Since the $2,000 mortgage is not in excess of the $2,000 adjusted basis, the mortgage would not be included with the $2,000 cash payments in the year of sale.

This principle was also expressed in Rev. Rul. 71-543, 1971-2 C.B. 223. The liabilities assumed need not bear any specific relation to the property that is sold and can be any liability of the seller. See Rev. Rul. 73-555, 1973-2 C.B. 159; but compare Rev. Rul. 76-109, 1976-1 C.B. 125. If at the time of the sale a seller is indebted to the buyer and that obligation is discharged as a part of the consideration for the installment sale, the amount of the obligation *is* treated as a payment. A sneaky taxpayer cannot wring out some cash with tax impunity by fancy footwork. The Treasury has properly so ruled. Rev. Rul. 71-515, 1971-2 C.B. 222. See also Reg. §15A.453-1(b)(3)(i). Cf. Big "D" Development Corp. v. Comm'r, 30 T.C.M. 646 (1971), aff'd per curiam, 453 F.3d 1365 (5th Cir. 1972), cert. den., 406 U.S. 945 (1972); and Rev. Rul. 76-398, 1976-2 C.B. 130.

In determining the ratio under § 453 of "gross profit" to "total contract price," the mortgage is subtracted from the "total contract price" so that $8,000/$8,000 of each payment would be taxed in each year. Reg. § 1.453-4(c). See also Reg. § 15A.453-1(b)(2)(iii). Seller would have a $2,000 LTCG in the year of sale and $2,000 LTCG in each of the succeeding three years, each from the sale of a capital asset held for 4 years. Although under *Crane* the mortgage represents a part of the

317

amount realized on the sale, it represents an amount that will not be received by Seller as payments. If the amount is not taxed at the time of the sale (and it is not because it is not treated as a payment) some means must be devised to account for it as actual payments are received. The device is a reduction of the "total contract price." This reduces the denominator in the critical fraction and, accordingly, increases the amount of each actual payment which must be reported as gain. A little exploratory arithmetic will show that the device works and is a suitable accommodation of the installment sales provisions to the *Crane* principle. See also Reg. § 15A.453-1(b)(5) Ex. (2).

1(g).   Under Reg. § 1.453-4(c) (see also Reg. § 15A.453-1(b)(3)(i)) the amount of the mortgage ($3,000) exceeds Seller's adjusted basis ($2,000) and the excess $1,000 is treated as a payment in the year of sale. The regulation in effect treats $2,000 of the mortgage as a mortgage and $1,000 of the mortgage as a receipt of cash in the year of sale. The ratio under § 453 of "gross profit" to "total contract price," is $8,000/$8,000 or 1. The amount of the mortgage actually treated as a mortgage ($2,000) is subtracted from the actual "total contract price" to compute "total contract price" under the formula. Reg. § 1.453-4(c). See also Reg. § 15A.453-1(b)(2)(iii). Thus 100% of all actual cash payments plus the $1,000 of the mortgage treated as a payment will be taxed as gain in the year of the sale. Seller will have $3,000 of LTCG in year one and $2,000 LTCG in years two and three and a $1,000 LTCG in year four, properly reflecting his overall gain of $8,000 when the *Crane* principle is taken into account. Each will be treated as LTCG from the sale of a capital asset held for 4 years. Cf. Reg. § 15A.453-1(b)(5) Ex. (3).

United Pacific Corporation, 39 T.C. 721 (1963), holds that if a purchaser does not take subject to or assume the mortgage, the excess of the mortgage over the adjusted basis is not a payment in the year of sale, even though there is an agreement that the buyer will subsequently assume the mortgage after payment of his purchase money mortgage. This does not mean that the principal of the mortgage is not a part of the amount realized by the seller, but only that it is not part of the amount reported on the sale. When the purchaser ultimately assumes the mortgage and begins making payments of principal, then the seller has additional income from the sale, which is reported on the installment method.

318

1(h). Seller's sale of Buyer's notes would constitute a § 453B(a) disposition of the notes, and Seller would be required to report gain in the year of the sale to the extent that the $7,000 amount realized on the notes (§ 453B(a)(1)) exceeds their $1,600 basis. Section 453B(b) defines the basis of a note to be the excess of the face amount of the note ($2,000) over the amount that would be returnable as income were the obligation satisfied in full ($1,600). Thus each note has a $400 basis and all four notes have an aggregate basis of $1,600. The gain would have the same character as if made on the original sale. § 453B(a), last sentence. Thus Seller would have a $5,400 LTCG from an asset held for 4 years on the disposition ($7,000 - $1,600).

1(i). Seller's gift of the notes would also constitute a § 453B disposition and Seller would be required by § 453B(a)(2) to report gain in the year of the gift to the extent that the fair market value of the notes (§ 453B(a)(2)) exceeds their bases. § 453B(b). The gain would have the same character as the gain on the original sale. § 453B(a), last sentence. Thus Seller would again have a $5,400 LTCG on the disposition: $7,000 (fair market value) less $1,600 (the § 453B(b) aggregate basis of the obligations).

Since the fair market value of each of the notes is $1,750 and Seller reports $7,000 on their disposition as if it were an amount realized, the disposition effects an instant increase in the basis for the obligations to $7,000. Consequently Daughter's § 1015 basis is $7,000, $1,750 for each note, see Rev. Rul. 79-371, 1979-2 C.B. 294, and cf. Shafpa Realty Corp., 8 B.T.A. 283 (1927). Thus Daughter has $250 of gain on the collection of each note. If each note is a capital asset, the issue whether there is a sale or exchange depends upon the application of § 1271(b). If the notes were issued by the Buyer after June 8, 1997, (see § 1271(b)(1)(A)), there is an exchange under § 1271(a). If the notes were issued prior to such date, there is no sale or exchange and Daughter has $250 of ordinary income on each note. Hudson v. Comm'r, 20 T.C. 734, aff'd. sub nom. Oglivie v. Comm'r, 216 F.2d 748 (6th Cir. 1954). If each $250 gain is a capital gain, Daughter's holding period for each note would tack Seller's holding period because Daughter's $7,000 basis was determined by Father's (after gross income inclusion) adjusted basis of $7,000. § 1223(2). Thus Daughter would have $250 LTCG on each note.

1(j).   These facts bring the rules of a second disposition by a related person into play. See § 453(e). Since the second disposition occurred within two years of the first sale (see § 453(e)(2)) and was made by a related person (§§ 453(f)(1) and 318(a)(1)(A)(ii)), § 453(e)(1) requires the amount realized on the second disposition (or fair market value where the disposition is not a sale or exchange, see § 453(e)(4)) to be treated as received at that time by the person making the first disposition. The § 453(e)(7)"no principal purpose" exception is assumed to be inapplicable here, and the § 453(e)(6) exceptions are also inapplicable. Note the special statute of limitations rules on such second dispositions. § 453(e)(8).

Under these facts Seller would have a $1,600 LTCG under §453(a)(1) on his first $2,000 of cash received. In addition, Seller would have $6,400 of LTCG at the time of Daughter's sale. Both would be from the sale of an asset held for 4 years. We first go to the § 453(e)(3) limitation computation where the amount treated as received by Seller at the time of Daughter's sale may not exceed the excess of:

(A).   The lesser of:

   (i)   the amount realized on the second disposition ($10,000) or

   (ii)   the total contract price for the first disposition ($10,000)

over

(B).   the sum of:

   (i)   The aggregate payments received with respect to the first disposition before the close of the year ($2,000), plus

   (ii)   The aggregate amount treated as received with respect to the first disposition for prior taxable years by reason of § 453(e) (zero)

Thus Seller is treated under § 453(e) as receiving $8,000 ($10,000 less $2,000).

Since Seller is treated as receiving $8,000, under Seller's § 453(c) ratio, Seller will be required to report a $6,400 LTCG.

Daughter would have no gain on her sale because her amount realized is equal to her basis in the property.

With respect to Seller's consequences on Daughter's payments of her obligations, see § 453(e)(5) and problem 1(m), below.

Does this all make sense? Sure. Congress is merely using a broad assignment of income theory where sales are made by related parties, generally within a two year period after the original § 453 sale. Incidentally, § 453(f)(1) defines a related person as "a person whose stock would be attributable under § 318(a) (other than paragraph 4) to the person first disposing of the property." Thus related persons include family members (not brothers and sisters), corporations, trusts, estates and partnerships.

1(k).   Using the same limitations rules of § 453(e), Seller would have $4,800 of LTCG under these facts in addition to the $1,600 of LTCG in the same year reported with respect to the $2,000 payment for the year. Each gain would be from the sale of an asset held for 4 years. Under § 453(e)(3) the amount realized would be $6000:

(A).   the lesser of:

      (i) $11,000 or

      (ii) $10,000

over

(B).   the sum of:

      (i) $4,000 ($2000 cash and payment of 1 $2,000 note. § 453(e)(3)(B)(i) includes all payments received during the year though they are received after the second disposition.)

      (ii)   zero

And 80% of that $6,000, $4,800 would be taxed as a LTCG under §453.

In addition, Seller would be taxed on $1,600 in year one and $1,600 in year two on actual payments received in the two years. Thus Seller will have recognized a total $8,000 LTCG.

Daughter would have a $1,000 LTCG on her sale of the property. Her holding period would be measured by her holding period for the property.

1(ℓ). If Daughter's sale were for only $9,000, then Seller's § 453(e)(3) receipt in the year of Daughter's sale would be $5,000:

(A).   the lesser of:

(i) $ 9,000 or

(ii) $10,000

over

(B).   the sum of:

(i) $4,000 and

(ii)   zero

And Seller would have a § 453(c) gain of 80% of $5,000 or $4,000, which again would be a LTCG. In addition, Seller would have recognized a total of $3,200 of LTCG on actual payments by the end of year two. Each gain would be from the sale of an asset held for 4 years.

Daughter would have a $1,000 LTCL under these facts. See problem 1(m), below, for the results to Seller on the subsequent collection of the remaining $6,000 of notes.

1(m). This problem illustrates § 453(e)(5) which, in effect, allows Seller a recovery of capital to the extent of the § 453(e)(1) amount received, prior to any § 453(c) treatment of Daughter's subsequent payments.

322

Thus in problem 1(j), above, when Seller receives the $8,000 of principal payments on the notes from Daughter, that $8,000 is treated as a recovery of capital and not as a receipt of payments under § 453(c). Seller thus recognizes no further gain.

In problem 1(ℓ), above, since Seller is treated as having received $5,000 under § 453(e)(1), the first $5,000 of note payments by Daughter are not treated as payments under § 453. Thus only the last $1,000 will be treated as a payment and Seller will recognize an $800 LTCG on the receipt of that payment from the sale of an asset held for 4 years.

Again, the results in problem 1(m) make sense. Seller recognized $3,200 of gain under § 453(c) on the first two payments, $4,000 of gain under § 453(e)(1), and $800 of § 453(c) gain on the final payment for a total $8,000, all of which was LTCG.

2.   The obligations received on the sale of the building meet the § 453A(b)(1) definition of nondealer real property installment obligations. When they are pledged as security and the $200,000 of loan proceeds are received, § 453A(d)(1) treats the proceeds as an imputed § 453 payment, subject to a § 453A(d)(2) ceiling equal to the unrecovered total contract price on the sale for the building (here $500,000).

Thus as a result of § 453A(d), Client is treated as receiving a $200,000 imputed § 453 payment in the year of sale. Three-fifths of that payment (gross profit of $300,000 over total contract price of $500,000) or $120,000 is included in Client's gross income in year one as a § 1231 gain. As a result of § 453A(d)(3) (which operates in a manner similar to § 453(e)(5)), Client is not treated as receiving any actual § 453 payments until Client recovers an amount equal to the previously imputed payment. Thus Client is not taxed again until payment of the third note in year four. When Client receives payment of the notes in years four, five and six, Client has $60,000 of § 1231 gain in each year. Note that if any of such § 1231 gain eventually makes its way into § 1(h), some of the gain may be taxed under § 1(h)(1)(C) and some under § 1(h)(1)(D) in which case the 25% § 1(h)(1)(D) gain must be included in income prior to the 20% § 1(h)(1)(C) gain. Prop. Reg. § 1.453-12(a). See Prop. Reg. § 1.453-12(d) Example 1.

3(a).   Although prior law would have allowed *Burnet v. Logan* open transaction results under these facts, § 453(j)(2) precludes such a result and requires a ratable basis recovery. Under a ratable basis recovery, Taxpayer would recover 1/25 of her basis or $4,000 of basis each year. The excess receipt of $11,000 each year would be included in income as a LTCG from the sale of an asset held for 3 years. Reg. § 15A.453-1(c)(3).

3(b)   No, same result. See the comment at the answer for problem 1(b), above.

3(c).   Since there is a maximum sales price, the gross profit method is to be used with the maximum sale price becoming the total contract price. See Reg. § 15A.453-1(c)(2) and cf. Reg. § 15A.453-1(c)(3)(i), first sentence. Thus as each payment of $15,000 is received 200,000/300,000 of each payment or $10,000 is included in income as LTCG from the sale of an asset held for 3 years.

If the maximum amount were not to be received in 25 years (for example, if only $10,000 were received in each of the 25 years for a total of $250,000), Taxpayer would have included in gross income 2/3 of that amount or $166,667 as LTCG from the sale of an asset held for 3 years and would have had only an $83,333 recovery of basis. In such situations the legislative history calls for a recomputation of the sale price in an earlier year and, if amounts in excess of recomputed income have been reported as income, Taxpayer would be permitted to deduct the excesses in the adjustment year as a loss. Seemingly, if no adjustment were made in earlier years, the $16,667 of basis that was not recovered but was treated as income would be deductible at the end of the 25 year period or reduce the final year's recovery to zero with an additional $10,000 loss. Cf. Reg. § 15A.453-1(c)(7)(ii).

Page 855:

The "Why?" question in the Text involves a *Burnet v. Logan* type transaction where there is no specific dollar amount of indebtedness (e.g., the amount to be received under a contract is based on a percentage of profits) but the transaction is "closed" and the amount estimated. If the amount properly received under the contract is less than the estimated amount, the difference in amount, which constitutes

324

a loss, likely takes its character from the original sale. This was an application of the *Arrowsmith* doctrine. Cf. Joe M. Smith, 48 T.C. 872 (1967), aff'd and rev'd on other issues, 424 F.2d 219 (9th Cir. 1970). Query whether the *Skelley Oil* case at page 744 of the Text alters that result. If there is an excess recovery, *new* income emerges which, lacking capital gain characteristics, can properly be called ordinary income. That result is established.

A similar situation arises, if either a cash or an accrual method taxpayer receives notes from an obligor on the sale of a capital asset, which are included in income in the year of the sale (see Chapter 24B2), and the obligor later fails fully to satisfy the obligation. Here we have a possible clash between the bad debt deduction provisions (see § 166)and the *Arrowsmith* doctrine. Because of the specificity of characterization in the bad debt characterization provisions, the lack of any judicial authority applying *Arrowsmith* in such situations is appropriate. The bad debt provisions apply.

PROBLEM

Page 858:

1(a).   These problems are intended to illustrate the application of the doctrine of *Burnet v. Logan*. § 453(d) must be elected in order to avoid the § 453 rules. If elected *and* if Taxpayer can demonstrate that the contingent payment obligation has no fair market value, then the results are spelled out below. Note under Reg. § 15A.453-1(d)(2)(iii), quoted above, this would also require a showing that the stock has no fair market value. If neither the value of the stock relinquished nor the amount to be received from its sale can be accurately determined at the time of the sale, the *Burnet v. Logan* doctrine is applicable. Under this doctrine, Taxpayer's receipts from the sale constitute a tax-free recovery of capital until they exceed her basis in the stock. Any excess over her basis is a LTCG because the stock was a capital asset in her hands. If this is an open transaction, Taxpayer would have a nontaxable recovery of capital in the amount of $50,000 in the year of sale and $2,000 in each of the twenty-five succeeding years. The payments received in each of the years succeeding the first twenty-five would be LTCG from the sale of an asset held for 3 years. Note Reg. § 1.1001-1(a), Rev. Rul. 58-402, 1958-2 C.B.15, and Reg. § 15A.453-1(d)(2)(iii),which express the Commissioner's position that property will be considered to have no ascertainable fair market value only in "rare and extraordinary cases." If the stock transferred were publicly traded or not of a merely speculative value, then under the principle of the *Philadelphia Park Amusement Co.* case, the amount to be received by Taxpayer would be assumed to have a value equal to the value of the stock, and the doctrine of *Burnet v. Logan* would be inapplicable. See the problem at page 860 of the Text which explores limitations on the open transaction doctrine and the gamble involved in making a § 453(d) election.

If Taxpayer did not elect under § 453(d), then § 453 applies and Reg. §15A.453-1(c)(4) requires a basis allocation (possibly reduced by the $50,000 initial payment) - over a 15 year period. Under the facts above, Taxpayer would potentially recover $3,333 of basis with respect to each $2,000 payment. However since that would result in a loss in each of the fifteen years ($3,333 - $2,000) the temporary regulations disallow any loss and the excess basis is reallocated over and beyond the 15 year period. Here, the end result would be identical to the result if § 453(d) was elected and *Burnet v. Logan* applied.

1(b). No. The doctrine of *Burnet v. Logan* applies to both cash and accrual method taxpayers and the results to Taxpayer are the same regardless of her method of accounting. Cf. Reg. § 15A.453-1(d)(2)(iii). If *Burnet v. Logan* was inapplicable, the results to Taxpayer are discussed at note 10 at page 860 of the Text.

PROBLEM

Page 860:

1(a). Since Seller elects under § 453(d), the amount realized attributable to the notes is the principal amount of the notes ($8,000) since the notes provide for adequate stated interest. Reg. §§1.1001-1(g)(1), 1.1274-2(b)(1). Seller would have an $8,000 LTCG ($10,000 amount realized less $2,000 adjusted basis) from the sale of a capital asset held for 4 years in the year of the sale. Note that Reg. §1.1001-1(g) supersedes the Section 453 regulations that would otherwise apply to this problem. See Reg. §1.1001-1(g)(3).

1(b).   If Seller is a cash method taxpayer, the results are the same as in problem 1(a), above. Reg. §1.1001-1(g) states that the amount realized attributable to a debt instrument is the issue price of the debt instrument. That determination is the same regardless of the taxpayer's accounting method.

1(c).   If the notes did not have the equivalence of cash, the result would nevertheless be the same as in problem 1(b), above. Under Reg. §1.1274-2(b)(1), the issue price of the notes is their principal amount. That determination is not dependent on a finding of cash equivalency.

Page 861:

For a detailed analysis of the OID rules with suggestions for improvements, see Sims, "Long-Term Debt, the Term Structure of Interest and the Case for Accrual Taxation," 47 *Tax L. Rev.* 313 (1992).

Page 869:

Another conversion transaction provision has been added to the Code under § 1260. This provision converts gains from "constructive ownership transactions" from long-term capital gains to ordinary income. The provision encompasses transactions involving a wide range of financial assets. See § 1260(c). A constructive ownership transaction involves a variety of derivative contracts such as: a long position under a notional principal contract with respect to a financial asset (§§ 1260(d)(1)(A), 1260(d)(3)); a forward or futures contract to acquire a financial asset (§§ 1260(d)(1)(B), 1260(d)(4)); the holding of a put or call option with respect to a financial asset where the options have substantially equal strike prices and substantially contemporaneous maturity dates (§ 1260(d)(1)(C)); and similar transactions with respect to financial assets, (§ 1260(d)(1)(D)). To the extent of the above gains, § 1260(a)(1) converts long-term capital gain to ordinary income, except to the extent that the taxpayer has "net underlying long-term capital gain" which is the amount of long-term capital gain the taxpayer would have had if the taxpayer had held the financial asset directly during the term of the derivative contract. § 1260(e). The taxpayer must prove the amount of the net underlying long-term capital gain by clear and convincing evidence or it is deemed to be zero. Id. Interest is charged on any amount that is taxed as ordinary income under the section. § 1260(b).

PROBLEM

Page 876:

1(a). If, under the test of Reg. § 1.83-7(b)(2), the option does not have a readily ascertainable fair market value, § 83 does not apply to the grant of the option and E will have no gross income from receipt of the option. E will have gross income only when the option is exercised (even though the exercise occurs after there is no substantial risk of forfeiture). Reg. § 1.83-7(a). In the fourth year when the option is exercised, the transfer of the Web stock will be subject to § 83(a) and, since there are no restrictions on the Web stock, E will have $850,000 of ordinary gross income (the difference between the stock's $1 million value and the $150,000 E pays for the stock) potentially taxed at the highest § 1 rates. The stock has a $1 million basis to E and a holding period which commences on the date of the exercise.

1(b). Again, the grant of the option again is not subject to § 83 because the option does not have a readily ascertainable fair market value. However, E immediately exercises the option triggering § 83(a) and (b). Under § 83(a), the acquisition of the Web stock is subject to a substantial risk of forfeiture and is not transferable, so E is not taxable at the time of the transfer. However, since E pays $1.50 per share for the stock (fair market value), this would be a good situation for a § 83(b) election. On making the election, E would have no gross income and the later appreciation could be recognized on a sale of the stock as long-term capital gain. In effect, the alternative plan would permit E to recognize $850,000 of gain as long-term capital gain rather than as ordinary income.

There are several issues for E in the alternative plan. First, when E purchases 100,000 shares of Web for $150,000, that investment is subject to the risk that Web will not be successful and E will lose the money. Another issue for E may be getting the $150,000 needed to purchase the Web stock. Companies sometimes lend funds to employees like E to take advantage of option plans.

328

1(c).   Although E transfers the option to Child this is not a disposition at arm's length under Reg. § 1.83-1(b)(1) but, instead, it is a Reg. § 1.83-1(c) disposition. Consequently, there are no § 83 consequences on the transfer. When Child exercises the option, E has $850,000 of ordinary gross income in the fourth year. Reg. § 1.83-1(c), -7(a). Child has a holding period for the stock which commences on the date of the exercise. See Priv. Ltr. Rul. 9722022 (May 20,1997).

Although it is beyond the scope of this course, the question of when E makes a gift to Child for gift tax purposes is important. If the gift occurs at the time of the transfer of the option, E makes a gift of zero, the $150,000 value of the stock less the $150,000 cost to purchase it; whereas, if the gift occurs at the time the option becomes substantially vested there is a gift of $850,000. The IRS takes the position that the gift occurs at the *later* of (1) the transfer, or (2) when the donee's right to exercise the option is no longer conditioned on the performance of services by the transferor. Rev. Rul. 98-21, 1998-1 C.B. 975.

Page 876:

A difficult problem is the proper means of providing some relief when an item of I.R.D. is included both under the income and estate tax. For instance, to allow a credit for the estate tax paid would, in effect, refund the estate tax paid. On the other hand, to allow no benefit would equate the I.R.D. item to already collected income items, without reducing the estate by the amount of income tax that would have been paid on the item. The allowance of an income tax deduction for the estate tax attributable to the item is an accommodation that does not pretend to precise doctrinal justification.

If taxpayer knows that the taxpayer is going to be taxed on an item of income (such as salary due the decedent at death) the taxpayer would prefer it to be I.R.D., because in that case, the taxpayer will at least get the § 691(c) deduction. Thus where something must be included in income in any event, a taxpayer will contend that it is I.R.D., if possible. See Hess v. Comm'r, 271 F.2d 104 (3rd Cir. 1959).

PROBLEMS

Page 880:

1(a).   An account receivable held by an attorney on the accrual method of accounting is not an I.R.D. item, because, under the accrual method, all events have occurred and the income was included in the attorney's gross income during life. In fact, the attorney would have a tax cost basis in the item.

1(b). An account receivable held by an attorney using the cash method of accounting would represent income not taken into attorney's gross income during attorney's life, and it is an I.R.D. item. Reg. § 1.691(a)-1(b)(1).

1(c). A contingent fee of an accrual method attorney that was not included in the attorney's income prior to death and becomes fixed after death is an I.R.D. item. Reg. § 1.691(a)-(b)(3).

1(d). Mere appreciated property (even recapture gain property) is not an item of I.R.D. It receives a stepped-up basis at the decedent's death.

1(e). The cash method taxpayer's installment sale obligation is an item of I.R.D. § 691(a)(4). However, to the extent of the decedent's basis in the obligation under § 453B(c), it is not an I.R.D. item and it is given that amount of basis. § 691(a)(4)(B). Furthermore, since under § 453(i) the recapture gain would have already been recognized by the decedent because § 453 is inapplicable to recapture gain, only the § 1231 unrecognized gain constitutes I.R.D.

2(a). Decedent's estate is taxed on $100,000 of ordinary income on its collection of the receivable. §§ 691(a)(1)(A), 691(a)(3).

2(b). Decedent's estate is taxed on the $100,000 of ordinary income on its transfer of the receivable in satisfaction of its obligation. §§ 691(a)(1)(A), 691(a)(3).

2(c). Child is taxed on the $100,000 of ordinary income on Child's collection of the receivable. §§ 691(a)(1)(C), 691(a)(3).

2(d). Child's estate is taxed on the $100,000 of ordinary income on the estate's collection of the receivable. §§ 691(a)(1)(C), 691(a)(3).

Chapter 25.   Disallowance of Losses

Page 885:

> Section 267 is not exclusive. Reg. § 1.267(a)-1(c) states that "no deduction for losses or unpaid expenses or interest arising in a transaction which is not bona fide will be allowed even though section 267 does not apply to the transaction." In Fender v. U.S., 577 F.2d 934 (5th Cir. 1978), the regulation was followed. The Commissioner was unsuccessful in arguing that the facts fell within the regulation in Widerner Trust v. Comm'r, 80 T.C. 304 (1983), acq. 1984-1 C.B. 2.

PROBLEMS

Page 887:

1(a).   Father's $10,000 loss on the sale to Daughter would be disallowed by § 267(a)(1) because it is a sale between members of a family. § 267(b)(1) and (c)(4). On Daughter's subsequent sale, § 267(d) applies and she will not be taxed on the realized gain of $5,000 ($45,000 - $40,000), because that gain does not exceed Father's previously disallowed loss of $10,000. Note that Daughter receives a cost basis in the stock under § 1012, Reg. § 1.267(d)-1(c)(1), and that § 267(d) merely provides that a taxpayer's gain from the sale or exchange of property shall not be recognized to the extent that a realized loss of the taxpayer's transferor was disallowed by § 267(a)(1).

1(b).   Daughter *realizes* a $15,000 gain which would be characterized as STCG. However, under § 267(d) she will be required to recognize only $5,000 of STCG. See Reg. § 1.267(d)-1(c)(3), which properly states that no tacking of holding periods is allowed.

1(c).   Daughter would have a $5,000 STCL. Section 267(d) applies only where the transferee sells or exchanges the property at a gain. It is worth remarking that § 267 does not contain a transferred basis rule.

1(d).   Son would have an $8,000 STCG. Under § 1015 and § 1223(2), Son would have a transferred basis (Daughter's $40,000 basis) and would be allowed to tack Daughter's holding period but still would not reach long term. The benefits of § 267(d) are applicable only to Daughter, the original transferee. See Reg. §§ 1.267(d)-1(a)(3) and (4) Ex. 3. Therefore, Son's entire realized gain of $8,000 is recognized.

2.   The issue is whether § 1041(a) is applicable to indirect transfers. Section § 267(a)(1) is expressly made applicable to both direct and indirect transfers, while § 1041 refers only to transfers. Nevertheless, the allowance of an indirect transfer can be read into § 1041 since congressional intent was to treat a transfer between spouses in the same manner as a gift. See § 1041(b)(1) and the Text at page 130. Cf. Reg. § 1.1041-1T(c).

Applying § 1041 to the *McWilliams*' trans-actions, the husband's loss which is realized on the sale of this stock is not recognized under § 1041(a)(1). The wife takes a transferred basis equal to the husband's adjusted basis in the stock. § 1041(b)(2). On the wife's sale of the stock she will recognize the loss subject to the limitations of §§ 165(f), 1211 and 1212. If § 1041 applies then § 267 is expressly made inapplicable. § 267(g). Note that if the wife recognizes a gain on the sale she does not get the benefit of the § 267(d) provision in which the gain is recognized only to the extent it exceeds the loss previously disallowed to the husband. But, as wife has the benefit of using husband's basis, she does not need § 267(d) assistance. Wife can also tack holding periods. § 1223(2). Holding periods are not tacked in § 267 transactions.

If § 1041 is inapplicable to indirect transfers, which seems highly unlikely, then the loss in the *McWilliams* case would still be disallowed by § 267(a)(1). If § 267(a)(1) applied, then, as seen above, the relief under § 267(d) is not as generous as the application of § 1041. Cf. § 1091. An argument can be made that the § 267(c)(4) retention of a spouse as a family member for § 267(c) purposes implies that § 267(a)(1) still has vitality with respect to some (indirect?) interspousal transfers. Note, however, that the § 267(c)(4) continued inclusion of a spouse is necessary for the attribution of ownership rules of § 267.

3.   The estate's basis for the land would be $100,000. § 1014(a)(1). On the sale of the land, the estate realizes a LTCL (see § 1223(11)) of $20,000. However, § 267 disallows the loss since the estate makes a sale (not in satisfaction of pecuniary bequest) to a beneficiary of the estate. § 267(b)(13).

332

4(a).   Taxpayer T's loss would be disallowed by § 267(a)(1). This is a transaction between persons in a relationship described by § 267(b)(2), that is, an individual and a corporation more than 50% in value of which is owned by that individual. Taxpayer is deemed to own:

Her own shares:	10%
Her son S's shares (§ 267(c)(2) and (c)(4)):	20%
Her proportionate share of the partnership shares (§ 267(c)(1)):	15%
Her partner X's share of the partnership shares (§ 267(c)(1) and § 267(c)(3); note that § 267(c)(5) does not preclude double attribution in this situation: "stock constructively owned . . . .by reason of . . .(1) shall, for purposes of applying . . . (3), be treated as actually owned by such person . . ."):	15%
Total	60%

4(b).   Again, § 267 disallows the loss and, again, the operative rule is § 267(a)(1) brought into play by § 267(b)(2). Taxpayer T "owns":

Her son S's shares by virtue of § 267(c)(2):	30%
Her proportionate share of the partnership shares. §267(c)(1):	15%
Her partner X's share of the partnership shares. § 267(c)(1) and (c)(3). The parenthetical here is inapplicable, because T "owns" shares under § 267(c)(1), not just (2). See Reg. § 1.267(c)-1(a)(2):	15%
Total	60%

4(c).   Finally T is home free, escaping the clutches of § 267. Taxpayer T now "owns":

Her son S's shares by virtue of § 267(c)(2):	30%
Her son S's share of the stock owned by the SX partnership. Paragraph (c)(5) permits the shares attributed to S from SX under (c)(1)(15%) to be reattributed to T under (c)(2).	15%

But X's shares are not attributed to T. This is because the attribution of X's shares to S by paragraph (3) cannot be used again to attribute them to T under paragraph (2). Paragraph (5) prohibits this.

	0%
Total	45%

5.   The issue raised is whether § 267 should apply to forced or involuntary sales. The court in *Merritt* disallowed the loss notwithstanding the involuntary nature of the sale. It indicated that although a primary goal of Congress in enacting § 267 was to prevent taxpayers from choosing their own time to realize a tax benefit, the crucial factors relevant in the application of § 267 are the taxpayer's retention of control and identity of interest.

The Fourth Circuit reached the opposite conclusion in *McNeill*. There the court considered voluntary tax avoidance to be the crucial factor and found such a motive lacking in a forced sale situation.

See also McCarty v. Cripe, 201 F.2d 679 (7th Cir. 1953), and Thomas Zacek, 8 T.C. 1056 (1947).

Page 889:

At a taxpayer's death, the § 1014 basis comes into play replacing any § 1091(d) basis. Its effect is to disallow permanently the § 1091 loss.

PROBLEMS

Page 889:

1(a).   Taxpayer's $10,000 LTCL on the December sale would be disallowed under § 1091(a), because she purchased "substantially identical" stock within 30 days of her sale.

1(b).   Under § 1091(d), her basis in the newly acquired shares is $65,000. The basis is determined by using the basis of the original stock ($60,000) and (1) increasing it by any excess cost of the replacement stock over the selling price of the original ($5,000) or (2) decreasing it by any excess of the selling price of the original stock over the cost of

334

the replacement stock (zero). The effect of § 1091(d) is to give her a basis equal to her total expenditures less her total receipts, neutralizing the transaction in which the loss is disallowed.

1(c).   Her holding period for the newly acquired shares as of January 1 of the next year is 24-1/2 months. Section 1223(4) permits tacking of the 24 month holding period of the original shares to the 1/2 month holding period of the replacement shares. Again, under § 1091, neutrality is the theme.

1(d).   Section 1091(a) applies only to loss situations. Taxpayer would therefore have $15,000 LTCG from an asset held for 2 years on the sale and a $65,000 cost basis and new holding period for the newly acquired stock.

1(e).   No. Section 1091 applies regardless of whether the purchase of new shares is prior or subsequent to the sale of the old shares if the purchase occurs within 30 days of the sale.

1(f).   Since taxpayer sold the shares to Son both § 1091 *and* § 267 would be applicable to disallow her loss. Both sections have relief rules relating to subsequent sales, one applicable to the transferee (§ 267(d)) and the other to the seller (§ 1091(d)) but, as only one loss has been disallowed, it is clear that only one such relief provision should apply. In such circumstances § 267(d), last sentence, expressly denies the usual relief to the transferee Son. Consequently Son will have a $5,000 STCG on his subsequent sale. It will be STCG because there is no tacking of holding periods; indeed, there would be no tacking even if § 267(d) were applicable. Reg. § 1.267(d)-1(c)(3).

On the other hand, upon disposition of the newly acquired stock, Taxpayer will get the benefit of the § 1091(d) basis rules and will determine holding period under the provisions of § 1223(4); and the result will be the same as problems 1(a) - (c), above.

1(g).   Section 1091 wash sale sanctions are less stringent than the sanctions of § 267 because: (1) § 1091(d) allows an exchanged basis (subject to adjustments) for the new stock as compared with § 267(d)'s limited relief from gain on subsequent sale; and (2) holding periods are tacked under § 1223(4) in a § 1091 transaction, but not in a § 267 transaction.

Reg. § 1.267(d)-1(c)(3) (not invariably advantageous of course). Although a kind of transferred basis concept is at work in § 267(d), there are obvious risks in permitting students to speak in these terms.

2(a).   Under Reg. § 1.1091-1(g), the date of the sale in a short sale situation is for purposes of § 1091 generally deemed the date of consummation of the short sale (i.e., June 15). Since Short purchased additional B shares within 30 days of the sale, § 1091 applies to disallow the loss deduction.

2(b).   In such a situation, known as a "sale against the box," Reg. § 1.1091-1(g) provides that the date of sale for purposes of § 1091 is deemed the date the short sale was entered into (i.e. June 1). Therefore, § 1091 does not apply since Short did not acquire additional shares within 30 days of June 1. For characterization as long-term or short-term gain or loss on a sale against the box, see § 1233(b).

Chapter 26.   Nonrecognition Provisions

Page 894:

> In Rev. Rul. 72-601, 1972-2 C.B. 467, the exchange of a remainder interest in real property for a life estate in real property was not considered a "like kind" exchange. The Ruling is discussed by Andrews in "Disposition of a Life Estate in Realty: What Are the Implications of Rev. Rul. 72-601?" 40 *J. Tax'n* 26 (1974).

Page 904:

> In Rev. Rul. 61-119, 1961-1 C.B. 395, which is discussed on this page, taxpayer set up two separate transactions in order to have a § 1231 gain qualifying for capital gain treatment on the sale of old equipment and a cost basis in new equipment that would support greater depreciation deductions from ordinary income than he would have had with a substituted basis determined under § 1031(d). The Ruling was prior to enactment of § 1245 which would have converted taxpayer's § 1231 gain in effect, to ordinary income anyway. The Commissioner would not be as interested in applying § 1031 to depreciable personal property today as he was in 1961.

Page 908:

> The second exception to the identification rule which creates an exception if, before the end of the exchange period (generally 180 days), the taxpayer actually receives timely identified property constituting at least 95 percent of the aggregate value of the identified properties, "the 95 percent rule" is a possible exception to the 3-property rule but would create an exception to the 200% rule only if the transferor contributed substantial additional cash to the transfer.

Page 909:

> In Rev. Proc.2000-37, 2000-2 C.B. ____, the Service provides a safe harbor under which it will not challenge a reverse like-kind exchange where a taxpayer acquires replacement property before giving up the relinquished property. The procedure is discussed in Lipton, "New

Revenue Procedure on Reverse Like-Kind Exchanges Replaces Tax Risk With Tax Certainty," 93 *J. Tax'n* 327 (2000).

Page 909:

> Under § 453(f)(6), applicable to § 1031 exchanges, the like kind property received is removed from the § 453 computation resulting in taxation only on the receipt of the boot property. This is done by excluding the like kind property from the total contract price and the gross profit, and by not treating its receipt as a § 453 payment. Prior law treated the receipt of the like kind property as a § 453 payment. See Rev. Rul. 65-155, 1965-1 C.B. 356. The provision merely alters the timing of income. For example, if one transferred a piece of like kind property with a basis of $40,000 and a value of $100,000 for another piece of such property worth $80,000 and two adequate interest bearing notes of $10,000 one to be paid in each of the two succeeding years, the $20,000 § 1031(b) gain on the two notes would be recognized only on their payment. Under § 453(f)(6): (A) the total contract price would be $20,000, (b) the gross profit would be $20,000, and (c) the only § 453 payments would be the note payments, each of which would be fully taxable in years two and three. Compare Reg. §§ 1.453-6(c) and 15A.453-1(b)(2) and (3) dealing with installment sales of property subject to a mortgage. Prior law would have treated the receipt of the like kind property as a § 453 payment and would have included 80% of the § 1031(b) gain on receipt of the like kind property or $16,000 in year one and $2,000 per year on payment of each of the notes in years two and three.

PROBLEMS

Page 910:

1. This problem illustrates the significant distinction between *Century Electric* and *Leslie*. In *Century Electric* and in *Rev. Rul. 76-301*, taxpayer's transfer of a property interest in return for some cash and a lease back constituted a like kind exchange under which loss is disallowed. This is so even though the taxpayer receives boot. See § 1031(c). If however, as in this problem, the taxpayer transfers a leasehold for its full fair market value and subleases back the area previously used, the *Leslie* case holds § 1031 inapplicable. See also

338

Jordan Marsh Co. cited in the *Leslie* case. Thus *Rev. Rul. 76-301* is inapplicable here, and X has a $50,000 loss under § 1231.

2(a). The results to T are as follows:

(1) T has a *realized* gain of $90,000 which if recognized would be a § 1231 main hotchpot gain.

(2) T would be required to recognize only $30,000 of § 1231 gain. Under § 1031(a) no gain is recognized if property held for productive use in trade or business or for investment purposes is exchanged solely for property of a like kind to be held for business or investment purposes. Note that property held for productive use in trade or business may be exchanged for like kind property held merely for investment and vice versa. Reg. § 1.1031(a)-1(a). "Like kind" is defined by Reg. § 1.1031(a)-1(b) specifically to include unimproved real estate for improved real estate, because the term relates only to the "nature or character of the property and not to its grade or quality." The *Crichton* case reaches an analogous result in an exchange of oil, gas, and mineral rights in unimproved land for an improved city lot. Section 1031(a) is inapplicable in this problem because this is not a solely like kind exchange. However, § 1031(b) comes into play when, in addition to property of a like kind, other property is received. It provides that gain is to be recognized only to the extent of the boot (property not of a like kind). In this problem the stock and cash received (the boot or "other property") are worth $30,000, and $30,000 is recognized, as that is less than the total gain on the exchange.

(3) T's basis for the stock received is $26,000. No basis is ever allocated to cash. Thus, in this type of exchange the cash portion is carved out and the matter treated, on our facts, as if $4,000 of the gain on the sale were received in the form of cash. Note that under § 1031(d) the basis to be allocated to property other than cash is reduced by the amount of the cash received. Essentially, § 1031(d) calls for a § 7701(a)(44) "exchanged" basis, substituting the basis for the like kind property transferred for the like kind property newly acquired. This is in keeping with the essentially deferral purpose of § 1031 (but

339

always recall § 1014) to postpone recognition of gain or loss by carrying along untaxed appreciation or undeducted loss on the old property through the exchanged basis device.

However, where some gain *is* recognized in a boot transaction, an upward adjustment of the basis otherwise carried over is obviously in order. Section 1031(d) recognizes this. Thus, on our facts, under § 1031(d) T's basis for the stock and like kind property together is $36,000 - the basis of the land ($10,000) less the money T received ($4,000) plus the gain T was required to recognize ($30,000). The second sentence of § 1031(d) requires the $36,000 to be allocated first to the non-like kind property received (in this problem the stock) in an amount equal to its fair market value on the date of the exchange ($26,000).

(4)   T's basis for the apartment building is $10,000. T's § 1031(d) basis remaining after allocating $26,000 to the stock ($36,000 - $26,000) is allocated to the like kind property received in the exchange. If more than one piece of like kind property is received the § 1031(d) basis of all the like kind property is allocated between or among the properties is accordance with their relative fair market values on the date of the exchange. See Rev. Rul. 68-36, 1968-1 C.B. 357. T's holding period of the old like kind property is tacked on to the new like kind property. § 1223(1).

(5)   The result above is logical because if T immediately sold the apartment and stock, T would have a gain (probably long term capital gain) of $60,000 on the apartment (holding periods are tacked under § 1223(1)) and no gain on the stock. T's total gain on the sale and the like kind exchange would be $90,000, equal to T's initial realized gain in problem 2(a)(1), above. In introducing § 1031 it may be well to stress that it is representative of several similar nonrecognition provisions each of which is supported by strong policy reasons for nonrecognition, and in which nonrecognition is coupled with an exchanged basis concept and, in turn, the exchanged basis is coupled with a tacking of holding periods.

2(b).   The results to B are as follows:

(1)   Preliminarily, notice that B is *within* § 1031(a)(1) to the extent that B has made a transfer of property (the apartment) for property of a like kind (the land). But B's exchange of stock for land is excluded from § 1031(a)(1) by § 1031(a)(2). B is outside §§ 1031(b) and (c), because neither applies unless in an exchange to which § 1031 otherwise applies the taxpayer has "received" property to be treated as boot, and B received only land, no boot, on the § 1031(a) exchange for the apartment. B has a $40,000 realized gain on the building and a $14,000 realized loss on the stock (assume LTCL).

(2)   Since B receives solely "like kind" property (the land) for the apartment, § 1031(a)(1) applies and B is not required to recognize any gain. However, B is allowed to recognize the $14,000 loss. Section 1031(c) is inapplicable to the loss. It applies only if boot is *received* in exchange for like kind property on which the taxpayer has a loss. Here B did not receive any boot and had no loss on the like kind property. Reg. § 1.1031(d)-1(e) Example. In substance B is deemed to have received $26,000 worth of land for B's stock and since the stock trans-action is outside the scope of § 1031, the loss is recognized. Similarly, gain would have been recognized by B if B's stock had appreciated in value. B has a $14,000 LTCL from an asset held for 3 years.

(3)   B's basis for the land is $60,000. Under § 1031(d), this is B's original basis in the properties, $70,000 ($30,000 + $40,000) plus the cash paid, $4,000, reduced by the loss recognized, $14,000. It is clear that under § 1031(d) B's $4,000 cash payment must be treated as a transfer of property with a basis equal to the amount of the cash. The language of § 1031(d) requires determination of a total basis for the like kind property received for like kind *and* other property even though in problem 2(b)(2), above, there was a theory of two separate transactions - building for land and stock for land. See Reg. § 1.1031(d)-1(a) (last sentence).

341

(4) If B had taken accelerated depreciation on the building and part of B's gain on a sale would have been a § 1250 gain, § 1250 could require recognition of the gain. In general under §§ 1250(a) and (i), the § 1250 gain will be recognized notwithstanding other provisions of the Code. However, § 1250(d)(4) provides as a limited exception to the application of § 1250, a § 1031 transaction.

B would be required to recognize all of that § 1250 gain under the facts of this problem. In general, § 1250(d)(4) allows postponement of B's § 1250 gain with the § 1250 gain taint carried over to the newly acquired property. However § 1250 (d) does require recognition of the § 1250 gain to the extent of the greater of:

(i) the gain recognized under § 1031 (zero in this problem) or

(ii) an amount determined under § 1250(d)(4)(C). That amount is the § 1250 gain less the value of § 1250 property received on the exchange. Since the land received by B is not depreciable, it is not § 1250 property (§ 1250(c)) and the full amount of B's § 1250 gain would be required to be recognized.

This is the typical now-or-never situation in which § 1250 must "getcha" now or the potential recapture is lost. Where § 1250 overrides § 1031 to require a recognition of gain, the amount recognized works an increase in basis in the old property which then carries over to the newly acquired property under § 1031(d).

(5) If B immediately sold the land he would have a $40,000 gain on the sale. Section 1223(1) would again tack B's holding period. B's total recognized gain and loss ($40,000 gain here and $14,000 loss in problem 2(b)(2), above) would equal B's gain and loss in problem 2(b)(1), above. However, the rate of tax on such gain might be altered. If B had merely sold the building as B's only § 1231 and then LTCG during a year, the § 1(h)(1)(D) rate of tax on the unrecaptured § 1250 gain would be

25%, whereas if B sold the replaced land, the § 1231 or LTCG would all be taxed at a 20% rate (possibly 18% depending on the years involved). This type of game playing may lead to Congress or the courts narrowing the broad definition of like-kind with respect to real estate. See problem 4, below.

3(a).   Section 1031(a) applies here. T has made an exchange of a building and land held as an investment for a replacement building and land to be held for the same purpose. The property is like kind property under the *Crichton* test and § 1031 applies.

3(b).   T's adjusted basis in the transferred property, $200,000 becomes T's basis for the replacement property. § 1031(d). The replacement property's $200,000 adjusted basis is allocated to the replacement building and the land in accordance with their relative fair market values. Rev. Rul. 68-36, 1968-1 C.B. 357. In this problem, the replacement building and the land are of equal fair market value, so T's $200,000 basis is allocated one-half each. As a result of a basis allocation of $100,000 to the replacement building, T may use the straight-line method to depreciate the $100,000 basis of the building over 39 years. §§ 168(b)(3)(A), 168(c).

It is significant in this problem that T depreciated the original building under the straight-line method. If T had used accelerated depreciation (applicable to real property placed in service before 1987), the difference between the accelerated depreciation actually claimed and a straight-line computation of depreciation would be subject to § 1250 recapture. Even if § 1250 recapture is not triggered in a § 1031 exchange (see § 1250(d)(4)), the § 1250 recapture amount does have a potential impact on basis allocation in a transaction similar to the one presented in this problem. If both § 1250 property (the building) and non § 1250 property (the land) are received in a § 1031 exchange, T's basis is allocated in accordance with the relative fair market values of the property received. However, the fair market value of the § 1250 property is deemed to be the excess of the fair market value of the § 1250 property received over the § 1250 recapture not recognized in the exchange. Reg. § 1.1250-3(d)(4)(ii) referring to Reg. § 1.1250-3(d)(2)(iii). The net effect of these regulations is to reduce the fair market value of § 1250 property received by the § 1250 recapture not

343

recognized, which means that a larger amount of T's basis would be allocated to the nondepreciable land.

4(a).   In view of the broad like-kind test applicable to real estate, this is a like-kind change. Taxpayer has a $4 million realized gain on the building and no gain on the land. Such gain is not recognized and Taxpayer acquires the replacement land with a $1 million substituted basis under § 1031(d) and a tacked 18-year holding period under § 1223(1). Note that if Taxpayer had recognized the gain on the building it would be a $4 million § 1231 gain converted to a LTCG and, under § 1(h)(1)(D), that gain would be taxed at a 25% rate or a tax of $1 million.

4(b).   Taxpayer would have a $5 million gain taxed under § 1(h)(1)(C) at a 20% rate resulting in a tax of $1 million. The ironic point is that the tax on the building would have been taxed at a 25% rate and the tax on the replacement land at a 20% rate, clearly a benefit to Taxpayer, raising an issue whether the like-kind test should be legislatively tightened up and perhaps a stricter "similar or related in service or use" test should be applied. Of course, Congress could legislatively enact a 25% tax taint on the replacement property, but this would add further legislative complexity.

5(a).   This is a sale and reinvestment. Section 1031 applies only to an exchange. Seller must recognize gain, and Seller takes the residential property with a cost basis and a fresh holding period.

5(b).   This problem follows Rev. Rul. 77-297 which holds that the transaction is an exchange, and Seller qualifies for § 1031 treatment - nonrecognition, exchanged basis, and a tacked holding period. §§ 1031(a) and (d); 1223(1).

The land and residential property satisfy the like kind test. See *Crichton* and Reg. § 1.1031(a)-1. Since the identification and exchange period requirements of § 1031(a)(3) are operative only upon a transfer by Seller of the property to Buyer, until the escrow closes, these requirements need not be satisfied.

5(c).   Here the transfer is complete on January 1 and in order to qualify under § 1031, § 1031(a)(3) must be satisfied. Students may question why some escrow arrangement is not provided to lengthen the time frame. The answer is that in this subpart there is a completed transaction, whereas in problem 5(b), above, there is no binding contract.

Section 1031(a)(3) is satisfied here: (1) The February 15 date satisfies the 45 day requirement of § 1031(a)(3)(A) known as the "identification period" requirement. See Reg. § 1.1031(k) - 1(b)(3) Example. (2) The regulations sanction identification of multiple properties (within limits). See Reg. § 1.1031(k)-1(c)(4). The identification of 3 properties here falls within the "3-property rule" of Reg. § 1.1031(k)-1(c)(4)(i)(A). (3) The June 15 date falls within 180 days of the January 1 transfer (§ 1031(a)(3)(B)(i)) and § 1031(a)(3)(B)(ii) is inapplicable because Seller is a calendar year taxpayer. In fact, the 180 day period is not tolled until June 30.

The fact that cash is put in escrow does not alter the result. There is no constructive receipt by Seller. See Reg. § 1.1031(k)-1(f)(2), and (3) Example (iii) as well as problem 5(d), below. See Cummings "How to Secure a Delayed Section 1031 Exchange," 70 *J. Tax'n* 230 (1989).

5(d).   Seller must recognize the gain as in problem 5(a), above. Although this may be an attempt to satisfy § 1031(a)(3), the attempt fails. Since Seller may demand the cash at any time, Seller has constructively received the cash at the time of the transfer of the land and § 1031(a)(3) is inapplicable. Moreover, under the regulations the transaction will be treated as a sale even if Seller ultimately receives like kind property. See Reg. § 1.1031(k)-1(f), especially 1(f)(3) Example (i) and (ii). See also Grob, Silverman and Gossett, "Deferred Like-Kind Exchanges of Real Estate Made Easier by Recently Issued Proposed Regulations," 68 *Taxes* 694 (1990).

6(a).   Note that though § 1031(d) refers to liabilities of the taxpayer being "assumed," the cross-reference in the Section to § 357(d) significantly expands the situations covered by the statute. Section 1031(d), last sentence, and § 357(d)(1)(B) treat B's taking the property subject to the $100,000 nonrecourse liability as an assumption of the liability and as a receipt of cash by A. As a result, A has a realized gain of $300,000, and a recognized gain of $100,000 (the liability relief) under § 1031(b). A's basis in the replacement property (determined under § 1031(d)) is $200,000: $200,000 - $100,000 (liability treated as cash) + $100,000 (gain recognized). A also is allowed a § 1223(1) tacked holding period. See Reg. § 1.1031(d)-2 Example (1).

B has a realized gain of $300,000, no recognized gain, a $200,000 exchanged basis (§ 1031(d)), and a tacked holding period (§ 1223(1)).

6(b). Things are a bit more complicated here. First, the regulations in effect treat only the *net* amount of the liabilities as cash boot. See Reg. § 1.1031(d)-2 Example (2)(c). As a result, A is treated as receiving $30,000 ($100,000 less $70,000) of boot. A has a gain recognized of $30,000 and a basis in the replacement property received of $200,000 ($200,000 - 100,000 + 70,000 +30,000) and a tacked holding period.

B is not treated as receiving any boot because B's liability relief ($70,000) is offset by B's liability assumption ($100,000). See Reg. § 1.1031(d)-2 Example (2)(b). The net liability assumption, $30,000, is added to B's adjusted basis of the transferred property so that B's basis in the replacement property is $130,000 ($100,000 - 70,000 + 100,000).

6(c). A is permitted to net the $50,000 of cash tendered against the $100,000 of mortgage relief. As a result, A is treated as receiving only $50,000 of boot. Reg. § 1.1031(d) - 2 Example 2(c). A has a realized gain of $250,000. A's amount realized is the $400,000 of real estate and the net $50,000 of liability relief and A's adjusted basis is $200,000, resulting in the $250,000 gain realized. A has $50,000 of gain recognized as a result of the liability (less cash transferred) relief. § 1031(b) and (d). A's basis in the newly acquired property is $200,000 ($200,000 less $50,000 (liability of $100,000 netted by $50,000 cash tendered) plus $50,000 (gain recognized)). § 1031(d). Again, A may tack A's holding period. § 1223(1).

B has an amount realized of $400,000 (building $350,000 plus cash $50,000) and an adjusted basis of $100,000, resulting in a gain realized of $300,000. On receipt of the cash, B has a $50,000 gain recognized. B's adjusted basis in the building received is $200,000 ($100,000 - 50,000 + 100,000 + 50,000) § 1031(d), and B may tack holding periods. § 1223(1).

Page 913:

Section 1033(h) provides that if a taxpayer's principal residence (having the same meaning as in § 121 except that taxpayer need not own the principal residence (see § 1033(h)(3)) or any of its contents is compulsorily or involuntarily converted as a result of a Presidentially declared disaster (see § 1033(h)(2)), the recovery of insurance proceeds gets special treatment under § 1033 as follows:

(1)   Insurance proceeds for personal property which was not scheduled property for insurance purposes are excluded from gross income. § 1033(h)(1)(A)(i).

(2)   Other insurance proceeds are treated as a common fund and if the proceeds are invested in a similar or related in service or use residence or contents, taxpayer may elect to recognize gain only to the extent that the total reinvestment. § 1033(h)(1)(A)(ii).

(3)   The reinvestment period is extended from 2 to 4 years. § 1033(h)(1)(B).

Page 913:

The cases and problems presented in this subpart all involve the application of § 1033 to outright owners of property or stock. However, § 1033 may also be elected by a lessee who receives a condemnation award for a leasehold interest in property. See Rev. Rul. 71-519, 1971-2 C.B. 309.

Page 914:

The *Masser* case was cited in Rev. Rul. 80-175, 1980-2 C.B. 230, which revoked Rev. Rul. 72-372, 1972-2 C.B. 471, and held that gain on a *voluntary* sale of timber downed in a casualty (hurricane) was not required to be recognized when the proceeds were reinvested in other standing timber.

Page 914:

See Yohe, "Income Tax Aspects of Condemnation Awards," 18 *Real Prop. Prob. and Trust J.* 532 (1983).

Page 921:

Two rulings continue the Service's attempt to limit the scope of the phrase "like kind." In Rev. Rul. 76-390, 1976-2 C.B. 243, a state condemned 10 acres of 15 acres of taxpayer's land used for a mobile home park. Taxpayer wanted to use the proceeds to build a motel on the remaining 5 acres. The Ruling held that the motel did not meet the "similar or related in service or use test" because under the owner-user test the motel did not have the same physical characteristics and same end use. In addition, it held under § 1033(g) the motel and the land it replaced were not "like kind" property, relying on *Rev. Rul. 67-255*, 1967-2 C.B. 270, which held that land is not of the same nature or character as a building or a storm drain, water system or a road. Rev. Rul. 76-391, 1976-2 C.B. 243, also relying on *Rev. Rul. 67-255*, held that a commercial building to be held for lease, which was constructed on taxpayer's land did not qualify as a § 1033(g) "like kind" replacement of condemned farmland that taxpayer leased.

The Service takes a more lenient although consistent position in Rev. Rul. 78-72, 1978-1 C.B. 258, holding that a long-term leasehold interest in improved real property and outright ownership of unimproved real property are "like kind" properties.

PROBLEMS

Page 922:

1(a). T has a realized and recognized gain of $4,000, all classified as ordinary income. T's full gain of $4,000 (the amount realized of $28,000 less the § 1016(a)(2) adjusted basis of $24,000) is ordinary income under § 1245(a), because the lesser of (1) the $40,000 recomputed basis or (2) the $28,000 amount realized exceeds T's adjusted basis of $24,000 by the full $4,000 amount. If the recognized gain had exceeded the § 1245 gain, the excess gain would have fallen within § 1231. Note that gains and losses from casualty type events

348

(but not those from a condemnation type conversion transaction) fall within the § 1231 subhotchpot. Such gains and losses from a condemnation transaction fall only into the § 1231 main hotchpot. It is obvious probably that § 1033 has no bearing on a *loss* problem.

1(b)(1). T has a recognized gain of $2,000 classified as ordinary income. T replaces the old equipment with new equipment which, under the "owner-user" test required by *Clifton Investment*, is "similar or related in service or use" to T. It is assumed that the replacement is timely, occurring within 2 years after the close of the first taxable year in which the gain was realized. § 1033(a)(2)(B)(i). Section 1033(a)(2)(A) does not allow T to escape tax on $2,000, the amount by which T's amount realized on the involuntary conversion of the old property exceeds the cost of the new property. (For a ruling involving the "amount realized" under § 1033, see Rev. Rul. 71-476, 1971-2 C.B. 308).

Although T's full realized gain was § 1245 gain (see § 1245(a)(1) and (d)), § 1245(b)(4) creates an exception to that section, which permits T to recognize the § 1245 gain only to the extent of the sum of:

(A)   the gain recognized under § 1033: $2,000, plus

(B)   the value of the non- § 1245 property acquired in excess of the § 1033 gain recognized to the extent that it has not been taken into account in determining gain recognized under § 1033: zero. (Reg. § 1.1245-4(d)(2) Example (2) illustrates the effect of the first clause of § 1245(b)(4)(B)).

Thus T would have to recognize $2,000 of ordinary income under §§ 1245(b)(4) and 1033(a)(2). A great place to ask the second "why?" Why does Congress add subparagraph (B)? We know, but only a good student will, that, unless the untaxed gain is carried forward in the low basis for § 1245 property, some § 1245 gain will permanently escape taxation.

1(b)(2). T's basis for the purpose of claiming depreciation on the new equipment is $24,000. § 1033(b)(2) provides that it is the cost of the new property ($26,000) less the gain not recognized on the old property ($2,000).

1(b)(3). If T immediately sells the new equipment for $26,000, T would have $2,000 of ordinary income. T's gain of $2,000 is § 1245 gain because T makes a sale of depreciable personal property and T's § 1245 gain is the lesser of:

   (A)   T's recomputed basis: $38,000 (As defined in § 1245(a)(2), this is T's adjusted basis plus post-1962 depreciation on the same or *other property* reflected in such property (nonrecaptured depreciation.) Reg. § 1.1245-2(c)(4)(i).) or

   (B)   T's amount realized: $26,000

minus T's $24,000 adjusted basis in the property. The result here reflects the fact that the replacement property carries over the old property's unrecaptured § 1245 taint. The result is proper since the theory behind § 1033 is that no conversion of property occurred (except to the extent of nonreinvested proceeds). The overall result is $4,000 of ordinary income which would be the same numerical result as the result if § 1033 had not applied. See problem 1(a), above.

Note that if the new equipment had immediately increased in value to $30,000 due to a shortage of supply, T's gain on an immediate sale for $30,000 would be $6,000, and it would all be § 1245 gain.

2.   No, the opinion in *Masser* implies that § 1033 applies only if circumstances beyond the taxpayer's control, such as an involuntary conversion, *require* a conversion of the property. In *Masser* there was what economically constituted a single piece of condemned property. In this problem the taxpayer has a choice whether to convert or repair the property, and the *Willis* case properly holds § 1033 inapplicable in such circumstances.

A result similar to *Masser* was reached in Rev. Rul. 73-35, 1973-1 C.B. 367, where a part of a taxpayer's business property was condemned. The proceeds from a sale of the remaining property were also treated as within § 1033, because it was impossible to restore the taxpayer's manufacturing complex as an economically profitable unit on the retained property. But see O.J. Smith, 56 T.C. 1249 (1971), aff'd per curiam, 459 F.2d 1043 (4th Cir. 1972).

3. If the taxpayer in *Clifton Investment* had bought a hotel, rather than stock in a hotel, § 1033(g) would have allowed the taxpayer to use either the "like kind" test or the "similar or related in service of use" test to be within § 1033(a). The "like kind" test would result in nonrecognition of the gain. Section 1033(g) does not apply if, as in *Clifton Investment*, controlling stock of a corporation owning "like kind" property is acquired. § 1033(g)(2).

4. The § 1033(g) "like kind" test would not apply in these circumstances because it applies only to involuntary conversions "as a result of . . . seizure, requisition, or condemnation, or threat or imminence thereof" and not to destruction, such as by fire or theft.

5. In general, the "like kind" test has always seemed broader than the "similar or related in service or use" test. But see *Rev. Rul. 71-41*. If "like kind" is the more lenient test, it is surprising that § 1031 makes it the criterion for *voluntary* conversions whereas § 1033, (with the exception of § 1033(g)) applies the more stringent similar-or-related test to *involuntary* conversions. As a policy matter it is difficult to justify this result. One may certainly raise the issue whether § 1033(g), applying only to real property and only to limited types of involuntary conversions (not including fire and theft, see problem 4, above, and not applying to stock control transactions, see problem 3, above), should be so narrowly restricted. One wonders whether § 1033 should apply a "like kind" test as an alternative to the "similar or related in service or use" test in all circumstances. The philosophy expressed in the first paragraph quoted from the committee report would seem to carry us well beyond the limited addition made in the form of § 1033(g).

Page 925:

The principles of Section 1038 discussed at this page of the Text may be seen at work in the following basic illustration which may be reproduced and distributed to students.

SECTION 1038

Assume T sold a piece of real estate with a basis to T of $60,000 for $100,000. $20,000 was paid in cash in the year of sale and the balance of the price was reflected in a note for $80,000, on which $20,000 was payable in each of the succeeding four years with interest on the unpaid balance (We now dismiss the interest, assuming it to be paid and taxed as due). The $80,000 note was secured by a mortgage on the property. Before any principal payments were made on the note and when the property had appreciated in value to $110,000 the buyer defaulted. T agreed to accept a reconveyance of the property in full satisfaction of the note and to pay the buyer an additional $30,000.[1] If there were no Section 1038, T would have had to report $32,000 of income on the disposition, computed as follows:

Portion of fair market value of property received for obligations on reacquisition ($30,000 was received for cash)	$80,000
Less basis for Section 453 obligations (Section 453B(b))	48,000
Income reportable	$32,000

This is the same amount as would have been reported if the purchaser had paid the obligations in full.[2]

T's basis for the reacquired property would be $110,000. As this is a fully taxable transaction T reacquires the property as if by purchase for a consideration equal to its fair market value at the time of acquisition.[3]

---

[1] It is assumed here that T is paying full value to re-acquire the property ($80,000 of purchaser's obligations, plus $30,000 cash equals $110,000). Realistically, the purchaser might accept less, because a force sale, the alternative to the voluntary arrangement, probably would yield less than the fair market value of the property. See Reg. § 1.1038-1(h), Example (1); and Cf., Reg. § 20.2031-1(b), differentiating "fair market value" and "forced sale price."

[2] See Reg. 1.453-5(b)(2).

[3] Reg. § 1.453-5(b)(6). As all of T's gain in the property ($40,000) has been taxed and T has invested another $ 10,000, the result is the same as if he had originally sold the property for $100,000 cash and has then added $10,000 to purchase new property at a cost of $110,000. Note that T has taken out $20,000 and put in $30,000 more for a net $10,000 increase in T's investment.

However, under Section 1038(b)(1), T's taxable gain is only $2,000, computed as follows:

Money and fair market value of property (other than obligations) received prior to the reacquisition	$ 20,000
Less prior taxed gain (Section 453(c) gain on the $20,000 was 40% x $20,000 = $8,000)	8,000
Gain taxed (Before the Section 1038(b)(2) limitation)	$12,000

On these facts, however, Section 1038(b)(2) limits the gain upon which T is taxed on the reacquisition to $2,000, computed as follows:

Excess of sale price over adjusted basis		$40,000
Reduced by: Gain taxed before reacquisition	$ 8,000	
Money paid by T upon reacquisition.[4]	30,000	
Gain taxed on reacquisition		38,000
		$ 2,000

Thus under Section 1038 T reports only $2,000, instead of the $32,000 otherwise reportable. The cost of this relief is a lower basis for the reacquired property, computed under Section 1038(c) as follows:

---

[4] This part of the limitations is not especially easy to understand. But notice that, if T had paid upon reacquisition only the same amount as T had withdrawn prior thereto ($20,000), the § 1038(b)(2) limitation would merely equal the amount taxable under § 1038(b)(1) ($40,000 less $8,000, less $20,000 equals $12,000). To the extent that T reinvests more than T has withdrawn, the amount taxed is reduced, because T has increased T's net investment, rather than having made a net cash bail-out.

Basis for the obligations (Section 453B(b))	$48,000
Plus gain taxed on the reacquisition (Section 1038(b))	2,000
Plus amount paid by the vendor in connection with the reacquisition of the property (Section 1038(b)(2)(B))	<u>30,000</u>
Basis	<u>**$80,000**</u>

A review of the entire transaction and its tax consequences to T will demonstrate the propriety of his new $80,000 basis for the property, which now has a fair market value of $110,000 and a potential $30,000 gain to T upon its sale. At the time of the sale, T had property in which T had a potential $40,000 gain (F.M.V. $100,000 less basis $60,000). T withdrew $20,000 of T's original investment of $60,000 but T was taxed on $10,000 of the amount withdrawn ($8,000 at time of sale plus $2,000 upon reacquisition). This should effect a net reduction of $10,000 in T's original investment (and basis) because only the $10,000 tax free withdrawal was in the nature of a return of his capital. At this point T's basis would have been $50,000 (original $60,000 less $10,000 return of capital). But T has also added $30,000 to T's investment ($10,000 of which took account of the post-sale appreciation). Thus T's basis becomes $80,000, and T remains potentially taxable on $30,000, the amount of T's gain on the original sale which, so far, has gone untaxed.

Chapter 27.   Computations

PROBLEMS

Page 941:

1(a).   T's tax liability under § 1(c) is $47,435. As is pointed out in the Note
        at page 932 of the Text, the special rates for non-surviving spouse, non-
        head-of-household singles were first added under the 1969 Act.

1(b).   T's tax liability under § 1(a) is $41,995.50. If married individuals meet
        the § 6013 requirements, they may file a joint return. Under §
        6013(d)(1)(A) marital status is determined at the end of the year and
        therefore T and Spouse may file a joint return.

1(c).   T's tax liability under § 1(a) is $41,995.50. The exception clause of §
        6013 (d)(1)(B) applies, and T is still treated as married in the year of
        Spouse's death. Spouse's executor or administrator and T may file a
        joint return for the year of Spouse's death. See § 6013(a)(3).

1(d).   T's tax liability under § 1(a) is still $41,995.50. In this situation, T is a
        "surviving spouse" as defined in § 2(a) and T may continue to use the
        § 1(a) rates. The following requirements of the § 2(a) definition of
        "surviving spouse" are met, viz:

        (1)   Spouse died in one of the two years immediately preceding the
                taxable year; § 2(a)(1)(A).

        (2)   T maintains a household providing over half of the cost of
                maintenance. § 2(a)(1) (last sentence).

        (3)   T's household constitutes the principal place of abode for § 151
                dependents of T who are children of T. The children are
                qualified dependents of T under § 152(a)(1) for whom T can
                claim deductions under § 151(c)(1). § 2(a)(1)(B)(i) and (ii).

        (4)   It is assumed that none of § 2(a)(2) limitations is violated.

1(e).   T's tax liability under § 1(b) is $44,457.50. T is a "head of household" as defined in § 2(b), because:

   (1)   T is not married at the close of the taxable year. § 2(b)(1).

   (2)   T is not a surviving spouse; see § 2(a). As Spouse did not die in one of the two immediately preceding taxable years, T does not qualify as a surviving spouse. § 2(a)(1)(A).

   (3)   T maintains a household and provides over half of the cost of maintenance. § 2(b)(1) (last sentence).

   (4)   T maintains as T's home a household which constitutes for more than one-half of the year the principal place of abode of T's children. § 2(b)(1)(A)(i).

   (5)   T does not fall within any of the § 2(b)(3) limitations.

1(f).   T's tax liability under § 1(d) is $51,752.30. Even though T supports two minor children in T's home, T does not qualify for the favorable "head of household" rate of § 1(b) because T is married at the close of the taxable year. See § 2(b)(1). See also §§ 1(d) and 7703(a)(1) concerning the time for determining marital status. If, however, T and New Spouse had lived apart during the entire taxable year, T could use the § 1(b) rates. See §§ 2(c) and 7703(b).

It may also be useful to compare the amount of T's liability as an unmarried person, computed in problem 1(a), above, with the higher amount T must pay now that T is married but filing separately. It might also be informative to point out that, under § 1(e), an estate or trust with $140,000 of taxable income would be liable for $54,595 of taxes.

2(a).   Husband and Wife have taxable income of $211,480. That amount of taxable income is computed as follows:

Gross income	$220,000
- § 62 deductions	- 0
Adjusted Gross Income	$220,000
- Standard deduction	- 5,000
- Personal exemptions	- 3,520

356

Equals taxable income of $211,480

The personal exemptions amount is 4 x $2,000 or $8,000; but that amount is reduced under § 151(d)(3) by an applicable percentage of 56%. The applicable percentage is computed as follows: $220,000 - $150,000 = $70,000 divided by $2,500 equals 28 x 2% = 56%. Thus the $8,000 of personal exemptions are reduced by 56% of $8,000 or $4,480 to result in a deduction of $3,520.

They would use the standard deduction of $5,000 (see § 63(c)(2)(A)), as it exceeds their total itemized deductions of $4,100, the total of the miscellaneous itemized deductions of $6500 which are subject to a $4,400 (2% of adjusted gross income, see § 67(a)) floor netting $2,100 plus the $2,000 of itemized deductions which are not subject to the 2% floor (see § 67(b)(2) and § 164(a)(1)). Since the standard deduction is used, no § 68 reduction is necessary.

Husband and Wife have $55,831 of tax liability computed under § 1(a) as follows: $41,995.50 plus $13,835.50 (35% of $39,530) equals $55,831.

2(b). Husband and Wife have taxable income of $190,880. That amount of taxable income is computed as follows:

Gross income	$220,000
- § 62 deduction	- 0
Adjusted Gross Income	$220,000
- Itemized deductions (see below)	- 25,600
- Personal exemptions (see problem 2(a))	- 3,520
Equals taxable income of	$190,880

They would elect to itemize their deductions. Their total itemized deductions after the 2% floor ($4,400) would be $30,600 less $4,400 plus $3,000 or $29,200. Under § 68, the amount of itemized deductions would be reduced by $3,600 (3% of adjusted gross income in excess of $100,000 or 3% of $120,000) from $29,200 to $25,600, which exceeds the $5,000 standard deduction.

357

Husband and Wife would have tax liability of $48,621, computed under § 1(a) as follows: $41,995.50 plus $6,625.50 (35% of $18,930) equals $48,621.

2(c).   If $100,000 of the taxpayers' gross income were made up of net capital gains, their taxable income would still be $190,880 as computed in 2(b), above. However, their tax liability would be computed using § 1(h) as follows:

§ 1(h)(1)(A): a tax under § 1(a) on $90,880, the *greater* of

(i)	$190,880 - $100,000 =	$90,880.
or		
(ii)	the *lesser* of:	
	(I) taxable income taxed at a rate below 25%, $46,700	
	(II) taxable income reduced by adjusted net capital gain, $90,880 ($190,880 less $100,000)	

The § 1(a) tax on $90,880 is $6,405 plus $18,333.60
$11,928.60 (27% of $44,180 ($90,880 less
$46,700)) or

Plus

§ 1(h)(1)(C): 20% of $100,000
         (taxable income in excess of $90,880) $20,000.00
Total tax $38,333.60

The effect here of § 1(h) is to impose a 20% ceiling on net capital gain which is made up of only adjusted net capital gain and which would otherwise be taxed at rates above 20%.

Alternative Problem 2:

If your students have had it with number crunching, you may want to assign Problem 2 disregarding § 68 and § 151(d)(3). If so, the answers to this problem are as follows:

358

2(a).   Husband and Wife have taxable income of $207,000. That amount of taxable income is computed as follows:

Gross Income	$220,000
- § 62 deductions	- 0
Adjusted Gross Income	$220,000
- Standard deduction	- 5,000
- Personal exemptions	- 8,000
Equals taxable income of	$207,000

The personal exemptions amount is 4 x $2,000 or $8,000 disregarding § 151(d)(3). They would use the standard deduction of $5,000 (see § 63(c)(2)(A)), as it exceeds their total itemized deductions of $4,100, the total of the miscellaneous itemized deductions of $6,500 which are subject to a $4,400 (2% of adjusted gross income, see § 67(a)) floor netting $2,100 plus the $2,000 of itemized deductions which are not subject to the 2% floor (see § 67(b)(2) and § 164(a)(1)). Since the standard deduction is used, no § 68 reduction is necessary.

Husband and Wife have $54,623 of tax liability computed under § 1(a) as follows: $41,995.50 plus $12,267.50 (35% of $35,050) equals $54,263.

2(b).   Husband and Wife have taxable income of $190,880. That amount of taxable income is computed as follows:

Gross Income	$220,000
- § 62 deduction	- 0
Adjusted Gross Income	$220,000
- Itemized deductions	- 29,200
(see below)	
- Personal exemptions	- 8,000
(see Problem 2(a) above)	
Equals taxable income of	$182,800

They would elect to itemize their deductions. Their total itemized deductions after he 2% floor ($4,400) would be $30,600 less $4,400 plus $3,000 or $29,200 disregarding § 68. The amount exceeds the $5,000 standard deduction.

Husband and Wife would have tax liability of $45,793., computed under § 1(a) as follows: $41,995.50 plus $3,797.50 (35% of $10,850) equals $45,793.

2(c).   If $100,000 of the taxpayers' gross income were made up of net capital gains, their taxable income would still be $182,800 as computed in 2(b), above. However, their tax liability would be computed using § 1(h) as follows:

§ 1(h)(1)(A): a tax under § 1(a) on $82,800 the *greater* of

(i) $182,800 - $100,000 = $82,800
or
(ii)   the *lesser* of:
       (I)   taxable income taxed at a
              rate below 25%, $46,700
       (II)   taxable income reduced by adjusted
              net capital gain, $82,800 ($182,800
              less $100,000)

The § 1(a) tax on $16,152 is $6,405 plus $9,747
(27% of $36,100 ($82,800 less $46,700)) or $16,152

Plus

§ 1(h)(1)(C): 20% of $100,000 $20,000
Total tax $36,152

The effect here of § 1(h) is to impose a 20% ceiling on the net capital gain, which is made up of only adjusted net capital gain which would otherwise be taxed at rates above 20%.

3(a).   Section § 1(g) applies to Joe because, as of the close of his taxable year, he is less than 14 years of age and has at least one surviving parent. § 1(g)(2). Joe's net unearned income (NUI) is $4,000, computed under § 1(g)(4) as follows:

Gross income which is not earned income as
defined in § 911(d)(2): $5,000

Less: Joe's standard deduction under § 63(c)(5)(A): $500

        plus: the greater of Joe's standard deduction
        ($500) or his itemized deductions connected
        with he production of NUI (O): $500   -1,000

        NUI: $4,000

The tax imposed by § 1(g) is $1,250, the greater of:

§ 1(g)(1)(A) tax: $450

Tax imposed without regard to § 1(g) = Gross income ($5,000)
less Joe's standard deduction under § 63(c)(5)(A) ($500) at the
§ 1(c) 10% rate.

or

§ 1(g)(1)(B) tax: $1,250

The sum of:

    § 1(g)(1)(B)(i): Joe's taxable income ($4,500) -
    Joe's NUI ($4,000) at § 1(c) 10% rate: $50

§ 1(g)(1)(B)(ii) (and § 1(g)(3)(A)):

    Tax on Parents' taxable income and Joe's NUI
    ($150,000 + 4,000 x § 1(a) rates = $39,610.50)
    less tax on Parents' taxable income ($150,000 x
    § 1(a) rates = $38,410.50) = $1,200

                                        $1,250

In short, $4,000 of the trust income to Joe is taxed at his parents' top rate of 30%. The remaining $1,000 less the standard deduction of $500 is taxed at Joe's rate of 10%. Note that Joe is not allowed an exemption amount under § 151(d) because his parents have claimed him as a dependent. § 151(d)(2).

3(b).   Section § 1(g) applies for the reasons stated in (a), above. Joe's NUI is $4,000, computed as in problem 3(a), above. The tax imposed by § 1(g) is $1,500, the greater of:

§ 1(g)(1)(A) tax: $750

    Tax imposed without regard to 1(g) = Gross
    income ($10,000) *less* Joe's $3,000 standard

deduction under §§ 63(c)(5) and 63(c)(2)(C)
($7,000) x § 1(c) rate ($600 + 15% of $1,000,
$150)

or

§ 1(g)(1)(B) tax:	$1,500

The sum of:

§ 1(g)(1)(B)(i): Joe's taxable income ($7,000) -
Joe's NUI ($4,000) x § 1(c) 10% rate = $300

§ 1(g)(1)(B)(ii) (and § 1(g)(3)(A)):
Tax on Parents' taxable income & Joe's NUI
(($150,000 + $4,000) x § 1(a) rates) =
$39,610.50) *less* tax on Parents' taxable income
($150,000 x § 1(a) rates = $38,410.50) = $1,200
                                                    $1,500

In short, $4,000 of the trust income is taxed at Joe's parents' top rate of 30%. The remaining $3,000 is taxed at Joe's rate of 10%. Note that the standard deduction of $3,000 is used to offset the earned income of $5,000. As in problem 3(a), above, Joe is not allowed an exemption amount. See § 151(d)(2).

3(c). Section 1(g) is inapplicable because Joe is 15 years of age. § 1(g)(2). Joe's tax liability will be $450 determined at the 10% rate under § 1(c) on $4,500 of taxable income.

Page 949:

The Job Creation and Workers Assistance Act of 2002 (Pub. Law No. 107-147 (2002)) added Section 1400L entitled "Tax Benefits for New York Liberty Zone" to the Code. In addition, the Victims of Terrorism Tax Act of 2001 (Pub. Law No. 107-134 (2001)) provided various types of tax relief for the victims of terrorist acts including the September 11, 2001 terrorist attacks. Section 1400L provides a broad range of tax incentives to provide economic incentives to repair and rebuild the damaged businesses and properties in the New York Liberty Zone (generally the area of the World Trade Center attacked on September 11, 2001).

Page 954:

1. Taxpayer would reduce the $100,000 of tax liability by utilizing the nonrefundable credits in the order in which they appear in the Code:

Credit	Amount	Remaining Liability
§ 21	$ 500	$99,500
§ 27	14,500	85,000

Although it would appear that Taxpayer would be allowed a Child Tax Credit under § 24, the credit would be phased out under § 24(b) and no credit would be allowed. We then reach the $82,000 § 38 general business credit which is a combination of the $2,000 research credit and the $80,000 investment credit. Since there is no alternative minimum tax liability, the § 38 credit can reduce tax liability only to the extent of $25,000 plus 75% of the remaining $60,000 of tax liability, or a total of $70,000. § 38(c). The remaining $12,000 general business credit ($82,000 less $70,000) is carried back 3 years (earliest year first) under § 39.

Returning to our chart:

§ 38	$70,000	$15,000

The remaining $15,000 of tax liability is consumed by the § 31 withholding credit, and Taxpayer is allowed a $5,000 refund for the excess of credit over remaining tax liability.

Thus, in summary Taxpayer has to pay no tax, has a $12,000 § 38 credit carryback, and a $5,000 tax refund.

2. Taxpayers' tax liability is determined as follows:

Gross Income	$18,000
Standard Deduction	[5,000]
Exemptions (5)	[10,000]
Taxable Income	$ 3,000
§ 1(a) Tax Liability (10% rate)	$ 300

§ 32 credit:

§ 32(a)(2)(A):
40% of $8,890 (§32(b)(1) and (2)) $3,556.00

§ 32(a)(2)(B):
21.06% of $5,390
($18,000 less $12,610 rounded)

Note: The phaseout amount is increased by $1,000 in 2002

(§ 32(b)(1)(A) and (2)(A) and (B)(i))   [1,135.00]

§ 32 credit: $2,421.00

Taxpayer will have no income tax liability and will instead receive a $2,121.00 refund ($2,421.00 less $300.00) from the government.

Although the problem does not call for the computation (and there are insufficient facts to make the computation), it should be pointed out that Taxpayer will likely receive an additional refund as a result of the child credit under § 24(d).

PROBLEM

Page 966:

1.   Taxpayer would be liable for $2,555 of AMT and $9,600 of regular tax, computed as follows:

     a. Regular tax under § 1(c):

     § 61: Gross Income: $200,000

     § 62 Deductions: -100,000

              § 162 expenses: $50,000
              § 168 depreciation: 50,000
         (There will be $30,000 of depreciation on the

364

pre-1987 property and $20,000 on the newly
acquired property ($550,000 divided by 27.5
straight-line life))

——————

Adjusted Gross Income: $100,000

    Itemized deductions (greater than
    the standard deduction): $ 50,000

        Charitable deduction (within 30% ceiling) $30,000

        Taxes: 10,000

        Miscellaneous

          expenses: 10,000

Exemption: -2,000

Taxable Income: $48,000

Under the assumed flat 20% rate,
the tax on $48,000 is $9,600.

Regular tax liability: $9,600

b. § 55 Alternative minimum tax:

Taxable income before adjustment by §§ 56 and 58: $48,000

§ 56(a)(1): The excess of regular tax depreciation of
$20,000 on the apartment less alternative depreciation
under § 168(g) which is $550,000 over a 40 year life
equals $13,750.

This results in a $6,250 difference which increases
taxable income: +6,250

§ 56(b): Miscellaneous itemized deductions as defined
in § 67(b) and taxes do not qualify as itemized
deductions under the AMTI: +20,000

§ 56(b)(1)(E): The personal exemption does not
qualify as an AMTI deduction. +2,000

Plus § 57 Tax preference items § 57(a)(5):
This normally tax exempt interest is a tax preference item: +3,750

The untaxed appreciation on capital gain property
contributed to charity is no longer a tax preference item:

§ 57(a)(6): Accelerated depreciation in excess of straight line
depreciation on pre-1987 real property is a tax preference item.
See I.R.C. (1954) § 57(a)(2):   +2,500

AMTI: $82,500

§ 55(d)(1)(B) exemption: -35,750
(There is no exemption reduction under § 55(d)(3)(B).)

Equals $46,750
The § 55(b)(1) alternative minimum tax rate is
26% of the $46,750 tax base or: $12,155

Finally under § 55(a) the AMT is $12,155 less the
regular tax liability of $9,600 or: $2,555

PART NINE: **PROCEDURE AND PROFESSIONAL RESPONSIBILITY**

Chapter 28.   Procedure and Professional Responsibility

Page 968:

> Fn. 1. See Martinez, "Federal Tax Amnesty: Crime and Punishment Revisited," 10 *Virg. Tax Rev.* 535 (1991), which concludes that tax amnesty is not a good idea for the Feds.

Page 974:

> A pair of 9th Circuit decisions has limited the right of a taxpayer to assert the Fifth Amendment privilege against self-incrimination when filing a tax return. In United States v. Neff, 615 F.2d 1235 (9th Cir. 1980), cert. den., 447 U.S. 925 (1980), the court ruled that the burden is on the defendant taxpayer to show that answers given on a return might be incriminating, unless the questions themselves and the surrounding circumstances are inherently threatening to the defendant's rights. In the absence of such a showing, the taxpayer's conviction for failure to file was upheld. Further, objections based on the privilege may properly be raised only in response to specific questions asked in the return; a taxpayer's "wholesale objection" to questions other than his name and social security number is not a valid claim of privilege. *Neff*, supra. at 1238; U.S. v. Turk, 722 F.2d 439 (9th Cir. 1983). The court went a step further in United States v. Carlson, 617 F.2d 518 (9th Cir. 1980), cert. den., 449 U.S. 1010 (1980), and decided that the public need to preserve the self-assessment system for collecting revenue outweighed the taxpayer's privilege against self-incrimination when claimed as an integral part of a scheme to frustrate the tax laws. Notwithstanding the fact that answering certain questions on the year-end return clearly might tend to incriminate the taxpayer of the crime of filing a false withholding exemption certificate, the asserted privilege was denied.

Page 974:

> See also Alter, "Shareholders Fifth Amendment Privilege Bars Summons of Corporate Records," 63 *J. Tax'n* 208 (1985); Cook, "The

I.R.S. and the Secret Agent," 35 *U. Fla. L. Rev.* 765 (1983); Rosenblatt, "Lawyer Beware: The Use of Counsel's Statements as Evidence Against his Client in Tax Fraud Cases", 63 *Taxes* 619 (1985).

Page 974:

A phone company that extends credit to its customers through use of credit cards is a third party recordkeeper under § 7609, regardless of whether the taxpayer uses the credit card. See U.S. v. New York Telephone Co., 682 F.2d 313 (2d Cir. 1982), discussed in Schwartz, "'Third-Party Recordkeeper' not Limited to Credit Card Transactions, says CA-2," 58 *J. Tax'n* 78 (1983).

Page 977:

In addition to the regular judges of the Tax Court, § 7443A provides that the Chief Judge of the Tax Court may appoint special trial judges. Initially such persons were called commissioners and were used to gather facts in complex factual situations. Since 1969, their role has been expanded and they are also used in judging § 7463 small tax cases discussed at page 977 of the Text. They may also hear other types of proceedings. See § 7443A(b).

Page 977:

Additional articles discussing the procedure for handling small tax cases are: Drennen, "The Status of the Tax Court", 29 *N.Y.U. Inst. on Fed.Tax.* 1017 (1971); Goldfein, "Some Tax Court Procedures Have Been Altered by the Revenue Act of 1978", 50 *J. Tax'n* 81 (1979).

Page 978:

For a discussion of refund suits, *see* Brennecke, "Taxpayers' Undeveloped Muscle -The Refund Suit," 47 *Notre Dame Lawyer* 304 (1971).

Page 981:

See Jones and Singer, "Changes in Procedure, Strategy Due in New Federal Circuit and Revamped Claims Court," 57 *J. Tax'n* 136 (1982).

Page 982:

Golsen and some of the inconsistencies it creates are the subject of commentary, see Note, "The Old Tax Court Blues: The Need for Uniformity in Tax Litigation", 46 *N.Y.U.L. Rev.* 970 (1971).

PROBLEMS

Page 987:

1(a).   In tax litigation, Taxpayers may obtain a jury trial only by means of a refund suit in the District Court.

1(b).   If Taxpayer has no money, Taxpayer must use the Tax Court deficiency procedures; payment is a prerequisite to a refund suit.

In this situation, if Taxpayer is held liable for the deficiency, § 6601(a) provides for interest from the due date of the tax until the date of payment, at a rate determined under § 6621. This does not, however, allow Taxpayer to get what in substance is a loan from the government if Taxpayer does not want to pay the taxes. Under § 6651(a)(2), if Taxpayer reports taxes on the return, but does not pay them, Taxpayer faces a penalty of 0.5% per month, up to a maximum 25%, subject to a minimum penalty. See § 6651(a), last sentence, and page 989 of the Text. Exceptions to the penalty exist for reasonable cause and lack of willful neglect.

1(c).   Taxpayer has the following alternatives:

(1)   Taxpayer may make payments *after* the issuance of the 90-day letter and still sue in the Tax Court (§ 6213(b)(4)). See also Rev. Proc. 84-58, 1984- 2 C.B. 501.

(2)   Taxpayer may make a "full" payment of the asserted deficiency (Flora v. U.S., 357 U.S. 63 (1958), on rehearing, 362 U.S. 145 (1960)), forego the Tax Court petition, and file a claim for refund after the Commissioner assesses the tax. If no assessment occurs after full payment, see the procedures of Rev. Proc. 84-58, Sec. 4.02, 1984-2 C.B. 501, under which the I.R.S. treats the payment as a deposit refundable, without interest, at

any time.

(3)   Under a procedure announced in Rev. Proc. 84-58, 1984-2 C.B. 501, Taxpayer may make a pre-assessment remittance on an anticipated deficiency. Such remittance must be designated as a cash bond and it will stop the running of interest on the amount of the payment. The cash bond is not treated as a payment subject to assessment, and it is recoverable by Taxpayer upon request.

1(d).   In this instance Taxpayer may want the tribunal with the most expertise in tax law. In general, the Tax Court is such a tribunal.

1(e).   The District Court and the Tax Court (*see Golsen*) are bound by the court of appeals. The Claims Court appears most promising. Taxpayer is no longer a step closer to the Supreme Court at the outset. If Taxpayer loses, the appeal is to the United States Court of Appeals in the Federal Circuit. See the manual Note for page 982 of the Text. If Taxpayer should sue in the Tax Court or the District Court, Taxpayer would probably have to reach the Supreme Court to win.

Further factors which Taxpayer might consider in choosing a tribunal:

(1)   Small case procedure in the Tax Court.

(2)   Convenience of forum.

(3)   Settlement possibilities during trial.

(4)   Cost and duration of litigation.

(5)   Appellate review possibilities.

2.   The obvious practical thought is that the Commissioner will not sit idly while the limitation period expires. Refusal to execute the Form 872 simply invites issuance of the 90-day letter. The 90 day letter tolls the running of the limitation period under § 6503(a). Executing Form 872 extends the chance for administrative settlement. If litigation involving other taxpayers is pending on issues involving T, the efforts of others may settle the matter in T's favor without the effort and expense of

litigation by T. If, however, T has no hope for administrative settlement and wishes to get to court to settle the controversy, T should decline to sign Form 872. Refusal to sign accelerates the 90-day letter, and potentially allows T to get to the Tax Court more quickly.

3. The execution of Form 870 under § 6213(d) merely waives T's right to a 90-day letter, the statutory deficiency notice. Also, it allows the Commissioner to assess the tax immediately. T will not receive a deficiency notice, so T may not file a petition to the Tax Court. McConkey v. Comm'r, 199 F.2d 892 (4th Cir. 1952), cert. den. 345 U.S. 924 (1953). Filing Form 870 precludes T from petitioning the Tax Court, but T may still use the refund procedures and file a claim for refund within two years of the payment of the tax. Form 870 expressly provides that it does not prevent an additional assertion of a deficiency for the year by the government. Form 870AD is distinguishable from a Form 870. A Form 870AD is a settlement form at the Appellate Division level. Under Form 870AD, T expressly agrees that no refund suit will be brought with respect to the asserted deficiency, and the government expressly agrees that it will not reopen the case in the absence of fraud or other malfeasance. Courts split on whether signing a Form 870 AD precludes taxpayers from bringing refund claims and suits. See Saltzman, IRS Practice and Procedure ¶ 9.08[2] (Warren, Gorham and Lamont 1991).

4. Section 6861(a) waives the normal procedures for assessment, and the Commissioner may make an immediate assessment if the Commissioner "believes that the assessment or collection of a deficiency . . . will be jeopardized by delay. . . ." § 6861(a). Thus, the Commissioner may make an assessment prior to any judicial action. However, § 6861(b) requires that if the jeopardy assessment occurs prior to the issuance of a 90-day letter, a 90-day letter must be issued within 60 days of the jeopardy assessment, giving T an opportunity to file a petition in the Tax Court.

One should probably emphasize the Commissioner's broad discretionary powers with respect to jeopardy assessments. Also note § 6863(a), allowing a taxpayer to file a bond to avoid collection of the assessment. Finally, distinguish Tax Court jurisdiction under a jeopardy assessment because a deficiency still exists from the factual situation of a case where payment prior to a 90-day letter wipes out the deficiency and precludes Tax Court jurisdiction. See *McConkey*, problem 3, above.

5(a).   The taxpayer should invoke the timely mailing rule of § 7502(a). The taxpayer's petition arrived at the Tax Court more than 90 days after the mailing of the deficiency notice. Using the timely mailing rule, the taxpayer should claim timely filing because of timely mailing. The question is not whether three *months* elapse, but specifically whether one files the petition within 90 *days*; we must actually count the days. See Minuto v. Comm'r, 66 T.C. 616 (1976). In this problem, June 28 is the 90th day after March 30. Deficient's petition is timely under § 7502(a). Note that the timely mailed/timely filed rule now applies to mailing using a designated private delivery service. § 7502(f).

5(b).   The 90-day letter must indicate the last date for filing under the 90-day period. The last sentence of § 6213(a) provides that if a petition is timely filed by the date on the notice, the petition is timely even though the date is improperly computed and is beyond the 90-day period. Again, the timely mailed, timely filed rule of § 7502(a) applies.

5(c).   If the date on the deficiency notice is inappropriately computed and is shorter than a 90-day period, a petition mailed by the proper date, June 28, 2002, should be timely.

5(d).   The timely mailing rule of § 7502 is of no avail if the taxpayer addresses the document improperly. The address of the Tax Court is the subject of Hoffman v. Comm'r, 63 T.C. 638 (1975); see also Minuto v. Comm'r, 66 T.C. 616 (1976).

5(e).   Deficient's petition will probably be untimely. Rev. Proc. 90-18, 1990-1 C.B. 491, provides that the Service will generally use the address on the most recently filed and properly processed return as the address of record for purposes of § 6212(b) and other notices specified in the revenue procedure. This result is consistent with Abeles v. Comm'r, 91 T.C. 1019 (1988), acq. 1989-2 C.B.1. A taxpayer who wishes to change his or her address of record must give clear and concise notification to the IRS Center serving taxpayer's old address or to the Chief, Taxpayer Service Division in the local district office. Taxpayers are able to use Form 8822 to send clear and concise notification of a change of address. Since Deficient's most recent tax returns have all been filed giving the Town Y address (and assuming proper processing), the Y address should be considered Deficient's last known address for purposes of § 6212(b)(1).

Assuming the Town Y address is Deficient's last known address, the issue is whether or not a deficiency notice which is not sent to taxpayer's last known address, but which is actually received by Deficient 17 days after it was sent, constitutes valid notice. In Mulvania v. Comm'r, 81 T.C. 65 (1983), the notice of deficiency was mailed to a former but not the last known address of the taxpayer. Taxpayer did not actually receive the notice until 16 days after it was mailed. The Tax Court held that the notice was valid even though it was not mailed to taxpayer's last known address and thus the taxpayer's petition which was filed more than 90 days from the date of mailing was untimely. The court interpreted § 6212(b)(1) as permissive rather than mandatory, actual notice in a timely manner being all the statute requires. The Court in *Mulvania*, agreeing with the 9th Circuit and quoting Clodfelter v. Comm'r., 527 F.2d 754 (9th Cir. 1975), cert. den., 425 U.S. 979 (1976) concluded that where the "mailing results in actual notice without prejudicial delay (as clearly was the case here), it meets the conditions of section 6212(a) no matter to what address the notice was successfully sent." Deficient's petition, not filed until July 10, is not filed within 90 days of March 29, the *Traxler* date of mailing. The validity of the notice to Deficient and thus the timeliness of the petition will depend on whether or not the 17 day delay is found to have been "prejudicial" to Deficient's ability to have filed a timely petition. Given *Mulvania*, a 17 day delay would not appear to be prejudicial.

5(f).   In problems (5)(d) and (e), above, Deficient is denied Tax Court jurisdiction, but: ". . . the petitioners will still be able to have their day in court by paying the deficiencies and bringing a suit for refund in the U.S. District Court." Baker L. Axe, 58 T.C. 256, 259 (1972).

Page 989:

The IRS is authorized but not required to abate interest attributable to its own errors or delays, § 6404(e), but the provisions apply only to Service failures to perform ministerial acts occurring after the Service contacts the taxpayer in writing. S. Rep. No. 313, 99th Cong., 2d Sess. 208 (1986).

In Francis M. Johnson, 34 T.C.M. 371 (1975), the taxpayer received written greetings from the Service. The greetings stated that she had overpaid her tax because of errors in her return and gave her a refund. Later, the Service realized they were in error and that the taxpayer originally was correct. The Service asserted a deficiency. The taxpayer claimed unfairness and hardship. The Tax Court, despite expressing displeasure over the Service's "bureaucratic bungling," found no other course open than to approve the deficiency. *Johnson* does not seem to be affected by the new legislation.

PROBLEMS

Page 991:

1(a). The Commissioner can make a timely deficiency assertion against T through April 15, 2006. There is a general three year limitation period for assessment in § 6501(a). If a taxpayer files the return early, the three year period runs from the last day prescribed for filing, i.e., April 15, 2003. § 6501(b)(1); see § 6072(a), fixing the due date for an individual's return. The result would not change even if April 15, 2003, were a Saturday, Sunday or holiday. See Rev. Rul. 81-269, 1981-2 C.B. 243, Situation 1; Cf. § 7503 and Situation 2 of the Ruling. The limitation on the early filing rule applies as well to any extensions of the date for filing. See Pace Oil Company, Inc. v. Comm'r, 73 T.C. 249 (1979).

1(b). The Commissioner can make a timely deficiency assertion against T through May 1, 2006. Section 6501(a) provides that the three year limitation period runs from the date the return was filed, "whether or not such return was filed on or after the date prescribed." § 6501(a). (But compare the early filing rule discussed in problem 1(a).)

   If a taxpayer mails a return timely by or before April 15, it is treated as timely "filed" even if not received until May 15. See Hotel Equities Corp., 65 T.C. 528 (1975), aff'd 546 F.2d 725 (7th Cir. 1976). The court in *Hotel Equities* held that the § 7502 date of timely mailing controls not only for purposes of a taxpayer's filing of a return, but also for the Commissioner's timely assertion of a deficiency under § 6501. Cf. Reg. § 301.7502-1(c).

1(c).   If the taxpayer files no return, assessment may occur at any time. §
        6501(c)(3). Emphasize this point, considering that the possibility of
        criminal prosecution is *not* so open-ended.

2(a).   Section 6501(e)(1)(A) provides that if the taxpayer omits an amount of
        gross income exceeding 25% of the amount of "gross income stated in
        the return", then a six year limitation period for assessment applies.
        Under § 6501(e)(1)(A)(ii), if the taxpayer discloses an item on the
        return, the item is not considered omitted even if not included in gross
        income. The University Country Club, Inc., 64 T.C. 460 (1975); see
        Erbacher, "When is Income Omitted from Gross Income for Purposes
        of Federal Statute of Limitations?," 8 *Cal. Western L. Rev.* 431 (1972).
        Under § 6501(e)(1)(A) and § 6501(b)(1), the limitation period would
        run on April 15, 2006. For an application of the six year period, see
        Adams v. Comm'r, 29 T.C.M. 476 (1970), aff'd per curiam, 456 F.2d
        259 (9th Cir. 1972).

2(b).   If an omission of an item is fraudulent (see § 6501(c)(1)), or if there
        is a willful attempt to defeat or evade tax (see § 6501(c)(2)), then
        assessment may occur at any time. For an application of § 6501(c)(1),
        see Nuckols v. Comm'r, 31 T.C.M. 761 (1972). In addition, even if a
        taxpayer subsequently files a nonfraudulent return, such filing does not
        cure the prior fraudulent filing, and assessment still may occur at any
        time. In such a case the regular statute of limitations never commences.
        Badaracco v. Comm'r, 464 U.S. 386, 104 S.Ct. 756 (1984). See Kahn,
        "The Supreme Court's Misconstruction of a Procedural Statute - A
        Critique of the Court's Decision in *Badaracco*," 82 *Mich L. Rev.* 461
        (1983).

        T may indeed be in more than mere financial difficulty. T certainly
        violates § 7206(1) by willfully filing a return containing a statement not
        believed by T to be true. T probably also violates § 7201, the general
        evasion statute. Unlike § 7206(1), conviction under § 7201 requires
        proof that T underpaid the tax. Violations of both sections are felonies.
        The sanctions are somewhat less severe under § 7206(1) than they are
        under § 7201. Easier proof of guilt under § 7206(1) frequently causes
        the Commissioner to use it as a backstop to § 7201.

PROBLEM

Page 994:

1. Mrs. T qualifies for innocent spouse relief under § 6015(a)(2). Under
    § 6015(c)(3)(A)(i)(II),Mrs. T has made an election and has not been in
    the same household as Mr. T for 18 (more than 12) months. The
    election is timely because it is made within 2 years after the Service
    has begun collection procedures. § 6015(c)(3)(B). Since Mrs. T was
    unaware of the omission when she filed the return, her election is valid.
    § 6015(c)(3)(C). In addition, neither § 6015(c)(3)(A)(ii) nor §
    6015(c)(4) would disqualify Mrs. T's claim.

    As a result of Mrs. T valid election under § 6015(c), Mrs. T is
    effectively allowed to file a separate return for the year. The $100,000
    of gross income omission creates a deficiency on Mr. T's separate
    return. See § 6015(d)(1), (d)(3)(A). Mrs. T must appraise Mr. T of
    Mrs. T's innocent spouse election. See § 6015(e)(4), (h)(2).

Page 997:

    Sections 1311-14 provide specific circumstances mitigating the effect
    of the normal three-year or other applicable statute of limitations. The
    provisions work both for the government and for the taxpayer, depend-
    ing on the circumstance of adjustment. See § 1312. If the taxpayer or
    the government cannot use the mitigation provisions, the defense of
    equitable recoupment may apply. See Bull v. U.S., 295 U.S. 247
    (1935); Stone v. White, 301 U.S. 532 (1937).

PROBLEMS

Page 998:

1(a). Under § 6511(a), Tex must file the claim within 3 years after filing his
      return. For purposes of § 6511, § 6513 treats a return that is filed early
      as filed on the last date prescribed by law for filing the return.
      Consequently, a claim filed by April 15, 2006, would be timely. See
      § 6072 (a), fixing April 15 as the filing date for income tax returns of
      calendar year individuals. The rule of § 6513 is one of convenience.
      Because of the rule, the taxpayer and the government need not worry

about the precise filing date, provided the taxpayer files his or her return on time.

1(b).   No express rule applies to late returns. In this problem, § 6513 has no application. Accordingly, the general three-year period for filing a refund claim runs from the date of actual filing of the return. See § 6511(a). Consequently, a refund claim filed by Tex on May 1, 2006, would be timely. But see § 6511(b)(2)(A) which may limit Tex's refund if filed after April 15, 2003 to only that amount of tax paid within three years of a claim for refund. For example, if Tex had made estimated payments during 2002, under § 6513(b)(2) the payments are deemed paid as of April 15, 2003 and not refundable if Tex makes a claim for refund after April 14, 2006.

1(c).   This circumstance invokes the two-year rule of § 6511(a). The presumptive three-year period would expire April 15, 2006. A timely refund claim could be filed June 1, 2006, two years after Tex paid the tax. If Tex does not file the claim by April 15, 2006, the refund may not exceed the portion of the tax paid during the two years immediately preceding the filing of the claim. See § 6511(b)(2)(B).

1(d).   This problem invokes a statutory exception to the presumptive three-year period of § 6511 (a). Claims based on worthless debts or securities have a special seven-year limitation period. § 6511(d)(1). The reason for this lengthy period is the difficulty in pinpointing the time a security or debt becomes worthless. Taxpayers otherwise waiting beyond the standard three-year period thereby receive relief from § 6511(d)(1). In this problem, a claim filed by Tex on or before April 15, 2010, would be timely.

2(a).   Refunder is a taxpayer filing a refund claim on which the Service fails to act. She is not required to wait forever to file suit. Under § 6532(a)(1), she may file suit six months after filing her claim, without regard to action by the government. § 6532(a)(1). She may file suit sooner if within the six-month period the Secretary renders a decision on her claim. Id.

2(b).   Section 6532 also sets a limitation period for filing refund suits. Section 6532 requires that taxpayers file suit not later than two years from the date the IRS mails the taxpayer a notice of disallowance of the claim. § 6532(a)(1). Under this rule, no limitation period runs against a suit until the Secretary denies the claim. Note that a taxpayer may prefer to defer filing suit, awaiting more settled or favorable judicial climates.

2(c).   If a taxpayer waives notice of disallowance of her claim for refund, the two-year limitation period for filing suit runs from the date of such waiver. § 6532(a)(3). Taxpayer must still wait until six months after filing her refund claim to file a refund suit. Reg. § 301.6532-1(c).

2(d).   No. If the taxpayer perceives gaining some advantage in settlement or compromise negotiations, or in interpersonal relations with the Service or the Department of Justice, perhaps the waiver is beneficial. Any such circumstances certainly would be governed by the particular circumstances of the case and should be assessed thoroughly by counsel.

3.   No. Taxpayers merely voluntarily, though mistakenly, overpaying taxes may file a claim for a refund. See § 7422(b). They may maintain such suits regardless of whether they pay the tax under duress or protest, seemingly making the issue irrelevant as a government argument.

4.   Section 6611 provides for the payment of interest on any overpayment of tax. The interest period generally runs from the date of the overpayment to the date of the recovery. But see § 6611(b)(2). Sometimes interest runs from a later date, as in the case of advance payment of tax. See § 6611(d). If a taxpayer files a return late, no interest is payable on an overpayment for the period prior to the date on which he or she files the return. § 6611(b)(3); see also § 6611(i). In addition, if a refund is paid within 45 days of the later of the due date of a return or the date the return is filed, no interest must be paid. § 6611(e).

         The Code provides for a single non-corporate interest rate. The single rate is the Federal short-term rate, plus three percentage points. § 6621(a)(1) and § 6621(b) (definition of Federal short-term rate). The interest rate is adjusted quarterly and is computed with daily compounding of interest (i.e., interest on interest). § 6622. For January 1, 2002 - March 31, 2002, the general rate (for both overpayments and underpayments) was 6%. Rev. Rul. 2001-63, 2001-2

C.B.___.

Page 1002:

1(a).   As an introduction to the problem, one should summarize Formal
         Opinion 85-352, Circular 230, and § 6694 (a). Under Formal Opinion
         85-352, an attorney may advise the statement of positions most
         favorable to the client if the lawyer has a "good faith belief" that those
         positions are warranted under existing law or can be supported by a
         good faith argument for extension, modification or reversal of existing
         law. Experts have suggested that a one-third chance of success is
         sufficient to support a reporting position under the standard of Formal
         Opinion 85-352. See Sax, Holden, Tannenwald, Watts, and Wolfman,
         "Report of the Special Task Force Report on Formal Opinion 85-352,"
         39 Tax Layer 635, 639 (1986). Circular 230 states that attorney may
         not advise a client to take a position on a return unless the attorney
         determines that the position has a "realistic possibility" of being
         sustained on the merits, or the position is not frivolous and the attorney
         advises the client of any opportunity to avoid the   § 6662 accuracy-
         related penalties by adequately disclosing the position and of the
         requirements for adequate disclosure. Circular 230 § 10.34(a)(1),
         (4)(ii). Circular 230 states that there is a realistic possibility of a
         reporting position being sustained on its merits if a reasonable and well-
         informed analysis by a person knowledgeable in the tax law would lead
         such a person to conclude that the position has approximately a one-in-
         three, or greater, likelihood of being sustained on its merits. Thus,
         while Formal Opinion 85-352 and Circular 230 state different
         standards, both are believed to require a reporting position to have an
         approximately one-third chance of success.

         Section 6694 (a) imposes a penalty on an income tax return preparer
         if (1) any part of any understatement of tax liability is due to a position
         for which there was not a realistic possibility of being sustained on its
         merits, (2) the income tax return preparer knew or reasonably should
         have known of the position, and (3) the position was not properly
         disclosed. The penalty does not apply if it can be shown that there is
         reasonable cause for the understatement and the preparer acted in good
         faith. An income tax preparer is defined to include any person who

prepares for compensation, or who employs one or more persons to prepare for compensation, any income tax return or a substantial portion of an income tax return. § 7701(a)(36). Because § 6694 (a) uses the same standard as Circular 230 ("a realistic possibility"), presumably a reporting position with a one-third chance of success also is protected from the § 6694(a) penalty.

On the facts of the problem, there is an argument that there is a one-third chance of Client's deduction being sustained because although the two Circuit Courts of Appeal would not allow Client to take the deduction, the Tax Court, which is generally well-versed in the tax law, has reached Client's result. Seemingly, although the courts have different status, the situation involves a one-third chance for Client's success and you may advise Client that she may take the deduction.

1(b).   Because this is a close case, it might be wise for the attorney to advise Client to adequately disclose the questionable position. Students, no doubt, will quickly see the downside of disclosure as it raises a red flag for the Service to audit Client.

Notes

Notes

Notes

Notes

Notes

Notes

Notes

Notes